Labour in Global Production Networks in India

Labour in Global Production Networks in India

edited by
Anne Posthuma
Dev Nathan

OXFORD
UNIVERSITY PRESS

YMCA Library Building, Jai Singh Road, New Delhi 110 001

Oxford University Press is a department of the University of Oxford.
It furthers the University's objective of excellence in research, scholarship,
and education by publishing worldwide in

Oxford New York
Auckland Cape Town Dar es Salaam Hong Kong Karachi
Kuala Lumpur Madrid Melbourne Mexico City Nairobi
New Delhi Shanghai Taipei Toronto

With offices in
Argentina Austria Brazil Chile Czech Republic France Greece
Guatemala Hungary Italy Japan Poland Portugal Singapore
South Korea Switzerland Thailand Turkey Ukraine Vietnam

Oxford is a registered trademark of Oxford University Press
in the UK and in certain other countries

Published in India
by Oxford University Press, New Delhi

© Oxford University Press 2010

The moral rights of the author have been asserted
Database right Oxford University Press (maker)

First published 2010

All rights reserved. No part of this publication may be reproduced,
or transmitted in any form or by any means, electronic or mechanical,
including photocopying, recording or by any information storage and
retrieval system, without permission in writing from Oxford University Press.
Enquiries concerning reproduction outside the scope of the above should be
sent to the Rights Department, Oxford University Press, at the address above

You must not circulate this book in any other binding or cover
and you must impose this same condition on any acquirer

ISBN-13: 978-019-806413-8
ISBN-10: 019-806413-6

Typeset in Aldine 401 BT 10/12.7
by Eleven Arts, Keshav Puram, Delhi 110 035
Printed in India by De Unique, New Delh 110 018
Published by Oxford University Press
YMCA Library Building, Jai Singh Road, New Delhi 110 001

CONTENTS

List of Tables	ix
List of Figures	xi
Foreword	xiii
Acknowledgements	xv

Introduction: Scope for Aligning Economic and Social   1
Upgrading within Global Production Networks in India
   Anne Posthuma and Dev Nathan

I: CONCEPTUAL AND GOVERNANCE ISSUES RELATED TO ECONOMIC
AND SOCIAL UPGRADING IN GLOBAL PRODUCTION NETWORKS

1. Global Aggregate Demand, Inequality, and the Prospects   37
   for Decent Work
   Dev Nathan

2. Beyond 'Regulatory Enclaves': Challenges and Opportunities   57
   to Promote Decent Work in Global Production Networks
   Anne Posthuma

3. Reach and Depth of Responsible Production: Towards a   81
   Research Agenda
   Peter Knorringa

II: SECTORAL CASE STUDIES OF ENGAGEMENT IN GLOBAL PRODUCTION NETWORKS

4. Global Production Networks and Decent Work in India and China: Evidence from the Apparel, Automotive, and Information Technology Industries
   Gary Gereffi and Esra Güler — 103

5. Decent Work in Global Production Networks: Challenges for Vulnerable Workers in the Indian Garments Sector
   Stephanie Barrientos, Kanchan Mathur, and Atul Sood — 127

6. Footloose Capital, Intermediation, and the Search for the 'High Road' in Low-wage Industries
   Meenu Tewari — 146

7. Labour Market Adjustment and Female Workers: Global Production and Expiry of Quotas in India's Textiles and Garments Industry
   Indira Hirway — 166

8. Global Agribusiness Value Chains, Small Producers, and Workers in India: Governance, Upgrading Opportunities, Policies, and Strategies
   Sukhpal Singh — 190

9. Gender, Labour, and Global Production Networks: Indigenous Women and NTFP-based Livelihoods
   Govind Kelkar, Meenakshi Ahluwalia, and Meenakshi Kumar — 212

10. Upgradation or Flexible Casualization? Exploring the Dynamics of Global Value Chain Incorporation in the Indian Leather Industry
    Sumangala Damodaran — 231

11. Cost Cutting Pressures and Labour Relations in Tamil Nadu's Automobile Components Supply Chain
    T.G. Suresh — 251

12. Small Producers and Labour Conditions in Auto Parts and Components Industry in North India
    Dinesh Awasthi, Sanjay Pal, and Jignasu Yagnik — 272

13. Taking the High Road? Labour in the Indian Software Outsourcing Industry
    Carol Upadhya — 300

14. Global Production Networks and Decent Work: Recent 321
    Experience in India and Global Trends
      Sandip Sarkar and Balwant Singh Mehta

Conclusion 348
  Dev Nathan and Anne Posthuma

Note on Contributors 372

TABLES

5.1	Examples of the Use of Vulnerable Labour in Global Production	129
5.2	Summary of Impacts at India Study Supply Sites	136
7.1a	Share of Women Workers in Unorganized Work and Home-based Work (in %)	179
7.1b	Growth of Home-based Workers from 1993–4 to 2000–1 (in %)	179
7.2	Trends in Average Daily Earnings by Gender in the T&G Industry (1974–9 to 2002–5)	182
7.3	T&G Wage Rates by Gender and by Organized/Unorganized Sectors (1999–2000)	183
7.4	Daily Wages of Home-based and Non-Home-based Workers in the T&G Industry, 1999–2000 (in Rs)	184
12.1	Sample Profile of Respondents	276
12.2	Recruitment Process in the Sample Firms	283
12.3	Base for Fixing Wages in the Sample Firms	284
12.4	Nature of Employment in the Sample Firms	285
12.5	Payment Terms in the Sample Firms	286
12.6	Incentive Structure in the Sample Firms	286
12.7	Working Hours in the Sample Firms	287
12.8	Health and Safety Practices in the Sample Firms	288
12.9	Welfare Measures in the Sample Firms	289
12.10	Social Security Measures in the Sample Firms	289

14.1	Profile of Workers in ICT Sector in 1999–2000, 2004–5	325
14.2	Pattern of Employment in ICT Sector and Sub-Sectors (in %)	326
14.3	Employment Growth in the ICT Sector during 1999–2000 and 2004–5 (Compound Annual Growth Rate in %)	326
14.4	Distribution of ICT by Formal and Informal Sectors (in %)	327
14.5	Distribution of ICT Workers by Formal and Informal States of Employment Contract (%)	328
14.6	Distribution of ICT Workers by Enterprise Type (%)	328
14.7	Distribution of Workers by Educational Level and Status (%)	329
14.8	Share of Graduates and Above in Different Segments of ICT	329
14.9	Daily Wages/Earnings by Formal/Informal Sector, 1999–2000 and 2004–5 (at 2004–5 prices)	330
14.10	Growth Rate of Wages during 1999–2000 to 2004–5 in the Formal Sector (%)	331
14.11	Daily Wages/Earnings by Enterprise Type, 1999–2000 and 2004–5, Constant Prices (2004–5 Prices) (in Rs)	332
14.12	Growth Rate of Wages during 1999–2000 and 2004–5 by Enterprise Type, Constant Prices (2004–5 Prices) (in %)	332
14.13	Daily Wages/Earnings by Education Level, 1999–2000 and 2004–5, Constant Prices (2004–5 Prices) (in Rs)	333
14.14	Growth Rate of Wages during 1999–2000 and 2004–5 by Educational Level, Constant Prices (2004–5 Prices)	333
14.15	Generalized Entropy Measures	335
14.16	Social Security Benefits of IT and Non-IT Sectors among Regular Workers (in %)	338
14.17	Nature of Job Contracts (in %)	339
14.18	Union Presence (in %)	340
14.19	Reasons for Change in Jobs	340

FIGURES

4.1	Types of Work and Economic Upgrading	110
4.2	Technological Composition of Exports: India and China	111
8.1	Value Chain Pressures Create Precarious Employment and Livelihoods	193
10.1	Hierarchy of Enterprises in Chennai and Kolkata	238
12.1	Value Chain Analysis (Firm catering to global supply chain)	279
12.2	Value Chain Analysis (Firm catering to domestic spares' market)	280
12.3	Auto Parts and Components Supply Chain	297
14.1	Kernel Distribution Graphs of Service Segment of Regular Workers (NSS 55th Round)	334
14.2	Kernel Distribution of Service Segment of Regular Workers (NSS 61st Round)	335
14.3	Relative Returns to Education (with respect to middle school) for 1999–2000	336
14.4	Relative Returns to Education (with respect to middle school) for 2004–5	337

FOREWORD

The rise of global production networks (GPNs), coordinated by transnational corporations, has linked firms and workers in diverse countries and distinct contexts within the same GPNs of goods and services destined for global markets. The opportunities as well as challenges of this process for developing countries are immense and require a deeper understanding of the conditions under which upgrading takes place for domestic industries and for workers. In this volume, such processes are referred to as *economic upgrading* (in which firms or industries raise their value-added with a GPN) and *social upgrading* (in which the terms and conditions of work are improved).

The vertical disintegration of segments of production in GPNs has enabled economic upgrading to be attained by some firms or producers in developing countries which have raised their value-added by moving into more technology- and knowledge-intensive segments, or shifting to more sophisticated processes and products. Some workers have also benefited from social upgrading when their skills, earnings, and conditions of work have improved, although informal work arrangements are also prevalent, particularly in the lower tiers of global value chains.

While the potential for economic and social upgrading exists, research has shown that not all firms have been able to capture these opportunities, nor have all workers shared in the gains of these processes. How economic and social upgrading can be attained, and particularly, how the relationship between both can be strengthened and made mutually-reinforcing, are crucial development issues within a global economy.

Policies have a central role to play in supporting a more integrated and inclusive upgrading process, and are complemented by the activities of employers' and workers' associations and organized civil society. The studies in this volume provide insights and implications that can influence such policies and strategies.

This volume opens with several thematic chapters which pose conceptual and governance issues related to economic and social upgrading in GPNs. The second part contains case studies which explore the impact of engagement in GPNs across a range of the major labour-intensive, capital-intensive, and knowledge-intensive sectors in the Indian economy. In this way, the volume provides a close examination of how firms and different categories of workers are affected in key sectors, while at the same time permitting cross-sectoral comparisons.

The studies reveal a complex interplay between forces which lead to upgrading or to downgrading trends in GPNs. These impacts vary across sectors and also between different tiers in global value chains. Yet, the chapters in this volume also shed light upon similarities and areas where policy interventions could be targeted in order to increase the gains and enhance their spillovers to a larger number of firms and workers otherwise excluded from economic and social upgrading processes. A number of policy-related issues are explored, such as: are informal forms of work declining, being created, or merely becoming embedded within GPNs? With economic upgrading, do developing countries obtain a greater share of profits earned within the value chain? Under what circumstances does economic upgrading lead to improvements in the terms and conditions of work in GPNs? Are these benefits confined to certain types of labour, such as skilled workers, or more widespread including low-skilled, female, casual, and contract workers, and those in small and unorganized units? What are the institutional and market factors involved in such improvements?

This volume is an important contribution to the growing literature on the impacts of global production upon labour in developing countries and provides detailed findings and analysis of interest for academics as well as policymakers.

Raymond Torres	Javeed Alam	Alakh N. Sharma
Director	Chairman	Director
IILS	ICSSR	IHD

ACKNOWLEDGEMENTS

This book is the product of a collaboration between the International Institute for Labour Studies (IILS) of the International Labour Organization (ILO), the Indian Council of Social Science Research (ICSSR) and the Institute for Human Development (IHD). The studies in this collected volume were written for an international workshop that addressed the issue of 'Global Production Networks and Decent Work: Recent Experience in India and Global Trends' held at the Institute for Social and Economic Change (ISEC) in Bangalore from 18–20 November 2007. The workshop brought together Indian and overseas scholars to present recent research findings regarding the impact of global production networks on Indian workers and firms. The discussions in this workshop have continued through on-going contact between its participants and have contributed toward a growing international research network in this field.

We are grateful to the institutional partners for their support which brought this book to fruition. We are particularly indebted to N. Jayaram, Former Director of ISEC and to S. Madheswaran and the staff for their most friendly and efficient hosting of the workshop. Thanks are also due to the contributors for their diligent revision of chapters. We would like to extend our gratitude to the anonymous external and internal readers whose valuable comments guided the revision of the draft manuscript. The ILO Subregional Office for South Asia in New Delhi provided support as well as information and comments on specific sections of the book for which we thank Leyla Tegmo-Reddy, Anjana Chellani, Akiko Sakamoto, and Coen Kompier. We owe many thanks to various readers for their comments on individual chapters, including Stephanie Barrientos, Franz

Ebert, Ann Herbert, Deirdre McCann, Frank Pyke, Arianna Rossi, Jean-Paul Sajhau, Emily Sims, and David Seligson. Special appreciation goes to Zeljka Kozul-Wright and Uma Rani Amara for stimulating discussions and suggestions while revising the text. We thank Charlotte Beauchamp and Alison Irvine-Moget of the Department of Publications at the ILO for their experienced guidance in this process. Warm gratitude is extended to the team at Oxford University Press in New Delhi which ensured capable and efficient preparation of the volume.

This entire process involved a truly collaborative effort on all sides, in which the IHD identified paper authors and organized the Bangalore workshop, while the ICSSR generously supported workshop expenses as well as travel of all Indian participants, and the IILS financed the Indian studies and travel of international participants.

Our special thanks are due to Raymond Torres, Director of the IILS and Gerry Rodgers, Former Director of the IILS, T.C.A. Anant and K.N. Jehangir of the ICSSR, and Alakh Sharma, Director, IHD, all of whom provided financial and institutional support as well as technical guidance at crucial points throughout this project.

Anne Posthuma
Dev Nathan

INTRODUCTION
Scope for Aligning Economic and Social Upgrading within Global Production Networks in India

Anne Posthuma and Dev Nathan

BACKGROUND

International trade, investment, and movement of goods have intensified at a faster pace than ever before, urged by the diffusion of new technologies, the relaxation of regulatory frameworks and the supply of low-wage labour in developing countries. Transnational corporations (TNCs) have been key drivers of this process through direct investments and international outsourcing, as they coordinate worldwide networks of suppliers that produce parts, components, final goods, and services for global markets. This coordinated sourcing is characteristic of global production networks (GPNs) which are estimated to account for one-third of world trade[1] (UNCTAD, 1999). The growth of GPNs has provided an important source of employment in many developing countries, but these are often low-waged and low-skilled jobs, involving poor terms and conditions of work. Despite the scale of these important changes, we do not fully understand their impacts upon firms and workers in developing countries.

During this same period, India has emerged as one of the fastest growing economies in the world, spurred first by reforms under its phase of domestic business-oriented liberalization and later by external market-oriented liberalization (Rodrik and Subramanian, 2004; Kohli 2006). Yet, this growth has brought mixed economic and social outcomes. On the one hand, recent studies show rising total factor productivity in Indian industry and exports have become more skill and capital intensive. This evidence suggests that some Indian products are moving into higher tiers of value chains and that companies are generating demand for more skilled workers (IMF, 2008; OECD, 2007). On the other hand, authors draw attention to problems of unbalanced growth between regions, the persistence of low quality informal work and adverse impacts of trade liberalization on more employment-intensive sectors and agriculture (Mazumdar and Sarkar, 2008; Pal and Ghosh, 2007). Given the rising prominence of India within the global economy and the need to create jobs for its large and heterogeneous labour force, we must know more about India's rising participation in GPNs and its potential to contribute toward more inclusive economic and social development.

The purpose of this volume is to present findings from selected sectoral studies and thematic texts to fill the gaps in knowledge in this still under-researched area. The studies in this volume show that the impact of participation in GPNs has been mixed. Upgrading opportunities do exist within GPNs, but the studies in this volume show that these opportunities tend to be concentrated among certain regions, sectors, firms, and workers rather than widespread. Furthermore, gains for companies do not automatically translate into gains for workers.

Participation in certain types of value chains has been found to provide latecomer firms with a fast track to process and product upgrading (Schmitz, 2004). This effect was confirmed among some domestic firms supplying to GPNs which improved their manufacturing process, enhanced product quality and sophistication, and raised productivity. Such firms have attained conformity with international technical and quality standards and increased their demand for skilled formal sector workers. These upgraded firms were mainly medium and large companies which had existing productive capacities and product development expertise prior to engagement with GPNs, or were companies which operate in higher technology and knowledge-intensive sectors such as information technology (IT). Positive spillovers were captured by smaller firms with adequate cash flow to invest in improved production practices and product quality, which also increased their requirements for skilled labour. Workers with technical and managerial skills, many semi-skilled workers, and those having opportunities to learn on-the-job also benefited.

Various exclusionary pressures also exist. Ponte (2008) draws attention to an 'adverse incorporation' of smaller firms and lower-skilled workers which has led to the embedding of informal and precarious work within global value chains (GVCs).[2] Firms in less technologically sophisticated sectors with limited productive capacities faced upgrading barriers as well. There are also costs involved in upgrading, such as investments to attain quality and product standards in the agrifood sector (Memedovic and Shepherd, 2009). In some forms of value chain governance, lead firms may prevent upgrading of suppliers, leading to 'lock-in' at low value-added, low-wage tiers (Schmitz, 2006; Gibbon and Ponte, 2005). Finally, the cost-cutting nature of much international outsourcing and fluctuations in order schedules put pressures upon suppliers to compete by keeping costs low, which includes low-wage, flexible labour practices.

While first-tier suppliers may gain under such circumstances, they survive by shifting price pressures and risks to smaller firms down their supply chain. These practices are described in the chapters on labour-intensive sectors such as garments, agriculture, and leather products as well as medium-technology sectors such as auto components. These negative externalities restrict profitability and inhibit the scope for smaller firms to invest in equipment, new practices, and quality certification. While many jobs have been created, studies provide evidence of the use of informal work throughout the tiers of many sectoral value chains, even among firms in the formal sector. Employment opportunities for women workers have been created in high tech sectors for more highly educated women, but the majority of these jobs are in labour-intensive, low-wage sectors.

Research is required to obtain a clearer understanding of the circumstances under which more inclusive and sustained upgrading in GPNs can be attained for local industry and workers. As part of this task, the chapters in this book contribute original research findings that shed light on several key questions of concern:

1. Is participation in GPNs contributing to technological upgrading among local companies and building their capacity to increase the range and sophistication of products, through mechanisms such as the transfer of technology, new production practices, and more exigent technical and quality standards? Are these processes involving smaller firms, even those in the unorganized economy?
2. Are domestic suppliers to GPNs generating higher skilled and quality jobs in India (involving standard employment contracts, payment of fair wages, and provision of adequate working conditions), or is the use of flexible and non-standard forms of work also present?
3. Is the integration of industrial clusters into GPNs more conducive to capturing and spreading positive spillovers to firms and workers, due to the distinctive features in clusters of dense inter-firm dependencies and 'thick' institutional structures of government and of business and labour associations?

The chapters in this book were written prior to the onset of the global crisis and collapse in global trade in late 2008 and early 2009. These events have exposed the vulnerabilities of export-driven development to exogenous shocks and have led to more critical review of the policy frameworks required to extract greater gains from global trade and production.

This introductory chapter is divided into two parts. The first part introduces the GPNs framework of analysis and the concepts of economic upgrading and social upgrading. The second part discusses the three sets of questions posed above in light of the findings from studies in this volume.

THE FRAMEWORK OF ANALYSIS: DEFINING ECONOMIC UPGRADING AND SOCIAL UPGRADING IN GPNs[3]

The term 'global production networks' (GPNs) is used in this volume to describe not only market-based relationships between global buyers, firms in their supply chain, and market intermediaries, but also the distinct institutional, political, and social settings of the different locations in which these productive relationships are embedded (Efendioglu et al., 2007; Barrientos et al., 2008). This framework has the advantage of enlarging the scope of analysis beyond the production chain itself. The GPNs framework takes into account the broader network of forces that impact upon the capacity of firms to improve their process and product technology and thereby move into higher value-added operations and enable workers to raise their skills and earnings, and access their labour rights. The GPNs framework comprises the two concepts of 'economic upgrading' and 'social upgrading'. These two concepts are briefly summarised below, before moving on to consider the relationship between both concepts.

Producers in developing countries pursue economic upgrading by using market linkages and new technologies to strengthen their existing productive capacities[4] in ways that enable them to raise productivity and thereby move into a higher value-added activity. Gereffi and Güler, in this volume, citing earlier literature, specify four channels of economic upgrading. Each of these four channels involves both a capital dimension and a labour dimension, which raises different implications for jobs and skills. The capital dimension entails the use of new machinery or advanced technology. The labour dimension refers to skill acquisition and labour productivity (in economic upgrading, labour is considered only as a productive factor).

1. *Product upgrading*—refers to improvements in the operation or design of an existing product, or innovations leading to the introduction of a more sophisticated product, and often requires more skilled labour;
2. *Process upgrading*—entails improvements in the production process to make it more efficient and productive. The improved production process may involve a substitution of capital for labour, which would imply a reduction of unskilled work;
3. *Functional upgrading*—involves a change in the range of activities performed by a firm or in a region that leads towards higher value-added stages in the production process (such as research and development activities, design, logistics, finance, marketing, or coordination of suppliers that provide the parts of a sub-assembly or full-package manufacturing). Moving from one segment of the value chain to another could be accomplished through vertical integration, which adds new skills and capabilities to a firm or cluster, or horizontal specialization; and
4. *Chain upgrading*—indicates the shift to a more technologically advanced production chain. New skills and technologies are frequently involved as the firm shifts into a new industry or product market.

Social upgrading refers to processes which enhance the quality of employment for workers, such as improved working conditions, skills acquisition, or higher earnings. It also involves the enhancement of social protection and workers' rights, particularly for more vulnerable categories of workers including women, children, migrants, and low-skilled workers. The broader term 'social' is used, because improved quality of work and labour rights can also impact positively upon workers' entitlements as social actors. Furthermore, this term recognizes that improved well-being of workers also affects the well-being of their dependents and may even have positive spillovers to their community. Social upgrading is comprised of two components:

1. *Measurable standards*—which involve quantifiable aspects such as the category of employment (whether regular or informal),[5] wage level, contract type, some aspects of social protection, and working hours; and
2. *Enabling rights*—which apply within the workplace and involve less quantifiable aspects such as freedom of association and the right to collective bargaining, non-discrimination, voice, and empowerment. (Elliot and Freeman, 2003; Barrientos and Smith, 2007).

The concept of social upgrading is closely related to the International Labour Organization (ILO) definition of decent work,[6] which involves both quantitative and qualitative aspects of work. Workers hired under regular employment contracts have greater ability to access their labour rights. In contrast, non-standard workers and those working in the informal economy have greater difficulty in accessing their rights or are outside the scope of national labour legislation (see further discussion in the chapters by Barrientos et al., and Damodaran and Awasthi et al. in this volume). Such workers are unlikely to avail of opportunities for social upgrading unless strategies and policies are directed toward their specific needs and circumstances.

To explore the relationship between economic and social upgrading, Milberg and Winkler (2008) studied a sample of 30 developing countries along a range of economic and decent work indicators. The study found a positive correlation between trade and economic upgrading, but not a significant link between economic upgrading and social upgrading. In the absence of more detailed data, the authors could only speculate as to the causes and consider the impacts of power and financial asymmetries between local suppliers and TNC buyers.[7] A key concern of these studies, and of future research, involves a clearer identification of factors required to strengthen the positive links between economic and social upgrading.

Global Value Chain (GVC) Analysis

As domestic firms integrate as suppliers into GPNs, their upgrading opportunities are determined not only by national policies or even by industrial categories, but increasingly by the position and role these local enterprises play within segments of GVCs. For this reason, the GVC analysis[8] is one of the core methods of analysis used within the GPNs framework. The GVC analysis highlights the linkages between lead companies and their suppliers in diverse countries involved in bringing a product or service through the stages from design and conception, through production to final markets. These relationships can range from arm's length market relations for standard products, to strategic outsourcing, or to more complex industry co-evolution as seen in the case of US buyers and Taiwanese contract manufacturers in the electronics industry (Sturgeon and Lee, 2006).

The earlier GVC literature distinguished between 'producer-driven' and 'buyer-driven' chains.[9] This distinction is still quite valid in more traditional and less technologically sophisticated sectors (Gibbon and Ponte, 2005). However, over time, the development of productive capacities and more advanced technological learning by some supplier firms and industries in developing countries have blurred this distinction (Sturgeon, 2009). More advanced suppliers may start to act like buyers, outsourcing their own production to suppliers which have demonstrated capacity to meet strict specifications and standards (ibid.). To understand how changes in technology, production complexity, or supplier competence may alter the relationship between lead firms and their suppliers, a typology of chain governance was developed (Gereffi et al., 2005).[10] Drawing upon this typology, both captive governance and relational governance characterize the inter-firm relationships described in labour-intensive and capital-intensive sectors examined in this volume. Meanwhile modular governance and some relational governance characterize the cases in the IT sector. This typology shows how the depth of technological exchange and inter-dependency between lead firms and suppliers may open up opportunities for economic upgrading by suppliers in developing countries. Within the GVC literature, some authors express greater optimism regarding upgrading opportunities for developing country firms, whereas other authors point toward situations where firms and workers have become trapped in lower value-added positions with little scope to upgrade (Ponte, 2008; Phillips and Henderson, 2009).

Labour and Gender Dimensions

The GVC analysis has most commonly been used to examine issues related to industrial upgrading. More recently, a set of authors has applied the GVC approach to examine the terms and conditions of work in production for export markets (Dolan and Tewari, 2001; Bair, 2005; Pegler and Knorringa, 2007; Barrientos, 2007a, 2007b; Nadvi, 2008). Such authors have used GVCs and other methodological approaches to provide detailed documentation of the circumstances in which precarious work is created in a variety of export sectors, including agriculture, garments, handmade carpets, yarn spinning, automotive components, and electronics (Rammohan and Sundaresan, 2003; McKay, 2006; Lee, 2007; Wick, 2007). Other authors emphasize the role of workers in global production as actors and draw attention to their strategies, collective action, and representative associations in promoting workers' rights and improving the conditions of work linked to global production (Lee, 2007; Seidman, 2008).

A related set of authors has examined public and private governance mechanisms operating at different levels, to promote compliance with labour standards within global production. Examples of such governance mechanisms include private voluntary initiatives and codes of labour practice adopted by TNCs, international framework agreements between TNCs and global union federations, and social and labour clauses in international trade agreements (to name only a few examples in this growing field:

Elliot and Freeman, 2003; Esbenshade, 2004; Barrientos and Smith, 2007; Locke et al., 2007; Schmidt, 2007; Meyer and Pickles, 2008; Papadakis, 2008; Knorringa, this volume; Posthuma, this volume).

The GPNs framework seeks to join these bodies of literature and research methodologies in order to create a multidisciplinary approach which can be used to study both economic and social processes within global production and to identify where policy and action can enhance the gains for domestic suppliers and workers in developing countries. Having introduced these concepts underpinning the GPNs framework, the following section now turns to the empirical findings in this volume by picking up three sets of issues which arise in the chapters comprising this volume: (a) the upgrading or downgrading role of inter-firm relations within GPNs; (b) the terms and conditions of work within GPNs; and (c) whether clustering among firms and the institutional environment surrounding the cluster are conducive to attaining economic and social upgrading in GPNs.

ECONOMIC UPGRADING AND SOCIAL UPGRADING AMONG INDIAN FIRMS IN GPNS

There is a continuing debate in the literature about the correct set of policies for developing countries to capture greater gains from participation in globalization. The prevailing development paradigm has advocated lowered government regulation of foreign investment, greater trade liberalization, and flexible labour markets as a key adjustment mechanism (World Bank, 2008). It was anticipated that these measures would unleash economic growth, raise the scale and productive capacities of domestic industry, and thereby enable countries with low-wage comparative advantage to create more skilled, productive and quality jobs.

Yet, various sectoral and cross-country studies show outcomes have been mixed (Gibbon and Ponte, 2005; UNCTAD, 2006 and 2007; Memedovic and Shepherd, 2009; UNIDO, 2009).[11] Instead, authors draw attention to the economic and social vulnerabilities that underlie export dependency and the unequal terms by which developing countries engage with the global economy (Stiglitz, 2002; Kozul-Wright and Rayment, 2007; United Nations, 2008). Milberg (2004) argues that the intrinsic structure and operation of global production exacerbate the uneven playing field for developing countries. In this context where TNCs hold a nearly oligopolistic bargaining position in relation to developing-country manufacturers of labour-intensive, low value-added goods, the margins of domestic industry decline and producers resort to competing on costs and low wages. As a consequence, the income of low-waged workers generates insufficient domestic aggregate demand to sustain the growth of local industries (Chan and Ross, 2003; Milberg, 2004).

Instead, other authors argue that the countries which have most benefited from opening to global production are those in which domestic companies have developed productive capacities and undertaken productivity-enhancing investments in equipment and innovation to shift into higher value-added segments which involve more sophisticated production processes and skilled labour (Cimoli, et al., 2009; UNCTAD, 2006). Authors supporting such a perspective emphasize the quality of foreign direct investment (FDI), more than its scale. Advocates of this perspective focus upon the policies and incentives that must be put in place to leverage positive impacts upon firm-level learning, the development of productive capacities, and demand for skilled labour (UNCTAD, 2006). Rather than reduced policy space among developing economies, on the contrary, upgrading in a global economy requires a more complete range of policy instruments and strengthened institutional capacity to promote firm-level capacities and ensure quality terms and conditions of work (Amsden, 2001; Akyüz et al., 2004; Rodrik, 2007; Chang, 2008; Berg and Kucera, 2008). The analytical framework of GPNs shares this perspective that policies and institutions play a pivotal role in harnessing the potential of global production to contribute to broader and sustained economic and social development (Efendioglu et al., 2007; Barrientos et al., 2008).

A number of important gains were found in all sectors examined in this book. Upgrading features included growth in the size and number of firms due to new opportunities in export markets, new investments by both foreign and domestic firms, rising output, increased employment and wages of skilled workers, and the creation of new jobs (often for women workers). Gary Gereffi and Esra Güler find these upgrading patterns were strongest in India's IT sector, but were also present for some firms and workers in the apparel and automotive industries. Meenu Tewari also identifies circumstances where economic upgrading positively reinforced social upgrading in the garments sector. Both chapters on automotive components, by T.G. Suresh and Dinesh Awasthi et al., describe economic upgrading among a core set of firms and workers in Chennai and the Punjab. These benefits tend to be concentrated rather than widespread among a broader range of firms and workers. These findings raise policy questions as to how more inclusive upgrading can be encouraged. The case studies of labour-intensive sectors (garments, leather products and agriculture), and of a medium-technology sector such as automotive components, describe the presence of negative externalities passed down to smaller firms in value chains and the use of informal and contingent labour. The following subsection will identify some of the factors leading towards these respective upgrading or downgrading patterns.

The Role of Inter-firm Relations in GPNs

Companies which benefited most from participation in GPNs had direct contact with their overseas clients and were either dynamic new entrants or incumbent firms that had built up productive capacities prior to exposure to export markets (we return to this issue later in this sub-section). Sourcing directly to the lead firm and possessing the necessary know-how to alter the form of incorporation within the value chain are recognized as significant upgrading factors (Schmitz and Knorringa, 2000; Nathan, this volume). The main success factors among upgraders included being a first-tier supplier, a large or medium-sized firm that could coordinate firms lower down the value chain and supplying to export markets, while also maintaining a foothold in the domestic market. Firm size was important in labour-intensive and price-sensitive sectors where scale economies and ability to coordinate a network of domestic suppliers are success factors. However, size was not always a determining factor for success. Smaller firms in direct contact with global buyers and possessing in-house skills with which to develop specialized products or services also raised their value-added and improved their market position. Although India's leading IT firms such as Infosys Technologies, Wipro, and Satyam Computer Services are large, niches also have been created for smaller, specialized IT service providers for overseas customers.

Process upgrading was observed in the chapters on garments, leather products, and automotive components, where firms moved from craft-like to assembly-line production. Automotive components firms replaced manual lathes with numerically-controlled machine tools (T.G. Suresh and Dinesh Awasthi et al., this volume; Unni and Rani, 2008). Even producers of agricultural and non-timber forest products were able to raise value-added of their products by increasing quality, grading, and processing of their products (Sukhpal Singh and Govind Kelkar et al., this volume). Firms were most amenable to product upgrading when they had developed firm-level capabilities. As observed in the chapter by Meenu Tewari, suppliers raised the design content of garments to access higher value-added markets and Gerefii and Güler noted a similar process in the high-end services offered by India's information technology sector. Examples of functional upgrading were less common, but were noted where firms provided full-package manufacturing to buyers both in leather shoes production (Damodaran, this volume) and the garments sector (Hirway, this volume; Tewari, this volume).

These cases demonstrate that domestic firms were often in a better position to extract benefits from global production when they already had acquired substantial productive capacities and technological know-how in their product lines, and where workers had specialized skills. This was observed in labour-intensive sectors (as seen in chapters by Tewari, Hirway, Singh, Kelkar et al., and Damodaran), in the automotive sector (T.G. Suresh, this volume), and the information technology sector (Sarkar and Mehta, this volume). These observations corroborate other studies which recognize that technology transfer and positive spillovers from TNCs are more effective in domestic firms with high absorptive capabilities (Chudnovsky et al., 2008).

A review of leading countries from globalizing Asia also suggests that the ability to harness greater gains from participation in global production—and to spread these benefits to a larger set of domestic firms—is largely determined by policies that support the ability of local firms to accumulate production capacities and compel innovative activities among leading national companies (Cimoli et al., 2008). A study of upgrading paths among Mexican firms reached similar findings that more advanced firms raised productivity and innovativeness under trade liberalization, but less advanced firms failed to keep pace (Iacovone, 2009). Policy support for domestic firms to shift from low-wage competition toward technological acquisition, skill development, and value addition would enhance the ability of domestic firms to benefit and learn from GPNs (Amsden, 2001; UNCTAD, 2006).

Evidence on the impact of the lead firm in a GPN is mixed. Case studies describe the dual role of lead firms as protagonist or impediment to economic and social upgrading in value chains. It is recognized that lead firms can play a positive role as the conduit for upgrading by transferring technology, standards, and new skill requirements as well as facilitating access to improved equipment by suppliers down the value chain (Gereffi, 1999). Under these conditions, GPNs can channel learning for domestic firms and raise the demand for skilled workers and more stable, standard employment contracts. Similarly, first-tier firms played a positive role in their supply chain when they helped smaller parts producers to adhere to strict quality and technical standards in Chennai and Punjab clusters (T.G. Suresh and Awasthi et al., this volume).

In this regard, Schmitz (2006) has noted the dual role of lead firms in 'captive' chains where participation may provide a fast track for latecomer suppliers to quickly attain process and product upgrading. In such cases, the lead firm also can block opportunities to upgrade into more profitable stages such as design, product development, marketing or branding. Downgrading pressures were prevalent in labour-intensive consumer goods, where buyers demand continuous price reductions, lead times are short, and design changes or seasonality contribute to fluctuating order volumes. Such factors are conducive to cost and risk shifting down the value chain, as illustrated when automotive assemblers in Chennai delayed payment to smaller suppliers or obliged them to hold inventories at their own expense (T.G. Suresh, this volume). Such examples reveal that upgrading trends can simultaneously be accompanied by downgrading pressures.

The chapter by Sukhpal Singh finds that medium and large farmers have benefited from participation in GPNs by raising output and productivity, improving agricultural practices and conforming to stricter technical and quality standards. In his view, the integration of small and marginal producers in rural areas within global food chains offers the potential to improve farming methods, raise product quality, and increase the incomes of rural households. Yet, the costs involved in upgrading areas such as processing, packaging, marketing, transport and standards present important entry barriers (also noted by Memedovic and Shepherd, 2009).

More than market access, Singh draws attention to the need to provide technical assistance and credit to small farmers, thereby enabling small producers to make new investments and acquire the knowledge and techniques necessary to supply higher quality markets. Singh doubts how global food chains alone could upgrade smaller producers and rural workers without strengthening their access to technical assistance and financial resources. Indeed, many smaller producers in India have been excluded from global food chains because they lack resources, knowledge, and techniques to enter higher value-added agricultural production. While competition between larger supermarkets and smaller local stores may improve quality standards, it also drives down prices which can impoverish rather than upgrade smaller producers in the value chain and run smaller local stores and vendors out of business.[12]

The discussion on production chains in agriculture is further extended to non-timber forest products in the chapter by Govind Kelkar, Meenakshi Ahluwalia, and Meenakshi Kumar. This chapter describes the various difficulties faced by indigenous women producers to obtain fair prices for their produce, or in controlling their own assets due to household gender relations. The chapter describes the results of a project where significant improvements were achieved with modest investments by empowering and organizing these women producers into groups (such as self-help groups). Through collective action, women producers strengthened their voice and improved their bargaining power in relation to buyers, while also enhancing their economic position in the household. While the cases described in this chapter refer mostly to domestic value chains, there are nevertheless important lessons that can be applied to upgrading in GPNs.

Sumangala Damodaran illustrates how cost-squeezing by global buyers and intense competition among exporting firms in the leather industry have driven down profits. Risks were passed to producers when a sample price is fixed and cannot be changed causing potentially large losses for producers if raw material prices rise. Cost cutting has become so pervasive that domestic market prices in the premium range sometimes may be higher than export prices. Damodaran recognizes the importance of non-price factors for suppliers to upgrade in GPNs (Humphrey and Schmitz, 2001) but shows that, instead, cost-based competition has predominated in India's leather industry. She argues this has reduced profitability and inhibited the ability of this sector to compete on the basis of innovation, skilled labour, and higher value-added products.

In his examination of the auto components industry in Tamil Nadu, T.G. Suresh highlights two elements: (*i*) shifts in the role of state-level industrial policies which shaped the character of this industry's development; and (*ii*) factors contributing to upgrading and downgrading patterns. The author argues that targeted policies and investments during the planning era built the infrastructure and institutions which nurtured the development of engineering-based manufacturing and highly-skilled labour. On this foundation, the state subsequently attracted foreign and domestic investment, under its new role as facilitator of capital investment. Reforms since the 1990s have streamlined the administrative structure for the approval of aspects such as incentives, land, and new infrastructure. Yet, public institutions responsible for labour regulations also have been reformed and weakened, thereby undermining a crucial mechanism for social upgrading within this local industry.

New investments and the diffusion of new production techniques and quality standards have enabled medium and large domestic firms to become major suppliers of high quality auto components. Regular workers in larger firms have benefited from economic upgrading, including a skill preium in some job areas. Yet, the author argues, upgrading spillovers to smaller firms were limited. Smaller firms have closed, shifted to the aftermarket, or become low-cost sub-contractors. Low wage informal work has grown and skilled workers have shifted to other industries. Development policies that relaxed labour legislation to attract new investment appear to have disembedded social upgrading from economic upgrading processes.

Sectoral differences matter when assessing the scope for upgrading in GPNs. The chapter by Gary Gereffi and Esra Güler provides insights in this regard by conducting a cross-industry analysis of India and China in three industries: apparel, automotives, and IT. The chapter shows that though a large number of new jobs have been created in both countries by supplying TNC lead firms, the quality of this work varies significantly. The authors present several important policy-relevant lessons for India. First of all, labour-intensive manufacturing will continue to be an important source of job creation. India must move beyond its reliance upon low-wage, low-skilled labour in industries such as apparel and address its urgent supply-side constraints (linked to low scale, lack of product diversification, and poor infrastructure). Second, consolidation of supply chains in the automotive industry has led to economic upgrading and improved job quality in assembly and first-tier companies, accompanied by poor wages and working conditions in lower tier firms. Shifting India's automotive industry toward high quality, value-added production will require more training in technical, design, and management skills, as well as greater public investments in infrastructure and electricity.

Third, despite the relatively small number of jobs in India's IT industry, the successful emergence of India as a global leader in knowledge-intensive sectors highlights the importance of domestic entrepreneurial capabilities and private sector training. A key role has been played by public sector investments in engineering colleges and science and technology institutions, as well as software technology parks. Overall, the authors find that both India and China face a common set of challenges: eroding labour-cost advantages, a shortage of highly skilled labour, and the need to move into higher value-added activities.

Scope for Small Firms to Upgrade in GPNs

Indian industry is composed mainly of small scale units which are estimated to account for nearly 80 per cent of total manufacturing employment, raising the question of how GPNs impact upon this set of firms. Indian small scale firms are traditionally characterized as labour-intensive and low-productivity units that use outdated machinery and provide poor wages and working conditions (OECD, 2007). However, recent studies reveal significant changes underway within India's small scale sector.

The gradual lifting of market reserve for small-scale industry, coupled with rising demand due to internal and external liberalization measures, appear to have encouraged firms to raise output, upgrade production practices, and hire more workers. Recent studies reveal that small firms are pursuing process upgrading, such as purchasing new equipment or importing second-hand equipment (Unni and Rani, 2008). Where firms are unable to invest in capital improvements, they may nevertheless improve operations by adopting new work practices (Saripalle, 2005). Many small-scale industries also seek internationally recognized certification such as ISO 9000/9001 and ISO 14001, or sector-specific certification such as ISO/TS16949 in the automotive industry to signal that they are able to produce at world-class standards.[13] Many small firms already export, although this varies widely across sectors (ISED, 2005).

The growth of subcontracting and outsourcing by Indian industry in recent years has linked small scale firms with larger export-oriented firms. A recent report found that the adoption of new production practices and technological change was greater among small firms working under subcontracting relationships, although it was not clear whether these firms were linked to export or domestic markets (ISED, 2005). Another study observed the growth of unorganized sector firms in the second and third tiers of auto components chains in the late 1990s. The same study found that process upgrading contributed to rising labour productivity which, in turn, encouraged improvements in the quality of employment (Rani and Unni, 2004).

In contrast, some contributors in this volume and other studies describe circumstances in which outsourcing by larger exporters to smaller unorganized firms involves shifting negative externalities down the value chain. Such examples, argue these authors, are incorporating precarious employment arrangements within export production (Nagaraj, 2007; Damodaran, 2009). Such practices were cited most frequently in labour-intensive and low value-added sectors where entry barriers are low and price competition is fierce (Barrientos, this volume; Damodaran, this volume; T.G. Suresh, this volume).

The evidence from studies cited above confirms differing tendencies. Some outsourcing relationships provided upgrading opportunities for small scale firms and their labour force. Yet, other studies find flexible and informal work at all levels, but especially in the lower tiers of GPNs. This is another area where further research is required to understand how upgrading and downgrading processes play out in subcontracting relationships between formal firms and small firms in the unorganized sector, and how this may vary across sectors.

The discussion above has shown that upgrading opportunities do exist within GPNs, but these are concentrated among certain firms and workers, rather than widespread. Furthermore, a number of factors were found to enhance positive externalities such as provision of technical assistance, availability of credit, existence of productive capacities, demand for workers with higher education and specialized skills, and conformity with international standards that require more skilled, formal sector workers. Cost and risk-shifting down value chains was most prevalent in price-sensitive, labour-intensive consumer goods industries. More specifically for workers, even where economic upgrading took place, this did not ensure an automatic link to upgrading in the terms and conditions of employment. The following section explores this latter issue in greater detail.

Social Upgrading in GPNs

Different factors have been associated with upgrading for workers in GPNs. The chapter by Meenu Tewari provides evidence showing how economic and social upgrading are linked, even among small and medium-sized firms in a labour-intensive sector. The author describes cases where Indian firms in the garments industry diversified their product mix and shifted to year-round production. More stable and higher value-added production, in turn, required more regular employment relationships, skilled labour and improved working conditions. Firms which undertook such changes reported lower turnover rates, reduced absenteeism and improved worker productivity, as well as rising profitability and export performance. This story recalls the chapter by Gary Gereffi and Esra Güler which notes the export advantage of Chinese garments producers that worked with a year-round product mix. Such cases show where social upgrading and economic upgrading are mutually-reinforcing processes.

Importantly, this positive relationship between economic upgrading and social upgrading was not due solely to market factors or inter-firm relationships in the value chain. Rather, Tewari draws attention to the central role of 'mediating institutions', which include state actors, new labour organizations, trade unions, non-profit organizations, and business associations. She describes how these mediating institutions play a role in shaping and sustaining social upgrading processes. In this context, the author describes new strategies adopted by the New Trade Union Initiative (NTUI) including a GVC approach to understand where precarious work is created in global production and how to overcome it. This approach led the union to adopt 'place-based' organizing strategies that reach out to workers in their communities—and involve issues that improve workers' lives, particularly for poor women workers—as well as organizing workers in the factories. This approach bridges both realms of work and family responsibilities of women workers. The NTUI has also campaigned to regulate labour contractors, an area which presents new challenges for organizing workers.

India has experienced rising demand for managerial, technical, and industrial skills in certain sectors and regions linked to export growth. This skills shortage—or more accurately, the skills mismatch—has called attention to the inadequacies of India's system of vocational and educational training (VET) to meet new skill requirements. This skills challenge involves raising both the quantity of graduates and the quality of training and technical skills acquired (NMCC, 2006).[14] In response, the government's National Policy on Skills Development has set three ambitious goals—expand the VET system, raise the quality and relevance of VET, and extend opportunities for skills development especially to youth and workers in the unorganized sector.

Tight labour markets for skilled workers have resulted in higher wages for skilled workers as noted by Dinesh Awasthi et al., in the Punjab auto components clusters. Meenu Tewari has observed that tight labour markets raise workers' bargaining power in relation to employers, as well as create a favourable environment for organizing workers. Yet, other authors note that rising demand for skilled labour has not necessarily led to more skilled and better-paid employment opportunities for women (Ghosh, 2004). Indira Hirway describes how rising capital-intensity and new skill requirements in the textiles and garments industry have tended to favour male workers in formal sector firms, while female workers are concentrated in lower-skilled and more flexible work in the informal sector.

The integration of low-cost and flexible workers into GPNs is facilitated by the size of India's unorganized sector, which is estimated at around 93 per cent of the national labour force (NCEUS, 2007, 2009).[15,16] A process of 'informalisation of the formal sector' is noted by various studies, in which compliance with labour legislation by registered firms is partial and affected employees receive only partial social security or other legally stipulated benefits (ibid.; Kundu and Mohanan, 2009). Informal and flexible employment arrangements also have been facilitated where states have relaxed the framework of labour regulation as part of the incentives to attract new domestic and foreign investment (Tendulkar, 2004).

The chapter by Stephanie Barrientos, Kanchan Mathur, and Atul Sood cites various studies that find the use of labour contractors to be intensifying in a range of sectors and countries engaged in GPNs. Furthermore, all levels of GVCs are affected: the authors find that precarious work tends to concentrate in lower tiers of GVCs, although casual and migrant workers were found even in upper-tier firms. This evidence has led the authors to argue that international outsourcing has created a situation where precarious work becomes endemic to global production.[17]

Similar circumstances were identified among studies in this volume. Sukhpal Singh notes that the rise of contract farming in agriculture has involved greater efforts to reduce labour costs. This has led to rising casualization of work and involvement of small producers as contract farmers as well as feminization of tasks, particularly in low-wage, low-skill, and seasonal jobs. With respect to the auto components industry in Chennai, the chapter by T.G. Suresh describes a widespread rise in part-time contracts, extension of trainee periods and subcontracting parts of production to smaller units. Other research found a significant share of informal and home-based enterprises and workers embedded in export production chains across a range of sectors, especially labour-intensive industries (Damodaran, 2009). In this regard, the NCEUS has recommended the provision of social security for all informal workers to strengthen the employment relationship between firms and informal workers and to ensure that global outsourcing takes place under clear contractual conditions and reasonable wages are paid on time (Government of India, 2008).[18]

India's textile and garments industry has grown rapidly after trade liberalization and the phase-out of quotas, becoming one of India's largest industries and a major source of employment. Yet, the chapter by Indira Hiraway shows the benefits of growth have impacted differently upon firms and workers, depending on the segment of production, firm size, whether the firm operates in the organized or unorganized sector, and whether female or male workers are involved. Organized sector firms have invested in capital deepening. In contrast, unorganized sector firms have remained labour intensive, with low productivity and higher female employment. The author shows that as the textiles and garments industry has raised exports for global markets, gender-based labour market segmentation has deepened. Larger formal sector firms have upgraded some jobs, making them more skilled, better-paid, and mostly male dominated. Meanwhile, outsourcing to informal production units resulted in new job creation mainly in informal, low-wage, low-skilled, and precarious jobs, primarily hiring women workers.

At the other end of the spectrum, the information and communication technology (ICT) sector best characterizes India's aspirations towards high-end participation in the global economy. Yet, questions are frequently raised regarding the extent to which this rising industry contributes to new job creation and good quality employment. Using data from the National Sample Survey for 1999–2000 and 2004–5 and other complementary data sources, Mehta and Sarkar (this volume) examine various aspects of decent work in the ICT sector. They provide evidence that every job in the ICT sector creates four other jobs in the wider economy and promotes high labour productivity. Formal, salaried employment is predominant, with little informality or subcontracting as compared to other sectors. Salaries are high and the sector attracts skilled and highly educated workers, although data show low unionization rates among ICT workers and that some categories of workers are not covered by social security benefits. Large differences in decent work were identified, especially for relatively lower-skilled segments of the IT-enabled services sector, such as call centres and business process outsourcing. Finally, the chapter points to changing trends in this sector, such as rising wage inequality among ICT workers.

Also related to the IT industry, Carol Upadhya provides a rare glimpse into the underside of India's high-tech miracle, based on qualitative interviews among Indian software professionals. Software developers are considered to be privileged workers who receive high salaries, work in pleasant surroundings, have opportunities to work abroad, and enjoy the satisfaction of skilled work. Instead, the author argues that India's position in the lower-end segment of software services contributes to flexibility and intensification of knowledge work. The implication here is that it is not only important to differentiate between types of industries in GPNs (for example, labour-intensive, capital-intensive, and technology-intensive). It is also important to examine whether firms specialize in production segments that are relatively higher or lower value-added.

Upadhya argues that India has carved a niche in the GVC of software production as a provider of outsourced, low-end IT services. By providing 'generic' services, Indian software firms accept a wide range of software development services in diverse 'domains', which in turn prevents software engineers from developing depth of expertise. India's 'global services delivery model' divides work across several locations and time zones, where work is carried out around the clock. This model translates into comparatively labour-intensive, low-cost, and low-skilled work that software professionals themselves describe as monotonous. Fragmentation of the work process and tight controls (including remote monitoring by overseas clients) reduce individual creativity. The dependency on overseas clients and uncertain orders results in insecure work, long and irregular working hours, intense work cycles, and high stress. All these factors contribute to high attrition rates and impact negatively upon the work–life balance of software engineers, particularly women employees.

Taking a broader perspective, Dev Nathan places the discussion of decent work within the expansion of GPNs and the question of where new sources of demand will emerge. Rising inequality and lowering of wages in order to become cost-competitive in a global economy ultimately reduce national accumulation in developing countries. The global economy is characterized by rising inequality, and changing patterns regarding where future sources of global aggregate demand will come from. Until the recent economic crisis, the expansion of global demand was dependent on US consumption and its payments deficit. However, emerging economies such as China and, to some extent, India are able to raise their domestic consumption. The future expansion of global demand, therefore, is linked to a reduction in inequalities and improved earnings of workers in developing countries, thus making the promotion of decent work an important economic policy as well as social policy.

Governance by State and Non-State Actors to Reinforce Social Upgrading

A number of state and non-state initiatives to promote better working conditions and labour rights for workers linked to global production have emerged in recent years. These initiatives seek to create new governance structures suited to the global economy (Mayer and Pickles, 2008).

The introduction of product standards and company codes of labour practice by global buyers has placed pressures on their suppliers to improve working conditions. The chapter by Stephanie Barrientos, Kanchan Mathur, and Atul Sood finds that such private codes of conduct have had varied impact, depending on which labour rights were promoted and what type of worker was covered. Drawing upon the findings from an impact assessment of codes of labour practice in the Indian garments sector, the authors conclude that codes are most effective when they seek to improve visual areas of labour conditions, such as health and safety. Codes were found to have limited impact, however, upon areas such as payment of minimum wages, social security protection, and provision of pension benefits. Moreover, codes had only minor impact on important working conditions such as hours, provision of regular employment, and harsh treatment of workers, and little or no impact on ensuring freedom of association. The study found that codes of labour practice were ineffective in promoting working conditions and labour rights for a large group of informal workers involved in these same supply chains. Based upon these findings, the authors recommend that supplier factories take more responsibility for contract workers, as a means to reduce vulnerability and to ensure that their legal entitlements are respected.

The chapter by Anne Posthuma assesses the experiences of public and private efforts to regulate labour conditions in global value chains. TNCs have gained experience and made some impact through private, voluntary codes of labour practice and social auditing. Yet, overall, many initiatives have been expensive, fragmented, and limited in their ability to impact beyond first-tier suppliers and formal workers. Public labour market institutions in developing countries are often under-staffed and under-resourced—although important trends are underway in some developing countries towards 're-regulation' and strengthening of the labour administration. The author identifies three regulatory gaps: between public and private regulation; between the protection of formal versus informal workers; and between the regulation of exporting firms and firms selling on the domestic market. In lieu of stronger public regulation in many developing countries, private sector initiatives have resulted in 'regulatory enclaves' which promote better conditions of work mainly for workers with formal employment contracts in first-tier supplier firms. Efforts to overcome regulatory enclaves will need to include more integrated, consultative, and systemic approaches. These new approaches will seek to join technical assistance with capacity building to help suppliers comply with labour standards and involve the respective strengths and capacities of public and private stakeholders.

In his chapter, Peter Knorringa focuses on fair trade and corporate social responsibility (CSR) initiatives aimed at promoting labour and environmental standards that surpass existing minimum legal requirements among firms producing for global markets. Knorringa poses two questions: 'can responsible production, as it has emerged in the industrialized countries, be mainstreamed among consumers in developing countries?'; and 'can this enhance development outcomes?' Such issues are pertinent in light of the emergence of middle-income consumers in key developing countries and the growing capacity of some suppliers to act as lead firms in their own global value chains. He asks whether middle-class consumers in developing countries would be inclined towards responsible consumption. The chapter concludes with the hypothesis that a more limited 'reach' of responsible consumption is likely to take hold in developing countries, mainly in a few pockets where 'depth' of responsible production may take root in local development strategies and could be promoted by local organizations of civil society.

In sum a positive relationship between economic and social upgrading has been achieved by some firms and sectors linked to GPNs. Furthermore, 'mediating institutions' play a role in reinforcing more balanced upgrading. However, other studies have highlighted the rising use of informal labour and informal work arrangements throughout all tiers of GPNs. Low road competitive strategies are pervasive, particularly in labour-intensive sectors. Different forms of public and private governance impact upon some working conditions among formal workers, but are limited or ineffective to improve the conditions of informal workers, particularly at lower tiers of value chains. The following section takes a different perspective, by exploring whether clusters of firms and their supporting institutions are effective in achieving more balanced economic and social upgrading in GPNs.

Do Clusters Contribute to More Balanced Economic and Social Upgrading in GPNs?

The literature on clustering and industrial districts argues that the distinct features of area-based sectoral agglomerations of firms and their socio-economic and industrial interdependencies are conducive to upgrading processes (Brusco, 1982). Central to this literature is the role played by 'thick' institutional structures of government, sectoral, and labour associations and other agencies that support economic and social upgrading in the productive sphere (Becattini, 1990). According to these authors, the embedding of clustered firms within formal and informal institutions fosters the conditions for firms to specialize and achieve collective efficiencies. Meanwhile, workers' associations struggle for quality terms and conditions of employment. Placing this literature within the context of globalized production, it is pertinent to ask if structures associated with clusters are more conducive to economic and social upgrading and can promote broader positive spillovers to smaller suppliers? Furthermore, do these circumstances enhance opportunities for training and creation of quality employment?

Some authors are sceptical, citing research findings that show upgrading of some firms does not necessarily upgrade others—on the contrary, some studies suggest upgrading of larger firms is related to the exclusion of weaker firms in the same chain or territory (Bair 2005; Dolan and Tewari, 2001). This mixed process of inclusion and exclusion is well illustrated in the case study by Dinesh Awasthi et al. that examines labour conditions among auto parts producers located in three Punjab clusters.

Two sets of value chains were examined: firms supplying to vehicle assemblers in domestic and export markets; and others serving the domestic replacement market (involving mainly unorganized sector firms). The study argues that upgrading was largely determined by the market served. Greater social upgrading took place in firms that supply to higher value-added markets (that is, the domestic and export assemblers). The diffusion of new production standards and rising output deepened rather than bridged this divide.

Firms supplying directly to higher value-added markets (involving around 400 large firms) experienced a strong upgrading 'pull' and received technical assistance from assembler clients when adopting new equipment and quality control systems. These firms had better working conditions, regular employment contracts, and on-going skills development. Meanwhile, nearly 10,000 micro, small, and medium sized suppliers to the domestic aftermarket continued using old machinery and visual quality inspection with high rejection rates of over 10 per cent. Poor working conditions were prevalent along various parameters of decent work for this latter set of firms. The lack of positive inter-firm spillovers from higher end suppliers to firms serving the domestic aftermarket, and the absence of local institutions that could provide training or other technical support for upgrading among smaller firms, showed little evidence of clustering benefits here.

A paradox is posed by Sumangala Damodaran in her study of three leather clusters. On the one hand, these clusters had manufacturing expertise, skilled labour, and decades of export experience prior to external liberalization. Furthermore, the industry enjoyed a favourable policy environment; the government was targeting incentives and assistance to induce economic upgrading in the leather industry in order to capture new export opportunities. On the other hand, and contrary to expectations, these clusters failed to raise the value-added of their products, and instead lost existing market share in various segments of the export market for leather products.

To explain this paradox, the author examines changes in the structure of production and conditions of work arising from engagement with GPNs. She attributes part of the industry's declining export performance to its reliance on low-cost labour which locked the industry into a 'low road' competitive strategy. Firms focused on cost-cutting and labour flexibility rather than investments in product and process upgrading. The study reflects upon the deleterious effects of price-based competition which inhibited upgrading even in clusters with firm-level expertise and a favourable policy environment. This case reinforces the lesson that clustered firms which followed cost-cutting, low-wage strategies, rather than investing in capabilities and skills, failed to mobilize positive inter-firm dynamics and avail of the institutional support believed to be conducive to more inclusive cluster upgrading.

In sum, the chapters in this volume show that economic upgrading has been attained by some Indian firms engaged in GPNs, but the upgrading effect has been mixed across regions, sectors, firms, and categories of workers. Gains were captured most readily by medium and large firms in direct contact with global buyers. Companies with existing productive capacities and in more knowledge-intensive and technologically sophisticated products and production segments also gained. Workers benefited most in this set of firms, which tended to offer better quality and skilled jobs with regular employment contracts. In addition, recent studies have revealed a new dynamism among small domestic firms that are undertaking even modest initiatives to attain process and product upgrading. Workers (especially skilled male workers), in this second set of firms also benefited from rising productivity, improved working environment, new skills requirements, and better wages. These upgrading efforts were reinforced by mediating institutions such as government agencies, workers' associations, trade unions, employers' associations, and non-governmental organizations.

At the same time, many firms have been excluded or incorporated under adverse conditions, which tend to lock them into low-wage, low-skilled forms of competition. Shifting of costs and risks down the supply chain have restricted small firms' capital for investments in product and process upgrading and driven them toward cost-based competition. Terms and conditions of work are poor in firms which rely on low wages and flexible labour practices to survive. Policies could provide an important support to upgrade such firms, by providing lines of credit and strengthening incentives for innovation. Asymmetries in GPNs, which enhance the bargaining position of TNCs and lead to price-driven outsourcing, present an enormous challenge for firms in developing countries. This volume has provided some examples where small producers raised scale, increased bargaining power, or enhanced value-added. More comprehensive policy responses are required to spread these benefits and attain more inculsive upgrading. Clusters of firms examined did not demonstrate any superior tendency to achieve more inclusive and widespread upgrading. Such cases point toward a role for policies to address negative externalities, induce a shift from dependence on low-wage costs to innovation and skills-based competition and strengthening of local support institutions.

Economic upgrading is not always accompanied by social upgrading. The growing use of informal labour, even among firms in the formal sector, has embedded precarious forms of work within GPNs. Workers with weak employer attachment have few means by which to access their labour rights. Public and private initiatives to promote labour standards in GPNs were found to be limited in their ability to improve the terms and conditions of a wide range of workers in GPNs. Some recommendations to enhance social upgrading were mentioned in this volume, including: the need for supplier firms to take responsibility for the legal entitlements of contract workers; and to ensure that outsourcing takes place under clear contractual conditions and that reasonable wages are paid. Clear regulations for labour contractors also are needed. The reforms underway in India's VET system to raising quality and widen access are very important and timely. Recommendations put forward by the NCEUS to strengthen the employment relationship where informal workers are hired, and to provide social security for all informal workers have significant implications to improve the protection of such workers.

The studies in this volume aim to contribute to the on-going debate regarding the potential and the challenges of participation in GPNs by developing countries and to inform policy considerations about how more inclusive economic and social upgrading can be attained in the global economy.

NOTES

1. Another third of world trade consists of intra-firm trade largely within TNCs, while the final third of world trade involves arm's length transactions through remote markets (UNCTAD, 2001).
2. As will be discussed later, the term 'global value chains' (GVCs) refers to the linkages between producers, workers, and other economic actors, across geographical locations, involved in the full range of activities to bring goods and services through the various stages from design, to production and consumption.
3. The discussion in this section draws upon a more detailed concept note by Barrientos et al. (2008), which presents the notions of economic upgrading and social upgrading and explores the relationship between both concepts.
4. Productive capacities have been variously described by different authors. Here we use the broader definition of productive capacities which includes 'the productive resources, entrepreneurial capabilities and production

linkages which together determine the capacity of a country to produce goods and services' (UNCTAD, 2006).
5. This involves casual and contract workers and informalization of formal labour markets.
6. Decent work is composed of four components: employment; standards and rights of work; social protection; and social dialogue. The definition of decent work involves work taking place under conditions of freedom, equity, security, and human dignity, in which rights are protected and adequate remuneration and social protection are provided (International Labour Organization, 1999).
7. Related to the effects of these asymmetries on upgrading possibilities of developing country firms, a study of the Mexican automobile industry found the rents of productivity growth attained by local suppliers were captured by TNC lead firms or passed on to consumers in the US and Europe, which resulted in a gap between productivity growth of domestic firms and wages (Palma, 2006).
8. We cite only a few works in this large body of GVC literature (Kaplinsky, 2000; Gereffi et al., 2001; Humphrey, 2004; Schmitz, 2005; Sturgeon, 2009) and global commodity chains literature (Gereffi and Korzeniewicz, 1994; Bair, 2005, 2009). For a comprehensive listing of the GVC literature, see www.globalvaluechains.org.
9. Producer-driven chains involve global production that is controlled by TNC manufacturers in capital and technology-intensive industries such as aircraft and automobiles. Meanwhile, buyer-driven chains are coordinated by lead firms such as large retailers, global brands, or supermarkets in labour-intensive consumer goods such as apparel, footwear, and agriculture that work with global sourcing networks with low-cost suppliers (Gereffi, 1994; Dolan and Humphrey, 2000).
10. Three (out of the original typology of five) forms of network governance are of greatest relevance to the sectoral case studies raised in this book, which involve coordinated relationships in GPNs. Between the extremes of hierarchy or market-based relationships, the other three governance forms include:
    a. Modular governance—where complex information regarding the transaction is codified and often digitized before being passed to highly competent suppliers;
    b. Relational governance—where information is exchanged between buyers and highly competent suppliers; and
    c. Captive governance—where less competent suppliers are provided with detailed instructions from lead firms who often dominate their supplier's business (ibid.; Sturgeon, 2009).
11. For example, an analysis of 24 value chains, covering two-thirds of the total merchandise exports of less developed countries (LDCs) in 2000–

2005, found that LDCs did not manage to significantly upgrade their specialization within these value chains (UNCTAD, 2006).
12. In this regard, Singh mentions cases where large buyers such as Carrefour, Asda, and Tesco have been charged with unfair business practices.
13. The Indian Ministry of Small Scale Industries has supported the wider dissemination of certification among small production units by providing reimbursement of consultant fees while preparing to apply for ISO certification. Firms which attain quality certification also lay the foundation for other competitive improvements, including technological and innovative capabilities that would permit a shift into higher value-added activities (Mani and Parameswaran, 2007).
14. Many small manufacturing firms in the automotive parts sector were found to be hiring migrant rural workers and providing on-the-job training, which suggests that official statistics may not be capturing the widespread process of informal training and skills development taking place among informal and small scale manufacturing firms that must meet their urgent and growing skills requirements (Unni and Rani, 2008).
15. India's 'Unorganized Sector' is a category of precarious and unprotected work that includes informal, unregistered workers, the self-employed, contract and casual labour, unorganized and own-account production units, almost all of the agricultural sector, small-scale industries, and home-workers. Unorganized workers have little bargaining power, particularly given India's labour surplus, and suffer low wages, poor working conditions, lack of income security or social security and are prone to unemployment and underemployment (NCEUS, 2006).
16. An estimated five-fold gap in earnings exists between the organized and unorganized sectors (Ray, 2004), reinforced by low productivity. These factors create an effective barrier against lifting workers out of poverty in the expanding unorganized sector (Papola, 2008).
17. Examining NSS data, Damodaran (2009) finds that about one-third of informal enterprises in India operate on contract, including a significant rise in small, own-account, home-based enterprises. The sectoral analysis confirms these practices in firms and sectors connected with GVCs.
18. The Unorganized Workers Social Security Bill approved by the Rajya Sabha and Lok Sabha in December 2008 is an example of setting a social floor for informal workers.

REFERENCES

Akyüz, Y., R. Kozul-Wright, and J. Mayer (2004), 'Trade and Industrial Upgrading in Developing Countries', in W. Milberg (ed.), *Labor and the Globalization of Production: Causes and Consequences of Industrial Upgrading*. New York: Palgrave Macmillan.

Amsden, A. (2001), *The Rise of 'The Rest': Challenges to the West from Late-Industrializing Economies*. New York: Oxford University Press.

Bair, J. (2005), 'Global Capitalism and Commodity Chains: Looking Back, Going Forward', *Competition and Change*, 9(2): 153–80.

Barrientos, S. (2007a), 'Migrant and Contract Labour in Global Production Systems—Addressing Decent Work for the Most Vulnerable Workers', Mimeo, February.

—— (2007b), 'Global Production Systems and Decent Work', Policy Integration Department, Working Paper No. 77. Geneva: International Labour Organization.

Barrientos, S., G. Gereffi, and A. Rossi (2008), 'What are the Challenges and Opportunities for Economic and Social Upgrading?', Concept Note presented at the 'Capturing the Gains Workshop', Manchester, December.

Barrientos, S. and S. Smith (2007), 'Do Workers Benefit from Ethical Trade? Assessing Codes of Labour Practice in Global Production Systems', *Third World Quarterly*, 28: 713–29.

Barrientos, S. and A. Kritzinger (2004), 'Squaring the Circle: Global Production and Informalization of Work in South African Fruit Exports', *Journal of International Development*, 16(1): 81–92.

Becattini, G. (1990), 'The Marshallian Industrial District as a Socio-economic Notion', in F. Pyke, G. Becattini and W. Sengenberger (eds), *Industrial Districts and Inter-Firm Co-operation in Italy*. Geneva: International Institute for Labour Studies.

Brusco, S. (1982), 'The Emilian Model: Productive Decentralisation and Social Integration', *Cambridge Journal of Economics*, 6(2): 167–84.

Chan, A. and R. Ross (2003), 'Racing to the Bottom: International Trade without a Social Clause', *Third World Quarterly*, 24(6): 1011–28.

Chang, H.J. (2008), *Bad Samaritans: The Myth of Free Trade and the Secret History of Capitalism*. New York: Bloomsbury Press.

Chudnovsky, D., A. López, and G. Rossi (2008), 'Foreign Direct Investment Spillovers and the Absorptive Capabilities of Domestic Firms in the Argentine Manufacturing Sector (1992–2001)', *Journal of Development Studies*, 44(5): 645–77.

Cimoli, M., G. Dosi, and J. Stiglitz (2009), 'The Future of Industrial Policies in the New Millenium: Toward a Knowledge-centred Development Agenda', in M. Cimoli, G. Dosi, and J. Stiglitz (eds), *Industrial Policy and Development: The Political Economy of Capabilities Accumulation*. Oxford: Oxford University Press.

Damodaran, S. (2009), 'Global Production, Employment Conditions and Decent Work: Evidence from India's Informal Sector', Paper presented at the Conference on Regulating for Decent Work, Geneva, 8–10 July.

Dolan, C. and J. Humphrey (2000), 'Governance and Trade in Fresh Vegetables: The Impact of UK Supermarkets on the African Horticulture Industry', *Journal of Development Studies*, 37(2): 147–76.

Dolan, C. and M. Tewari (2001), 'From What We Wear to What We Eat: Upgrading in Global Value Chains', *IDS Bulletin*, 32(3): 94–104.
Efendioglu, U., A. Posthuma, and A. Rossi (2007), 'Decent Work in Global Production Systems: An Integrated Approach to Economic and Social Upgrading', Draft working paper, March. Geneva: ILO.
Elliott, K. and R. Freeman (2003), *Can Labor Standards Improve under Globalization?* Washington D.C.: Institute for International Economics.
Esbenshade, J. (2004), *Monitoring Sweatshops: Workers, Consumers and the Global Apparel Industry*. Philadephia: Temple University Press.
Gereffi, G. (1999), 'International Trade and Industrial Upgrading in the Apparel Commodity Chain', *Journal of International Economics*, 48(1): 37–70.
Gereffi, G., J. Humphrey, R. Kaplinsky, and T. Sturgeon (2001), 'Introduction: Global Value Chains and Development', *IDS Bulletin*, 32(3): 1–9.
Gereffi, G., J. Humphrey, and T. Sturgeon (2005), 'The Governance of Global Value Chains', *Review of International Political Economy*, 12(1): 78–104.
Gereffi, G. and M. Korzeniewicz (eds) (1994), *Commodity Chains and Global Capitalism*. Westport: Praeger.
Ghosh, J. (2004), 'Globalisation, Export-Oriented Employment for Women and Social Policy: A Case Study of India', in S. Razavi, R. Pearson, and C. Danloy (eds), *Globalization, Export-Oriented Employment and Social Policy: Gendered Connections*. Houndmills: Palgrave.
Gibbon, P. and S. Ponte (2005), *Trading Down: Africa, Value Chains and the Global Economy*. Philadelphia: Temple University Press.
Government of India (2008), *Economic Survey 2007–2008*, New Delhi: Ministry of Finance (available at http://indiabudget.nic.in/, accessed on 7 April 2009).
Government of India, Planning Commission (2008), *Eleventh Five Year Plan 2007–12, Volume 1: Inclusive Growth*. New Delhi: Oxford University Press (available at http://planningcommission.nic.in/plans/planrel/fiveyr/11th/11_v1/11th_vol1.pdf, accessed on 7 April 2009).
Humphrey, J. (2004), 'Upgrading in Global Value Chains', Working Paper No. 28. Geneva: Policy Integration Department, ILO.
Iacovone, L. (2009), 'The Better You Are, The Stronger it Makes You: Evidence on the Asymmetric Impact of Liberalization', Policy Research Working Paper 4930. Washington D.C.: Development Research Group, The World Bank.
ISED (2005), *India: The State of Development of Small and Medium Enterprises*. New Delhi: Institute of Small Enterprises and Development.
IILS (International Institute for Labour Studies) (2008), *World of Work Report: Income Inequalities in the Age of Financial Globalization*. Geneva: ILO.
Kaplinsky, R. (2000), 'Spreading the Gains from Globalisation: What can be Learned from Global Value Chain Analysis?', IDS Working Paper No. 110. Brighton: Institute of Development Studies.
Kohli, A. (2006), 'Politics of Economic Growth in India, 1980–2005' (Parts I and II), *Economic and Political Weekly*, 1 and 8 April, Part I: 1251–59, Part II: 1361–70.

Kozul-Wright, R. and P. Rayment (2007), *The Resistible Rise of Market Fundamentalism: Rethinking Development Policy in an Unbalanced World*. London: Zed Books and Third World Network.

Kundu, A. and P.C. Mohanan (2009), 'Poverty and Inequality Outcomes of Economic Growth in India: Focus on Employment during the Period of Structural Adjustment', OECD Seminar on Employment Outcomes and Inequality: New Evidence, Links and Policy Responses in Brazil, China, and India, 8 April, Paris.

Lee, C.K. (2007), *Against the Law: Labor Protests in China's Rustbelt and Sunbelt*. Berkeley: University of California Press.

Mani, S. and M. Parameswaran (2007), 'The Other Side of the Story: Industry Standards and Technological Capability Building at the Industry Level: A Study Based on the Indian Automotive Industry', Paper presented at the Globelics Conference.

Mayer, F. and J. Pickles (2008), 'Governance and Implications for Decent Work in Global Production Networks', Concept Note prepared for DFID grant, 'Capturing the Gains: Economic and Social Upgrading in Global Production Networks', November.

Mazumdar, D. and S. Sarkar (2008), *Globalization, Labor Markets and Inequality in India*. New York: Routledge and IRDC.

McKay, S.C. (2006), *Satanic Mills or Silicon Islands? The Politics of High-Tech Production in the Philippines*. Ithaca: Cornell University Press.

Mehrotra, S. and M. Biggeri (eds) (2007), *Asian Informal Workers: Global Risks, Local Protection*. Routledge Studies in the Growth Economies of Asia. London: Routledge.

Memedovic, O. and A. Shepherd (2009), 'Agri-Food Value Chains and Poverty Reduction: Overview of Main Issues, Trends and Experiences', Working Paper 12. Vienna: Research and Statistics Branch.

Milberg, W. (2004), 'Globalized Production: Structural Challenges for Developing Country Workers', in W. Milberg (ed.), *Labor and the Globalization of Production: Causes and Consequences of Industrial Upgrading*. New York: Palgrave Macmillan.

Milberg, W. and D. Winkler (2008), 'Measuring Economic and Social Upgrading in Global Production Networks', Concept Note presented at the 'Capturing the Gains Workshop', Manchester, December.

Ministry of Labour and Employment, Government of India and ILO Subregional Office in India (2008), 'National Policy on Skills Development' (draft), New Delhi.

Nadvi, K. (2008), 'Global Standards, Global Governance and the Organization of Global Value Chains', *Journal of Economic Geography*, 8(3): 323–43.

Nagaraj, R. (2004), 'Fall in Organised Manufacturing Employment: A Brief Note', *Economic and Political Weekly*, 39(30): 3387–90.

—— (2007), 'Labour Market in India: Current Concerns and Policy Responses', Seminar on Labour Markets in Brazil, China, and India, OECD, March.

Nash, J. (1953), 'Two-person Cooperative Games', *Econometrica*, 21(1): 128–40.

NASSCOM–Mc Kinsey Report (2005), *Extending India's Leadership of the Global IT and BPO Industries*.
Nathan, D., D.N. Reddy, and G. Kelkar (2008), *International Trade and Global Civil Society*. New Delhi: Routledge.
NCEUS (National Commission on Enterprises in the Unorganized Sector) (2006), 'Redefining of Unorganized Sector in India', Paper No. 2. New Delhi: Expert Group on Informal Sector Statistics.
NCEUS (2007), *Report on Conditions of Work and Promotion of Livelihoods in the Unorganized Sector*. New Delhi: NCEUS.
––––– (2009), 'The Challenge of Employment in India—An Informal Economy Perspective'. New Delhi: NCEUS.
OECD (Organisation for Economic Co-operation and Development) (2007), *Economic Survey of India*. Paris: OECD.
––––– (2008a), 'The Social Impact of Foreign Direct Investment', OECD Policy Brief. Paris: OECD.
––––– (2008b), *Employment Outlook 2008*. Paris: OECD.
Pal, P. and J. Ghosh (2007), 'Inequality in India: A Survey of Recent Trends', DESA Working Paper No. 45, July, New York.
Palit, A. (2008), 'Evolution of Global Production Systems and Their Impact on Employment in India', Draft Working Paper. New Delhi: ILO Subregional Office.
Palma, J.G. (2006), 'Globalizing Inequality: Centrifugal and Centripetal Forces at Work', DESA Working Paper No. 35, ST/ESA/2006/DWP/35. New York: United Nations.
Papadakis, K. (ed.) (2008), *Cross-Border Social Dialogue and Agreements: An Emerging Global Industrial Relations Framework?*. Geneva: International Institute for Labour Studies and ILO.
Papola, T.S. (2008), 'Employment Challenge and Strategies in India', ILO Asia-Pacific Working Paper Series. New Delhi: ILO Subregional Office for South Asia.
Pegler, L. and P. Knorringa (2007), 'Integrating Labour Issues in Global Value Chain Analysis: Exploring Implications for Labour Research and Unions', in V. Schmidt (ed.), *Trade Union Responses to Globalization*. Geneva: ILO.
Phillips, R. and J. Henderson (2009), 'Global Production Networks and Industrial Upgrading: Negative Lessons from Malaysian Electronics', *Austrian Journal of Development Studies*, Special Issue on 'Understanding Uneven Development in the Global Economy', 2: 38–61.
Ponte, S. (2008), 'Developing a "Vertical" Dimension to Chronic Poverty Research: Some Lessons from Global Value Chain Analysis', Working Paper No. 111, Manchester: Chronic Poverty Research Centre, University of Manchester.
Prebisch, R. (1960), *The Economic Development of Latin America and its Principle Problem*. New York.
Rammohan, K.T. and R. Sundaresan (2003), 'Socially Embedding the Commodity Chain: An Exercise in Relation to Coir Yarn Spinning in Southern India', *World Development*, 31(5): 903–23.

Rani, U. (2008), 'Impact of Changing Work Patterns on Income Inequality', Discussion Paper No. 193. Geneva: International Institute for Labour Studies, ILO.

Rani, U. and J. Unni (2004), 'Unorganized and Organised Manufacturing in India: Potential for Employment Generating Growth', *Economic and Political Weekly*, 39(41): 4568–80.

Ray, S.R. (2004), 'Unorganized vis-à-vis Organized Manufacturing Sector in India', Indian Ministry of Statistics and Programme Implementation, November (available at http://mospi.nic.in/mospi_seminarseries/nov04_3_6_final.pdf, last accessed 10 August 2009).

Rodrik, D. (2007), *One Economics, Many Recipes: Globalization, Institutions and Economic Growth*. Princeton: Princeton University Press.

Rodrik, D. and A. Subramanian (2005), 'From "Hindu Growth" to Productivity Surge: The Mystery of the Indian Growth Transition', IMF Staff Papers, 52(2). Washington D.C.: International Monetary Fund.

Sakamoto, A. (2008), Background Paper on Skills Policy, presented to the Indian Government, New Delhi.

Saripalle, M. (2005), 'Competing through Costs Versus Capabilities: Organisational Transformation of the Indian Automobile Industry', Mimeo, June.

Sayeed, A. and R. Balakrishnan (2004), 'Why do Firms Disintegrate? Towards an Understanding of the Firm Level Decision to Sub-Contract and Its Implications for Labor', in W. Milberg (ed.), *Labor and the Globalization of Production: Causes and Consequences of Industrial Upgrading*. New York: Palgrave Macmillan.

Schmidt, V. (ed.) (2007), *Trade Union Responses to Globalization*. Geneva: ILO.

Schmitz, H. and P. Knorringa (2000), 'Learning from Global Buyers', IDS Working Paper No. 100, Brighton: Institute of Development Studies, University of Sussex.

Seguino, S. and C. Grown (2006), 'Gender Equity and Globalization: Macroeconomic Policy for Developing Countries', *Journal of International Development*, 18(8): 1081–104.

Seidman, G. (2007), *Beyond the Boycott: Labor Rights, Human Rights and Transnational Activism*. New York: American Sociological Association, Rose Series/Russell Sage Foundation.

Singh, A. (2009), 'The Past, Present and Future of Industrial Policy in India: Adapting to the Changing Domestic and International Environment', in M. Cimoli, G. Dosi, and J.E. Stiglitz (eds), *Industrial Policy and Development: The Political Economy of Capabilities Accumulation*. New York: Oxford University Press.

Stiglitz, J. (2002), *Globalization and its Discontents*. New York: W.W. Norton and Company.

Sturgeon, T. and J. R. Lee (2006), 'Industry Co-Evolution: A Comparison of Taiwan and North American Electronics Contract Manufacturers', in S. Berger and R. Lester (eds), *Global Taiwan: Building Competitive Strengths in a New International Economy*. New York: M.E. Sharpe.

TeamLease Services (2007), 'India Labour Report 2007: The Youth Unemployability Crisis' (available at www.teamlease.com, last accessed 10 August 2009).

Tendulkar, S.D. and T.A. Bhavani (2007), *Understanding Reforms: Post 1991 India*. New Delhi: Oxford University Press.

United Nations (2008), *World Economic and Social Survey: Overcoming Economic Insecurity*. New York: Department of Economic and Social Affairs, United Nations (available at http://www.un.org/esa/policy/wess, accessed on 8 October 2009)

UNCTAD (1999), *World Investment Report: Foreign Direct Investment and the Challenge of Development*, Geneva.

——— (2006), *LDC Report 2006: Developing Productive Capabilities*, Geneva.

——— (2007), *LDC Report 2006: Knowledge, Technological Learning and Innovation for Development*, Geneva.

UNIDO (2009), *Industrial Development Report 2009: Breaking in and Moving Up*, Vienna.

Unni, J. and U. Rani (2008), *Flexibility of Labour in Globalizing India: The Challenge of Skills and Technology*. New Delhi: Tulika Books.

Wick, I. (2007), 'Aldi's Clothing Bargains: Discount Buys Discounting Standards? Working Conditions in Aldi's Suppliers in China and Indonesia'. Siegburg: SÜDWIND Institut für Ökonomie und Ökumene.

World Bank (2008), *India Country Strategy 2009–12*. Washington, D.C. (available at http://go.worldbank.org/5IWA37WFB0, accessed on 8 October 2009).

World Bank (2008), *Doing Business 2009*. Washington D.C.: The World Bank, the International Finance Corporation, and Palgrave Macmillan.

I

Conceptual and Governance Issues Related to Economic and Social Upgrading in Global Production Networks

1 GLOBAL AGGREGATE DEMAND, INEQUALITY, AND THE PROSPECTS FOR DECENT WORK

Dev Nathan[*]

THE QUESTION OF AGGREGATE GLOBAL DEMAND

Global production networks (GPNs) exist within the context of international trade. In fact, the very definition of GPNs relates to the location of segments of production processes in different national arenas. As a result of this, a product enters into international trade at different stages of production, and not just at the beginning and the end. But it is the demand for the final commodity that determines the demand for its different components. The scale or extent of production at different stages of a GPN then depends on the final demand for the product that is put on the market.

In this elementary way, global demand for a product determines the extent to which capital will employ labour. But capital does so in the context of investment and production decisions themselves based on the market and expectations about the market. And, as we all know now after Keynes, there is no reason why investment should always equal savings; as a consequence of which there could be a shortfall in aggregate demand.

To put the same problem in the context of global production systems, any one firm or country can increase its production of traded commodities. But there is no assurance, rather it is unlikely, that there will always be

---

[*]Thanks to T.S. Papola and Sandip Sarkar for discussions at various times. Thanks most of all to Govind Kelkar for pointing out that, with the feminization of agriculture in China and India, contemporary rural–urban inequality in these countries is a matter of gender inequality.

sufficient demand to absorb all of the increased production. The expansion of production in GPNs thus depends on the expansion of global demand. But with competitive cost-cutting pressures, wages will be pushed down. For each firm this may be a profitable strategy, but in the aggregate this can lead to a shortfall in demand (unless investment covers up for all the increase in profits). The likely reduction in aggregate demand in the subsequent period would reduce the demand for labour and thus adversely affect labour market conditions. This is the crucial Keynesian market failure, reproduced on a global scale and affecting the prospects for decent work.

Along with the aforementioned cost-cutting tendency of competition, it may be pointed out that the world economy is currently in a phase of an increase in productivity due to the application of information technology (IT). This is a general-purpose technology, such as the steam engine or electricity. As it is applied to production in general, the resulting increase in productivity would itself require an expansion of the market, even to sustain levels of production. At the same time, the effect of the increase in productivity would be to decrease employment per unit of output, and thus tend to reduce the employment of labour. Offsetting this tendency would be the income effect of an increase in productivity, which would increase the demand for labour.

There are three sources of demand. The first is investment by capitalists, whether due to the pressure of competition (in order not to lose competitive position in the market), to replace stock and machinery, or to utilize anticipated increases in the market. The second is consumption by workers and others. Fordism is not only mass production, it is also mass consumption required to sustain the increases in production. But all of this may still be insufficient to sustain the market for the increased volume of production. A third source of demand is the extension or widening of the capitalist market into new areas. The first two constitute the deepening of capital, while the third is the extension of capital. The importance of capitalism extending its frontiers was recognized by Rosa Luxemborg (1968) as a crucial factor for the sustainability of capital accumulation. Market expansion, however, is achieved not only through the export of goods and capital but also through national accumulation in developing countries.

The best promise of massive market expansion would seem to be in the incorporation of more and more countries to global growth, investment, production and consumption. Growth in the larger countries of the developing world, together with China, Russia and the ex-socialist group of Eastern Europe, could serve as a first tier to pull the others forward. It is quite obvious that these potentially huge markets are a very long way from stagnation (Perez, 2002: 167).

In the current scenario, however, the expansion of global demand is crucially dependent on the US payments deficit. This, of course, cannot continue for ever. There are already signs that growth in Asia, particularly China and to an extent India, is beginning to take up some of the slack from American slowdown. But does the current importance of the US deficit mean that any self-diffusion of capitalism must come to a halt, as argued by Patnaik (2007)? No, what it does mean is that in order to sustain the continued diffusion of capitalism, the international financial system will have to undergo a change to continue the expansionist course. Such a change has occurred before—from the gold and the gold–sterling standard during the British Empire to the gold–dollar and then a dollar–oil standard after the 1970s, during US hegemony. The growth of Asia is now increasing pressure for another change in the world's financial system, moving from a dollar-based standard to an SDR-based or some other such standard. There is also need for a change in the distribution of global savings, with an increase in savings in the US and a possible reduction in China.

How this change will come about—whether in the national-capital manner of the first half of the twentieth century, or with the transnationalization of capital itself holding sway in the formation of appropriate institutions of global capital, or with an altogether new and different type of economic system—is something that remains to be seen. The current global recession has sparked off debate on what is needed for global regulation and on what the shape of Bretton Woods II will be.

GLOBAL INEQUALITY

The question of changing the regime of global accumulation is not only one of a new financial architecture. There is also the question of inequality in the global economy and the manner in which it might impact on the stability of accumulation and growth. A feature of growth in the current period of globalization of production networks (that is, post 1973, or post the OPEC [Organization of the Petroleum Exporting Countries] oil shock, which brought to an end the post-Second World War golden age of capitalism) is the growth of inequality in the world economy.

An increase in global inequality would mean an increase in the share of profits (or property incomes) and a reduction in the share of wages in total income (or non-property incomes). In classical economic analysis (including in this Keynesian analysis), workers are assumed to consume all their income and save nothing, while capitalists save all their income. Investment by capitalists then has to equal savings, if there was not to be a deficit in effective demand. Without sticking to the assumption of workers consuming all they earn, it is still correct that savings out of wages would be much less than savings out of profits. In which case an increase in inequality, leading to an increase in profit share, would require a corresponding increase in investment.[1]

For individual economies, an excess of savings over investment can always be transferred to another country, for example, by buying government bonds in that country. This is most famously the case of excess Chinese savings being transferred to the US, which has net negative savings. Such shifts would lead to accumulations of claims in one country on another. For any individual country it is possible for there to be such an excess of savings over investment, without a deflationary effect. But for the world as a whole, investment must equal savings; else such an excess of savings over investment will have a deflationary effect. There is a real sense in which there is a global economy—investment will need to equal savings over the world as a whole, if demand is to equal production. A shortfall of global savings over global investment will result in global effective demand less than production, with all its consequences for global employment and decent work.

Investment is inherently unstable, depending not only on the current economic situation but also on expectations about the future. A high level of inequality, leading to a high savings rate and thus requiring high investment, is an unstable situation. Of course, high savings and high investment are conducive to high rates of growth, of the type the world has seen for more than a decade. But the high investment requirement of high inequality makes for an unstable economic situation. The higher the amount of investment needed to maintain employment, the more unstable the economic situation would be. A transition to a lower level of global inequality, on the other hand, would increase the component of consumer demand in total aggregate demand and, thus, reduce reliance on uncertain investment.

The former chairman of the US Federal Reserve, Alan Greenspan, frequently referred to 'irrational exuberance' (something that Keynes referred to as 'animal spirits') to account for over-investment during the dot-com bubble (see Shiller, 2000). But such animal spirits or, to put it a less metaphorical manner, capitalists' expectations of the future market, are a key factor in investment. With a higher share of profits, there is more to invest. It is fine so long as investors' expectations of the growth of the market continue to keep them investing enough to cover savings. But the greater the extent of inequality, the more the investment required, and the greater the potential impact on employment of even small shortfalls in investment.

FEATURES OF GLOBAL INEQUALITY

The issues of the extent of global inequality and whether it is increasing or decreasing are then relevant to the prospects of global employment. So far the reference has been to inequality as though there is only one such measure of global inequality. However, there are three such measures. It is necessary to clarify which one is relevant for the macroeconomic considerations being discussed here.

There has been a heated debate on the question of international inequality, what Branko Milanovic calls 'the mother of all inequality disputes' (2005: 87). The dispute lies between using two concepts of international inequality. Concept 1 is a simple calculation of inequality based on countries' unweighted income levels. Concept 2 is a population-weighted comparison of countries' income levels. In a Concept 1 calculation (or the United Nations General Assembly calculation, as Malinovic refers to it), Sierra Leone's income level would count for the same as China's; while in a Concept 2 calculation, China's income level, based on the relative populations, would count for more than 200 times that of Sierra Leone.

On the basis of the Concept 1 calculation, there has been an increase in unweighted international inequality from 1960 onwards. The inter-country Gini increased by 20 per cent from 1965 to the end of the century (Milanovic, 2005: 39). The reasons for this increase in inequality lie in the poor performance of Africa, where 24 countries in 2000 had a per capita gross domestic product (GDP) that was less than 20 years ago, and the decline of incomes in the Latin American countries in the 1980s and in the former Soviet bloc in the 1990s. Asia, which on the whole did better than the above poorly-performing countries, does not count for as many countries as the latter.

However, the picture changes if we weight countries' mean incomes by their population. Now the Asian countries, particularly the growth of China and later India too, have an enormous impact on inter-country inequality. The sustained higher growth of the Asian economies compared to the Organisation for Economic Co-operation and Development (OECD) countries means that the gap between these two groups has become less than it was, contributing to a decline in inter-country inequality. In brief, it may be said that this reduction in inter-country inequality is due to the spread of technology and of labour and management capacities, so that what was earlier a monopoly of Euro-America is now more widely distributed. As a UNU/WIDER study sums it up, 'Evidence to date...indicates a steady reduction in inequality between countries during the period 1960s to 1998' (Chotikapanich et al., 2007: 1). Glenn Firebaugh (2003) refers to this as 'The New Geography of Global Income Inequality'.

But, along with a decline in inequality between countries, as witnessed in the rise of Asia, there has also been growing inequality within key countries; for example, China, India, and Brazil. Inequality in China (measured by the Gini coefficient) had reached 0.472 by 2004, as against 0.469 in the US in 2005.[2] This is somewhat more than India's 0.36 in 2004 and the European Union's 0.31 in 2005. Inequality in Brazil (0.634) is by far the highest among the major economies. Inequality in developed countries has also increased, particularly in the US and the UK. This, of course, is part of the new geography of global income inequality (Firebaugh, 2003), as within-country inequality becomes more important than between-country inequality.

The situation of global inequality is well summarized as, 'If the world were a single country, it would be one of the worst distributed, with a Gini coefficient of 0.68, well above the world's simple average of 0.39 and the population weighted average of 0.35' (Bussolo et al., 2008: 15). As the authors point out, only Haiti with a Gini coefficient of 0.71 showed more inequality than the world as a whole in 2000.

In dealing with the macroeconomics of the global economy, what is relevant is the third concept of inequality—which, in a sense, deals with each person (rather, household) in the world on an equal basis. For an analysis of the changing shares of profits and wages in total income, in a broad sense, it is distribution of global income among all households that is relevant. Growing income inequality can be taken as an indicator of an increase in the share of profits (or, of non-labour income generally). The spread of corporate shareholding through mutual funds and pension fund investments means that workers also get a share of property income. But in any case, an increase in income inequality can be taken as an indicator of an increase in the share of profits (property income).

The wage data, as calculated from the United Nations Industrial Development Organization (UNIDO) manufacturing wage figures (Galbraith, 2007), also show an increase in wage inequality (the ratio of wages of skilled or high-skilled labour to unskilled or low-skilled labour). The increase in wage inequality holds both for developed and developing countries; or to use terms that more accurately represent the nature of the changes, industrialized and industrializing countries. Further, as pointed out by Galbraith, there has been a clear increase in inequality from the late 1980s onwards.

Growing inequality means that the share of consumer demand will fall and the share of investment in aggregate demand needs to correspondingly increase. That is the macroeconomic relation that makes the current course of accumulation unstable.

WHY IS INEQUALITY GROWING?

There are broadly two types of analysis of the reasons for the existence and even growth of inequality. One looks at the nature of current labour market situations, the growth in demand and supply for skilled labour of different types, and related matters like the type of labour market transactions. The other type of analysis situates labour market changes within broader historical transitions. The two types of analysis are not necessarily exclusive, and the second can be seen as placing changes in the first within the context of broad historical changes in the economic structure.

It has been argued that with globalized production there has been an increase in demand for skilled labour—for example, in Feenstra and Hanson (1997) for Mexico and Hseih and Woo (2005) for Hong Kong—and that this is due to the growth of production-sharing or the spread of GPNs. With global production sourcing, the basic unit of economic organization becomes the 'networked firm' composed of a variety of networked organizations (Castells, 1996: 199). Power relations suffuse networks and the key functions, such as design (or the creation of new products and technologies), branding, and marketing, are monopolized while manufacturing functions are distributed.

For the nodal firms there is an increase in average skill requirement, as medium- or low-skill segments, such as manufacturing functions, are outsourced. On the other side,

> [W]hile products shifted to developing countries would be characterized as unskilled-labor-intensive from a developed country's perspective, they appear skilled-labor-intensive when compared with existing domestic production from the developing country's point of view. As a result, 'outsourcing' increases the average skill intensity of production in both the developed and developing economies, inducing an increase in the skill premium in both places (Goldberg and Pavcnik, 2007: 62).

With GPNs, there is an increase in the skill intensity of production and the demand for skilled labour, leading to an increase in the skill premium. But, along with this, there is also the entry of large numbers of workers in developing countries into the low-skilled category of labour. This is the process of transfer of surplus labour from developing-economy agriculture into industry. It keeps the wage rate at the lower end of the wage structure.

The second strand of analysis starts out by asking if there is a historical specificity to this structure. Or, is it a structure that is set in stone for all of capitalism's history? Simon Kuznets (1955) first drew attention to the relation between income level and income inequality: as income rose from a low level, there was an increase in inequality, which stabilized at a medium level of income and then fell as income increased. This inverted-U is an empirical observation. Having observed this empirical relation, Kuznets then went on to hypothesize a reason for it. He found it in the inter-sectoral transition that characterized the process of industrialization.

The phase of growing inequality is that of the industrial transformation of an agrarian society. There is a growing inequality between town and countryside. Within industry there is growing employment. But there is an increase in both income inequality and wage inequality. On the one hand, capital accumulation is reflected in a higher share of profits. On the other hand, the bottom wage in industry, though it may be higher than what could have been earned in the agrarian economy, is held down by the shift of workers from agriculture to industry and from rural to urban areas. At the same time, as the demand for high-skill labour grows and outstrips its supply, there is also an increase in the skill premium in wages. Thus, along with an increase in income inequality there is also an increase in inequality in wages in industry.

What brought about the transition, that Kuznets saw from the data, from high to lower inequality? In the usual neo-classical analysis, if at all this happened, it would be due to the growing skill intensity of labour, and so on; that is, to basic demand and supply factors in the labour market. But Kuznets found the reason for the change in the movement of inequality in the political economy process—the spread of education, democratization, the growth of trade unions as a countervailing power to capital, and the intervention of the state. '[C]ountervailing power, modern industrial relations, democratization and the rise of the welfare would assure, past a certain point, declining inequality in the overall structures of pay. From this, Kuznets inferred that the relationship between income and inequality would follow an inverted "U" shape: first rising, and then falling, as the ordinary process of industrialization unfolded' (Galbraith, 2007: 588).

The transition that Kuznets observed in individual countries is now taking place on a global scale. It is not just that China and India are industrializing, but also that in this process there has been an increasing rural–urban divide in these economies and this affects the global distribution of income. Malinovic

(2005: 115) points out, '[W]e seem to be in the presence of an interesting situation where world inequality is driven by what happens to the relative incomes of the three large areas: (1) the rich countries of the West, (2) urban incomes in China and India, and (3) rural incomes in these countries. The ratio between 2 and 3 has been rising'. This trend of growing urban–rural inequality in China and India is only representative of what is happening in other countries, such as Thailand, Indonesia, or Bangladesh. The crucial 'swing' factor is the ratio of (2) to (3): if that increases, world inequality goes up; if that decreases, world inequality goes down.

INEQUALITY TRANSITIONS AND THE LABOUR MARKET

How do the factors of transitions in inequality impact on the labour market? This needs to be looked at in both global and national locations and the interaction between the two.

The inter-sectoral transition that Kuznets observed was also analysed by Arthur Lewis (1954). Lewis saw a shift of surplus labour from agriculture at a near constant wage rate as the source of labour supply for industrialization. This labour supply could be related to two factors. One, the demographic dividend, as birth rates fall and the proportion of working age population increases, leading to a higher supply of labour in the market (see Cai Fang, 2008). Along with this, there could also be a process of depeasantization, with the growing landless population (or, as more accurately in the case of China, the small peasants who are unable to make an adequate living from agriculture) seeking urban employment. This also led to the growing urban–rural divide since rural incomes stagnated while urban incomes rose.

But there would be a point at which there would cease to be surplus labour to shift from agriculture. With this Lewisian turning point (see Cai Fang [2008] for an analysis of this for China), the economy's period of surplus labour would come to an end. 'A shortage of migrant workers was evident in the Pearl River Delta region as early as 2003, and the phenomenon has spread to the Yangtze River Delta region, even to provinces in central China, the origin of many migrant labourers' (Cai Fang, 2008: 9). There may be disagreements over whether China has or has not reached such a situation of an end to the surplus labour regime, but there is no denying the analytical hypothesis: that at some time, a shortage of rural migrant labour is likely to develop.

With this, there is likely to be an increase in wages. While earlier the rise in wages could have been confined to highly skilled workers, with labour shortage, a rise in wages could extend down the line and lead to an increase ages of low-skilled workers. With this, there would be a decrease in quality—provided policies are geared to maintaining full employment. he Lewisian turning point is then related to the Kuznets' shift from increasing to decreasing inequality (Cai Fang, 2008).

The inequality that is of greatest concern from a welfare point of view is that between wages at the base and the rest. In the wages at the base there is a connection between rural and urban sectors. Low-skilled migrants in urban areas, with little or no education, who are recent migrants from the countryside, can easily be substituted by other, more-recent migrants from the countryside. As a result, bottom wages (or earnings) in urban areas may be just a bit more than rural wages. The floor of urban wages is set by the prevailing rural wage.

At one level it would seem that it is possible to secure an increase in wages at the bottom only after the Lewisian turning point has been reached. But if we see the rural connections of the base urban wage, then it can be seen that measures that lead to an increase in rural wages and incomes will have their effect on urban wages. India's National Rural Employment Guarantee Act (NREGA) is one such measure. It provides 100 days of employment to any rural household that wants it. Just after the first year of implementation, reports (see studies by IHD [2008] and newspaper reports) suggest that there has been a fall in migration from the main labour supplying areas, such as Bihar. A land reform that provided small plots of land to landless agricultural labour would also push up the wage rates in rural areas with spillover effects, through the reduction in migration to urban areas. Where the households that provide migrant labour already possess land, as is most often the case in China, an increase in productivity of peasant agriculture would provide a similar upward push to rural incomes and rural wages. The current shift in the terms of trade between food and non-food commodities in favour of food will also increase rural incomes and reduce, at least for some time, rural–urban inequality.

The rural–urban inequality that has been referred to so often is also a gender inequality. With the increasing feminization of agriculture in China, India, Vietnam, and other such countries, women are the main recipients of low rural incomes and wages. Thus, reducing this inequality is also a matter of reducing gender inequality in ownership of land, access to productive resources, and so on.

The aforementioned can be summed up in terms of the social minimum. Increasing the social minimum would be a step in increasing incomes at the base and thus also have an effect on inequality. An implication of this is that in pushing an economy from a 'low road' to a 'high road' in the industrialization process, agricultural productivity can play a key role. Alternatively, a high level of migration with relatively high incomes, relative to the rest of the economy, can also leave only the possibility of a 'high road'.[3]

Brazil, notorious as one of the most unequal countries in the world, has begun to see some reduction in this inequality. This reduction has been brought about by two measures that raised the social minimum—an increase in minimum wages and the cash transfer programme to families below the poverty line. There was a stronger decline in inequality in rural areas promoting a, possibly limited, rural–urban convergence and a reduction in the Gini. 'Although the cash transfer program (*Bolsa Familia*) introduced in the nineties and consolidated during the government of Luis Inacio Lula da Silva contributed to the decrease in poverty in the countryside, increase in minimum wages remained the major factor for this positive development' (de Medeiros, 2008: 6).

Even on approaching or going beyond the Lewisian turning point, it is not that changes in the distribution of income will come about automatically. The distribution of income is subject to the institutional framework of the economy. A situation of labour shortage creates a favourable condition for interventions that reduce inequality—government policies and legislation that support workers' struggles to increase wages, improvements in social welfare, and so on. But these do not come about automatically. It requires political and social change—basically one of intervening in those matters that were formerly left to the market; that is, of shifting from governance as a purely market facilitation role to adding on a market regulatory role.[4] There is the example of South Korea, where in the late 1980s systematic labour shortages prevailed, but the government policies still favoured the dualism of the earlier period (Freeman, 1993; Cai Fang, 2008). Only intense struggles between the working people and the government led to changes in policy more conducive to allowing for a role of trade unions in negotiating changes in labour conditions.

'THE GREAT TRANSFORMATION'

The whole gamut of political changes summarized by Kuznets in the term 'democratization' could come about with the Lewisian turning point—a strong role for trade unions, national wage bargaining, etc. Along with a change in the mode of accumulation (from extensive methods based on cheaper labour to intensive methods of increasing total factor productivity, nowadays summarized as upgrading), there is a substantial shift from an almost unfettered market system to one substantially regulated. The regulation of the market system is not in micro-matters, but in setting minimum labour, environmental, and other standards. This is what Karl Polanyi (1944: 30) called 'The Great Transformation'—the shift from a 'self-regulating market economy ...[which] could not exist for any length of time without annihilating the human and natural substance'.

Polanyi's Great Transformation took place substantially in the period after the Great Depression and the Second World War. Keynesian macro-policies for maintaining full employment were combined with social welfare policies. The latter included regulation of conditions of work, the provision of a social minimum, and regulation of monopolies. All this was brought about again not by any requirement of the regime of accumulation, even if they contributed to changing it, but 'because people *combined* to bring about change that would control or even replace the market' (Stewart, 2006: 13).

The important question is: would it be possible in the present context of globalization to create the type of consensus (or, Great Transformation) that led to what is commonly called the 'Golden Age of Capitalism'? There are two important aspects of the present situation that should be noted.

First, the forms of existence of labour are being globally connected. The splitting up of a production chain into parts located in different countries leads to a globally social form of existence of labour. Labour is becoming more and more globally social, cooperating in productive networks. The social nature of labour is easily seen in immaterial production—ideas develop in a social, collective process. There is individuality but also a collectivity in this process. The social nature of labour is less easily seen in the case of material production. But the global spread of production processes makes more obvious the social nature of this labour too.

Second, the globalization of production networks has a distributional consequence: if various national sections of labour collaborate in the making of a product, and one cannot attribute the product to any one part of that labour, then the manner in which net income is distributed cannot be a matter of so-called marginal productivities. Rather it is a matter of bargaining relations and strength along that chain. This, of course, can lead to competition as different sections of workers try to get as much as possible. But the point here is that even in such competition lies the base of a globally cooperative social existence.

This global existence is also brought out starkly in negotiations and even in failures. Wages in China and India do come into wage negotiations in the

US or Europe. They are taken to account for the failures of some workers to retain their jobs. The global existence of workers is present in not just national but even factory locations.

At the same time, numerous forms of transnational coordination and contact have proliferated. There is now an international, better called transnational (as it does not join together national forms but transcends national forms), practice of advocacy and struggle. Every sort of group with a 'claims' function (see Stewart, 2006: 14) works in and with transnational networks. Women, indigenous people, street dwellers, homeworkers, trade unions—all are increasingly part of a transnational practice of advocacy, support, and struggle. There are international instruments for almost every conceivable problem and these international instruments are used in struggles in various locations. There is a 'thickening' of global organizations and interactions of various types.

In developing a self-consciously transnational practice, however, a number of measures would still need to be undertaken. The most important is a methodological one—of overcoming what has been called 'methodological nationalism' (see Sassen, 2007). Methodological nationalism is no longer a matter of actually thinking that solutions can be national, but more and more has become merely a lamenting the passing of that age, without attempting to work out a programme for the current situation. This does not mean that there is no need or scope for national action. In fact, as will be seen later, a lot of required action is national. But in taking up these actions, whether of a minimum wage or a social minimum, it is necessary to be conscious and take account of the international implications and connections of these actions. What, for instance, is their impact on competitiveness? This can be used as an excuse to plead for no action; it can also be used to inform the types of actions taken. As Bowles and Gintis (1998) point out, particularly in the context of globalization, asset redistribution would be superior to income redistribution, as the former is likely to have positive incentive effects in increasing the productivity of labour unlike the latter. In an open economy, productivity effects become more of a concern than in relatively closed economies.

But it is also true that countries have not lost all the ability to determine policies. Overall government spending is limited by the size of the budget feasible without an adverse impact on inflation and exchange rates. But there are still many things that can be possible within that range. Large economies such as China, India, and Brazil would have more of a leeway than smaller countries. Not only do they have greater fiscal strength, but their overall attractiveness for capital is also not likely to be easily nullified by certain changes. For instance, all three countries have adopted redistributive measures that would favour agricultural labour—the *Bolsa Familia* conditional cash transfer programme in Brazil, the National Rural Employment Guarantee Scheme (NREGS) in India, and a whole range of redistributive measures in China, including increased compensation for farmers losing their lands, and some subsidies for rural education and health care. All of these measures will have an effect on rural–urban inequality in these countries. These were undertaken without any measure of coordination between these countries. Of course, as mentioned earlier, these are large economies and so have substantial fiscal capacity. The important point, however, is that one should not exaggerate the lack of ability to determine redistributive policies. The limits of such policies are greater than in the case of relatively closed economies, but, as the aforementioned experiences of China, India, and Brazil show, the degree of freedom is not trivially non-zero.

There is a parallel in the case of workers and trade unions. Global competition does limit the extent of possible wage increases. In a closed economy, companies can carry on cost-plus pricing to maintain profits. But in an open economy, prices have to be taken as given. In which case, it is price minus wages (and other costs) that equal profits. There is pressure to reduce costs. Does this mean that there is no flexibility in wage bargains? There is a reduced degree of flexibility, but it does not disappear. In those corporations that are price-makers in oligopolistic markets, there would be more scope for workers to bargain increases. In those corporations that are price-takers in competitive markets, there would be less scope for such bargaining. But in each case it would be necessary for workers to limit their demands for wage increases to something less than the increase in productivity.

The most important factor for the move towards a Polanyi moment (one of re-regulating the market to take account of crucial market failures) is the depth of the current global downturn. With the massive bailout of the US financial system and the substantial stimulus packages in all major economies around the world, it is clear that the Washington Consensus of market fundamentalism has lost its hegemony over global policy-making. There is a striking difference between the current stimulus packages and the insistence of the US and the International Monetary Fund (IMF) to not allow stimulus packages during the Asian and other crises earlier on.

At the same time, there is a form of nationalism in the types of interventions being carried out. The US is clearly concerned at Asian and other sovereign wealth funds getting bigger shares in US financial organizations and, most evidently, in the bailout of the American car companies, meaning in effect protecting them from a sell-out to other capitals. In this again, the US government is doing what it pressured the South Korean and other Asian governments not to do during the Asian crisis—not to take measures to protect their 'national' capitals from being taken over by other solvent capitalist groups.

GLOBAL COORDINATION?

The problem of growing global inequality, it was pointed out earlier, is a problem of growing inequality within countries. For countries such as China, India, and Brazil, and similar economies like Indonesia, Thailand, and Malaysia, measures to raise the floor of the agrarian income can be taken at the national level. In developed OECD countries, the issue is more of raising wage incomes at the bottom.

Actions can be taken at national levels to deal with these issues. But they would mean taking substantial redistributive measures. The irony is that major developing countries, such as China, India, and Brazil, are taking some such measures, as mentioned earlier, however inadequate they may be. But in the US the political and intellectual current opposed to redistributive measures holds sway. However, the current major crisis, as is unfolding with the expanding US recession, seems likely to force a change in policy. Barrack Obama fought and won the US presidential campaign on the promise of redistributive policies. It remains to be seen the extent to which stimulus is combined with redistribution.

But all of these measures would have fiscal implications. Their extent, unless they raise productivity, would be limited by the constraints on fiscal balances in open economies. But there are other institutional changes, chiefly in labour relations or in the taxation system, that may not be as easy at the national level because of the fear of capital flight. Of course, capital in direct investment would not be as mobile as portfolio capital. But there would nevertheless be the problem of keeping a country as attractive an investment destination as possible.

With the growing transnationalization of corporations, even from developing countries, the necessity of remaining attractive for capital is relevant even for 'national' capital. For instance, when an Indian IT company, such as Infosys, decides on investing in its next centre, it looks at the whole world, the distribution of markets, the facilities available, the labour supply and market positions, and so on. It looks to get the maximum out of an investment decision and ceases to be guided by national considerations.

Measures to reduce inequality are not normally popular to capital—until, as at present (late 2008), capitalists realize, or are forced to realize by demand crises, that too much inequality is not a good thing for the stability of growth. The problem is that this is essentially a global macroeconomic issue. For any one country, able to export, there is no reason to worry that exports are a large or growing percentage of GDP. But for the whole global economy, there has to be some way of equating production with demand. The market, especially with the volatility of investment, based on animal spirits, cannot be expected to automatically perform this function.

Is international coordination on global aggregate demand likely or possible? Global aggregate demand is not an issue before any organization, though there is much discussion about global inequality. But there clearly have been moves to increase the extent of global coordination—both in monetary policies and in fiscal stimulus packages. The crisis of global accumulation has clearly increased the momentum for global coordination.

The push for global coordination to overcome problems of shortfalls in global aggregate demand did not come about so easily; that is, without a new crisis. Not that one wants such a crisis of accumulation. But it is good to remember Eichengreen's analysis that it was the experience of the Great Depression that was the important motivation for the Roosevelt-era and post-Second World War compact that brought about the Great Transformation (Eichengreen, 2007). Again, it was only after the disastrous effects of contractionary policies during the Asian and subsequent Latin American crises that the necessity of some measure of restrictions on short-term capital mobility has come to be accepted.

Right now capital, even in India and China, is not so sanguine about the prospects of continuing with high rates of growth. The US sub-prime and subsequent financial crisis (also a result of trying to push for housing market growth in the face of growing inequality[5]) has had an impact on many parts of the world's financial system. Whether there will be enough appreciation of the instability of high growth based on and, in turn, contributing to growing inequality is open to question. But the current major crisis of accumulation is leading to very Keynesian fiscal stimulation in almost every country around the globe.

At the same time, there is certainly considerable coordination, with power equations included, in international policy. Most of this coordination used to focus on the G-8, with China and India sometimes added to the list. But now with Brazil, Mexico, and South Africa too in the list, the G-20 has to occupy centre stage in global coordination. Central banks do, even if largely informally, coordinate interest rate changes. But it seems likely that we will see coordinated action to reduce global inequality and deal with the global Keynesian problem of aggregate demand; in a sense, there is now a Polanyian turning point in global governance of the economy.

What is clear is that there is currently a grave deficit in global institutions, which are lagging behind when compared to the globalization of the economic system. The Keynesian market failure of insufficient aggregate demand can and does occur on a global scale. But there is no global Keynesian authority. Other than through markets themselves, right now global economic issues are managed through consultations between the triad (US, EU, and Japan) or between the G-20 countries. But this is still an ad hoc form of decision-making, with power residing with the major economies and, importantly, struggles between them. It is not yet clear what the shape of Bretton Woods II will be like.

In this panorama, however, there are not just the two actors of capital and states, but also the growing countervailing power of global civil society, including trade unions and other forms of organized labour, along with other forms of organized producers, consumer unions, and so on. This countervailing power of global civil society, however, has not made itself felt in the arena of global financial management. In fact, one might say with Ulrich Beck (2005: 15) that 'it [global countervailing power] does not exist as such, and that it first has to define, orientate and organize—that is, constitute—itself politically against all manner of resistance in the global arena of action'.

CONCLUSION

What growing inequality possibly shows is that, besides an agenda for a social minimum, there is also need for a decrease in wage/profit inequality within enterprises. If the share of capital (through profits) keeps rising, then at some time, it is likely to affect demand. Further, inequality can fuel social tension within and even between countries, besides being morally repugnant. Chinese premier Wen Jiabao referred to the threat that might be posed by China's migrant workers ending up in a 'miserable plight as described in the novels by Charles Dickens and Theodore Dreiser'. The recent winner of the Booker Prize, Arvind Adiga's *The White Tiger*, captures better than any economic treatise, the extreme inequalities characterizing India today. There is a need to deal with not just inter-country inequality (as measured by inequality between countries) but also with inequality within countries. The successes of some developing countries in 'catching up' with the developed countries raises new problems of the distribution of income within those countries. Of particular global importance are the rural–urban gaps in China and India (Milanovic, 2005), which, with the generally recognized feminization of agriculture in these countries, are gendered gaps. Dealing with the rural–urban gaps in developing countries, with the gap between women and men overall, and with the falling share of wages in global income, become crucial not only for justice but also for the stability of global growth, itself related to the prospects for decent work.

NOTES

1. Before proceeding, it is necessary to consider one question: Is an increase in inequality necessary to bring about an increase in investment? It would be so, only if we hold to the classical assumption—that all wages (or non-property incomes) are consumed and all profits (or property incomes) are invested. An increase in investment in such an economy could only be brought about by an increase in the share of profits and a decrease in the share of wages. This is an old 'Victorian' argument in economic analysis.

    But in the contemporary world, a large part of savings actually comes not out of profit, but out of household incomes, in large part non-property incomes. For instance, in the India, the steady rise in household savings from 6.6 per cent of GDP in the 1950s to 23.8 per cent of GDP in 2003–4 to 2006–7, contributes substantially to investment (Mohan, 2008).

    The proportion of income saved is certainly likely to be higher in the case of profits than wages, as it would generally be so for higher incomes compared to lower incomes. But there are considerable savings out of household income and this enables the corporate sector and government investments to be greater than their own savings.
2. The Gini figures in this paragraph are from Eloi Laurent (2007).
3. This might tell us something about why Kerala did not take the 'low road' but is now taking the 'high road' to industrialization.
4. See Gereffi (2006) for a discussion of market governance roles as comprising facilitation, regulation, and redistribution.
5. The US Congressional Budget Office releases authoritative data on household distribution of pre- and post-tax income. Its reports reveal that 'the increase in income inequality (both pre- and post-tax) as measured by

the change in the shares of income going to different income classes, was greater from 2003 to 2005 than over any other two-year period covered by the CBO data' (Bernstein 2007).

REFERENCES

Beck, Ulrich (2005), *Power in the Global Age*. Cambridge: Polity Press.
Bernstein, Jared (2007), 'Updated CBO Data Reveal Unprecedented Increase in Inequality', Economic Policy Institute Issue Brief #239, 13 December (available at www.epi.org, accessed on 12 December 2008).
Bowles, Samuel and Herbert Gintis (1998), *Recasting Egalitarianism: New Rules for Communities, States and Markets*. London: Verso.
Bussolo, Maurizio, Rafael E. de Hoyos, Denis Medvedev, and Dominique van der Mensbrugge (2008), 'Global Growth and Distribution: Are China and India Reshaping the World?', Research Paper No. 2008/29. Helsinki: UNU-WIDER.
Cai Fang (2008), 'Approaching a Triumphal Span: How Far is China Towards its Lewisian Turning Point?', Research Paper No. 2008/09. Helsinki: UNU-WIDER.
Castells, Manuel (1996), *The Network Society*. Oxford: Blackwell Publishers.
Chotikapanich, Duangkamon, D.S. Prasada Rao, William E. Griffiths, and Vicar Valencia (2007), 'Global Inequality: Recent Trends', Research Paper No. 2007/1. Helsinki: UNU-WIDER.
de Medeiros, Carlos Aguiar (2008), 'Growth Patterns, Income Distribution and Poverty: Some Lessons from the Latin American Expereince', The IDEAS Working Paper Series No. 02/2008 (available at www.networkideas.org, accessed on 12 December 2008).
Eichengreen, B. (2007), *European Economy since 1945*. Princeton University Press.
Feenstra, Robert C. and Gordon H. Hanson (1997), 'Foreign Direct Investment and Relative Wages: Evidence from Mexico's Maquiladoras', *Journal of International Economics*, 42: 371–94.
Firebaugh, Glenn (2003), *The New Geography of Global Income Inequality*. Cambridge, MA: Harvard University Press.
Galbraith, James K. (2007), 'Global Inequality and Global Macroeconomics', *Journal of Policy Modelling*, 29(1): 1–13.
Gereffi, Gary (2006), *The New Offshoring of Jobs and Global Development*. Geneva: ILO Social Policy Lectures, IILS.
Goldberg, Pinelopi and Nina Pavcnik (2007), 'Distributional Effects of Globalization in Developing Countries', *Journal of Economic Literature*, XLV (March): 39–82.
Freeman, Richard (1993), 'Labor Market and Institutions in Economic Development', *American Economic Review*, 83(2): 403–8.
Hseih, C.T. and K.T. Woo (2005), 'The Impact of Outsourcing to China on Hong Kong's Labour Market', *American Economic Review*, 95(2). 1673–87.

IHD (Institute for Human Development) (2008), *Understanding the Process, Institutions, and Mechanism of Implementation and Impact Assessment of NREGA in Bihar and Jharkhand*, Mimeo, March. New Delhi: IHD.

Kuznets, Simon (1955), 'Economic Growth and Inequality', *American Economic Review*, 45(1): 1–28.

Laurent, Eloi (2007), 'Globalization: End of the Beginning or Beginning of the End?', *The Globalist*, 11 September (available at www.theglobalist.com, accessed on 12 September 2007).

Lewis, Arthur (1954), 'Economic Development with Unlimited Supplies of Labour', *The Manchester School of Economics and Social Studies*, 22: 139–91.

Luxembourg, Rosa (1968), *The Accumulation of Capital*, New York: Monthly Review Press.

Mohan, Rakesh (2008), 'Growth Record of the Indian Economy, 1950–2008: A Story of Sustained Savings and Investment', *Economic and Political Weekly*, 49(3): 61–71.

Milanovic, Branko (2005), *Worlds Apart: Measuring International and Global Inequality*. Princeton and London: Princeton University Press.

Patnaik, Prabhat (2007), 'A Model of Growth of the Contemporary Economy', *Economic and Political Weekly*, 42(22): 2077–81.

Perez, Carlota (2002), *Technological Revolutions and Financial Capital: The Dynamics of Bubbles and Golden Ages*. Cheltenham, UK, and Northhampton, USA: Edward Elgar Publishing House.

Polanyi, Karl (1944), *The Great Transformation*. Boston: Beacon Press.

Sassen, Saskia (2007), *A Sociology of Globalization*. New York and London: W.W. Norton.

Shiller, Robert, (2000), *Irrational Exuberance*. Princeton: Princeton University Press.

Stewart, Frances (2006), 'Do We Need a New "Great Transformation"? Is One Likely', Research Paper No. 2006/36. Helsinki: UNU-WIDER.

Thompson, Edward (1964), *The Making of the English Working Class*. London and Harmondsworth: Penguin Books.

2

BEYOND 'REGULATORY ENCLAVES'
Challenges and Opportunities to Promote Decent Work in Global Production Networks

Anne Posthuma*

INTRODUCTION

Participation in global production networks (GPNs) has provided an important source of employment creation in developing countries. Export production has incorporated many new types of workers into the global labour force, including young women and migrant workers. These jobs have opened an important source of income for workers and their families. Yet, the pay and terms of employment, as well as working conditions, may be poor—a large number of workers have been drawn into insecure and unprotected forms of work, particularly in lower tiers of global value chains (GVCs), limiting the ability of these workers to access decent work.[1]

Under pressure, particularly from trade unions, consumer groups, and non-governmental organizations (NGOs), global corporations have responded by developing codes of labour practice and implementing social auditing programmes. Numerous private sector initiatives have been created and expertise has been garnered in this area. Conditions of work have improved for some workers as a result of these corporate-led initiatives, but the conditions of many workers remain largely unaffected by these efforts.

*I would like to thank Stephanie Barrientos, Franz Ebert, Malcolm Gifford, Sangheon Lee, Deidre McCann, Frans Röselars, Arianna Rossi, Andrew Schrank, Emily Sims, Raymond Torres, and Maria Luz-Vega for their valuable perspectives, comments, and suggestions received during the development of this chapter. I am solely responsible for any errors and the views expressed herein; this chapter does not necessarily reflect the views of the ILO.

A phenomenon that could be termed 'regulatory enclaves' has emerged, where most improvements are concentrated among the group of employees with formal contracts in larger and first-tier supplier firms in GPNs.

The term regulatory enclaves is used to describe the limited coverage of much private and public regulation in relation to the full range of workers in global supply chains. By identifying the set of workers which are protected, the term regulatory enclaves also aims to draw attention to workers engaged in less visible and unprotected forms of work linked to global production. Diverse forms of informal work arrangements have become embedded within global supply chains, both in first-tier supplier firms themselves, as well as in outsourced firms down the supply chain. Regulatory gaps have formed between regular and informal workers in the same firm or in different tiers of the same global supply chain.

Other factors leading to regulatory enclaves relate to the that has formed rift between private voluntary initiatives and public labour administration and inspection. Despite substantial financial expenditures by transnational corporations (TNCs) in initiatives to improve working conditions in their global supply chains, challenges remain to achieve social upgrading[2] for workers in smaller firms and for the contract, casual, and migrant workers linked to production for global markets. Private sector monitoring is frequently found to be costly and uncoordinated across different company programmes, selective in the labour standards monitored, and generally conducted without consultation with public labour administration, workers, or their representatives. On the other hand, labour market institutions in most developing countries lack the capacity, resources, and new types of skills required to effectively regulate the diverse types of work situations within global supply chains. After over 15 years of such initiatives, both private and public actors recognize that individually no actor can single-handedly regulate working conditions in global supply chains. How to bridge private and public regulatory efforts and build capabilities to overcome enclaves in ways that improve the ability for more workers embedded in global value chains to access decent work?

This chapter begins with a summary of key features concerning how global production impacts upon local labour markets and workers in global supply chains. The subsequent sections draw upon existing literature to examine some of the main factors constraining the ability of both private and public regulation to achieve more widespread improvements for workers in global supply chains. The final section turns to recent initiatives that suggest we might be at an inflection point where one generation of labour regulation in global supply chains is passing to another generation which may be able to move beyond regulatory enclaves and promote better labour standards for a broader segment of workers.

GLOBAL PRODUCTION AND IMPACTS UPON LOCAL LABOUR MARKETS

One important feature of the current phase of globalization is the rise of international outsourcing. In contrast to TNC production in developing countries via subsidiaries, franchises, and other similar arrangements, the growing practice of international outsourcing involves suppliers with whom TNCs have little or no fixed investments, formal ownership, or legal ties. International outsourcing especially in price-sensitive and labour-intensive goods has been found to involve informal and precarious forms of work within value chains. Over time, the practice of international outsourcing has spread from price-sensitive, labour-intensive consumer goods to other sectors including agro-business and high-end technology services, raising questions about how far higher skilled jobs and knowledge-intensive work also could be affected (Dossani and Kenney, 2007; World Bank, 2007).[3]

International outsourcing places pressure on local firms to compete by using flexible and informal work arrangements in which workers are inadequately protected or not covered by existing legal and regulatory institutions. Differing labour practices may co-exist within the same supplier firm or within the same global value chain, forming regulatory gaps between regular and casual or contract workers.

For example, situations are documented in which regular and informal labour work side-by-side in the same factory performing similar tasks, yet informal workers are engaged under different contractual arrangements and do not share the same benefits, labour rights, or means to improve their working conditions (Barrientos et al., 2008). In cases where contract labour is provided by third-party agencies and work is conducted outside of the supplier's factory, it is virtually impossible for the working conditions of these workers to be monitored.

Global producers set standards for their supplier firms that have differing implications for labour. On the one hand, rigorous technical and quality standards of international clients are conducive to a more skilled and stable labour practices. On the other hand, some buyer practices raise uncertainty or shift cost and risk to suppliers down the value chain. For example, suppliers maintain delivery schedules despite changes in order volumes due to seasonality, changing consumer demand, and design changes. Suppliers commonly lack longer-term contracts that ensure a lasting business relationship; instead, they are under pressure to reduce costs in order to retain clients, thereby slicing down their profit margins. Under such conditions, flexible labour practices become an important means of reducing fixed costs[4] and coping with uncertainty. Overtime is common and informal labour processes are introduced even within formal employment (Damodaran, 2008).

Companies maintain a core labour force of skilled workers under more stable employment conditions, complemented by a peripheral labour force on temporary, part-time, or casual contracts that provide flexibility in hiring or shedding labour during upswings and downturns. Sometimes, labour contractors and labour agencies provide seasonal and short-term labour (Barrientos, 2007b). Tewari (in this volume) notes that employers in south Indian garment firms expressed a preference for hiring young, semi-skilled female workers who could be paid less than men and were less likely to organize. Smaller second- and third-tier firms, as well as subcontracted firms, embed unregistered and informal work into lower tiers of value chains, sometimes involving home-based, migrant, and even child labour (Barrientos, 2007a, 2007a; International Metalworkers' Federation, 2007; Wick, 2007). In precarious forms of work, it is difficult to establish the employment relationship and provide legally sanctioned protection and rights to workers (ILO Recommendation No. 198, 2006d; ILO, 2006b).

PRIVATE VOLUNTARY INITIATIVES AND CSR: LIMITS OF CODES AND SOCIAL AUDITING

Since the early 1990s, consumers concerned about reports of poor labour standards in global factories have formed NGOs and staged campaigns that pressured TNCs to take responsibility for labour conditions in their global value chains. Transnational corporations have often responded quickly to protect their reputation. Where public regulatory capacity was weak, companies designed their own codes of labour practice and social auditing systems for implementation within their value chain. Private codes of labour practice have proliferated and the multiplicity of different company-level auditing programmes has given rise to a multi-billion dollar corporate social responsibility (CSR) industry.[5]

After over 15 years, a number of challenges have been identified by trade unions, academics, NGOs, and companies themselves regarding the development and application of private sector codes of labour practice, including:

1. *High cost*: Monitoring labour conditions in supplier factories across the globe can involve substantial human and financial resources. For example, Nike reportedly invests over US$ 10 million per annum and involves roughly 100 employees in its worldwide monitoring programme (Locke et al., 2007).
2. *Uncoordinated*: The lack of coordination between different private codes and auditing systems, even among companies using the same suppliers or within the same sector,[6] gives rise to duplication and conflicting standards. Global suppliers may be caught in a regulatory paradox, involving different code requirements and additional costs. Local suppliers ask why a unified code cannot be formulated.[7]
3. *Selective standards, mixed results*: Private codes and monitoring programmes involve different standards regarding workers' rights, terms and conditions of employment, and occupational safety and health. They are often selective in relation to national labour law and even the Core Labour Standards.[8]
4. *Limited reach to informal work and subcontracted firms*: Private sector auditing and CSR initiatives are rarely designed or conducted in ways that effectively identify informal work arrangements. Auditing rarely extends below first-tier suppliers, overlooking subcontracted firms further down the supply chain where most cases of casual labour, homeworking, migrant workers, and child labour, are found (CCC, 2005). While first-tier suppliers speak of 'auditing fatigue', smaller subcontracted firms down the supply chain would rarely be included in audits.
5. *The auditing process fails to capture workers' viewpoint*: Auditing visits are frequently announced in advance, enabling suppliers to prepare and coach workers how to respond, if questioned. Auditors are not trained to identify specific labour violations, especially in areas such as freedom of association. Finally, interviews with workers may be conducted on site, making their identity known to management, thereby inhibiting honest and confidential responses (O'Rourke, 2003; Barrientos and Smith, 2006; Business for Social Responsibility, 2007).
6. *Corporate-driven codes create a parallel system to national legislation, trade unions, or supplier input*: Private codes are typically developed and

implemented without consultation with public labour administration, suppliers, representatives of workers, or workers themselves. This approach deprives public authorities access to valuable information that could help to improve regulatory practices and update national legislation[9] and fails to build capacity of the public labour inspection in ways that could, in turn, benefit the private sector itself.[10] For suppliers, if codes are introduced without a positive incentive for improvement—such as guaranteed future orders or technical assistance—then audits turn into an obligation or a test to be passed, rather than an opportunity to invest time and resources in structural changes (Sims, 2005). Trade unions and workers' organizations fear that private codes and auditing schemes may undermine, or seek to replace, their role in promoting workers' rights and improving working conditions (Schmidt, 2007).

This quick review of the performance of what might be considered a 'first generation' of private codes of labour practice and social audits highlights their limitations to promote deeper processes necessary to correct endemic, structural problems. Private regulation, operating in isolation from other public, trade union, or multi-stakeholder initiatives, is a limited tool to achieve the goal of raising labour standards in GPNs and leads to regulatory enclaves. Indeed, companies themselves have come to this conclusion. In a shift from the earlier preference for self-regulation, companies now realize that they 'cannot do it alone' (BSR, 2007) and recognize the regulatory role of the government,[11] indicating a need to develop new models that will be a part of the next generation of regulatory approaches. We will return to the issue of new regulatory approaches later in this chapter.

PUBLIC REGULATION OF LABOUR IN DEVELOPING COUNTRIES

In many developing countries, various factors contribute to weak labour market institutions and low compliance with labour standards. Key factors include poor capacity and limited resources to fulfil their mandate, labour law that requires updating or may be unclear to employers, under-resourced institutions with staffing and infrastructure needs, and concern that strict labour law enforcement might deter foreign investment (ILO, 2006c, 2008: 6). The expansion of GPNs has coincided with the predominance of a policy framework which prescribes the reduction of state regulation.[12]

Some developing countries have begun reviewing their labour legislation in light of new trends and challenges arising from expanded international trade and global production. Recent studies reveal changes underway to strengthen the resources and capacity of the Labour Administration[13] and Labour Inspectorate,[14] which are mandated to regulate labour conditions and employment relations at the national level. The original concept and definition of the labour inspectorate's role and function did not contemplate the work arrangements, and transnational structure of global production that exist today. Adequate enforcement of labour law also may require changes in legislation, the structure of labour inspection, as well as staff preparation to fulfil this role. Some countries, regions, or states are implementing change that reveals what might comprise the next generation of public labour regulation.

Some authors claim a 'regulatory renaissance' is underway in southern Europe, North Africa, and Latin America (Piore and Schrank, 2008). Labour laws are being updated in various countries to reinforce public labour administration and its functions in a process that could be described as 're-regulation' (Berg and Kucera, 2008; Bronstein, 2009). Some outdated legislation is being removed or revised, other laws are being flexibilized where needed, and yet other laws that are weak or had been de-regulated are being strengthened. Nevertheless, reform of labour legislation is a slow and contested process and occasionally may contain some incoherence with other policies designed to attract foreign investment, facilitate trade, and shape business practices (Human Rights Council, 2008).

In Latin America, this review of labour legislation has been driven in large degree by concern over the impacts of trade liberalization and global production.[15] Labour code reforms in Latin America address a range of areas, including the terms of employment (such as hiring and firing practices), conditions of employment (such as working hours, wages, and legislation for small businesses), and collective labour relations (such as freedom of association, collective bargaining, and the prevention or resolution of conflicts) (Vega-Ruíz, 2008: 235). In Asia, where the number of labour inspectors and frequency of inspections have declined over many years and little social dialogue has existed traditionally between the ministry of labour and social partners, new integrated labour inspection policies have been introduced. These new inspection policies involve key stakeholders and hold the potential to improve implementation of existing labour laws and promote compliance with labour standards[16] (Casale et al., 2006). China's revised labour legislation introduced in January 2007 specifies improved defence of workers' rights within the context of export production (http://www.labournet.com.cn/english). In Africa, the role of labour inspectors has been strengthened, especially in Ghana, South Africa, Kenya, and Uganda (Casale et al., 2006).

The debate over rigidity versus flexibility of labour legislation has shifted towards concern over its application and enforcement, drawing attention to the role of labour inspection. Recent studies have examined labour law enforcement and efforts to strengthen labour administration and inspection in selected countries of Latin America (Jatoba, 2002; Amengual, 2007; Marshall, 2007; Piore and Schrank, 2008; Pires, 2008; Schrank, 2009). A distinction is made in this literature between the Anglo-American approach to enforcement (rooted in deterrence, sanctions, and fines with a rigid division of labour between areas of inspection) and the Franco-Iberian tradition (based upon conciliation, training, and a unified system of work inspection that draws upon all areas of labour law to bring companies into compliance). Schrank and Piore (2007) argue that the latter model is more conducive to reconciling respect for labour standards with competitiveness, especially in developing countries heavily engaged in global production. Other authors such as Pires (2008) argue for a hybrid approach that blends elements of both models, noting that efforts to promote labour standards are most successful when they join punitive and pedagogical elements of labour monitoring (Pires, 2008).

Efforts to strengthen and professionalize labour inspectorates in developing countries reveal several immediate challenges to tackle. First of all, the ratio of labour inspectors in relation to the size of the labour force is generally very low in most developing countries. Information for the period 2003–6 indicates many cases where the ratios of labour inspectors to overall workforce fall below International Labour Organization (ILO) benchmarks.[17] The low ratios in Asia are striking, considering the elevated levels of foreign direct investment and international outsourcing of goods and services taking place in this region.

Second, beyond quantity, equal importance must be given to the quality of staff and resources. Labour inspectors often report being overwhelmed by their case loads, short of resources and means of travel, poorly paid, subject to bribes, and under pressure to not undertake inspections that might damage the investment climate. A third challenge concerns the differing organization of labour inspection across countries and whether the remit of labour inspectors is defined in broader or more specific terms.

The cross-border nature of global production exceeds the scope of state regulation and may involve different regulatory structures among countries involved in the same supply chain, highlighting the need for new governance structures that are appropriate to the reality of a global economy (Mayer and Pickles, 2008).

Finally, changes in the organization of production, where layers of subcontracting embed unregulated work and precarious groups of workers down global supply chains, pose new challenges for labour inspectors. Public labour inspectorates have difficulty monitoring work in the informal economy, in micro-enterprises, small workshops, and even home-based and piece-rate work which are linked into GVCs. It is difficult to regulate work in such circumstances due to their small size and relative invisibility; or because scarce resources require setting of priorities to inspect larger, formal sector firms; or because labour legislation itself does not cover work in such small production units—comprising another regulatory gap.[18] In India, the Factories Act of 1948 still regulates basic conditions of work and specifies that labour regulation does not apply to enterprises employing under 10 workers (if the company has electricity) or under 20 workers (if the factory does not use electricity). As a result, Indian labour inspectors rarely operate beyond organized urban workplaces, leaving out workers in rural areas and in smaller production units at the lower end of supply chains. In some developing countries, the labour administration considers micro and small enterprises as falling outside the scope of regulation.

Both public and private mechanisms for regulating work are limited in relation to workers in smaller production units, in the informal economy, and rural workers.

Challenges to Labour Regulation in the Informal Economy

Market relations between the modern productive sector and informal activities are rising, particularly in countries where fiscal discipline is poor and inspection capabilities are limited (Tokman, 2006).[19] The International Labour Conference in 2002 recognized the increasing prevalence and variety of situations of informal work and the blurred boundaries between so-called formal and informal labour, thereby widening its definition to the informal economy.[20]

Informal workers may be deprived of their labour rights for several reasons. First, workers might not be declared by their employers or are engaged in clandestine forms of work. In these cases, labour inspectors may have the formal authority to act in cases of non-compliance with existing law, although in practice, they may have limited opportunities to do so. One key precondition is that an employment relationship must be determined in order to apply labour laws (ILO, 2006b). Second, workers might be considered to be excluded from the scope of labour and social security laws. Where no legal basis exists for protecting such workers and their economic activities are not covered by law, inspectors have no legal authority to act (Daza, 2005). Some informal activities are the result of limited compliance with legal and procedural requirements, where firms meet some registration prerequisites but may neglect their tax obligations or compliance with labour law (Tokman, 2006). Finally, in other circumstances, revised labour laws make it easier for entrepreneurs to hire workers under fixed-term contracts, with reduced levels of social and labour protection (Tokman, 2006).

Governments may provide an incentive for small and micro producers by organizing initiatives (sometimes in consultation with workers' and employers' representatives) aimed at improving their business skills and productivity. Related programmes may involve extension of social protection to workers in the informal economy. In addition, new partnerships are being formed with informal economy organizations such as cooperatives, community groups, and small traders' and labour associations in order to build awareness and provide information regarding the advantages as well as the responsibilities of formal registration (ILO, 2002a; 2002b). India is outstanding for its efforts in this regard, with the establishment in 2004 of the National Commission for Enterprises in the Unorganized Sector (NCEUS) as an advisory body and watchdog for the informal economy (http://nceus.gov.in).

Challenges to Extend Protection to More Workers

The preceding discussion has shown that the reach of labour regulation to promote labour standards for a large share of workers linked to GPNs is still limited, despite years of private voluntary codes of labour conduct and auditing efforts. The recent strengthening of public labour inspection services in many countries has improved regulatory capacity, but the cross-border nature of global production poses challenges for national inspectors.

As seen above, a rift has formed between public and private labour regulation in global supply chains. Voluntary corporate initiatives can play a role in the promotion of labour standards in global production, but as one element among other initiatives by government, workers' associations, employers' associations, and civil society. Greater communication and coherence needs to be built between initiatives by TNCs to promote labour standards in their supply chains and public regulatory institutions which enforce national labour legislation in the domestic economy. Improved coordination could potentially reduce costs and induce positive spillovers to smaller firms in supply chains—eventually impacting positively upon firms engaged in production for domestic markets. Yet, in practice, most private voluntary initiatives to improve labour conditions have focused on first-tier suppliers, missing out smaller firms and informal workers down the supply chain, and are conducted without consultation with public inspectors or trade union counterparts.

This situation has led to what could be called 'regulatory enclaves' where audits and codes of labour practice have mostly targeted workers with regular employment contracts, in first-tier supplier firms, engaged in export production. The restricted coverage of such initiatives fails to address adequately the substantial use of subcontracted firms and of contract, casual, and migrant workers in informal work arrangements within global supply chains.[21] This is an area where greater communication between private initiatives and public regulatory bodies could potentially unleash positive improvements for a much broader set of workers. Policymakers may consider incentives that could further encourage greater interaction between private and public regulation, in order to achieve more far-reaching and lasting impacts for workers. The following section considers whether several recent initiatives might offer elements for a next generation of labour regulation.

BEYOND 'REGULATORY ENCLAVES': ELEMENTS FOR A NEXT GENERATION OF LABOUR REGULATION?

What can be learned from recent studies and evaluations to indicate what might comprise a next generation of labour regulation? First, there is emerging consensus that no single actor has all the knowledge required to solve complex and dynamic problems in the workplace, nor the overview necessary to employ all instruments needed to achieve the type of labour regulation required in a global economy (Black, 2002). Corporate codes of labour practice and social auditing may be useful tools for promoting labour standards in global production, but they are not the only ones (Barrientos and Smith, 2007). A broader range of stakeholder involvement, partnerships, and additional tools are required and new relationships and forms of coordination are needed. An approach that promotes an integrative theory of transnational labour regulation may be possible, where the expertise and positive impacts of non-state systems can play a dynamic role in building state regulatory capacity (Kolben, 2007, 2009).

Another aspect concerns the limitations of a sanctions-based approach. Codes and audits that are imposed unilaterally or that are coercive are limited tools alone to induce lasting change. Supplier firms require positive incentives, such as technical support, to adopt productive practices that integrate compliance with labour standards, or assured sourcing contracts from buyers to induce a process of deeper structural change. Capacity-building and training are important components of initiatives that put into place the policies, procedures, and controls for factories to comply with labour standards (Locke et al., 2008). This implies a shift of resources from auditing to remediation and capacity-building (ibid.).

Corporate codes of labour practice should be seen as a complement to, not a substitute for, public legal regulation (Jenkins, 2001; ILO, 2006a). Nevertheless, different actors may hold diverging views as to the role that public regulation should play in promoting labour standards in the framework of global production.

As noted earlier, codes of labour practice and social auditing are frequently implemented without consultation with workers and their representative organizations concerning their own working conditions. The strengthening of enabling rights could play a key role in remedying the unilateralism of CSR initiatives and their lack of engagement with workers and other stakeholders (CCC, 2005; ETAG, 2006). While official trade unions emphasize the limitation of codes, the latter are recognized to be valuable, particularly in poorly organized supply chains where workers have no other recourse of action (Miller, 2008). Helping workers to access enabling rights, including freedom of association and legitimate forms of worker representation, can lay the foundation for greater dialogue between the company and workers and build greater complementarities between company codes and the improvements in working conditions that trade unions aim to achieve. Low trade union density prevails in apparel factories supplying to global markets (estimated at below 10 per cent in most cases) as well as anti-trade union activities or the prevention of worker organization (ibid.). Innovative examples such as the framework agreement between the global union International Textile, Garment and Leather Workers Federation and the Spanish multinational Inditex, aim to demonstrate that labour standards can be promoted in a global supply chain by putting in place management systems that are backed up by industrial relations training (as the step towards developing an industrial relations system in factories where one is absent) (Miller, 2008).

Also, ethical consumption can impact corporate behaviour by signalling that a market exists for products made in accordance with verified social and environmental standards. Tools to support this process, such as transparent auditing and reporting mechanisms (Sabel et al., 2000), are important for companies, public labour inspectors, workers' representative organizations, as well as ethical consumers. The questions regarding how far ethical consumption may be taken up by developing-country consumers are also pertinent (as seen in the chapter by Knorringa in this volume).

Finally, the growing recognition among companies and multi-stakeholder initiatives that community-based monitoring methods should be included (Casey, 2006) underscores the fact that, in addition to the workplace, workers' concerns are also linked to issues in their household and community where they live.

New Directions in Private and Public Sector Labour Regulation Initiatives

Will the evolution of the next generation of labour regulation in GPNs address these challenges? New directions taken by global buyers to move beyond codes and social audits provide some insights.

Companies are changing their value chain practices. If the consolidation of the value chain concentrates larger orders among fewer first-tier suppliers, then this may reduce the direct cost of auditing and ease the burden of regulating compliance with labour standards. However, consolidation of the global value chain alone will not overcome the creation of informal work arrangements. Polarized impacts were identified in the Indian leather industry and readymade garments industry where both regular employment and self-employment rise, but informal work arrangements also rise within them. The growth of large firms (centralization) was mirrored by the growth of tiny household enterprises (decentralization) (Damodaran, 2008), which suggests that consolidation of value chains may still involve shifting of costs and risks to suppliers. A similar process of consolidation of sourcing partners, but with decentralization via unofficial subcontracting, was also found in a study of Moroccan apparel suppliers engaged in global value chains (Rossi, 2009).

Some TNCs were reportedly providing technical support based on lean manufacturing concepts to raise the capacity of their supplier network to schedule work, improve quality, and raise efficiency (seen as some of the root causes of poor working conditions). This type of 'commitment model' that emphasizes information sharing, joint problem-solving, and new management techniques to help suppliers to improve production practices may also promote good labour practices in global value chains (Locke et al., 2008). However, suppliers need positive incentives, including stable or higher prices, as well as assurance that sourcing contracts will be guaranteed despite drops in productivity that may occur in the transition to new production practices. Questions also remain regarding who would bear the cost of remediation and capacity-building (Casey, 2006). Finally, capacity-building among suppliers would imply similar changes in TNC sourcing practices to avoid sudden surges in order volume or in production programming and price squeezing that are key factors which encourage subcontracting and which work down the global value chain.

As a third example, companies are forming collaborations with other stakeholders. A number of large firms such as Nike, Adidas, Reebok, and Gap have built partnerships with local trade unions and NGOs (CCC, 2005: 76). Multi-stakeholder initiatives (MSIs) have been set up in apparel and sporting goods, cocoa and chocolate manufacture, and the tobacco industries. International Framework Agreements (IFAs) are creating channels for social dialogue between TNCs and Global Union Federations to promote labour regulations and improved conditions of work across borders in the respective countries where global value chains of the same TNC operate (Papadakis, 2008). At the local level, partnerships with local organizations such as NGOs provide corporations with knowledge regarding the real working and living conditions of workers. This partnership model will take different forms, depending on which organizations a global corporation prefers to work with and whether an industrial relations structure exists at the local level.

These changes in private sector regulation of labour in global value chains may provide some idea of what next generation regulatory approaches will involve. Changes in public regulation signal similar shifts.

Initiatives to Strengthen Public Labour Inspection

Changes in how labour inspection is conducted also constitute a major area of transformation that can move from a focus on sanctions and penalties to include broader functions of the inspector and technical support to help companies come into compliance. In some countries the remit of labour inspectors is focused on safety and health issues in the workplace. Other traditions of labour inspection may include areas such as conditions of work, forced labour, child labour, employment relations, social security, gender equality and discrimination, illegal employment, and even specific sectoral functions (such as agriculture, construction, mining, maritime, and railways). Additional duties may also extend to include the control of immigration, the informal economy, registration of small enterprises, and HIV/AIDS in the workplace. Other differences include whether action is initiated in reaction to complaints and occupational accidents, or as part of regular prevention and control activities (ILO, 2005). A broader remit enables labour inspectors to take a more integrated approach to improving conditions of work at the firm level.

Reforms that have been introduced to improve the competence, independence, and impartiality of inspectors include:

1. competitive examinations for recruitment;
2. job security and improved wages that provide recognition of the importance of this function;
3. training and education for inspectors to update their knowledge and skills as regards new patterns of work, using the perspective of lifelong learning;
4. improved equipment, means of communication, and record-keeping that support effective inspections and follow-up action;
5. adequate transportation budget for inspectors to visit factory sites; and
6. inter-ministerial cooperation to link labour inspectors with related parts of government such as enterprise development and vocational training.

(ILO, 2006a, paragraph 13; Schrank and Piore, 2007; Gifford, 2008).

Changes in the organization of production and embedding of informal work arrangements down global value chains pose new roles for labour inspectors, to regulate working conditions in ways that join the workplace with the household, communities where workers live, and broader social relations. Indeed, in the Indian state of Karnataka, recent research indicates that the remit of labour inspectors is starting to evolve in the direction of addressing these regulatory gaps as regards informal workers and those in the domestic economy (Srinivas, 2008).

CONCLUSION

Engagement in GPNs has provided an important source of job creation in developing countries. Yet, the quality of these jobs has been questioned as evidence of poor working conditions in global factories has come to light. Under pressure from trade unions, NGOs and consumer groups to improve labour conditions in their value chains and finding generally weak public labour law enforcement in developing countries, many TNCs have designed and implemented voluntary initiatives such as codes of labour practice and social auditing. Studies and experience reveal that individual codes have been largely uncoordinated even between firms in the same sector and selective in the labour standards audited. Furthermore, social audits are often limited to first-tier supplier firms and miss informal and unprotected work prevalent in lower tiers of their value chains.

Gaps have formed between public and private labour regulation, between regulatory initiatives extended towards regular versus informal workers, and between private corporate auditing programmes aimed at first-tier suppliers in export production and labour in smaller and informal enterprises, also producing for the domestic market. This chapter argues that these gaps have led to the formation of 'regulatory enclaves'. The term regulatory enclaves aims to draw attention to the fact that the potential of private sector efforts to improve the conditions of work remains largely confined to a sub-set of workers in GVCs. Studies have shown such initiatives face difficulties to reach informal workers embedded in lower tiers of global value chains or to build collaborations that could develop capacity of public regulatory agents.

Yet, changing approaches by both public and private actors suggest that we may be at an inflection point of change towards another generation of labour regulation in GPNs. New approaches will involve more than merely refining previous practices. They will likely comprise more integrated, consultative, and systemic processes that build on the respective strengths of public, private, and civil society stakeholders. Rather than parallel processes, greater communication and coordination between private and public labour regulation as well as representative workers' associations may help to build capacity, bring greater coherence between private codes and national legislation, and possibly stimulate positive spillovers to smaller firms and their workers. Some of these new approaches will join technical assistance and capacity-building with sanctions in order to encourage suppliers to come into compliance. The use of multi-stakeholder consultation that involves workers and their representative trade unions is another area where important progress is being made toward strengthening compliance with labour standards, labour rights and in improving workers' access to decent work. The effectiveness of new regulatory approaches will be gauged *inter alia* by their cost-effectiveness and replicability among smaller domestic firms with limited resources and their coordination with companies in the same sector or region. How these collaborations will operate, the partners involved, and the respective expertise contributed will comprise a large part of the new regulation agenda for labour in global production.

A final word is in order, as regards possible implications of the current economic crisis and how it may impact upon CSR initiatives. Private regulatory initiatives are withstanding a test during this period of declining market demand in the industrialized countries. Perhaps this context provides an opportunity (rather than an obstacle) to conceive of new governance mechanisms at the national and transnational levels aimed towards regulation of working conditions in GPNs.

NOTES

1. The concept of 'decent work' refers to work taking place under conditions of freedom, equity, security, and human dignity, in which rights are protected and adequate remuneration and social coverage are provided (ILO, 1999). The promotion of decent work includes efforts to improve conditions for those working in informality, such as unregulated wage workers, the self-employed, and homeworkers (ibid.).
2. The term *social upgrading* refers to improvements in the quality of work as well as the capabilities and entitlements of workers themselves. This term includes *measurable standards* such as the category of employment, wage level, contract type, social protection, and working hours. Social upgrading also involves *enabling rights* which involve less quantifiable aspects of work such as freedom of association, the right to collective bargaining, and non-discrimination (Barrientos et al., 2008).
3. The outsourcing of higher skilled work may serve as a platform to stimulate learning and backward linkages necessary to strengthen domestic sectors in developing countries. However, concerns are also raised to avoid a negative consequence that outsourced jobs which are well-paid by local standards might displace scarce qualified professionals from essential services such as education and medical care.
4. Whether overtime is voluntary or compulsory, paid or unpaid, and in compliance with or violation of national law is an important issue in export processing zones (EPZs) (Amengual, 2007; ILO, 2008) as well as in export-oriented companies outside of EPZs (Wick, 2007).
5. Many codes are audited by companies that are hired by the factories they inspect, calling into question the objectivity of the reporting practices and

creating a need for independent verification and certification (Polaski, 2003; Mamic, 2004).
6. Notable exceptions include the Global e-Sustainability Initiative (GeSI) that establishes a base code for companies in the electronic sector, and the Multi-Fibre Arrangement (MFA) Forum for the textiles and apparel industry. Transnational Companies also may meet among themselves to exchange information and form joint initiatives, as done in India by global brands including Ikea, Gap, Adidas, Levi, Tesco, H&M, and Walmart.
7. The Joint Initiative on Corporate Accountability and Workers' Rights (JO-IN) is an attempt to create a common code using multi-stakeholder participation.
8. An impact assessment of the Ethical Trade Initiative (ETI) Base Code of labour practice among 29 member companies showed wide variation between suppliers on their compliance with a number of labour standards. Greatest impacts were obtained in the areas of health and safety, elimination of child labour, non-excessive working hours and payment of national minimum wage. Meanwhile, limited impact was observed in areas such as respect for freedom of association and collective bargaining, reduced discrimination, provision of regular (rather than temporary or contract) employment and harsh treatment of workers (Barrientos and Smith, 2006:14–19). Similarly, a detailed analysis of factory audits conducted among global suppliers to Nike shows that such private sector monitoring did not identify important differences in working conditions and in employment status between different workers. Nor did these audits involve capacity building or technical assistance related to remediation which would enable firms to come into compliance (Locke et al., 2007).
9. ILO Convention 81 encourages sharing of information on labour standards gathered from private audits and recognizes the public labour inspectorate as the authority to promote effective cooperation with private institutions engaged in similar activities (Convention 81, Art. 5(a)).
10. This spirit of coordination is foreseen in the Labour Administration Convention No. 150 (from 1978) that provides a general framework in which different public and private agencies can work in a coordinated manner to promote labour standards and compliance with national labour law.
11. The tripartite conclusions of a recent ILO discussion on the promotion of sustainable enterprises emphasized the regulatory role of government, including labour law enforcement through efficient labour administration and labour inspection systems. The conclusions called for special attention to extend labour law coverage to all workers, including women and men in the informal economy or workers in disguised employment relationships (ILO, 2007).

12. For example, the *Doing Business Report* of the World Bank suggests that labour market institutions that provide protection for workers are a cost and competitive disadvantage to business. Its Employing Workers Index downgrades the ranking of countries with strong labour legislation (Berg and Cazes, 2007).
13. The Labour Administration Convention No. 150 (1978) and accompanying Recommendation No. 158 set out the overall duties of a labour administration, including labour inspection.
14. See the Labour Inspection Convention No. 81 (1947) and the Labour Inspectorates (Non-Metropolitan Territories) Convention No. 85 (1947), as well as the Labour Inspection (Agriculture) Convention No. 129 (1969) and the accompanying Protocol of 1995 to the Labour Inspection Convention No. 81.
15. Including concern to avoid potential trade sanctions by the United States government over labour violations and to respond to changing patterns of labour use that have proliferated under global production, including informal work, outsourcing, disguised employment relationships at lower levels of supply chains, self-employment and difficult areas such as domestic workers.
16. But difficult cases persist, as in Pakistan where the state has withdrawn itself from monitoring the implementation of labour laws through the suspension of labour inspection (Casale et al., 2006).
17. While no official definition exists for a sufficient number of labour inspectors at the national level, the ILO has set benchmarks regarding the number of labour inspectors in relation to number of workers: 1/10,000 in industrial market economies; 1/15,000 in industrialising economies; 1/20,000 in transition economies; and 1/40,000 in less developed countries (ILO, 2006a, paragraph 13). Ratios of labour inspectors to workforce vary widely between countries and regions. Using ILO data for 2003–2006, Gifford (2008) estimates the ratios at approximately 1/25,000 in Latin America, 1/35,000 in Middle East and North Africa countries, over 1/85,000 in Asia and the Pacific, and 1/90,000 in Sub-Saharan Africa. Within Latin America, recent estimates indicate intra-regional differences, ranging from 19/100,000 in Chile, 4/100,000 in Honduras, and 0.5/100,000 in Ecuador (Schrank and Piore, 2007:22).
18. The wording of the Occupational Safety and Health Convention, 1981 (Convention number 155) intends that firms should not deny employees protection under the law because of the size of the production unit where they work (Gifford, 2008).
19. Some authors hold 'burdensome' labour regulations responsible for rising informality (World Bank, 2008:190), although reduced regulation has not proven effective at reducing the informal economy.

20. This broader definition includes all unprotected labour, even those working in enterprises with over five employees, in addition to the informal sector as previously defined (ILO, 2002).
21. Most workers in informal work arrangements lack protection under either private or public regulation, and thereby need to build their own forms of workplace or community-based organization in order to achieve voice and access to their labour rights, as well as more general citizenship rights.

REFERENCES

Amengual, M. (2007), *A Survey of Labor Standards and Working Conditions in Export Processing Zones*, Report prepared for the ILO InFocus Initiative on EPZs, October.

Barrientos, S. (2007a), 'Migrant and Contract Labour in Global Production Systems—Addressing Decent Work for the Most Vulnerable Workers', Mimeo, February. Geneva: Integration Department, ILO.

—— (2007b), 'Global Production Systems and Decent Work', Policy Integration Department, Working Paper No. 77, May. Geneva: International Labour Organization.

Barrientos, S., G. Gereffi, and A. Rossi (2008), 'What are the Challenges and Opportunities for Economic and Social Upgrading?', Concept Note developed for the 'Capturing the Gains' workshop held in Manchester, December.

Barrientos, S. and S. Smith (2006), 'The ETI Code of Labour Practice: Do Workers Really Benefit?', London, Ethical Trading Initiative (available at www.ethicaltrade.org/d/impactreport, last accessed 18 June 2009).

—— (2007), 'Do Workers Benefit from Ethical Trade? Assessing Codes of Labour Practice in Global Production Systems', *Third World Quarterly*, 28(4): 713–29.

Berg, J. and S. Cazes (2007), 'The Doing Business Indicators: Measurement Issues and Political Implications', Economic and Labour Market Papers, No. 6. Geneva: ILO.

Berg, J. and D. Kucera (eds) (2008), *In Defence of Labour Market Institutions: Cultivating Justice in the Developing World*. Geneva: Palgrave Macmillan and International Labour Office.

Black, J. (2002), 'Critical Reflections on Regulation', Mimeo. London: London School of Economics and Political Science.

Bronstein, A. (2009), *International and Comparative Labour Law: Current Challenges*. Geneva: ILO.

Business for Social Responsibility (BSR) (2007), 'Beyond Monitoring: A New Vision for Sustainable Supply Chains', BSR Occasional Papers, 5 July, San Francisco.

Casale, G., A. Sivananthiran, and C.S. Venkata Ratnam (2006), *Re-engineering Labour Administration to Promote Decent Work*. New Delhi: International Labour Office and Indian Industrial Relations Association.

Casey, R. (2006), 'Meaningful Change: Raising the Bar in Supply Chain Workplace Standards', Working Paper 29. Cambridge, MA: Kennedy School of Government, Harvard University.

Clean Clothes Campaign (CCC) (2005), 'Looking for a Quick Fix: How Weak Social Auditing is Keeping Workers in Sweatshops', Report. Amsterdam: Clean Clothes Campaign.

Damodaran, S. (2008), 'Linking Employment Trends and Industrial Structure: Two Cases of Global Value Chain Incorporation in India', Paper presented at Conference organised by the Society for the Advancement of Socio-Economics (SASE), 21–23 July, Costa Rica.

Daza, J.L. (2005), 'Informal Economy, Undeclared Work and Labour Administration', Dialogue Paper No. 9, June. Geneva: ILO.

Dossani, R. and M. Kenney (2007), 'The Next Wave of Globalization: Relocating Service Provision to India', *World Development*, 34(5): 772–91.

Ethical Trading Action Group (ETAG) (2006), 'Transparency Report Card', December (available at www.maquilasolidarity.org, accessed on 3 July 2009).

Gifford, M. (2008), 'Labour Inspection: Fresh Initiatives', seminar presentation, Geneva, 9 April.

Human Rights Council (2008), *Protect, Respect and Remedy: A Framework for Business and Human Rights*, Report of the Special Representative of the Secretary-General on the issue of human rights and transnational corporations and other business enterprises, document A/HRC/8/5. 7, Geneva, 24 June.

International Labour Organization (ILO) (1999), *Decent Work*, Report of the Director General, Geneva.

—— (2002a), 'Resolution Concerning Decent Work and the Informal Economy', Report IV, adopted at the International Labour Conference, 90th Session, June.

—— (2002b), 'Decent Work and the Informal Economy', Report VI, International Labour Conference, 90th Session, Geneva.

—— (2005), *Unity beyond Differences: The Need for an Integrated Labour Inspection System (ILIS)*, Final report of the conference organized by the Luxembourg Presidency of the Council of the European Union, Luxembourg, 9 March.

—— (2006a), 'Strategies and Practice for Labour Inspection', ESP Committee, Governing Body document GB.297/ESP/3, November.

—— (2006b), 'The Employment Relationship', Report V(1), International Labour Conference, 95th Session, Geneva.

—— (2006c), 'The End of Child Labour: Within Sight', Report by the International Programme for the Elimination of Child Labour. Geneva: International Labour Organization.

—— (2006d), International Employment Relationship Recommendation No. 198 (available at http://www.ilo.org/iloex/cgi-lex/convde.pl?R198, accessed on 18 June 2009).

—— (2007), 'Conclusions Concerning the Promotion of Sustainable Enterprises',

International Labour Conference, Document number ILC96-VI-2007-06-0147-2, Geneva.

ILO (2008), 'Employment and Industrial Relations: Promoting Responsible Business Conduct in a Globalising Economy', Background Paper prepared for the ILO-OECD Conference on Corporate Social Responsibility, 23–24 June, Paris.

International Metalworkers' Federation (2007), 'Survey on Changing Employment Practices and Precarious Work'. Geneva: IMF.

Jatobá, V. (2002), 'Labour Inspection within a Modernised Labour Administration', IACLM-ILO Working Paper 148. Geneva: ILO.

Jenkins, Rhys (2001), 'Corporate Codes of Conduct: Self Regulation in a Global Economy', Business and Society Programme Paper No. 2, April. Geneva: United Nations Research Institute for Social Development.

Kolben, K. (2007), 'Integrative Linkage: Combining Public and Private Regulatory Approaches in the Design of Trade and Labor Regimes', *Harvard International Law Journal*, 48(1): 203–56.

—— (2009), 'Towards an Integrative Theory of Transnational Labor Regulation', Paper presented to the Regulating for Decent Work Conference, July, Geneva.

Locke.R., M. Amengual, and A. Mangla (2009), 'Virtue out of Necessity? Compliance, Commitment and the Improvement of Labour Conditions in Global Supply Chains', *Politics and Society*, 37(3): 319–51.

Locke, R., T. Kochan, M. Romis, and F. Qin (2007), 'Beyond Corporate Codes of Conduct: Work Organization and Labor Standards at Nike's Suppliers', *International Labour Review*, 146(1–2): 21–37.

Mamic, I. (2004), *Implementing Codes of Conduct: How Businesses Manage Social Performance in Global Supply Chains*. Geneva: ILO.

Marshall, A. (2007), 'Explaining Non-Compliance with Labour Legislation in Latin America: A Cross-Country Analysis', Discussion Paper 184. Geneva: International Institute for Labour Studies.

Mayer, F. and J. Pickles (2008), 'Governance and Implications for Decent Work in Global Production Networks', Concept Note prepared for DFID grant, 'Capturing the Gains: Economic and Social Upgrading in Global Production Networks', November.

Miller, D. (2008), 'The ITGLWF's Policy on Cross-Border Dialogue in the Textiles, Clothing and Footwear Sector: Emerging Strategies in a Sector Ruled by Codes of Conduct and Resistant Companies', in K. Papadakis (ed.), *Cross-Border Social Dialogue and Agreements: An Emerging Global Industrial Relations Framework?*, pp. 161–90. Geneva: International Institute for Labour Studies and ILO.

O'Rourke, D. (2003), 'Outsourcing Regulation: Analyzing Non-governmental Systems of Labor Standards and Monitoring', *Policy Studies Journal*, 31(1): 1–29.

Papadakis, K. (ed.) (2008), *Cross-Border Social Dialogue and Agreements: An Emerging Global Industrial Relations Framework?*. Geneva: International Institute for Labour Studies and ILO.

Piore, M. and A. Schrank (2008), 'Toward Managed Flexibility: The Revival of Labour Inspection in the Latin World', *International Labour Review*, 147(1): 1–23.

Pires, R. (2008), 'Promoting Sustainable Compliance: Styles of Labour Inspection and Compliance Outcomes in Brazil', *International Labour Review*, 147(2–3): 199–229.

Polaski, S. (2003), 'Trade and Labour Standards: A Strategy for Developing Countries', Carnegie Endowment Report, Washington, D.C., January.

Rossi, A. (2009), 'Economic and Social Upgrading in Global Production Networks: The Case of the Garment Industry in Morocco', D.Phil thesis, Institute of Development Studies, University of Sussex.

Sabel, C., Dara O'Rourke, and Archon Fung (2000), 'Ratcheting Labour Standards: Regulation for Continuous Improvement in the Global Workplace', Social Protection Discussion Paper No. 11. Washington D.C.: The World Bank.

Schmidt, V. (ed.) (2007), *Trade Union Responses to Globalization*, Geneva: Global Union Research Network and ILO.

Schrank, A. (2009), 'Professionalization and Probity in a Patrimonial State: Labour Inspectors in the Dominican Republic', *Latin American Politics and Society*, 51(2): 91–118.

Schrank, A. and M. Piore (2007), 'Norms, Regulations and Labour Standards in Central America', *SÈrie Estudios y Perspectivas number 77* (Studies and Perspective Series, Number 77), Sub-Regional Office of the Economic Commission for Latin America and the Caribbean, Mexico City, February.

Sims, E. (2005), 'Private Regulation of Employment Relations: What Role for CSR?', Mimeo. Geneva: ILO.

Srinivas, S. (2008), 'Labour Regulation and Inspection: An Indian or Karnataka Model? Initial Reflections', Draft paper, June.

Tewari, M. (2007), 'Footloose Capital, Intermediation and the Search for the "High Road" in Low-Wage Industries', Paper prepared for the IILS–ICSSR–IHD International Workshop on 'Global Production Networks and Decent Work: Recent Experience in India and Global Trends', Bangalore, 18–20 November.

Tokman, V. (2006), 'Integrating the Informal Sector in the Modernization Process', Paper prepared for the Department of Economic and Social Affairs (DESA), Development Forum on Productive Employment and Decent Work, 8–9 May.

Vega-Ruíz, M.L. (2008), 'New Trends in Latin American Labour Reforms: The Law, Its Reform and Its Impact in Practical Terms', in J. Berg and D. Kucera (eds), *In Defence of Labour Market Institutions: Cultivating Justice in the Developing World*, pp. 233–63. Geneva: Palgrave Macmillan and International Labour Office.

Wick, I. (2007), 'Aldi's Clothing Bargains: Discount Buys Discounting Standards? Working Conditions in Aldi's Suppliers in China and Indonesia', Working Paper. Siegburg: SÜDWIND Institut für Ökonomie und Ökumene.

World Bank (2007), 'New Pressures in Labour Markets: Integrating Large Emerging Economies and the Global Sourcing of Services', *Global Economic Prospects*. Washington D.C.: The World Bank.

World Bank (2008), *Doing Business 2009*. Washington D.C.: The World Bank, International Finance Corporation, and Palgrave Macmillan.

3   REACH AND DEPTH OF RESPONSIBLE PRODUCTION[1]
Towards a Research Agenda

Peter Knorringa

INTRODUCTION

Corporate social responsibility (CSR) is a hot topic for both business managers and development professionals. Business managers and a small army of consultants are busy developing and implementing a multitude of standards and codes of conduct to convince consumers and civil society organizations (CSOs) of their companies' responsible behaviour. This responsibility is usually operationalized in terms of respecting and enhancing labour and environmental standards in the production processes of their suppliers in developing countries. This chapter raises two basic questions in order to begin assessing the development relevance of responsible production. First, how likely is it that responsible production becomes increasingly mainstreamed? Second, to what extent can we expect the 'tool' of responsible production to enhance developmental outcomes? In other words, these questions explore the quantitative (reach) and qualitative (depth) importance of responsible production for development.

In exploring these questions, two broad trends need to be taken into account. First, China and India will act not only as the workshops of the world, but increasingly also as the lead actors in major global value chains. For example, Chinese value chain organizers are increasingly setting standards and/or making existing standards applicable or irrelevant, and we do not know enough about how the entry of China and India in the global economy affects the relevance of, for instance, International Labour Organization (ILO) and Forest Stewardship Council (FSC) standards (Schmitz, 2006: 55).

Second, a significant number of new middle-income consumers from 'production' countries are entering the global consumption market. So far, attention on the consumer side has focused on the roughly 800 million middle-income consumers in countries of the Organization for Economic Co-operation and Development (OECD). However, another 600 million to 1.5 billion middle-income consumers from the Global South (most visible in countries like China, India, South Africa, and Brazil) are likely to have started to significantly influence global consumption patterns. As compared to middle-income consumers in OECD countries, we do not yet know much about the extent to which these new middle-income consumers from the Global South are more or less or similarly inclined to responsible consumption behaviour, nor do we know much about whether CSOs in these 'new' consumption countries will be able to effectively wield their potential 'power of activism' (Spar and La Mure, 2003) to push companies towards more responsible production. Moreover, one can assume that the lead actors in the global production system will anticipate newly evolving global consumer patterns. In short, we need additional insights in these interconnected trends of global production and consumption patterns to be able to better assess the potential reach and depth of labour standards.

This chapter is structured as follows. The next section provides definitions of responsible production, Fair Trade, and CSR. It briefly contrasts the models and realities of Fair Trade and CSR, and introduces the role of civil society and state actors in responsible production. Moreover, it presents the optimistic 'business case' for mainstreaming responsible production. However, the section that follows it puts forward some sobering thoughts to the idea that responsible production will be the way of the future, by showing how the rise of China and India as centres of global production and consumption may well limit the reach of responsible production. Nevertheless, the next section argues that it might be feasible to develop 'pockets' of responsible production that may provide relevant examples of how localized depth in responsible production can be achieved. The last section concludes and presents some preliminary hypotheses that could be addressed by future research.

RESPONSIBLE PRODUCTION: DEFINITIONS, ACTORS, AND MANIFESTATIONS

Confusion about Definitions

Defining responsible production, Fair Trade, and CSR seems a simple first step in developing this chapter. However, the confusion in the discussion on the definitions reflects the overall confusion in this area of work. Instead of getting drawn into a survey of the definitional issues in this booming literature, this chapter begins by briefly highlighting the often implicit discourse clashes that thwart agreement on straightforward definitions. Responsible production refers to those situations where the lead actors of supply chains make a deliberate effort to include, throughout their supply chain, labour and environmental standards that go beyond the existing minimum legal requirements. In this way, responsible production is used as an umbrella term, encompassing both Fair Trade and CSR initiatives. While CSR is particularly important to investigate the likelihood of broadening the reach of responsible production as it involves usually large brand-sensitive corporations, Fair Trade initiatives are inherently niche activities that may provide significant demonstration effects of localized depth of responsible production when investigating how to enhance its developmental relevance.

Many definitions of CSR by management scholars not only include that firms need to go beyond what is required by law, but also to go beyond the interest of the firm (McWilliams et al., 2006).[2] This is counter-intuitive and counter-productive, as the more sustainable achievements in responsible production most feasibly are to be found in situations where firms can actually increase long-term profitability and sustainability by engaging in CSR as a way to differentiate themselves and their products. In a very critical, forcefully argued recent survey, *The Economist* (20 January 2005) even went one step further and argued that *only* the type of CSR where both profits and social benefits increase makes sense. Given their dislike of the CSR terminology, they prefer to label the situation where higher profits and increased social benefits go together as 'good management', so as to differentiate it from three other types of CSR which they feel are flawed.[3] This type of 'good management' is what is referred to as the 'business case for CSR' in much of the business-school CSR literature. This implies a win-win situation, often without much emphasis on the inherent conflicts of interests among the different 'stakeholders' in such initiatives. Another recent special issue of *International Affairs* (2005, Vol. 81, No. 3) on CSR by development researchers sheds a very different light on the debate (see, for example, Blowfield, 2005; Jenkins, 2005). They argue that the development relevance of CSR will remain inherently limited in terms of reach as long as only internationally operating brand-sensitive firms in consumer markets are pushed to behave responsibly, and depth remains limited as long as private sector actors can get away with defining, implementing, and evaluating what is socially responsible.

The official definition of Fair Trade has been the result of fierce discussions within the movement, and is currently formulated as follows: 'Fair Trade is a trading partnership, based on dialogue, transparency and respect, that seeks greater equity in international trade. It contributes to sustainable development by offering better trading conditions to, and securing the rights of, marginalized producers and workers—especially in the South' (FINE, 2001).

The reality of Fair Trade, inevitably, is more unruly. Even for the star product of coffee, it seems clear that it is far from easy to deliver on the very ambitious claims made in Fair Trade documentation.[4] Moreover, and this is probably more important and structural, with their modest turnover and the volatility in consumer tastes, Fair Trade marketing channels simply cannot guarantee a regular demand for particular upgraded indigenous handicrafts from specific groups of specialized artisans from the South. Fair Trade can and does aim to upgrade such producers, and in some cases succeeds in assisting them to 'get on the radar screen' of mainstream buyers. Nevertheless, the overall picture seems to indicate that for local development in the South, in whatever sector, on its own Fair Trade cannot achieve significant reach in terms of mainstreaming responsible production.

These intrinsic problems related to the model and reality of Fair Trade do not render it useless. On the contrary, they have played a crucial role as norm entrepreneurs, setting an example of how international trade can (at least aim to) be done 'differently'. Fair trade has played a catalytic role in raising consumer awareness, especially among middle-class consumers in Europe and the US. It can be argued that the present trend of CSR being in vogue among leading companies can at least partly be attributed to the pioneering role of Fair Trade. One of the questions to answer is: In what ways and to what extent Fair Trade can play an equally catalytic role among 'new' middle-income consumers from the Global South.[5]

Also, the CSR reality is quite different from its model and has many faces. The last two decades have seen a bewildering proliferation of standards and codes, many of which relate to responsible production. A good and still relatively recent overview of various types of standards is given in Nadvi and Waltring (2004). Probably the best known example of CSR with a supply-chain focus is the Ethical Trading Initiative (ETI), in which a group of well-known brand-name companies work together with trade unions and non-governmental organizations (NGOs) to ensure that labour conditions of suppliers 'meet or exceed international labour standards'. An in-depth, independent study on the ETI indicates that such international labour standards are successfully met for core workers in core supplier firms, but that the picture becomes more variegated for indirectly employed workers or for smaller firms and farmers who supply to core suppliers of global buyers (Barrientos and Smith, 2006; www.ethicaltrade.org). While ETI has perhaps received the most publicity, many other multi-stakeholder initiatives (MSIs) exist. Among MSIs, a convergence towards some of the ILO core standards can be seen. Most MSIs include regulations on health and safety, working hours, equal treatment of women, and child labour. The operationalizations of freedom of association, wage levels (minimum vs prevailing vs living), and the scope of non-discrimination clauses remain controversial (O'Rourke, 2006). Further and broader convergence of labour standards is in the air, as many existing initiatives may be absorbed in the upcoming new guideline to be issued by the International Organization for Standardization, which will be known as ISO 26000, and is expected to be launched in 2010.

The Role of CSOs in Responsible Production

Next to private and state actors, a variety of CSOs—like NGOs, labour or trade unions, community-based organizations, social movements, and consumer organizations—can play a role in responsible production. CSOs possess fewer sources of power as compared to governments and private sector companies.[6] Nevertheless, CSOs have often succeeded in making a difference and in effectively wielding their power of persuasion and threat of exposure (Spar and La Mure, 2003), even to the extent that some of the more recent literature points at the often assumed but unsubstantiated legitimacy of CSOs to speak on behalf of 'the poor' or 'the oppressed' or 'the concerned' or other relatively vague constituencies (Gereffi et al., 2001). In any case, it seems safe to assume that CSOs have played, and will continue to play, an important role in the area of promoting responsible production and consumption, as soft power plays a crucial role in consumption behaviour. CSOs have the potential to act as catalysts of change in introducing new norms in consumption behaviour, to punch beyond their weight, and to push for norms to become more mainstreamed.

Norm Life Cycle Model

A useful tool to analyse the process of how new norms can become mainstreamed is the norm life cycle model by Finnemore and Sikkink (1998: 898).[7] The model distinguishes three stages: norm emergence, norm cascading, and norm internalization, with a key role assigned to the 'norm tipping' that takes place between the first and second stage (Segerlund, 2005: 5). In the first stage of norm emergence, altruism, empathy, idealism, and commitment are seen as the main motives for 'norm entrepreneurs' to push, for example, for better labour standards. Once a certain critical mass of key companies have adopted such a norm, 'norm tipping' brings us to the second stage of norm cascading in which legitimacy, reputation, and esteem become the main motives of companies to join what is now seen as 'the right thing to do'. In the third stage of norm internalization, the new norm has become a generally accepted minimal standard that all participants need to conform to; at this stage, for example, new laws on minimum labour standards can further institutionalize the now generally accepted new norm.

A CSO Classification

This schematic norm life cycle model can help to position the various roles of CSOs in responsible production and consumption. Some CSOs are squarely placed in the first stage of norm emergence, where they aim to show how 'it' can be done differently. For example, Fair Trade aims to show how international trade with poor producers in developing countries can also be based on more equal, more respectful trading relationships with an explicit aim to deliver more benefits to local producers. Next, action/campaigning organizations like Greenpeace use a 'blaming and shaming' approach to force mainstream companies to behave in a more socially responsible manner. Others like the Clean Clothes Campaign aim to push forerunner companies involved in MSIs to play a role as trendsetters with a focus on depth and norm setting, as part of creating a critical mass to bring us closer to the 'norm tipping point'. In contrast, other CSOs, like Solidaridad, might aim predominantly for increased reach and can be positioned in the norm cascading stage, where they aim to convince broader (and more 'conservative') mainstream business initiatives of the need to 'join the responsible crowd' and to adopt 'realistic minimal' standards in order not to jeopardize their legitimacy and reputation.[8]

Role of Government in Responsible Production

The role of the state in responsible production is often forgotten or dismissed, but there is no way around including state actors. Private sector actors need government to set the rules to which private actors can comply. This quite basic observation seems to have gone out of fashion and hardly gets any attention in much of the CSR literature.[9] Still, I would not be surprised when both Karl Marx and Adam Smith would have agreed that the role of the government is crucial in enforcing responsible production and ensuring developmental outcomes, even though their argumentation would differ. Marxists would argue that the dominant logic of individual capitalists is to maximize profits in the short run, and that they assume that all other capitalists will behave in the same way. Therefore, they will collectively drive wages down below the reproduction wage and thus destroy longer term productive labour. This process can only be reversed when the state steps in to regulate, and/ or when workers can enforce 'higher' wage levels through collective bargaining.

Classical economists would argue that the invisible hand in the market would ensure developmental outcomes, given a 'few' preconditions: economic interaction is voluntary, competition is allowed to function properly, and externalities are addressed. Governments have a key role in ensuring these preconditions: for example, to provide independent judiciary to ensure voluntary economic interactions; to fight anti-competitive behaviour in, for example, cartels; and to regulate how to address and compensate for externalities. In short, to ensure the development relevance of responsible production, a key role of state actors is inevitable. The question is not whether the government should be involved in these processes, but how to work towards a more feasible and effective role for governments in responsible production (Fox, 2004; Moon, 2004; Graham and Woods, 2006), which will be elaborated upon in the section on 'Depth: How to Increase the Developmental Relevance of Responsible Production'.

The Business Case for CSR and the Race to the Top

Optimism reigns within both the CSR-minded business community and among NGOs engaged in stimulating responsible production. They differ on how fast and how deep responsible production should or could penetrate, but they agree on the logic of the basic direction. While many business managers are wary to go 'too fast' and to run 'ahead of the troops', most NGOs feel that changes come too slowly. Nevertheless, most NGOs also feel that they are on the right track, and that what needs to be done is to get more companies to embrace more responsible standards as the way of the future.

The underlying business logic, next to the social or environmental benefits, is that of high-road causality thinking, which is based on the idea that in situations of quality-driven competition it pays to invest in workers—and thus offer relatively better labour conditions—in order to achieve continuous improvements. Such workers become increasingly skilled, relatively scarce, and possess significant tacit knowledge. Such a conceptualization of workers clearly has its merits in an increasingly knowledge-intensive globalizing economy. However, one should be careful not to over-generalize the extent to which such a conceptualization offers a useful model to understand labour conditions in developing economies (Knorringa and Pegler, 2006). The high-road causality logic holds in some sub-sectors and for specific higher market segments, but amounts to wishful thinking for the bulk of labour-intensive, low-cost, export-oriented production.

Another key problem with the high-road causality logic is that it seems to require already a certain critical mass of responsible producers, that is, the norm cascading stage, so that many not-yet responsible producers with self-respect feel inclined to join the high-road. This also becomes clear in the, to my knowledge, most forceful formulation of the business case for responsible production, which has been made by Sabel et al. (2000). They use the language of the new competition and total quality management to put forward the idea of a race-to-the-top by companies competing not only on quality, diversity, innovation, and price, but also on their social achievements. In their words:

The impressive gains that have been achieved in product quality, diversity, price, and innovation in global markets can, we assert, be extended to focus these disciplines on the improvement of labour and environmental conditions, and social performance more generally. We offer 'Ratcheting Labour Standards (RLS): as a regulatory strategy that...attempts to redirect some of these energies towards the advancement of social ends. (Sabel et al., 2000: 1)

Basically, they put forward the idea that when labour and environmental concerns are integrated into the core business model of private sector companies, the business community can and will mainstream responsible production.[10]

Unlike a fixed-rule regime, which aims to ensure that all facilities exceed minimum thresholds, RLS establishes an on-going competition in which laggards pursue leaders and leaders attempt to out-do themselves because they know that no particular performance level confers lasting ascendancy. Though RLS begins with consumer taste and public pressure as its drivers, it should in time include the forces and resources of national governments and international organizations. (Sabel et al., 2000: 2)

Therefore, the RLS approach assumes a critical mass of 'ethically sensitive customers', towards achieving norm cascading in which legitimacy and reputation become the main motives for companies to want to join a self-reinforcing process of high-road competition. Unfortunately, it seems rather far fetched to imagine such a process to simply take hold at the global level. The next section aims to put the mainstreaming optimism into perspective, using observations from the Asian Driver discussion.

REACH: SOME SOBERING THOUGHTS ON THE LIKELIHOOD OF MAINSTREAMING RESPONSIBLE PRODUCTION

While the previous sub-section presented the possibility of a self-reinforcing race to the top, in this section I will put forward some sobering observations. In the following I introduce four main reasons, all of them related to the rise of China and India in the global economy, to be kept in mind when assessing the potential for an increased reach of responsible production. The first two issues are related to production and the last two issues relate to consumption.

Production Issues

First, globalization requires firms to be more flexible. Basically, the need for more flexibility at the firm level is 'passed on' to workers in terms of more insecure and precarious labour conditions. Moreover, while core workers in final product producers and key supplier firms may enjoy responsible standards and improved employment conditions, the proportion of such core workers seems to be decreasing due to increased outsourcing. The overall picture is of fewer core workers at the global level and more differentiation through various layers within firms, through local subcontracting arrangements and through international relocation of economic activities.

Moreover, some observers stress that firms and production countries are also facing the pressure of what is called 'immiserising growth',[11] where: 'growing...participation in industrial activities—reflected in the level of industrial activity, the growth in physical trade and the increase in industrial employment—may in fact become associated with declining overall standards of living' (Kaplinsky, 1998: 4). This negative macro effect is not because of an inefficient allocation of resources, but because of the pressures arising from economic globalization. Kaplinsky concludes that: '[I]n previous eras, participation in industrial segments of the value chain provided the source for sustainable income growth. But, increasingly, in a globalising economy these industrial niches have become highly competitive, raising the spectre of immiserising growth' (1998: 31). He argues that firms or countries need to identify and exploit specific rents from competitive advantages, but that the main lesson from recent history is that all rents are transitory and that new suppliers in global value chains (GVCs) basically carry out 'rent-poor' activities. Again, escaping from this immiserizing-growth trap is something that might be achieved by some individual firms or countries, but the general trend is expected to be one of 'declining real wages and declining real incomes in those countries specialising in rent-poor products.... The challenges thus confronting producers everywhere is to upgrade by appropriating whatever categories of rents are within their grasp, but to do so more rapidly than competitors in the knowledge that a rate of innovation lower than the average will result in immiserising growth' (Kaplinsky, 1998: 34).

Many observers may feel that the image of immiserizing growth paints too pessimistic a picture, especially when looking at dynamic growth in China and India. This is not the place to get into this debate. It suffices here to state that our argument does not hinge on immiserizing growth to become more or less widespread. To assess the likelihood of mainstreaming responsible production, we simply need to be aware of the basic capitalist business model, which implies that a majority of firms in a particular sub-sector do not produce A-brands with high image vulnerability, but will continue to look for the cheapest acceptable price/quality mix. Given the continued abundant availability of cheap and easily trained labour for labour-intensive production phases in GVCs, the market wage for this type of labour is not likely to rise in the foreseeable future.

A second issue on the production side is that Asian (especially ethnically Chinese) intermediaries increasingly play a more central role in many GVCs. Though the role of these lead actors has so far remained rather invisible, they are increasingly taking a leadership role in the governance of a wide variety of GVCs, for both branded and unbranded consumer goods (Schmitz, 2006). While A-brand consumer goods and A-brand retailers are very vulnerable to the 'power of activism' and have in recent years become pro-active in terms of responsible standard setting, this applies much less to the rather invisible Asian intermediaries who are more likely to downplay these logistically more complicated and cost-raising concerns and be at best reactive in terms of responsible standard setting. Given the increasingly dominant role of Asian intermediaries and their minimalist approach to responsible standard setting, this also makes it increasingly difficult for others to remain competitive through following a higher road towards responsible standards setting, except in premium market segments.

Consumption Issues

I would also like to raise two issues related to the rise of China and India as global centres of consumption. The first is the overestimation of the relative importance that most consumers would attach to the labour and environmental impacts of the production and distribution of goods they (do not) purchase. Many of the new middle-class consumers in the Global South, but also many consumers in OECD countries, probably attach very limited importance to these 'additional attributes' of the products they buy, if it means paying a somewhat higher price, except perhaps for identity products like clothing and shoes, and possibly for food and health products. Research indicates that relatively few (around 5 per cent) of consumers actually use their 'consumption as voting' (Shaw et al., 2005), while it needs to be stressed that this type of research is still in its early stages and has an almost complete OECD focus. We face a serious lack of knowledge about the extent to which especially new middle-class consumers from the Global South are inclined to buy responsibly produced products. This would be an important area for new research on global production networks and decent work, as without this information on consumer behaviour, predictions about the potential reach of responsible production are anybody's guess. Therefore, assessing consumer behaviour needs to play a key role in any convincing value chain analysis that aims to promote decent work.[12] Moreover, we need to investigate to what extent and in what ways consumer and development organizations in, for example, India and China can play a pro-active role in reinforcing consumer preferences towards responsibly produced products.

The second issue is an implication of the 'bottom of the pyramid' thinking (Prahalad, 2005). The bottom of the pyramid debate focuses on bringing another 4 billion relatively poor consumers into the global market realm by 'simplifying' existing consumer products, to produce them at cost levels within reach of relatively poor consumers. From the perspective of this study, one might argue that such a simplification of product attributes would probably leave no space for 'luxury' responsible attributes like an FSC label. In other words, branded products will also increasingly need to find a way to produce a broader variety of simpler products at lower price ranges.

Adding up these two production and two consumption related points leads to a picture in which we are probably more likely to experience a further rise in low-road production and an increased differentiation within low-road production, instead of an inevitable spreading of higher road production. Next to this increasing share of low-road production we could envisage a significant market segment for some middle- and upper-income citizens who consume responsibly produced goods supplied by A-branded retailers, and an even much smaller niche for Fair Trade products consumed by particularly concerned and action-oriented citizens.

Moreover, the fact that two large developing countries will join the ranks of the superpowers will not automatically lead to more developmental GVC governance. Instead, it is perhaps more likely to lead to more hard-nosed capitalism and ruthless competitive behaviour in a broader range of product varieties and market segments. What we may expect is a quite long and potentially volatile transition period in which the new global power structure works itself out (Humphrey and Messner, 2006). In conclusion, there seems to be very little reason to assume that a drive towards mainstreaming responsible production will gain dominance in this volatile situation.

DEPTH: HOW TO INCREASE THE DEVELOPMENTAL RELEVANCE OF RESPONSIBLE PRODUCTION

The previous section argued that widespread mainstreaming is unlikely. However, this is not the end of the story. Somewhat similar to arguments made by Evans (1996) and Moore (1994), one might envisage a catalytic role of a number of successful 'pockets' of effective responsible production, if and when it can be shown that localized depth of responsible production provides developmentally relevant inputs to processes of local development. Going against the odds, such 'pockets' of effective responsible production could set best practice examples, may stimulate further debate, and provide CSOs with ammunition to influence public opinion and politicians on the need for more stringent government policies and laws to enforce compliance with specific labour and environmental standards. Such a strategy aims to reinforce norm emergence and get us closer to the norm tipping point. Such a strategy implies, at least for the time being, a shift away from thinking primarily in terms of reach of responsible production, to thinking in terms of the depth or developmental relevance of responsible production.

Not much work has been done on this perspective, but a few authors have started to at least raise the issue. For example, Locke et al. (2006), after studying one of the show cases of CSR—Nike—conclude that the existing codes of conduct, even when followed through consistently, do not seem to be very significant in terms of achieving developmental impacts. This is at least partly a result of the fact that the issues included in most codes reflect the interest of companies to be able to show potential consumers they behave responsibly, and do not often seem to reflect either the priorities of poorer segments in the local workforce or local development priorities (Blowfield, 2005; Jenkins, 2005).

In other words, private sector actors have been successful in setting the agenda and determining the indicators to measure responsible behaviour, but in order for responsible production to gain more developmental relevance, other actors like local CSOs, development professionals, and engaged government officials need to find a way to start co-moulding this agenda and determining future indicators. Moreover, we need to recognize that these types of standards or codes can only be one element in a broader development strategy (Barrientos, 2000). Codes that lead to improved labour standards in the export-oriented local factories can be a catalytic point of departure for other pro-poor development interventions, only if and when other local or national developmental actors can and will use this as a lever.

However, at present MSIs seem, in line with private actors' priorities, to focus almost exclusively on monitoring direct improvements in the workplace. This anomaly is illustrated nicely by a recent interview by the author with the director of a well-known NGO dealing with verification of codes of conduct in global garment supply chains, on 21 September 2007. We discussed in detail the need to localize items for verification, such as wages, toilet facilities, overtime regulations, freedom of association, and we discussed the ins-and-outs of their monitoring system. When we started to discuss the difference between output, outcome, and impact indicators, the discussion took a surprising turn as he basically said that what they really meant to achieve ('impact') was to 'contribute to an emerging social dialogue by providing an example of how combined NGO–buyer pressure can be used to improve employment conditions and relations'. However, the output and outcome indicators all focused on issues related to direct employment conditions and labour relations in the monitored factories. This anomaly seems to be indicative of the present situation. While CSOs involved in MSIs ultimately aim at economic, social, and political empowerment of poorer groups at the local level, their direct activities are limited to monitoring conditions of workers in specific factories that are part of their initiative.

Such a strategy is also risky, as higher standards may well push out weaker and often smaller suppliers that pay lower and more irregular wages to poorer workers. In response to standards by outside buyers, local firms tend to concentrate production in easier-to-monitor places of work and cut off smaller subcontractors from their supply chain, either for real or only on paper. A similar process occurs in terms of labour contracting, where permanent workers or middlemen contract casual workers (often [seasonal] migrants) to take care of the more tedious work, without enjoying the benefits of working in a responsible chain. This may increase the gap between a relative elite of local firms supplying to GVCs with improved labour conditions and a mass of local firms ruled by low-road production in which labour conditions are not likely to improve (Gibbon and Ponto, 2005).

Instead, in order to work towards a more localized and broad-based 'race to the top', one might think of a localized version of the 'ratcheting labour standards' idea (Sabel et al. 2000, discussed in the section 'Responsible Production'). In some localities it might be feasible to mobilize (among state, private, and civil actors) the critical mass needed for norm tipping and subsequent norm cascading at the local level. In trying to achieve such localized depth in responsible production, we face a paradox. What matters most is not the highest standards but a way to optimize the linkages with other local initiatives, to achieve broader and deeper localized impacts.

From the supply chain perspective, responsible production will only start to really make a difference when firms integrate responsible attributes in their purchasing practices (Barrientos and Smith, 2006; Locke and Romis, 2006). Moreover, based on a case study of footwear suppliers to Nike in Mexico, Locke and Romis (2006) go one step further in arguing that this integration is achieved more easily in supply chains that are more quality-driven (as opposed to price-driven) and where relationships are more long term and less asymmetric.[13]

Therefore, to strengthen localized depth in responsible production, some local–global responsible catalysts need to convince and cajole local and supply chain actors to build realistic coalitions. One element in pushing forward such a strategy could be to connect to the emerging field of a more localized and actor-specific manifestation of the broader discourse on ethics and morality in development (Proctor, 1998; Gasper, 2005).[14] This would also be a modest but important step in 'universalizing' decent work standards at the local level (ILO, 2002).

In this process of constructing pockets of responsible production, government actors need to play a crucial but not necessarily labour-intensive role. In essence, governments need to set minimum standards, private sector acts as engine of growth and employment, while NGOs primarily act as watchdogs. In terms of the role of government, it is often mentioned that governments might be relatively good in setting standards and producing laws and regulations, but that the main problem lies with enforcement. Some innovative work seems to argue for giving other actors a role in enforcement, giving government actors the possibility of concentrating more on setting the standards. Weil (2005), based on a case study related to informal garment manufacturing in Los Angeles, argues that involving the buyers in monitoring minimum wage regulations in small subcontractor firms reduces the number of violations in paying minimum wages, and that using buyers to monitor increases the 'credible threat' to subcontractors. Again, this seems to work best in situations where buyers and suppliers have (a perspective of) a more long-term relationship. The key point for experiments with increasing the depth of responsible production is that this illustrates how one might creatively look at new delineations in the complementary roles of private, state, and civil actors.[15]

While present initiatives predominantly rely on voluntary civil regulation, state actors need to play a regulatory role to ensure minimum standards across the board. In short, while the whole debate on mainstreaming responsible production is dominated by private actors, with CSOs 'breathing down their neck', the issue of strengthening the developmental relevance of responsible production inevitably brings state actors back into the equation. Finally, future research would need to systematically distinguish between the regulatory roles of state actors at various levels of analysis. At present, most regulatory power rests with national governments, while the main challenges of regulation in the context of responsibility in GVCs seem to be at the global level (to regulate buyer behaviour) and at the local level (to regulate producer behaviour).

CONCLUSION AND HYPOTHESES FOR FUTURE RESEARCH

Non-governmental organizations working to mainstream responsible production face an uphill battle with an uncertain outcome but with potentially important developmental implications. A key challenge for future research is to confront the upbeat discourse on how NGOs play a catalytic role in mainstreaming labour and environmental standards, with the sobering Asian Drivers and bottom of the pyramid discourses that predict, for the foreseeable future, that Asian wages will not increase and that GVCs will experience an increasing share of low-road production in which 'luxury' responsible attributes are not to be expected. In the end, this is an empirical question; so a key issue for further investigation will be to explore, in specific locations and sectors, the net effects in terms of reach and depth of responsible production. Of particular importance in exploring the potential reach of responsible production is to develop research on the extent to which new middle-class consumers in the Global South are inclined to buy responsible products and how such inclinations might be harnessed.

Based on the little we know about the development relevance of responsible production, we can expect that the interaction between (*i*) the doubling in numbers of middle-income global consumers and (*ii*) the changes in GVC governance will lead to:

1. a *reduced* overall reach of enforcing minimum labour standards in the global economy, and
2. an *increased* depth of labour standards in some alternative niches and in the supply chains of major A-brands for consumer goods.

This also means that the 'gap' between responsible and 'normal' or 'market-based' labour standards will increase further. This will be most visible in developing localities where the first and second tier suppliers of A-brands are located next to producers for other markets. In general, it seems highly unlikely that CSR initiatives of major brand-name companies will play a norm-setting role in local economies, which also reduces the relevance of such standards as a way to enhance broader developmental goals such as reducing income poverty. While this seems the most likely overall trend, significant exceptions to the rule might still be used to demonstrate the situations in which responsible production can actually provide a stimulus to and become part of local development strategies that do enhance broader developmental goals. Such good practice examples of pockets of effective localized responsible production most likely will reveal innovative private–state–civil actor coalitions, cooperating where possible and recognizing different interests where necessary.

Therefore, future research into such good practice examples could well provide policy-relevant insights on where and when selective CSO pressure is more likely to generate positive developmental impacts. Moreover, such research would also contribute to a better understanding of the newly emerging 'division of roles': the structurally complementary as well as partly conflicting roles of government, private sector, and civil society in enhancing development in a globalizing world with new anchors.

NOTES

1. An earlier version of this essay was presented at a workshop on 'Global Production Networks and Decent Work: Recent Experience in India and Global Trends', 18–20 November 2007, Bangalore, India, Session III: 'Governance Challenges to Economic and Social Upgrading in Global Production Networks'.
2. McWilliams, Siegel, and Wright, as guest editors of a special issue on CSR in the *Journal of Management Studies*, one of the top business school journals, define CSR as 'actions that appear to further some social good, beyond the interests of the firm and that which is required by law' (2006: 1).
3. These three situations are: (*i*) 'pernicious CSR', where profits increase but social benefits decrease (this is where governments have failed to appropriately regulate the economy); (*ii*) 'borrowed virtue CSR', where profits decrease and social benefits increase (this is where shareholders fail to control managers who spend excessively on social programmes); and (*iii*) the worst case scenario is both a reduction in profits as well as social benefits which *The Economist* labels as 'delusionary CSR' (20 January 2005).
4. Especially in non-food products, it is often impossible to actually pay a premium. For a recent study on Fair Trade in the Netherlands, see Knorringa (2003).
5. The follow-up questions could be: What role do NGOs in the Global South play and how can global civil society alliances support the mainstreaming of labour and environmental standards? More specifically, what role can we

expect, for example, Chinese NGOs to play, as compared to, for example, Indian NGOs, given the different trajectories and room to manoeuvre of civil society in these two main consumption as well as production countries?

6. Traditional international relations literature identifies a hierarchy of sources of power (*i*) military power, (*ii*) economic resources, (*iii*) soft power, such as moral authority and persuasion (Florini, 2000: 10). While governments can use all three of these powers, private sector companies can still use the second and the third, and CSOs are basically confined to using only soft power (Segerlund, 2005: 25).
7. This model was developed in the context of analysing state behaviour.
8. One important insight to take from this model is that various CSOs may play complementary roles in furthering the responsible production agenda. Unfortunately, many staff members in CSOs look at this through a more competitive lens and put time and effort in arguing about which role is more important or more politically correct, while a recognition of these complementarities might be a first step towards developing more effective (tacit) liaisons, like the harmonized division of labour between Greenpeace and the World Wildlife Fund (WWF) in dealing with companies while working towards mainstreaming the FSC label.
9. For a notable early exception, see Fox et al. (2002).
10. Interestingly and ambitiously, they spend a separate section on explaining how it will be more difficult but not impossible to launch a similar process in the informal sector.
11. The phrase was initially coined by Bhagwati in 1958, and further developed in Bhagwati (1987).
12. However, value chain analysis has only recently begun to address the need to connect to consumer behaviour. For an early and interesting attempt, see Pelupessy and van Kempen (2005).
13. A study on comparing two footwear suppliers in China gave similar results in terms of better employment conditions in the factory with more network-type of relation with the main buyer (Frenkel, 2001).
14. This would be one way to address the present situation in which development standards are set and implemented by private sector actors (Blowfield, 2005).
15. For an innovative approach on how governmental and non-governmental actors may fill state capacity deficits, see Braithwaite (2006). For a case on government as a possible driver of CSR, see Moon (2004).

REFERENCES

Barrientos, S. (2000), 'Globalization and Ethical Trade: Assessing the Implications for Development', *Journal of International Development*, 12: 559–70.

Barrientos, S. and S. Smith (2006), *Evaluation of the Ethical Trading Initiative*. Brighton: Institute of Development Studies.

Bhagwati, J.N. (1987), 'Immiserizing Growth', in J. Eatwell, M. Milgate, and P. Newman (eds), *The New Palgrave Dictionary of Economics*. London: Macmillan.

Blowfield, M. (2005), 'Corporate Social Responsibility: Reinventing the Meaning of Development?', *International Affairs*, 81(3): 515–24.

Braithwaite, J. (2006), 'Responsive Regulation and Developing Countries', *World Development*, 34(5): 884–98.

Evans, P. (1996), 'Government Action, Social Capital and Development: Reviewing the Evidence on Synergy', *World Development*, 24(6): 1119–32.

FINE (2001), Definition of Fair Trade, (available at http://en.wikipedia.org/wiki/FINE#Definition_of_Fair_Trade, accessed on 24 November 2006).

Finnemore, M. and K. Sikkink (1998), 'International Norm Dynamics and Political Change', *International Organization*, 52(4): 887–917.

Florini, A.M. (2000) *The Third Force: The Rise of Transnational Civil Society*. Washington DC: Carnegie Endowment for International Peace.

Fox, T. (2004), 'Corporate Social Responsibility and Development: In Quest of an Agenda', *Development*, 47(3): 29–36.

Fox, T., H. Ward, and B. Howard (2002), *Public Sector Roles in Strengthening Corporate Social Responsibility: A Baseline Study*. Washington DC: The World Bank.

Frenkel, S.J. (2001), 'Globalization, Athletic Footwear Commodity Chains and Employment Relations in China', *Organization Studies*, 22(4): 531–62.

Gasper, D. (2005), *The Ethics of Development: From Economism to Human Development*. New Delhi: Vistaar.

Gereffi, G., R. Garcia-Johnson, and E. Sasser (2001), 'The NGO–Industrial Complex', *Foreign Policy*, 125 (July/August): 56–65.

Gibbon, P. and S. Ponto (2005), *Trading Down? Africa, Value-chains and Global Capitalism*. Philadelphia: Temple University Press.

Graham, D. and N. Woods (2006), 'Making Corporate Self-Regulation Effective in Developing Countries', *World Development*, 34(5): 868–83.

Howell, J. and J. Pearce (2001), *Civil Society & Development: A Critical Exploration*. London: Lynne Rienner Publishers.

Humphrey, J. and D. Messner (2006), 'China and India as Emerging Global Governance Actors: Challenges for Developing and Developed Countries', *IDS Bulletin*, 37(1): 107–14.

ILO (2002), *Decent Work and the Informal Economy*. Geneva: ILO.

Jenkins, Rhys (2005), 'Globalization, Corporate Social Responsibility and Poverty', *International Affairs*, 81(3): 525–40.

Kaplinsky, R. (1998), 'Globalisation, Industrialisation and Sustainable Growth: The Pursuit of the Nth Rent', IDS Discussion Paper No. 365, p. 43. Brighton: Institute for Development Studies.

Knorringa, P. (2003), *Fair Trade Effect Study: Pilot-phase Synthesis Report*, Report for the Dutch Fair Trade Organisation., The Hague: Institute of Social Studies.

Knorringa, P. and L. Pegler (2006), 'Globalisation, Firm Upgrading and Impacts on Labour', *Journal for Social and Economic Geography*, 97(5): 468–77.

Locke, R. and M. Romis (2006), 'Beyond Corporate Codes of Conduct: Work Organization and Labor Standards in Two Mexican Garment Factories', MIT

Sloan Working Paper No. 4617–06. Cambridge: MA: MIT Sloan School of Management.

Locke, R., F. Qin, and A. Brause (2006), 'Does Monitoring Improve Labor Standards? Lessons from Nike', MIT Sloan Working Paper No. 4612–06. Cambridge, MA: MIT Sloan School of Management.

McWilliams, A., D.S. Siegel, and P.M. Wright (2006), 'Guest Editors' Introduction: Corporate Social Responsibility, Strategic Implications', *Journal of Management Studies*, 43(1): 1–18.

Moon, J. (2004), *Government as a Driver of Corporate Social Responsibility*. Research Paper Series, No. 20–2004, International Centre for Corporate Social Responsibility, Nottingham University Business School.

Moore, M. (1994), 'How Difficult is it to Construct Market Relations? A Commentary on Platteau', *Journal of Development Studies*, 30(3): 818–30.

Nadvi, K. and F. Waltring (2004), 'Making Sense of Global Standards', in H. Schmitz (ed.), *Local Enterprises in the Global Economy*, pp. 53–94. Cheltenham: Edward Elgar.

O'Rourke, D. (2006), 'Multi-stakeholder Regulation: Privatizing or Socializing Global Labor Standards?', *World Development*, 34(5): 899–918.

Pelupessy, W. and L. van Kempen (2005), 'The Impact of Increased Consumer-Orientation in Global Agri-food Chains on Smallholders in Developing Countries', *Competition and Change*, 9(4): 357–81.

Prahalad, C.K. (2005), *The Fortune at the Bottom of the Pyramid: Eradicating Poverty Through Profits*. Upper Saddle River: Wharton School Publishing.

Proctor, J.D. (1998), 'Ethics in Geography: Giving Moral Form to the Geographical Imagination', *Area*, 30(1): 8–18.

Sabel, C. D., O'Rourke, and A. Fung (2000), 'Ratcheting Labour Standards: Regulation for Continuous Improvement in the Global Workplace', KSG Working Paper No. 00–010. Cambridge, MA: John F. Kennedy School of Government, Harvard University.

Schmitz, H. (2006), 'Asian Drivers: Typologies and Questions', *IDS Bulletin*, 37(1): 54–61.

Segerlund, L. (2005), *Corporate Social Responsibility and the Role of NGOs in the Advocacy of New Norms for Transnational Corporations*. Licentiate's Thesis, Department of Economic History, University of Stockholm, Sweden.

Shaw, D., T. Newholm, and R. Dickenson (2005), *Consumption as Voting: An Exploration of Consumer Empowerment*, Mimeo. Glasgow: Caledonian University.

Spar, D.L. and L.T. La Mure (2003), 'The Power of Activism: Assessing the Impact of NGOs on Global Business', *California Management Review*, 35(3): 78–101.

The Economist (2005), The Good Company, Survey on Corporate Social Responsibility, 20 January (available at www.economist.com/surveys, accessed on 12 November 2006).

Weil, D. (2005), 'Public Enforcement/Private Monitoring: Evaluating a New Approach to Regulating the Minimum Wage', *Industrial & Labor Relations Review*, 58(2): 238–57.

II

Sectoral Case Studies of Engagement in Global Production Networks

4 GLOBAL PRODUCTION NETWORKS AND DECENT WORK IN INDIA AND CHINA
Evidence from the Apparel, Automotive, and Information Technology Industries

Gary Gereffi and Esra Güler

INTRODUCTION

A striking feature of contemporary globalization is that a very large and growing proportion of the workforce in many global industries is now located in developing economies. From the point of view of international development, offshoring of manufacturing and service work is important because it can help to spur industrialization and upgrading processes in developing countries. Hence, many governments pin their hopes on global outsourcing as a key driver for economic development. Nevertheless, while engaging in global production networks (GPNs) is becoming an important source of income and employment generation for developing economies, it is 'decent and productive' employment that matters, not jobs alone.

Given the frequent criticisms of a low-wage and low-skill trap in GPNs and the fact that high-paying and skilled jobs have remained rooted in advanced economies, the complexities of the ongoing job shifts need unpacking. Using country and industry comparisons, this chapter seeks to gain a fuller understanding of the conditions under which growth is taking place through GPNs, and the extent to which this growth can be a vehicle for genuine economic and social upgrading with improved employment, sustainable incomes, and protection for workers.

The first section will offer a new conceptualization of jobs in the global economy. In the second section, we will specifically look at the cases of India and China using the framework of global value chains (GVCs). The country cases will cover a broad range of industries, including apparel as a typical low-technology buyer-driven chain, automotive as an example of a medium-technology product in producer-driven value chains, and the information technologies (IT) sector representing high-technology goods and services. All three industries have undergone significant changes over the past decade, witnessing a rapid expansion of global outsourcing and the movement of jobs, notably to India and China. In particular, we will address two main questions: To what extent have the emerging economies of India and China succeeded in becoming trade and production hubs in diverse sectors? Do the accomplishments of India and China in these industries mark significant improvements in employment and working conditions?

THE NEW GLOBAL LABOUR MARKET

What began as simple offshore assembly work in the 1960s and 1970s has rapidly spread up and down the value chain into a wide range of goods and services. Virtually all consumer products sold by developed-country retailers today are made entirely or to a significant extent by workers in offshore factories in developing countries. Even products that require advanced manufacturing capabilities, such as hard disk drives and semiconductors, are becoming hi-tech commodities made in capital-intensive facilities in Southeast Asia and elsewhere (McKendrick et al., 2000). Certain kinds of software programming and hardware design can now be done more cheaply in places like India, Taiwan, South Korea, and the Philippines than in the United States, Europe, or Japan. A growing array of knowledge-intensive business services—such as engineering, design, accounting, legal and medical advice, financial analysis, and business consulting—are now moving offshore as well (Engardio et al., 2003).

In 2004 (January–March), it was estimated that China accounted for all US production shifts in sporting goods and toys; 40 per cent of production in electronics and electrical equipment, apparel, and footwear; and one-third of US production shifts in aerospace, appliances, household goods, and wood and paper products. Meanwhile, India was the destination for all the offshore shifts in finance, insurance, and real estate, and one-third of those in communications and IT. For 2004, total US job loss due to offshore production shifts was estimated to reach 406,000, of which 99,000 went to China and 47,000 to India (Bronfenbrenner and Luce, 2004: 29, 55).

There have been several factors that underlie the size and composition of job shifts in the global labour market. First, following the break-up of the Soviet Union in 1989 and the end of the Cold War, about 3 million workers from China, India, Russia, and Eastern Europe—half of the world's labour force—joined the capitalist world economy, creating a labour supply shock on a scale unlike anything experienced before. Second, technological changes associated with the internet allowed a dramatic expansion of outsourcing and offshoring options in services as well as manufacturing, and this real-time connectivity has converted what were once segmented national labour markets into an integrated, global production system. Third, transnational corporation business strategies have been unrelenting in their search for new efficiencies, especially on the labour side where substantial cost gains can be found. As a result, offshore outsourcing is no longer considered merely an option, but 'an increasingly urgent survival tactic for companies in the developed economies' (Roach, 2003: 6).

ECONOMIC AND SOCIAL UPGRADING AND A TYPOLOGY OF JOBS

In order to evaluate the implications of the new global production system on the developing world, it is essential for us to know not only the quantity of jobs that are affected, but also the quality of jobs being created. The important question is whether it is possible to simultaneously improve both the quantity and quality of employment in GPNs. To examine the linkages between the two, and how they relate to a broader strategy of sustainable development, we explore further the concepts of economic and social upgrading.[1]

Economic upgrading is defined as 'the process by which economic actors—nations, firms, and workers—move from low-value to relatively high-value activities in global production networks' (Gereffi, 2005: 171). The concept of upgrading is now used beyond the manufacturing sector, including agriculture and service sectors. Basically, economic upgrading has four strands:

1. *Product upgrading*: introduction of a more advanced product;
2. *Process upgrading*: changes introduced in the production process with the objective of making it more efficient and productive;
3. *Functional upgrading*: a change in the mix of activities performed by a firm or a locality towards higher value added stages in the production process (for example, research and development, design, logistics, finance, or marketing);
4. *Chain upgrading*: a move towards a more technologically advanced production chain.

The main motivation in economic upgrading is to improve economic performance such as production, exports, profits, or technological capabilities, whereas in social upgrading it is to enhance the capabilities and entitlements of workers as social actors and improve the *quality* of their employment. Social upgrading involves access to better work, which might result from economic upgrading, but it also includes enhancing working conditions via better wages, benefits, standards, social protection, social dialogue, and worker rights (at a minimum defined by core International Labour Organization [ILO] Conventions) in the value chain.

Social upgrading is comprised of two components: (*i*) measurable standards, which are quantifiable aspects such as category of employment (regular or irregular), wage level, contract type, social protection, working hours, and health and safety levels; and (*ii*) enabling rights that are less quantifiable aspects, such as freedom of association and the right to collective bargaining, non-discrimination, voice, and empowerment. The definition of social upgrading relates to the ILO's decent work concept, which constitutes four main pillars: employment, standards and rights at work, social protection, and social dialogue. Decent work helps to frame social upgrading as it covers both quantitative and qualitative aspects of jobs (Barrientos et al., 2008).

Economic upgrading and social upgrading are interlinked, and upgrading requires a balanced and integrated approach between the two. In the best-case scenario, economic upgrading and social upgrading work hand-in-hand and it is implicitly assumed that moving up in the chain leads to higher–value added activities and higher profits, and these translate into higher wages and better work conditions. However, the two do not always work in tandem, nor do they have to come at the expense of the other.

The development trajectories and dynamics of economic and social upgrading in the GPNs of the developing world are determined by the character of jobs in GVCs—whether the jobs are mere assembly activities, advanced manufacturing of components and finished products, or product development, design, and engineering services. From a GVCs perspective, jobs are not tied to particular locations or industries, but to certain economic activities that cut *across* industries. Based on this classification, five types of jobs exist in the global economy (Gereffi, 2006: 9; Barrientos et al., 2008):

1. small-scale, household-based work, which usually includes agricultural production and labour-intensive or artisanal types of manufacturing;
2. low-skilled, labour-intensive assembly work in export processing and subcontracting industries, which is factory-based;
3. moderately skilled, full-package manufacturing work (original equipment manufacturing or OEM), which is associated with the production of finished consumer goods;

4. advanced production work, which usually involves original design manufacturing (ODM) and own brand manufacturing (OBM) of key components or sub-assemblies to large manufacturers; and
5. knowledge-intensive work, which is linked to the offshore provision of research and development, IT, and business process services.

Small-scale, household-based work is often found at the base of many GPNs in developing economies. The workers are small-scale producers, outgrowers in agricultural production, or homeworkers in more labour-intensive or artisanal types of manufacturing. They usually have access to their own assets and means of subsistence. Production takes place in or around the household residence, with limited separation between commercial productive activity and unpaid reproductive activity. The work involves both paid and unpaid family labour, including child labour.

Low-skilled, labour-intensive assembly jobs were generated in the first wave of offshore production in the 1960s and 1970s by the transnational corporations' search for low-wage, labour-intensive production, especially in light consumer goods industries such as apparel, sporting goods, housewares, and toys. In many developing nations, these jobs were the first stage of export-oriented industrialization, most commonly located in export processing zones (EPZs) or in extended supply chains locally, in which plants are provided with inputs for assembly. In 1975, there were close to 80 EPZs in 25 countries; by 1997, there were 93 countries with 845 EPZs. In 2006, the figures grew to 3,500 EPZs in 130 countries. In terms of employment, the number of workers in EPZs tripled from 22.5 million in 1997 to 66 million in 2006, with China alone accounting for 60–70 per cent of the global EPZ workforce—approximately 40–45 million workers (Singa Boyenge, 2007). Thus, assembly jobs continue to play a vital role in the global economy.

Assembly jobs in EPZs are useful in attracting investors, ramping up output, and meeting international quality standards for a variety of export products, and they tend to have a relatively large and positive impact on job creation, especially for female workers. However, assembly work is repetitive and fragmented, and highly vulnerable to the purchasing preferences of global lead firms. These tend to be footloose jobs, characterized by minimal local linkages to the host economy and poor working conditions. Furthermore, they are often low paying, not unionized, and involve temporary, informal, and contract work. While women do a significant portion of low-skilled, labour-intensive assembly work, they usually have insecure, low-paid jobs. Considering the negative social features of this type of work, many developing economies are now trying to move beyond assembly to more stable forms of integration with GVCs.

Moderately skilled, full-package production (OEM) jobs have emerged with the rise of 'global buyers', including giant discount chains, department stores, and brand marketers (so-called 'manufacturers without factories') (see Gereffi, 1994, 2005; Dolan and Humphrey, 2000). The key difference between assembly jobs and OEM jobs is who supplies the inputs and coordinates the production process: in assembly production, manufacturers in advanced industrial countries control the inputs and the orders; in full-package production, while global buyers provide the orders, developing-country suppliers coordinate the supply of inputs, make the final product, and send it to the buyer. As developing-country firms increase their coordination capacity in the full-package process, they can improve their bargaining power and gain higher margins.

The likelihood of social upgrading is a direct consequence of the relationship between suppliers and buyers. Consequently, the full-package system has clear advantages over assembly work. The introduction of product standards and company codes of labour practice by buyers has led to pressure on full-package suppliers for decent conditions with higher worker compensation, job security, and skill improvement. However, except in relatively advanced economies (such as South Korea, Taiwan, Hong Kong, and Singapore in the 1980s and 1990s), OEM firms are often not able to participate in more profitable stages such as design, product development, and branding because these activities are retained by global buyers. Besides, with growing demand by lead firms for flexibility, full-package jobs may also involve temporary, contract, or casual work.

Advanced production jobs arose in conjunction with a different set of offshore activities that emerged in the 1980s and 1990s. Lead firms in capital- and technology-intensive value chains, such as automobiles and electronics, set up international production networks not only to assemble and deliver their finished goods, but also to develop a supply base for key intermediate products and sub-assemblies. A good example of this form of production is the rise of global contract manufacturers in the electronics industry and 'mega suppliers' in the automotive industry (Sturgeon and Lester, 2004). The opportunities for developing-country suppliers are related to the process of supplier-oriented upgrading, which can improve technology learning and knowledge spillovers. However, large and technologically sophisticated first-tier suppliers tend to concentrate 'good' jobs in relatively few locations. In the case of the hard disk drive industry, design jobs remained rooted in the US, which accounted for nearly 80 per cent of the wage bill, despite the fact that 80 per cent of the jobs were in Southeast Asia (McKendrick et al., 2000). Another problem is that supplier-oriented upgrading has a built-in contradiction. The lead firms are reluctant to have suppliers learn too much, and thereby try to curtail their power to set the knowledge parameters essential for product innovation. Overall, these jobs are well-paying, productive, and relatively secure, but flexible as demand shifts.

Knowledge-intensive jobs are being created by a new wave of offshoring in services. White-collar outsourcing started with simple service jobs, like call centres and telemarketing, but it now includes more advanced business services such as finance, accounting, software, medical services, and engineering.

One of the best measures of expanding knowledge-intensive work in developing nations is newly emerging research and development (R&D) centres. In India, according to the Organization for Economic Co-operation and Development (OECD), there are over 100 R&D centres built by multinational firms and the country ranked as the sixth most-favourable location in a recent survey of the world's largest R&D corporate investors (*The Economist*, 2007). In China, the figure is much higher with nearly 1,000 R&D centres (Gereffi et al., 2008: 20). Knowledge-intensive service jobs are increasingly seen as an opportunity for the developing world to attain both economic and social benefits with technological learning and knowledge spillovers, better income, and good export prospects. However, on average, the size of employment in this job category is relatively small, considering the requirements for high skills and advanced degrees, mainly in science and engineering. The McKinsey Global Institute (Farrell et al., 2005) estimates that in 2008 the number of service jobs in low-wage developing countries would reach 4.1 million, which is only 1.2 per cent of the total number of service jobs in developed countries. The unskilled majority in developing countries is excluded from the desired employment opportunities provided by knowledge-intensive work.

Figure 4.1 highlights a key dimension of our typology of work. If we compare different industries within agriculture, manufacturing, and services, all five types of work are present in each industry. However, there are significant differences in the proportions of each type of work across these industries. Within manufacturing, if we compare industries that can be classified as relatively low-tech (apparel), medium-tech (automotive), and hi-tech (electronics), the low-skilled and household-based types of work decrease and the relative importance of knowledge-intensive and highly skilled work increases. This progression at the work level is associated with economic upgrading.

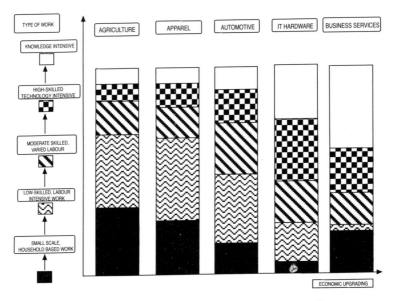

Figure 4.1: Types of Work and Economic Upgrading

Source: Barrientos et al. (2008).

COMPARING NATIONAL UPGRADING TRAJECTORIES: INDIA AND CHINA

Characterized by extensive economic diversification and booming merchandise exports to all parts of the world, China currently is one of the world's fastest growing economies, relying heavily on foreign direct investment (FDI) to fuel its export growth since the 1980s. India, by contrast, was until the early 1990s an inward-oriented economy, but it has now become a major player on the global economic stage, sparked to a large degree by the stellar performance of its IT sector and its dynamic business service exports. Services have grown faster than manufacturing in the Indian economy, which highlights a divergent development path compared with China. Moreover, unlike China, India relies more extensively on home-grown entrepreneurs rather than foreign capital to spur development (see Huang and Khanna, 2003).

How are these two different patterns reflected in China's and India's upgrading trajectories? One of the ways that we can assess industrial upgrading for export-oriented economies such as China and India is to look at the shifts in the technology content of their exports over time. We divide exports into five product groupings, which are listed in ascending levels of technological content: primary products, resource-based products, and low-, medium-, and high-technology manufactures.[2]

From Figure 4.2, we see that in 1988, more than one-third of India's exports to the world were low-technology products (mainly textiles and apparel), followed by primary and resource-based products. In the early 1990s, following the liberalization period, low-technology products moved

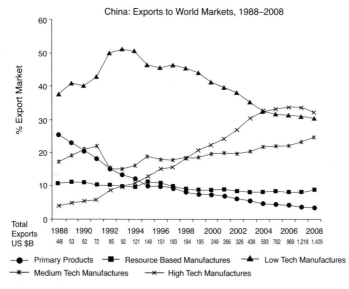

Figure 4.2: Technological Composition of Exports: India and China
Source: UNCOMTRADE (2009).

further ahead of other categories in India's export mix, while the medium-technology manufactures (mainly automotive products) grew slowly. By 2008, nearly 40 per cent of India's exports of $182 billion were in resource-based manufactures (mainly refined petroleum products and precious and semi-precious stones that rebounded in the late 1990s), whereas low-technology manufactures declined to 22 per cent and medium-technology manufactures were 18 per cent of the total. Thus, in the last 20 years, India did not increase the technological sophistication of its manufacturing exports, except the rise in automotive products and, to a limited extent, high-technology manufactured items (7 per cent).

Unlike India, the composition of China's exports to the world during 1988–2008 was transformed from a profile based on low-technology and primary products to one dominated by medium- and high-technology manufactured items. In 1988, the leading product category was low-technology manufactures, mainly a wide variety of light consumer goods: apparel, footwear, toys, sporting goods, housewares, and so on. These products accounted for half of China's overall exports in the early 1990s, and then started to decline sharply. By 2008, high-technology exports from China had increased their share to nearly 33 per cent of the country's overall exports, and already passed low-technology exports for the top spot in China's export mix. Furthermore, medium-technology exports increased their share to 25 per cent of China's total exports of $1429 billion in 2006.

While both economies have increased the diversification of their export profiles in the last 20 years, it is clear that China has performed better than India in the technological sophistication of its manufacturing exports. China has experienced a more rapid and decisive growth in the share of medium- and high-technology manufactured products in its export mix.

Nevertheless, a word of caution is needed in using exports as an indicator of economic and social upgrading. The problem with export statistics is that we have no way of knowing the degree to which these economies are carrying out the labour-intensive and low-technology processes, which are associated with lower wages and poor working conditions, versus skill-intensive and high value-added tasks. We need to link more precise employment data with disaggregated trade statistics and analyse industries from the GVCs perspective. Most developing countries do not collect such data in a systematic fashion. Thus, with the data available to us, the next section carries out a cross-industry analysis for India and China.

APPAREL INDUSTRY

Prior to the phase-out of the Multi-Fibre Arrangement (MFA) in 2005, apparel had become one of the most geographically dispersed of all industries, with over 100 exporting countries and 20 million registered workers producing textiles and apparel worldwide[3] (Gereffi and Memodovic, 2003; UNCTAD, 2005; Dicken, 2007: Chapter 9). As in many developing countries, textiles and apparel constituted one of the largest and most dynamic sectors in the economies of India and China. In India, it is estimated to account for 4 per cent of GDP, 26 per cent of manufacturing output, 15 per cent of exports, and 18 per cent of industrial employment (Tewari, 2008).In China, despite its less strong share due to steep rise of technology-intensive manufacturing, the apparel industry still produced 2.9 per cent of GDP, 7 per cent of industrial output, and around 15 per cent of total exports in 2005 (Ramasamy and Yeung, 2008).

China's spectacular performance in the apparel industry has been driven by global sourcing strategies. According to the most recent statistics released by the World Trade Organization (WTO), the value of Chinese textile and apparel exports jumped from less than $17 billion in 1990 to over $171 billion in 2007, increasing its share in world exports from 7.9 per cent to 25.1 per cent, and making China the world's second-largest textile and apparel supplier and the number one apparel exporter. India has also built a strong position, but it is less dominant in the global market. India's textile and apparel exports rose from $4.7 billion to $19.1 billion between 1990 and 2007, ranking the country as the fifth-largest textile and apparel supplier and the sixth apparel exporter.

Why has India been unable to more effectively utilize its comparative advantages in textiles and apparel, including an abundant supply of low-skilled labour, a long history of textile and apparel production, and the world's largest land area for cotton production? Comparing these two countries, first, China has sought to leverage its huge economies of scale, illustrated by the growth of China's mega-factories and single-product clusters called 'supply-chain cities' (Gereffi, 2009: 46–8). In contrast, except for a few large firms (for example, Arvind, Raymond, Gokaldas, and Karle) and some small firms organized in clusters (for example, Tiruppur), the apparel industry in India is characterized by small fragmented units reserved until 2001 under the long legacy of the government's small-scale industry (SSI) policy.

Second, China has made major investments in infrastructure and logistics to lower transportation costs and shorten the time to market. Thus, despite labour costs in India ($0.38/hour) being lower than those in China ($0.88/hour), Chinese firms have significantly higher competitiveness in non-labour components of their costs than their Indian counterparts. For instance, shipping containers of apparel products from Mumbai/Chennai to the east coast of the US is 37 per cent more expensive than shipping the same products from Shanghai (Adhikari and Weeratunge, 2006).

Third, China has a coherent upgrading strategy to diversify its product mix, including cotton and synthetic fibre apparel; but India has long focused on low value-added cotton-made and seasonal apparel such as summer and spring clothes with limited demand throughout the year. As long as these supply-side constraints persist, the export gap between India and China may not be narrowed in the foreseeable future.

The next issue is to identify if and how the economic gains of these countries translate into real advantages for the Indian and Chinese workers in terms of quantity and quality of employment. It is hard to say how many jobs their integration into the global apparel chain has spawned, but increased exports have undoubtedly facilitated a surge in employment. According to United Nations Industrial Development Organization (UNIDO) country statistics, this was most impressive in China, where apparel employment increased from 1.75 million in 1995 to 3.78 million in 2006, raising apparel's share in manufacturing employment from 3 to 6 per cent. Though lagging behind China, India registered an increase in apparel jobs from 276,000 in 1998 to 449,000 in 2004, with a rise in the share of apparel employment in total manufacturing employment from 3.5 to 5.5 per cent (UNIDO, 2009).

Regarding the quality of employment, there are various aspects to consider. First, there has been a rise in real wages of apparel workers in India, as reported by a recent occupational wage survey (GoI, 2008). However, despite the wage increases, apparel workers remain among the worst paid of all workers in the manufacturing sectors of both India and China. In India, although the gap between apparel and average manufacturing wages narrowed, the ratio still corresponds to 58.7 per cent, whereas in China it is 38.7 per cent for 2003 (Ernst et al., 2005).

Second, the apparel industry is often recognized as one in which female workers predominate. In India, the gender composition in the organized apparel sector shows that the majority of workers are women, nearly 60 per cent on average, but it is much higher in certain regions, especially the southern states like Tamil Nadu and Karnataka, where respectively 84 per cent and 79 per cent of all apparel employees are female (GoI, 2008). The challenge with female apparel workers is that they are mostly concentrated in low-paying, less-skilled job categories like helper, marker, sorter, and sweeper; they also earn less than men in almost all occupations.

Third, shortened lead times by global apparel brands and retailers affect employment contracts in supplier firms, which tend towards greater use of temporary, contract, and casual workers, as well as transferring production itself through mechanisms of subcontracting to the unorganized sector—that is, home work and child labour in some instances. In the case of India, besides quick response trends, seasonal and small-scale orders, and the historical legacy of SSI policy, another underlying factor for flexible work is the country's rigid labour laws like the Industrial Dispute Act requiring firms with more than 100 workers to get permission for lay offs. Indian firms often transfer jobs to the unorganized sector to get around such laws, leading to a polarization in the industry. While we can be more or less certain that upgrading to full-package production in India has pushed up working conditions in the large, export-oriented firms in the organized sector, a decent work deficit exists lower down in the supply chain.

Looking at China, which relied for a long time on the low-cost strategy, many firms operating in the country are now facing rapidly climbing costs, mainly due to raw material prices and wages in coastal sites, along with rivalry from emerging low-wage apparel exporters like Vietnam and Bangladesh bidding down the already razor-thin margins. However, China's recent policy initiatives to increase value-added and address poor working conditions signal that the 'low road' is no longer the first option for China. 'The List of Restricted Commodities in Processing Trade' that came into effect in 2007 requiring the move of labour-intensive production from coastal areas to inland and undeveloped areas, and the Labour Contract Law which came into effect in 2008 to discourage the use of contract labour and support unionization, are two critical developments in China. We believe that such efforts reflect a window of opportunity for China and they will be essential for economic and social upgrading of other global apparel suppliers. In fact, among those suppliers, India will be under increasing pressure to take the 'high road' and 'race to the top' strategies.

AUTOMOTIVE INDUSTRY

Hindustan Motors of India produced its first car, the Ambassador, in the 1950s, when Toyota began to produce in Japan. After 50 years, Toyota's car production reached 5 million units, while the output of Hindustan Motors was 18,000 cars with no change in the Ambassador's original model (Du Pont, 2002). For China's first automobile manufacturer, First Auto Works (FAW), the trend was not much different from India's. Founded in 1953 in China's northern city of Changchun, Jilin Province, the FAW began to produce its Jiefang (Liberation) trucks in 1956 with 1,600 assembled units and this product had not been changed for nearly 30 years (Holweg et al., 2009).

However, today total vehicle output is climbing rapidly in both India and China. According to production statistics of the International Organization of Motor Vehicles Manufacturers (OICA, 2007), with its 8.9 million vehicles in 2007, China was the third-largest vehicle producer after the US and Japan, surpassing Germany; India was the tenth-largest automotive manufacturer supplying 2.3 million vehicles.

The offshore investments and 'follow sourcing' strategies of global firms have been of paramount importance for the restructuring and incorporation into GVCs of the Chinese and Indian automotive industries. Today, driven by the demands of the world's leading automakers to establish local manufacturing capacity, first-tier component suppliers like Bosch, Johnson Controls, Lear, Siemens Automotive, Magna, TRW, Denso, and others have attained supply-chain consolidation and a global footprint. By the same token, India and China, with their huge and rapidly growing domestic markets, low-wages,[4] and abundant engineering skills, became two of the largest destinations for expanding investments by global automakers, and consequently by many of their established first-tier suppliers from the late 1990s onwards (Sturgeon and Lester, 2004; Dicken, 2007: Chapter 10).

Over the past decade, the composition of Indian component exports has upgraded from the lower-value 'after-market' for repair parts to higher value-added parts for the auto assemblers (OEMs), particularly engine parts. While the 'after-market' auto parts had been dominant in the total auto component exports with a 65 per cent share in the 1990s, the OEM parts attained the leading share of 75 per cent as of 2007 (ACMA, 2008). In China, the move from the production of labour-intensive parts (like wiring harnesses and brake parts) to higher technology-intensive and value-added components (particularly engines) is being reported. In late 2003, the joint venture between the Shanghai Automotive Industry Corporation (SAIC) of China and General Motors (GM) began making engines to be installed in the 2005 Chevrolet Equinox built in Canada (International Metalworkers' Federation, 2006, 2007).

Emerging Chinese and Indian auto companies are even coming up with their own brands and models in global markets. Chery Automobile from China already began exporting its low price, branded cars to new markets in the Middle East and Asia. Tata Motors of India is also a successful example with many domestic designs and brands, with the Nano model launched in the domestic market in 2009 and planned for future expansion to global markets. Many Indian and Chinese automotive firms now aim to develop their own capacities in design and engineering activities.

Indeed, as a way to achieve higher design and engineering capabilities, the research centres of foreign investors are global pacesetters in India and China. In the case of China, GM is the most aggressive foreign firm in transferring technology to the country. Under the joint venture with the Chinese SAIC automotive firm, GM's research centre in Shanghai employs 1,300 people, localizing the design of Western models. GM is now building its own research centre in China to develop hybrid technology and other designs (Bradsher, 2007).[5]

Looking forward, expectations are for strong continued growth of the Indian and Chinese automotive industries. Yet, questions remain about the widely touted weaknesses of the two countries' automotive sectors. While India's automotive manufacturers are now all private firms,[6] the state-owned enterprises of China including the 'top three'—SAIC, FAW, and Dongfeng Motor Corporation—create vulnerability for operational efficiency and competitiveness. Also, both countries suffer from remaining trade barriers, skill shortages, and rising wages, as well as a fragmented structure of component suppliers, a majority of which are still labour-intensive and low quality with weak technological and managerial capacities.

The Chinese government called for a massive consolidation and restructuring, in its 2001–5 auto industry plan, which intended to cut 118 automakers to only three, and reduce the number of component suppliers from hundreds to five to ten large firms (International Metalworkers' Federation, 2004). However, it is still uncertain whether the Indian component industry will achieve critical mass. Also, India's higher cost of production due to its poor infrastructure and high electricity costs, and its sizeable but much poorer domestic market, are the other chief obstacles for further growth and upgrading.

What are the social impacts of the rising automotive industry in India and China, in light of the recent global integration driven by foreign firms? Employment in the Indian automotive industry rose from 257,000 in 1998 to 337,000 in 2004, increasing the share of the automotive sector in total manufacturing employment from 3.2 to 4.2 per cent (UNIDO country statistics for India). Despite overall wage gains under global insertion, wage levels are still low in India, and remaining wage gaps between motor vehicle assembly and parts jobs are considerable. China is also reported to have very low wages. According to data for 2002, the hourly wage in China was as low as $0.50 whereas wages were $31.67 in the United States and $5.04 in

Mexico (Holweg et al., 2009). However, due to increased output and the concentration of production facilities in certain urban areas, there has been a shortage of qualified employees, and as a consequence of this, a trend of booming wages for skilled workers. As Holweg et al. (2009) mentioned, Volkswagen has complained that in Shanghai, due to the shortage of qualified managers, wage levels are catching up to European levels.

Another dimension of job quality is employment arrangements. According to the International Metalworkers' Federation (2007), there is a widespread and growing use of contract workers in the automotive industry. Some assembly and parts-making operations in China are staffed almost entirely by workers on fixed-term contracts. In many cases, almost half of the workforce is in precarious jobs, receiving much lower compensation and social benefits than regular employees, unequal or inadequate access to facilities, and worse conditions of work. Similarly, in the case of India, a permanent worker at the Hero Honda Gurgaon operation can draw a monthly wage of up to Rs 40,000, compared to only about Rs 6,700 for contract workers, with some earning only Rs 2,200 (International Metalworkers' Federation, 2006). However, a study by Okada (2004) shows a contrary picture about flexible employment in India, suggesting that in response to increased competition in the liberalization period of the 1990s, the demand for casual workers of component suppliers to Maruti Suzuki and Tata Motors (Telco) fell and employers increasingly chose regular long-term employment, mainly to improve product and process quality standards. There was also a clear upward shift in the educational level of the workforce (even in small suppliers) and more focus on formal in-firm training programmes.

While we can expect that the major automotive companies and first-tier suppliers would probably score well on decent work dimensions, there is less certainty with respect to labour practices in second- and third-tier suppliers both in India and China.

IT SECTOR

Offshore outsourcing in India's IT sector is considered by many as a globalization success story. IT services have been advantageous for the Indian economy, being less capital-intensive and requiring far fewer economies of scale coupled with India's good pool of low-wage scientists and engineers[7] and high proficiency in English. The IT sector's contribution to India's GDP has steadily increased from 1.2 per cent in 1998 to 5.2 per cent in 2007. It generated around $40 billion export earnings in 2008 with a growth of

36 per cent, thereby boosting the foreign exchange reserve of the country (NASSCOM, 2008).

The difficulties of climbing the IT value chain, especially with regard to technology, are well known. Traditionally, almost all of the research and development was done in the US, and India remained largely separated from the cutting-edge activities. However, by the early 2000s, India had begun to offer higher-level services, such as systems architecture, design, and technology strategy services (Chadwick, 2003). While around 90 per cent of exports were onsite projects in the late 1980s, in 2005 this share decreased to 30 per cent as offshore development accelerated (Altenburg et al., 2008). India has gained considerable autonomy from customers in managing projects independently (ibid.). Furthermore, India has emerged as a global leader in workforce development for the knowledge workers, and its R&D labs are associated with the largest multinational and domestic IT firms (Wadhwa et al., 2008).

The IT cluster in Bengaluru (earlier Bangalore), the so-called 'Silicon Valley of India' that accounts for 40 per cent of India's software exports with 140 transnational development centres and 750 large and small domestic IT firms, mirrors the rapid trend of India's upgrading. Firms in this city reportedly moved from labour-intensive activities—including coding, testing, and maintenance—to skill-intensive and high value-adding activities, like design and requirement analyses, as well as from on-site to offshore services. The Bengaluru software cluster has benefited from public sector investments in technology-intensive industries; a significant number of engineering colleges and science and technology institutions; software technology parks established in the early 1990s with high-speed communication links; and incentives such as tax concessions, flexible labour regulations, and private sector training for global IT subsidiaries (Vijayabaskar, 2005; Wadhwa et al., 2008).

While India is the centrepiece of global IT services, China is known as the global factory for IT hardware. Particularly in its Pearl River Delta region, China is now the largest exporter of IT goods, surpassing the US and up from a world ranking of tenth in the year 2000. Indeed, the huge FDI inflow for high technology exports is the key to China's integration in GPNs. In 2005, 88 per cent of high-technology exports from China were made by foreign-invested enterprises, which produced 58 per cent of the country's total exports (Ernst, 2007). The largest IT product exporters are still foreign-owned in China, but similar to India's indigenous software corporations, China has witnessed the emergence of its own IT global manufacturers, like Huawei Technologies, the major domestic telecommunication networks provider in China, and Lenovo, which became a global IT firm with its acquisition of IBM's personal computer division in 2005, including IBM's international research facilities.

The remarkable upgrading of China, with its exposure to foreign firms' cutting-edge technology and management approaches, is supported by many exemplary companies as well as a wide range of highly sophisticated products. China's export bundle now resembles a country with a per capita income that is three times higher than that of China. According to Rodrik (2006:18), 'China has steadily moved away from being simply an assembler of components. Increasingly, production is integrated backwards and the supply chain is moving to where the assembly is undertaken'. However, contrary to those findings, Koopman et al. (2008) argue that sophisticated or high-skilled sectors in China, such as computers, electronic devices, and telecommunication equipment, tend to have low shares of local content, particularly in foreign invested firms' exports.

The booming growth of India's and China's IT and allied sectors, despite being relative newcomers, has created significant employment opportunities. In India, IT employment reportedly crossed the 2 million person mark in 2007, with an increase of about 389,000 jobs in one year (NASSCOM, 2008). Of course, 2 million jobs could appear insignificant in terms of India's total population of 1.1 billion. In the case of China, electrical–electronic manufacturing employment (used as a proxy for IT employment) for 2002 was around 3 million people. It then rose to over 6 million employees in 2004, accounting for 35 per cent of the total world employment in this sector (ILO, 2007). As illustrated by China's employment, the IT hardware industry generates more jobs than software. Thus, recent initiatives in India, such as the project in Hyderabad to develop a semiconductor manufacturing industry, can help India to create more jobs and also extend the country's presence throughout the IT value chain.

Despite their large labour pools, most of the engineering graduates from India and China are not considered suitable for working in foreign firms inside the country or abroad. A 2005 McKinsey Global Institute's survey of corporate human resource managers revealed that only about 25 per cent of the Indian engineering graduates and 10 per cent of Chinese engineers would qualify for such jobs (Farrell et al., 2005). Furthermore, adding to the bottleneck of skilled personnel, both India and China suffer an outward migration of graduates to the US and elsewhere (Tschang, 2003).

In both India and China, IT employees consist of a small and relatively well-educated portion of the labour force with technical, managerial, or communication skills and often fluency in English. IT employees are usually natives of the urban areas where the most popular IT companies are located. In India, for instance, these locations are Bengaluru, Delhi, Mumbai, Kolkata, Chennai, and Hyderabad.

Moreover, employment in IT is not gender neutral. Women tend to cluster at the lower end of the job hierarchy, leading to the feminization of certain service activities. Particularly in call centres where communication skills are critical, there are many job opportunities for females. In higher-skilled IT jobs, the challenge is that females are disadvantaged with their lower enrolment rates, especially in technical education. Even when they qualify for higher-skilled jobs with equal responsibilities as men, their returns are inequitable. Studies on India also highlight other aspects of IT jobs, such as the lack of trade unions and collective mobilization, mainly due to gaps in legislation and the individualized nature of work, and the burdens of continuous overtime and night work to meet tight project deadlines (see Rothboeck et. al., 2001; Varma and Sasikumar, 2004).

CONCLUSION

While China and India have pursued distinct economic trajectories, in both countries international trade and foreign investment have played a major role in upgrading selected industries, such as apparel, automotive, and IT. Considering China's more rapid industrialization, India certainly can learn from China's experience. Reducing the constraints in exports by promoting large-scale production and improving competitiveness in the non-labour areas, such as infrastructure and energy, are examples of areas where India can learn from China's policy initiatives.

Looking at the tremendous job creation in China over the past decade in all three sectors, India cannot underestimate the importance of labour-intensive manufacturing to create sustained employment and incomes for its large poor population, which still depends on agriculture. Perhaps it can be valuable to examine the potential links between the currently booming services sector and labour-intensive manufacturing in India. Yet, China also has much to learn from the Indian experience, particularly if it wants to improve its position in the global IT services sector. However, the ripple effect of current events in the US financial market on Indian IT companies, which are dependent on serving the US market, also shows the limits of IT service–oriented upgrading. In addition, the growth of India's indigenous private sector can provide important lessons for China, which lacks such dynamism.

The analysis in this chapter reveals that India's and China's integration into GPNs has not been merely a race to the bottom, but it has offered considerable opportunity for creating high-quality jobs. However, delivering decent work is not an automatic outcome of global integration; indeed, a number of structural factors exist to achieve economic and social upgrading. This chapter provides a summary of each country's upgrading process based on its structural and factor conditions; the job, industry, and value chain characteristics; and the policies of government and international and private parties. In apparel and automotive industries, China has advantages over India mainly due to its factor endowments and proactive government policies, whereas in the IT sector, particularly with respect to IT services, India has a stronger profile with its workforce development, export orientation, and the government's appropriate policies. However, currently the two countries face a host of new economic and social challenges, including eroding labour-cost advantages, shortage of high skills, poverty, unemployment, and the need to move high-value activities.

Production in China and India for GVCs has been linked to the emergence of a more flexible labour force, which generally includes a high share of female and migrant workers. Drawing on the lessons from the Chinese model of exports and employment promotion, India might be able to reduce economic and social problems, including a huge reliance on foreign investment and assembly work, large regional income disparities, and massive rural to urban migration associated with poor working conditions. China's recent policy initiatives to address these issues should be borne in mind too. Nonetheless, for other developing countries, India and China are clearly atypical cases because their huge domestic markets and labour forces allow them to challenge and redefine some rules of the game in GVCs in an effort to promote indigenous innovation and sustainable local development. Adapting global lessons to local conditions is an ongoing challenge for all nations in the global economy.

NOTES

1. This section draws upon ideas discussed more fully in Barrientos et al. (2008).
2. Sanjaya Lall (2000) developed this technological classification of exports based on 3-digit Standard International Trade Classification (SITC) categories. His article provides the detailed list of products under each category.
3. The true employment including unregistered workers is much higher.
4. The hourly labour cost comparison from KPMG (2007) is: United States, $22.70; China, $1.50; and India, $1.60.
5. Nevertheless, this centre is wholly owned by GM which might reflect its control over the knowledge parameters for product innovation.
6. The auto sector is now entirely in the private sector following the decision by India's cabinet at the end of 2006 to sell the government's remaining 10.3 per cent stake in Maruti Udyog.

7. Computer-science and IT graduates at the bachelor's level were nearly 220,000 in 2005–6 for India and 575,000 for China, compared to 129,000 in 2005–6 for the US (Gerffi et al., 2008: 16–17).

REFERENCES

ACMA (Automotive Component Manufacturers Association of India) (2008), *Global Competitiveness of Indian Auto Component Industry & Its Sustainability, Status of Indian Automotive and Auto-Component Industry: Status Report* (available at http://acmainfo.com/docmgr/Status_of_Auto_Industry/Status_Indian_Auto_Industry.pdf, accessed on 21 July 2009).

Adhikari, Ratnakar and Chatrini Weeratunge (2006), 'Textiles & Clothing Sector in South Asia: Coping with Post-quota Challenges', in B.S. Chimni, B.L. Das, S. Kelegama, and M. Rahman (eds), *Multilateralism at Crossroads: Reaffirming Development Priorities*, South Asian Yearbook of Trade and Development, pp. 109–45. Delhi: Centre for Trade and Development and Wiley, India.

Altenburg, Tilman, Hubert Schmitz, and Andreas Stamm (2008), 'Breakthrough? China's and India's Transition from Production to Innovation', *World Development*, 36(2): 325–44.

Barrientos, Stephanie, Gary Gereffi, and Arianna Rossi (2008), 'What are the Challenges and Opportunities for Economic and Social Upgrading?', Concept Note prepared for 'Capturing the Gains', International Labour Organization Workshop, Manchester, UK, December.

Bradsher, Keith (2007), 'G.M. will Build Its Own Research Center in China', *New York Times*, October (available at http://www.nytimes.com/2007/10/30/business/30auto.html, accessed on 21 July 2009).

Bronfenbrenner, Kate and Stephanie Luce (2004), 'The Changing Nature of Corporate Global Restructuring: The Impact of Production Shifts on Jobs in the U.S., China, and Around the Globe', US–China Economic and Security Review Commission, October.

Chadwick, William Jr. (2003), 'Global Trends in the Information Technology Outsourcing Services Market', *Industry Trade and Technology Review*, Publication No. 3661, November, Washington D.C.: Office of Industries, USITC.

Dicken, Peter (2007), *Global Shift: Mapping the Changing Contours of the World Economy*, 5th edition. London: Paul Chapman.

Dolan, Catherine and John Humphrey (2000), 'Governance and Trade in Fresh Vegetables: The Impact of UK Supermarkets on the African Horticulture Industry', *Journal of Development Studies*, 37(2): 147–76.

Du Pont, Pete (2002), 'On History's Ash Heap: Socialists Promised Heaven, but Their Heads were in the Clouds', *Wall Street Journal*, Opinion Archives, May.

Engardio, Peter, Aaron Bernstein, and Manjeet Kripalani (2003), 'Is Your Job Next?' *Business Week*, 3 February, pp. 50–60.

Ernst, Christoph, Alfonso Hernández Ferrer, and Daan Zult (2005), 'The End of the Multi-Fibre Agreement and Its Implication for Trade and Employment',

Employment Strategy Papers 2005/16. Geneva: International Labour Organization.

Ernst, Dieter (2007), 'Beyond the "Global Factory" Model: Innovative Capabilities for Upgrading China's IT industry', *International Journal of Technology and Globalisation*, 3(4): 437–59.

Farrell, Diana, Martha A. Laboissière, and Jaeson Rosenfeld (2005), 'Sizing the Emerging Global Labor Market', *The McKinsey Quarterly*, 3: 92–103.

Farrell, Diana, Martha A. Laboissière, Jaeson Rosenfeld, Sascha Stürze, and Fusayo Umezawa (2005), *The Emerging Global Labor Market: Part II—The Supply of Offshore Talent*. San Francisco: McKinsey Global Institute.

Gereffi, Gary (1994), 'The Organization of Buyer-Driven Global Commodity Chains: How US Retailers Shape Overseas Production Networks', in Gary Gereffi and Miguel Korzeniewicz (eds), *Commodity Chains and Global Capitalism*, pp. 95–122. Westport: Praeger.

____ (2005), 'The Global Economy: Organization, Governance and Development', in Neil J. Smelser and Richard Swedberg (eds), *The Handbook of Economic Sociology*, 2nd edition, pp. 160–82. Princeton: Princeton University Press and Russell Sage Foundation.

____ (2006), *The New Offshoring of Jobs and Global Development*. Geneva: International Institute for Labour Studies.

____ (2009), 'Development Models and Industrial Upgrading in China and Mexico', *European Sociological Review*, 25(1): 37–51.

Gereffi, Gary and Olga Memodovic (2003), 'The Global Apparel Value Chain: What Prospects for Upgrading by Developing Countries?' United Nations Industrial Development Organization (UNIDO), Sectoral Studies Series (available at http://www.unido.org/doc/12218, accessed on 21 July 2009).

Gereffi, Gary, Vivek Wadhwa, Ben Rissing, and Ryan Ong (2008), 'Getting the Numbers Right: International Engineering Education in the United States, India, and China', *Journal of Engineering Education*, 97(1): 13–25.

GoI (Government of India) Labour Bureau (2008), *Report on Textile Garments Industry*. Occupational Wage Survey, Sixth Round (available at http://www.labourbureau.gov.in/OWS%202K8%20Gar%20Contents.htm, accessed on 21 July 2009).

Holweg, Matthias, Jianxi Luo, and Nick Oliver (2009), 'The Past, Present and Future of China's Automotive Industry: A Value Chain Perspective', *International Journal of Technological Learning, Innovation and Development*, 2(1&2): 76–118.

Huang, Yasheng and Tarun Khanna (2003), 'Can India Overtake China?' *Foreign Policy*, 137(July–August): 74–81.

International Labour Organization (ILO) (2007), *The Production of Electronic Components for the IT Industries: Changing Labour Force Requirements in a Global Economy*. Report TMITI2007. Geneva: International Labour Office.

International Metalworkers' Federation (2004), *Auto Report 2004*. Geneva: International Metalworkers' Federation (available at http://www.imfmetal.org/main/files/AR2004_english.pdf, accessed on 21 July 2009).

____ (2006), International Metalworkers' Federation News Article: 'Honda Workers in India Strike', 11 April. Geneva: International Metalworkers' Federation. (available at http://www.imfmetal.org/main/index.cfm?id=47&l=2&cid=13749, accessed on 21 July 2009).

International Metalworkers' Federation (2007), *Auto Report 2006/07*, April. Geneva: International Metalworkers' Federation.

International Organisation of Motor Vehicles Manufacturers (OICA) (2007). *Production Statistics* (available at http://oica.net/category/production-statistics/, accessed on 21 July 2009).

Koopman, Robert, Zhi Wang, and Shang-jin Wei (2008), 'How Much of Chinese Exports is Really Made in China? Assessing Foreign and Domestic Value-Added in Gross Exports', Office of Economics Working Paper No. 2008-03-B, March. Washington D.C.: U.S. International Trade Commission.

KPMG International (2007), *India Automotive Study 2007: Domestic Growth and Global Aspirations*. India and Germany.

Lall, Sanjaya (2000), 'The Technological Structure and Performance of Developing Country Manufactured Exports, 1985–1998', *Oxford Development Studies*, 28: 337–69.

McKendrick, David G., Richard F. Doner, and Stephan Haggard (2000), *From Silicon Valley to Singapore: Location and Competitive Advantage in the Hard Disk Drive Industry*. Stanford: Stanford University Press.

NASSCOM (National Association of Software and Services Companies) (2008), 'Key Highlights of the IT-BPO sector performance in FY 2007–08', *Strategic Review* (available at www.nasscom.in/upload/5216/Strategic_Review_Feb2008.pdf, accessed on 21 July 2009).

——— (2008), *Indian IT/ITES Industry: Impacting Economy and Society 2007–08*. A NASSCOM-Deloitte Study. New Delhi: NASSCOM

Okada, Aya (2004), 'Skills Development and Inter-firm Learning Linkages under Globalization: Lessons from the Indian Automobile Industry', *World Development*, 32(7): 1265–88.

Ramasamy, Bala and Matthew Yeung (2008), 'Does China have a Competitive Advantage in the Low-end Garment Industry? A Case Study Approach', pp. 111–128, in *Unveiling Protectionism: Regional Responses to Remaining Barriers in the Textiles and Clothing Trade* (ST/ESCAP/2500), United Nations Economic and Social Commission for Asia and the Pacific (UNESCAP), Trade and Investment Division (available at http://www.unescap.org/tid/publication/tipub2500_pt1chap4.pdf, last accessed on 21 July 2009).

Roach, Stephen (2003), 'Outsourcing, Protectionism, and the Global Labor Arbitrage', Morgan Stanley Equity Research, Special Economic Study, 11 November, New York.

Rodrik, Dani (2006), 'What's So Special About China's Exports?', CEPR Discussion Paper No. 5484, January. London: Centre for Economic Policy Research.

Rothboeck, Sandra, M. Vijayabaskar, and V. Gayathri (2001), 'Labour in the New Economy—The Case of the Indian Software Labour Market', Background paper for the *World Employment Report*. Geneva: International Labour Organization.

Singa Boyenge, Jean-Pierre (2007), 'ILO Database on Export Processing Zones' (Revised). Sectoral Activities Programme Working Paper No. 251. Geneva: International Labour Organization.

Sturgeon, Timothy J. and Richard K. Lester (2004), 'The New Global Supply Base: New Challenges for Local Suppliers in East Asia', in Shahid Yusuf, M. Anjum Altaf, and Kaoru Nabeshima (eds), *Global Production Networking and Technological Change in East Asia*, pp. 35–87. Washington, DC: The World Bank and Oxford University Press.

Tewari, Meenu (2008). 'Deepening Intraregional Trade and Investment in South Asia: The Case of the Textiles and Clothing Industry'. ICRIER Working Paper No. 213. New Delhi: Indian Council for Research on International Economic Relations (available at http://ideas.repec.org/p/ind/icrier/213.html, last accessed on 21 July 2009).

The Economist (2007), 'Technology in India and China, Splendid Miscegenation', 8 November, *The Economist* Newspaper Limited, London.

Tschang, Ted (2003), 'China's Software Industry and Its Implications for India', OECD Development Centre Working Paper No. 205 (formerly Technical Paper No. 205), DEV/DOC(2003)03.

UNCTAD (United Nations Conference on Trade and Development) (2005), *TNCs and the Removal of Textiles and Clothing Quotas*. New York and Geneva: UNCTAD.

UNCOMTRADE (United Nations Commodity Trade Statistics Online Database) (2009), United Nations Statistics Division (available at www.comtrade.un.org/, last accessed on 15 October 2009).

UNIDO (United Nations Industrial Development Organization) (2009), Industrial Statistics, Country Brief (available at http://www.unido.org/index.php?id=4879, last accessed on 21 October 2009).

Varma, Uday Kumar and S.K. Sasikumar (2004), *Information and Communication Technology and Decent Work: Study of India's Experience*. Research Report prepared under the auspices of ILO/JILPT Networking of National Institutes of Labour Studies in the Asia Pacific Region. NOIDA: V.V. Giri National Labour Institute, India.

Vijayabaskar, M. (2005), 'Governance of Flexible Accumulation in Clusters: Can It Create 'Decent Work' in Low-income Regions?', Paper for the QEH 50th Anniversary Conference, 'New Development: Threats and Promises', Queen Elizabeth House, Oxford, 4–5 July (available at http://www.qeh.ox.ac.uk/dissemination/conference-papers/vijayabaskar.pdf/, last accessed on 21 July 2009).

Wadhwa, Vivek, Una Kim De Vitton, and Gary Gereffi (2008), *How the Disciple Became the Guru: Workforce Development in India's R&D Labs*. Report funded by the Ewing Marion Kauffman Foundation, 23 July (available at http://papers.ssrn.com/sol3/papers.cfm?abstract_id=1170049, last accessed on 21 July 2009).

World Trade Organization (WTO) (2008), *International Trade Statistic* (available at http://www.wto.org/english/res_e/statis_e/its2008_e/its08_toc_e.htm, last accessed on 12 July 2009).

5 DECENT WORK IN GLOBAL PRODUCTION NETWORKS

Challenges for Vulnerable Workers in the Indian Garments Sector

Stephanie Barrientos, Kanchan Mathur, and Atul Sood

INTRODUCTION

The challenges of addressing decent work in the context of global production networks (GPNs) and economic liberalization are immense. Global production is largely based on outsourcing and the coordination of supply networks across countries, in which the dominant companies are not themselves direct employers. The use of irregular workers is intensifying and labour is rapidly becoming more mobile physically and geographically in employment linked to global production. Workers often have low employer attachment and are recruited through labour agents or contractors. Many governments have pursued labour market deregulation combined with a 'low road' cheap labour strategy to export competitiveness, and have little control over foreign buyers whose commercial requirements underpin employment practices. All these factors have contributed to undermining the rights and protection of workers and have provided a fertile environment for the persistence of poor working conditions. How can new channels be opened up and what are the leverage points through which to address decent work for more vulnerable workers in the context of global production?

Over the past decade, there have been an increasing number of 'voluntary' initiatives to address poor working conditions within global production. The drive behind such initiatives has been campaigns by non-governmental organizations (NGOs) and trade unions, and adverse media coverage of brand-name buyers. In consequence, many thousands of companies have now introduced codes of labour practice that address minimum labour standards. A significant number of multi-stakeholder initiatives (MSIs) have been launched involving companies, trade unions, and NGOs, as well as initiatives by multilateral organizations. These have led to some improvements for regular workers, and in relation to more visible issues such as health and safety. But initiatives of multi-stakeholders and multilaterals have failed to reach the more vulnerable workers. Despite increasing commitment by some individual companies to work with trade unions and NGOs to address workers' rights, incidences of labour abuse in global production continue to surface amongst the more vulnerable, mobile, and irregular workers.

A key challenge is to better understand how the dynamics of global production are underpinning a commercial environment in which poor working conditions and labour abuse thrive, in order to inform a more effective strategy of decent work for all. This chapter contributes to this process by focusing on the more vulnerable casual, contract, and migrant workers. It is here that some of the greatest challenges exist, and where enhancing decent work could have the greatest impact. First, the chapter asks why the use of vulnerable workers is endemic within global production, from the top tiers of suppliers through to lower tier sub-contractors. Second, it examines the challenges for addressing the rights of such workers. This draws on findings from a case study in the Indian garments sector, carried out as part of an impact assessment for the UK Ethical Trading Initiative. Third, it asks how decent work can be enhanced for such workers in the context of GPNs.

VULNERABLE WORKERS IN GLOBAL PRODUCTION

Globalization has led to an expansion of waged labour employed in export production in many developing countries. It is estimated that there are 40 million workers engaged in garment production globally (Hale and Wills, 2005). Women form a significant portion of the labour force in many countries exporting consumer goods in buyer-led global value chains (GVCs). They are often concentrated in casual work and face some of the poorest conditions of employment (Dolan and Sorby, 2003; Hale and Wills, 2005). Much work in global production is insecure, involving a variety of employment categories. Many workers are employed on a temporary or casual basis, sometimes for up to 12 months a year without a permanent contract. The use of migrant labour (international or internal) is common in many sectors. Increasingly, workers are recruited through third-party

Table 5.1: Examples of the Use of Vulnerable Labour in Global Production

Country	Sector	Type of Vulnerable Labour	Note on Known Recruitment Methods
India (Delhi)	Garments	Internal migrant, male from rural areas	Direct and labour contractors
Bangladesh	Garments	Internal migrant, female from rural areas	Direct (some informal labour contractors)
South Africa	Fruit	Internal migrant, male and female, from different regions	Direct and labour contractors
Costa Rica	Fruit	Internal and international migrant	Direct and labour contractors
Vietnam	Garments and Footwear	Internal migrant and female, mainly from rural areas	Direct
China	Garments	Internal migrant, from rural areas, significant female	Direct and informal labour contractors
UK	Agriculture	International migrant, male and female, from wide number of countries	Direct, seasonal workers' schemes and labour contractors (providers)

Source: Adapted from Barrientos (2006). For further information on all these case studies, see Theron and Godfrey (2000); Barrientos and Kritzinger (2003); Singh et al. (2003); Kabeer and Mahmud (2004); Frances et al. (2005); Barrientos and Smith (2006); Deshingkar (2006); Pollard (2006).

labour contractors that remain separate from the producer, who takes no responsibility for their employment (Barrientos and Dolan, 2006). Measuring the number of these workers is difficult because they are often excluded from census surveys or employer lists. Table 5.1 provides examples of the use of vulnerable workers (migrant, casual, and contract labour) across a number of sectors. This is based on case studies carried out for different projects in a number of countries across agricultural and manufacturing sectors. The question is why the use of vulnerable workers appears to be widespread, and, in some cases. intensifying.

Global brands and retailers rarely own production or are direct employers within their sourcing countries. They increasingly outsource production to networks of global suppliers (Dicken et al., 2001; Efendioglu et al., 2007; Gereffi, 2006). Within GPNs, increasing dominance of corporate buyers is characterized by the commercial power they exert over suppliers. Suppliers that are dependent on sales to large corporate buyers are caught in this complex web of shifting sourcing, competitive pricing, and rising standards (Acona, 2004). In their commercial relations, dominant firms often strive to offset any risks of production (such as a fall in demand, shifting consumer trends, and poor quality) onto their suppliers. Examples include shortening lead times, refusing deliveries on spurious 'quality' grounds in the food sector because of over supply, reducing prices paid to suppliers, requiring suppliers to fund 'special offers', or lengthening payment times (Oxfam, 2004). At the same time, buyers are able to exploit their position to increase the economic rents they extract, either through branding or upgrading their position, or simply through reducing input prices. Brands and dominant firms argue that they are responding to the pressures of a competitive global economy, and efficient suppliers are able to improve productivity to meet more exacting commercial demands and remain competitive. But many suppliers are caught in a pincer movement between increasingly stringent commercial demands and rising quality standards required by buyers (Barrientos and Kritzinger, 2004).

These competitive pressures affect the basis on which employment takes place within GPNs. The decisions and actions of buyers and their agents can have direct implications for production operations and working conditions. One strategy by suppliers to cope with increasingly competitive cost pressures and tightening production schedules is the use of third-party labour contractors. Labour contractors are separate agents who coordinate the supply of labour often at short notice, facilitating rapid fluctuations in labour use to meet buyer demands.[1] This also helps to reduce labour cost, not only through low wage levels, but also the more 'efficient' use of labour that is only on site for specific periods, with few non-wage costs such as social insurance payments. Labour contractors operate in different ways. Some are involved in recruitment alone, but increasingly the labour contractor acts also as the employer when workers are on a production site. Some labour contracting is carried out by reputable agencies, but often informal labour contractors include unscrupulous employers who exploit workers through illicit wage deductions for transport or housing and violation of basic workers' rights. The most vulnerable workers, including migrant, female, and child labour, are often recruited through contractors, with little or no protection (Martin, 2005; Plant, 2007; Barrientos, 2008).

In nation-states where export production is premised on foreign direct investment and outsourcing by foreign firms, global buyers are beyond the reach of government regulation in the countries from which they source. Many governments have created export processing zones in which labour regulations are relaxed in order to reduce costs and attract global buyers. Corporate codes of labour practice arose as a result of trade union and NGO pressure on corporate brands and retailers because of poor working conditions in their GPNs. Global trade unions and NGOs now play an increasingly important role in holding corporate buyers to account for labour standards observed by their suppliers. They are able to mobilize consumer campaigns and fuel adverse media publicity against brands and retailers who fail to ensure minimum labour standards in their global sourcing base (Oxfam, 2004; ActionAid, 2005).

Corporate buyers and their suppliers now devote large resources to the monitoring of codes of labour practice. This has spawned an industry engaged in social compliance and independent social auditing. Multistakeholder Initiatives promote alliances between suppliers, independent trade unions, NGOs, and government to provide a more collaborative approach to improving labour standards. One such initiative in the UK is the Ethical Trading Initiative (ETI). Its membership is made up of companies, NGOs, and trade union organizations. In 2003, it commissioned an impact assessment to examine how effective corporate codes of labour practice are for improving employment conditions and the lives of workers in member company supply chains.

The ETI impact assessment involved in-depth case studies on 25 supplier sites and interviews with 418 workers in manufacture and agriculture in Costa Rica, India, South Africa, UK, and Vietnam (plus a scoping study in China).[2] Across all countries, the assessment found that codes of labour practice were having a positive effect on improving certain 'visual issues'. The biggest impact was on health and safety, with positive changes found on 20 out of 25 sites. This led to improvements in the lives of workers' families through observance of health and safety at home. For example, banana workers no longer hugged their children in overalls used for pesticide spraying. Other changes were in better adherence to legal minimum wages and documented employment benefits for regular workers. Codes are also helping to raise awareness of the need to comply with national regulation. But codes have had little impact on the improvement of 'less visual issues' such as the freedom of association and no discrimination. On no site did workers feel able to join a trade union as a result of codes (although unions had already existed prior to codes on some sites in the study). Codes had had little effect on discrimination in the hiring, training, and promotion of women and migrant workers.

An important finding in the study was that regular and permanent workers were most likely to have benefited from changes resulting from codes. Casual and migrant workers (international or internal) were found in the upper tiers of the supply chain in all case study countries, and the use of third-party labour contractors was found in most, except Vietnam. These workers were least likely to have benefited from the implementation of codes of labour practice, and on many sites they faced significant issues. In fact, workers hired through third-party labour contractors faced the greatest problems of code violation. They normally have no security, can face illicit wage deductions, and can be subject to harassment or abuse by contractors. Many such workers receive no employer or state protection. They are most vulnerable in the event of illness, injury, lack of mobility, old age, childbirth, and carer responsibilities. In the India case study, the use of internal migrant workers and third-party labour contractors was found to be prevalent, with many associated problems for workers. We will further examine the findings from the Indian case study to explore some of the complexities and challenges of addressing the rights of vulnerable workers in global production.

ETHICAL TRADING INITIATIVE IMPACT STUDY IN THE INDIAN GARMENTS SECTOR[3]

Background to the Delhi Garments Sector

Readymade garment exports from India have grown rapidly over recent decades. Garment exports were virtually non-existent prior to 1960. Between 1970 and 2000, the share of garment exports in total exports grew from 1.89 per cent to 12.5 per cent (Singh et al., 2003). India's share in world garment exports also rose from 1.8 per cent in 1980 to 2.34 per cent in 1990, and stood close to 2.82 in 1999. In 2003, India ranked as the sixth largest garment exporter to the European Union, with a 5.6 per cent market share, which has been increasing.[4]

It is estimated that in 1999–2000, there were approximately 30,472 garment enterprises in Delhi. Of these, 675 garment enterprises were registered under the Factory Act and 29,797 were unregistered garment enterprises. Thus, nearly 98 per cent of the estimated garment units in Delhi are in the unorganized sector. Delhi accounts for a little over 13 per cent of the all-India registered sector garment enterprises and 3.84 per cent of the unregistered enterprises. In terms of the total all-India production in rupee terms, Delhi produces roughly 19.2 per cent of the total value of output in the registered sector and 16.54 per cent of the output in the unregistered sector (see CSO, 1999; NSSO, 1999–2000).

The setting up of the New Okhla Industrial Development Authority (NOIDA) in 1976 was an experiment in developing a modern township under the Uttar Pradesh Industrial Area Development Act. NOIDA is a well-planned township 12 km away from the centre of Delhi. Phase II of NOIDA includes an export processing zone and a hosiery complex. Textiles and readymade garments are among the areas of special focus. However, while planning the industrial township housing, no space was allocated for workers. This has resulted in emergence of slums and 'unauthorized' residential colonies of the poor.

Gurgaon is located in the state of Haryana and is 32 km from Delhi. Udyog Vihar, a part of Gurgaon, is an area earmarked for industrial units. Industrial plots are of reasonable size. Here, readymade garments have also been identified as a sector of potential development. Gurgaon again has no provision for workers' housing. Delhi employs an estimated 1.02 lakh[5] workers in the garment industry. Of these, it is estimated that only 21,469 workers are in the registered garment sector and 80,051 workers are in the unregistered sector. The total garment sector employment in Delhi is roughly 5.82 per cent of the all-India garment sector employment (see Singh et al., 2003: 30 [Table 2]).

The gender distribution of the estimated workforce suggests that in the unorganized garment workforce, men form roughly 97 per cent of the total garment employment in Delhi. The share of women is barely 3 per cent. In relation to all India, it is estimated that Delhi employs roughly 6 per cent of the total garment workforce, 7 per cent of the total male, and 1.5 per cent of the total number of female workers in the garment sector. In India, currently there are nearly 40 labour laws. These laws are fairly progressive and guarantee protection of labour rights. Labour legislation applies to all factories and, contrary to commonly held belief, differ very little with factory size and whether registered with the Factories Act or not. A major issue though is lack of registration or enforcement of legislation (ibid.).

ETI Case Study Findings in Delhi Garments Sector

In order to examine whether and to what extent the ETI Base Code has impacted on Indian garment suppliers and workers, research was undertaken which involved the selection of three contrasting ETI member value chains (see Barrientos et al., 2006). Two were retailers and one a brand. One chain was fairly complex, involving intermediaries; one chain was more direct, with a social compliance officer based in Delhi; the final chain was even more integrated, also with a social compliance officer based in Delhi. One of the companies was relatively new to the ETI, but had had a code similar to the ETI Base Code for a number of years. The case study traced the selected garment value chains from the UK to Delhi. It also covered adjoining areas within the National Capital Region including Gurgaon in Haryana and NOIDA in Uttar Pradesh. From the three ETI company value chains, six suppliers were selected. The main criterion for selection was to ensure a cross-section of suppliers from the three value chains based on size, product range, share of buyer volume, and length of association with the buyer. Although we traced the firms through selected ETI company value chains, between them they supplied a total of seven ETI member companies and many other buyers.

The six units covered by our sample belonged to the big and medium categories in the Delhi garments sector.[6] They also represent the complexity of production organization prevalent in the sector. The production process in our sample units was mostly assembly line. Production work in times of high demand is often outsourced to smaller units called the fabricating units. Each supplier has multiple units, a total of 31 units for the six suppliers in our sample. Three of the six suppliers are relatively old companies and were established between 1970 and 1980. Two of them have been working for the past two decades. Only one of them is relatively new. All of the sample companies were 100 per cent export-oriented garment manufacturing units. The sample units reported a total of 5,143 workers. All supplier companies had other units that were not included in our study. They supplied up to 30 buyers per company (ETI and non-ETI) and had multiple codes. They dealt directly with their buyers and their awareness of the ETI was limited or minimal. Only half the suppliers in our study had heard of the ETI, and it was difficult for managers to distinguish between different company codes (whether or not they were members of the ETI).

The case study involved interviewing the three ETI member companies and key intermediaries within their value chains as well as key informants from trade unions, NGOs, and professionals well versed with the garment sector. For each of the three ETI member companies, two sites were chosen. Within the six sites, interviews were carried out with managers, senior managers, and workers, recording histories and experiences of suppliers.[7] In each of the units, a total of 25 workers from among various categories of workers were identified and selected for filling the questionnaire/schedule. One hundred and fifty workers were interviewed out of a total of 5,143 workers in the main units. On each site, three focus group discussions

(FGDs), one each with male and female workers and one with a mixed group of workers (both male and female), took place. Relatively fewer women workers were employed in the sample units.

Approximately 15 per cent of the workers in the six units in our study were regular/permanent workers and 85 per cent were either temporary or contract workers hired through third-party contractors.[8] In written documentation we were not informed of contract workers; however, site interviews with management and workers revealed that all but one of the units in our study employed contract labour. Many workers were internal migrants from outside Delhi who returned to their villages for festivals. Out of a total of 150 workers, 101 were male and 49 female. The lower number of female workers interviewed reflected the fact that employment is predominantly male in the Delhi garments sector.[9]

The caste profile of workers revealed that 50 per cent of workers belonged to the general castes, that is, Brahmins and Rajputs; 22 per cent of the workers belonged to other backward castes, that is, Yadavs, Kumhars, Jats, and Patels; 14 per cent of the workers belonged to and minority groups, that is, Muslims and Christians. The percentage of Scheduled Caste workers in the sample was 8.6 per cent, mainly belonging to the Harijan and Koli castes. Approximately 3 per cent did not know/specify the caste group they belonged to.

The aim was to select for the FGDs workers who had spent more than two years in either the same factory or similar garments units. This was to ensure that the workers had adequate experience of working in ETI code supplier companies and could comment on impact. The workers' perception was further strengthened by visits to two workers' colonies where the workers from the sample units and those who participated in the FGDs were living. The interactions with these workers took place in their homes. Contract workers from one of the sample units were also interviewed off-site with the help of a prominent trade union. To better understand the general perceptions of workers in the garments sector in Delhi and to triangulate information gathered from the workers in the sample units, a few workers were also interviewed from one of the larger workers' colony in Delhi.[10]

Table 5.2 summarizes the impacts reported by management and workers in each of the nine areas of the ETI Base Code. 'Major' indicates that widespread and significant change has occurred across several or all case-study worksites (for example, reductions in working hours at over half the sites). 'Minor' indicates that changes were reported at only a few sites or had minimal impacts on workers (for example, introduction of age documentation at one or two sites). An asterisk next to either 'Major' or

Table 5.2: Summary of Impacts at India Study Supply Sites

ETI Base Code Principle	Management	Workers
Freedom of employment	0	0
Freedom of association	0	0
Health and safety	Major	Major
Child labour	Minor	0
Living wage	Minor	Minor
Working hours	Minor	Minor*
Discrimination	Minor	0
Regular employment	Minor	Minor
Harsh treatment	Minor	Minor

Notes: Major: major and/or multiple impacts across several worksites; Minor: minor impacts and/or impacts at isolated worksites only; *Impact perceived as negative by at least some interviewees; 0: No impact reported.

'Minor' implies that the change was viewed as negative for at least some of the people interviewed. Zero means that no change was reported, but this does not necessarily imply that there were non-compliances with the Base Code.

The study found that the main impact of codes of labour practice in India has been on health and safety. There have been some impacts in relation to the payment of minimum wages, and particularly the payment of social and pension benefits. There have been minor impacts on working hours, regular employment, and harsh treatment, although these varied by factory. There has been little or no impact on freedom of association and discrimination, which remain significant issues in the Delhi garments sector. It should be emphasized that impacts are not necessarily exclusively a result of implementation of the ETI Base Code. It was sometimes impossible to separate changes brought about by company codes of labour practice from other influences, but all impacts reported here were considered to be at least in part related to code implementation.

The study found that permanent/regular workers have seen the most positive impacts from buyers' codes of labour practice, particularly in relation to the payment of the minimum wage, statutory benefits, and premium for overtime hours.[11] Temporary workers have experienced some positive impacts. But some suppliers rotate temporary workers between factories. Formally they then work less than 240 days and do not get permanent benefits.

The least impact of codes was experienced by contract workers.[12] The position of contractual workers remains a significant issue on all but one site. They are employed through the contractor, which drastically reduces the responsibility of the unit owners towards them. Pay slips are given to the contractual workers by the contractor. But often no proper written records are maintained for contractual labour. They may work on a separate floor within the premises of the same factory, and have a separate entrance. Offsite responses of contractual workers revealed that they are often not paid minimum wages, payment is delayed or not on time, and made in instalments. In one case, workers reported that the contractor had absconded without paying full wages. Some workers reported a system of double bookkeeping. In reality they do not receive benefits or allowances. But a separate record is kept for buyers and labour inspectors showing that they do.

In FGDs, contract workers gave the following examples of complaints:

1. 'Contractors do not pay workers total wages at the end of the month; only a part of the wages are paid to workers. The remaining money is paid to workers in instalments. Workers are not given pay-slips but are made to sign in a register.'
2. 'Overtime hours are normally put in till 9 pm in case a shipment is stuck. Our workday ends at 6 pm and we usually put in three hours' overtime. Overtime is not voluntary; if a worker refuses to do overtime hours the same day, they risk losing their job. We are given Rs 25 as food allowance on days that we have to work overtime. However, if overtime extends from 9 pm to 11 pm or 11pm to 2am, we are not given any further additional food allowance. We also have to report for work the following day at 9:30 am.'
3. 'When buyers come for inspections to the unit, we are told to leave the premises for some time and take a break and have tea or there is no more work on that day. We are made to exit from the back gate of the unit and not paid on these days. Since we work on a separate floor, we usually have no access to other workers in the factory.'

One site does not use contractors any more because they were underpaying workers and not making deposits under the Employees' State Insurance'Corporation (ESI) and provident fund (PF). Another site switched 2,500 tailors hired from the gate and were placed under the direction of a contractor who has made on agreement on compliance issues. The company pays contract workers, not the contractor. Therefore, ultimate control remains with the company. Before codes, only permanent workers had appointment letters; now their contract workers also get them. Factories taking greater responsibility for contract workers is an important way of ensuring that legal entitlements are extended to these workers.

No obvious discrimination was observed in the factories based on caste or religious grounds. However, gender discrimination was observed in most factories. A fewer number of women were employed compared to the number of men. They were concentrated in semi-skilled jobs whereas men were mostly in skilled jobs. Women are taken in as casual workers and invariably the first to be thrown out when work reduces. Women workers were articulate and confident, but even after a lot of persistence from the members of the research team, generally refused to say anything openly against the management. However, they said that they had never been promoted despite putting in five to nine years of work in the same factory and did not receive any training that could equip them to take up 'better/skilled' work in the same factory. Women workers in some of the units said that a token system operates for visiting the toilets in order to ensure that only one or two workers visited the toilets at any one time, reducing the impact on production. This creates a problem for women who are menstruating or are pregnant and might need to use the toilets frequently. Often strict vigil is kept on them and they are ticked off if the supervisors feel that they spend too long in the toilets.

A visit by members of the research team to two of the colonies where a large number of workers from garment factories reside (including those in the research study) revealed that the living conditions of regular workers are definitely better than those of the contract workers. They keep their homes clean, own household appliances like TV and radio, and are well turned out. The houses of these workers were fairly clean and they were well dressed. Some workers linked improvements in their living conditions to improvements in conditions in their factories. Receipt of ESI and PF benefits means that they will now also receive support in case of old age or ill health.

In contrast, a visit to a colony of contract workers in Tehkand area of Delhi revealed the appalling conditions in which they survive. A majority of the workers are migrant labourers and live in squalor. Some of the people residing here have built a set of 70–75 living quarters specifically catering to such a population. A worker pays a monthly rent of Rs 700 per month on an average. There are heaps of garbage in the colonies. They live in a near slum existence. The living quarters are roughly 6 ft by 7 ft in size, with cooking facilities inside the room where at times 2–4 members live. While most of the male workers are tailors, women were piece-rate or daily wage workers. Some of them are also involved in doing embroidery on a piece-rate basis. Where they do not receive ESI or PF, these workers are likely to face extreme poverty in the event of old age or ill health.

CHALLENGES FOR REACHING VULNERABLE WORKERS

The reasons why codes of labour practice are failing to reach more vulnerable workers are complex. Here we will highlight some key issues and policy recommendations that arose from the ETI Impact Assessment.

Complex Value Chains

A few of the largest brands and retailers source from highly integrated value chains and have close relationships with their suppliers. They are in a better position to influence adherence to their codes of labour practice. But many companies operate in complex value chains, where suppliers deal with multiple buyers and agents. Many suppliers have limited direct engagement with their buyers on codes, and the attitude of agents and intermediary companies can be very variable. Any one buyer has limited influence on its own. However, the study found that suppliers are more likely to respond when a critical mass of buyers requests codes of labour practice. Collaboration between buyers can help to enforce the message of codes of labour practice. If buyers jointly emphasized that codes apply to all workers on any site, including those employed casually or by third-party labour contract, this could help to extend the reach of codes.

Communication and Capacity Building

Some buyers provide good information and support to their suppliers on codes. However, communication and capacity building by buyers with their suppliers is often patchy or poor. Agents can also act to block communication channels to suppliers. Supplier engagement is enhanced where buyers organize local supplier conferences, bringing together a number of suppliers, and work with other local stakeholders. Communication and training materials developed to support the implementation of codes could place greater emphasis on the importance of addressing the rights of women, casual, and migrant workers, including those employed through third-party labour contractors.

Monitoring

All the sites in the ETI Impact Assessment had fulfilled either a self-assessment or been monitored through social audits in relation to their 'buyers' codes'. Yet, the research found issues of non-compliance on many of the sites in the study. While snapshot social auditing has been fairly successful at identifying visual issues such as health and safety, it is failing to pick up more embedded issues such as discrimination and freedom of association that are central to workers' rights. The weaknesses of current monitoring systems have been raised in other studies.[13] Casual, migrant, and contract workers are often overlooked in social audits. Some suppliers send such workers away during buyer or audit visits, or use 'double book-keeping' to mask code violation. Social auditors need to be much more vigilant about including casual, migrant, and contract workers in monitoring, and engaging with trade unions and NGOs who are aware of the use of such workers.

Integration into Business Practice

A complaint made vocally by many suppliers in the ETI study was about the pressure they are under from buyers to reduce prices, carry more of the costs, and meet tighter delivery deadlines. Some complained of the double standards of many global brands and retailers. Buyers often make commercial demands that undermine observance of their own company code of labour practice. A prime example is orders placed at short notice that necessitate extra overtime. Many suppliers use casual workers and labour contractors to cope with volatile orders, meet sudden production surges, and keep labour costs down. Yet, it is amongst these workers that code violation and even labour abuse are more likely to be found. Global buyers need to integrate the principles of ethical trade into their core business practices to support the application of their codes to all workers. This includes linking code compliance to buyer incentive systems, enhancing supplier relations, and ordering and pricing systems.

PROMOTING DECENT WORK FOR VULNERABLE WORKERS

Labour contracting is likely to persist, given the demand for flexible labour generated by global production and the commercial imperatives of global buyers. Here, we will examine some approaches that have been developed, often as a result of pressure from civil society organizations, to address decent work for contract workers.[14]

Given that labour contracting is embedded in GPNs, relying on voluntary actions by individual suppliers is very unlikely to be sufficient. Labour contractors themselves need to be harnessed through wider MSIs and regulatory measures. Pressure to advance down this route is increasingly coming from different sources: trade unions, NGOs, and even some retailers fearful of exposure for abusive practices labour contracting in their value chains can encompass.

In order to access their rights, migrant workers need to have greater information and the ability to organize independently for their rights. One challenge has been the difficulty for trade unions to organize contract or migrant workers. The mobility of workers, their lack of attachment to any one employer, poor language skills, and fear of the consequences of being linked with trade unions are all factors inhibiting organization. Trade unions have traditionally focused on permanent or regular workers, and are often distant from contract or migrant workers. Increasingly, trade unions are recognizing the importance of developing innovative strategies to support and organize migrant workers, and have played an important role in campaigns to regulate labour contractors. A challenge for trade unions is whether they could begin to organize workers through labour contractors. This would depart from the production site as the point of organization, but would help them organize workers irrespective of their mobility between sites.[15]

The MSIs provide one form of independent monitoring of labour contractors, but will only ever cover those labour contractors who wish to opt into the system. They will always be under pressure from less scrupulous contractors who undercut them. Ultimately, therefore, regulation has to play a role if decent working conditions are to be ensured under a labour contracting system. Martin (2005) has argued that addressing labour contractors alone is insufficient, without also including the producers who hire them. Drawing on the US example, he has highlighted three levels of regulation: registration, where all labour contractors are legally bound to register with an approved authority; bonds, which can be used as insurance if labour contractors do not pay legal wages and entitlements; and joint liability between labour contractors and producers, so that the latter are also liable if a labour contractor fails to fulfil legal requirements for workers on a site.

Similar moves have also been made in South Africa and the UK. In South Africa, where labour contracting has expanded in a number of sectors, the government amended the Basic Conditions of Employment Act (BCEA) to include labour brokers or contractors, and extend joint liability to the producer, even if they are not the direct employer, for all workers on their site. Under the BCEA, even where an employee is employed by a labour contractor or broker, they and the client are jointly and severally liable if the labour contractor does not comply with the BCEA (Taylor, 2003). A big challenge, however, is lack of enforcement given lack of sufficient resources for labour inspection. In the UK, following the Morecombe Bay tragedy in 2004, where 23 undocumented Chinese cockle pickers died, pressure mounted on the government to introduce the Gangmasters (Licensing) Act (Pollard, 2006). This was passed through parliament in 2004 and came into force in 2006. Under this Act, all labour contractors have to be registered and monitored by the Gangmasters Licensing Authority and producers have been made jointly liable if they do not use registered contractors. There are criticisms, however, that the Act is not extensive enough in its scope. It only covers agriculture, not the food processing industry or other sectors such as construction, hotels, and catering, which also make extensive use of contract labour. These acts provide legal measures to ensure producers are not able to circumvent their legal obligations in relation to employment conditions and standards through the use of outside contractors.

CONCLUSION

Research based on case studies cited earlier indicates that the use of labour contractors is intensifying in GPNs. Commercial pressure appears to be driving greater reliance by suppliers on outside contractors to coordinate their labour supply to meet insecure orders and keep labour costs down. More systematic research is needed to establish how generalized this trend is becoming. However, from the information we have, it is clear that there a number of serious challenges to addressing the rights of vulnerable workers, especially those recruited through labour contractors. These workers often face high levels of exploitation by unscrupulous agents. Their high levels of insecurity and mobility between production sites and low employer attachment mean that they largely fall outside established channels for union organization and government protection. New innovative strategies are being developed to enhance decent work for this type of labour. But to date, these are the exception rather than the norm. More coherent strategies are needed, based on the changing dynamics of global production, if the rights of such workers are to be more systematically addressed.

NOTES

1. Note that by labour contracting we are not referring here to a legal contract of employment between an employer and worker, but to the practice of using separate third-party agents to recruit and increasingly employ workers so that the worker ceases to be a direct employee of the company on whose site they are working.
2. For the full findings and country reports, see www.ethicaltrade.org/d/impactreport. The views expressed here do not necessarily represent the views of ETI or of its member organizations, nor does ETI take responsibility for the accuracy of information contained in this chapter.
3. This section draws on Barrientos et al. (2006). Atul Sood and Kanchan Mathur were the lead researchers who carried out the India Case Study as part of the ETI Impact Assessment.

4. Background information on Delhi garments is drawn from Singh et al. (2003).
5. A lakh is a unit in a traditional number system still used in India, and is equal to a hundred thousand.
6. Units that have a turnover of more than Rs 1,000 million are considered big firms in the market, often employing more than 2,000 workers. Units with a turnover of less than Rs 100 million are considered as small units in the industry.
7. Within our sample, two suppliers said that they do not sub-contract out work because of the codes, while the others did. The research team was unable to obtain contact details for sub-contractors at the lower levels of the chain, or to obtain agreement to carry out interviews at that level.
8. The percentage of workers in the study sites reported as permanent was contradictory—in written tables, management reported all workers as permanent, but in verbal interviews, all but one factory HR manager reported using temporary and contract labour (this one factory used to employ temporary and contract workers but had ceased to do so because of problems with the contractor). The likely reason for contradiction is that they would not write down having temporary and contract labour for fear of coming under pressure from the Labour Inspectorate.
9. The dominance of male workers in the Delhi garments sector is particular to north India, where the percentage of women employed in any sector is low compared to other regions in India.
10. This was a case study, and the sample was not statistically representative of all suppliers to ETI companies, or the Indian garments sector as a whole. Not all suppliers who were approached agreed to participate in the study. There was a problem on one site of management controlling availability of workers for research, with the team only able to conduct interviews on days when permanents selected by management were available. Consequently, off-site interviews were conducted separately with contract workers contacted through a trade union.
11. Any worker who has been employed for a duration of 240 days is a permanent worker. They are also entitled to 1.75 per cent ESI (Employees' State Insurance Corporation), 12 per cent provident fund, and gratuity after five years plus employment.
12. The contract arrangements vary: (*i*) recruit workers at gate, contractor supervises, workers paid by company; (*ii*) recruit at gate, contractor supervises, contractor pays workers; (*iii*) recruited and paid by contractor.
13. For example, Locke et al. (2006).
14. This section draws on Barrientos (2008).
15. There is information that unions in the US have begun to pursue this strategy. In the UK, the Transport and General Workers Union (now part of Unite) has been developing pilot programmes to support migrant workers often recruited via labour contractors.

REFERENCES

Acona (2004), *Buying Your Way into Trouble? The Challenge of Responsible Supply Chain Management*. London: Insight Investment Management Ltd.

ActionAid (2005), *Power Hungry: Six Reasons to Regulate Global Food Companies*. London: ActionAid.

Barrientos, S. (2006), 'Migrant Workers and International Labour Standards: Examining the Challenges in Global Production Systems', Paper to DFID Labour Standards Forum, Department for International Development, London, May.

Barrientos, S. (2009), 'Bottom of the Food Chain: Contract Labour in South Africa and UK Agriculture', in D. Hulme, D. Lawson, and I. Matin (eds), *What Works for the Poorest?* West Hartford: Kumarian Press.

Barrientos, S. and C. Dolan (eds) (2006), *Ethical Sourcing in the Global Food System*. London: Earthscan.

Barrientos, S. and A. Kritzinger (2003), 'The Poverty of Work and Social Cohesion in Global Exports: The Case of South African Fruit', in D. Chidester, P. Dexter and J. Wilmot (eds), *What Holds Us Together: Social Cohesion in South Africa*, pp. 102–99. Cape Town: HSRC Press.

Barrientos, S. and A. Kritzinger (2004). 'Squaring the Circle—Global Production and the Informalisation of Work in South African Fruit Exports', *Journal of International Development*, 16: 81–92.

Barrientos, S. and S. Smith (2006), 'The ETI Code of Labour Practice: Do Workers Really Benefit?', Summary Report, London: Ethical Trading Initiative, www.ethicaltrade.org/d/impactreport.

Barrientos, S., A. Sood and K. Mathur (2006), *The ETI Code of Labour Practice: Do Workers Really Benefit?*. India Report, London: Ethical Trading Initiative (available at www.ethicaltrade.org/d/impactreport, accessed on 1 June 2009).

CSO (1999), *Annual Survey of Industries 1998–99*, New Delhi: Central Statistical Organsiation, Department of Statistics, Ministry of Planning.

Deshingkar, P. (2006), 'Internal'Migration, Poverty and Development in Asia: Including the Excluded through Partnerships and Improved Governance', Background Paper for the Asia 2015 Conference, DFID, London.

Dicken, P., K.O. Kelly, K. Olds, and H.W.C. Yeung (2001), 'Chains and Networks, Territories and Scales: Towards a Relationional Framework for Analyzing the Global Economy', *Global Networks*, 1(2): 89–112.

Dolan, C. and K. Sorby (2003), *Gender and Employment in High-Value Agriculture Industries*. Washington DC: World Bank.

Efendioglu, U., A. Posthuma, and A. Rossi (2007), 'Decent Work in Global Production Systems: An Integrated Approach to Economic and Social Upgrading', Draft working paper, March. Geneva: ILO.

Frances, J., S. Barrientos, and B. Rogaly (2005), *Temporary Workers in UK Agriculture and Horticulture*, Report by Precision Prospecting for the Department for Environment, Food and Rural Affairs, London.

Gereffi, G. (2006), *The New Offshoring of Jobs and Global Development*. Geneva: ILO.

Hale, A. and J. Wills (eds) (2005), *Threads of Labour: Garment Industry Supply Chains from the Workers' Perspective*. Oxford: Blackwell Publishing.

Kabeer, N. and S. Mahmud (2004), 'Globalization, Gender and Poverty: Bangladeshi Women Workers in Export and Local Markets', *Journal of International Development*, 16: 93–109.

Locke, R., F. Qin, and A. Brause (2006), 'Does Monitoring Improve Labour Standards? Lessons from NIKE', MIT Working Paper No. 4612–06. Cambridge, MA: MIT.

Martin, P. (2005), 'Merchants of Labor: Agents of the Evolving Migration Infrastructure', Discussion Paper, DP/158/2005, Geneva: IILS.

NSSO (1999–2000), *Informal Sector in India*, Report No. 459 (55/2/2), July 1999–June 2000, 55th Round. New Delhi: National Statistical Organisation.

Oxfam (2004), *Trading Away Our Rights*. Oxford: Oxfam International.

Plant, R. (2007), 'Forced Labour, Slavery and Poverty Reduction: Challenges for Development Agencies', Background Paper for FCO High Level Conference on Poverty, Slavery and Social Exclusion, London.

Pollard, D. (2006), 'The Gangmaster System in the UK—The Perspective of a Trade Unionist', in S. Barrientos and C. Dolan (eds), *Ethical Sourcing in the Global Food System*, pp. 123–40. London: Earthscan.

Singh, N., R. Kaur, and M. Kaur Sapra (2003), 'Continents Wide and Layers Deep: The Ready-made Garment Industry in the Times of Restructuring', Mimeo. New Delhi: National Council of Applied Economic Research.

Taylor, N. (2003), 'Briefing on Wine Industry Ethical Trading Initiative', Mimeo. Cape Town: Wine and Agriculture Ethical Trading Association.

Theron, J. and S. Godfrey (2000), 'Protecting Workers on the Periphery', Monograph 1. Cape Town: Institute of Development and Labour Law.

6

FOOTLOOSE CAPITAL, INTERMEDIATION, AND THE SEARCH FOR THE 'HIGH ROAD' IN LOW-WAGE INDUSTRIES[1]

Meenu Tewari

INTRODUCTION

Why and under what conditions do some firms adopt labour-friendly business practices in the face of intensified global competition and neoliberal pressures, while others in the same sector and region do not? Drawing on field research conducted in the Indian textile and apparel industry, I examine a set of mediating conditions that explain some of these differences, including the role of new labour market intermediaries (especially 'new' unions, community groups, public sector agencies, and/or buying agents or brokers) who directly or indirectly step in to negotiate on behalf of labour. The chapter's main argument is that the link between industrial upgrading and improved labour conditions is not inevitable or automatic even when firms see improved labour standards as a source of increased productivity. Not only do mediating institutions play a critical role in shaping and sustaining these—labour-friendly employment relationships, but important and ongoing linkages between formal organizations and informal practices in the labour market are important to altering the trajectory of industrial relations and sustaining the gains to labour.

THE PUZZLE

Does improved competitiveness in labour-intensive industries—such as apparel and clothing—require an inevitable race to the bottom? This question has recently been asked by many researchers (see Tendler, 2005;

Teitelbaum, 2006), policymakers, and non-governmental organizations (NGOs) involved in understanding the changing nature of global manufacturing and its consequences for labour and employment. The fraught discussion on labour standards and compliance in the context of trade and development illustrates the sharp tensions within this debate. One strand of the literature, representing the position of advanced countries, argues for 'harmonization' of labour standards and has sought to tie market access to improvements in labour market outcomes in supplier countries (Rodrik, 1997; Badrinarayan, 2005; Harrison and Scorse, 2004). Another strand shows that many developing countries have pushed in the opposite direction, seeking to liberalize their labour markets even further on the assumption that maintaining a low-cost advantage will help promote exports and gain market share (Flanagen, 2003; cf. Badrinarayan, 2002). Recent academic scholarship (such as by Besley and Burgess [2004], Sachs and Bajpai et al. [2002], among others) has added to the view that stringent labour laws (such as those in India) undermine economic performance, undercut exports, and impede the adoption of growth-enhancing reforms.

Yet, a growing number of empirical studies are beginning to provide evidence to the contrary—that export growth even in labour-intensive sectors such as apparel can be associated with improved rather than reduced labour protection, higher rather than lower labour standards, and more inclusive worker training initiatives than segmented and exclusionary access to skill formation. Challenging conventional wisdom, Teitelbaum (2006), for example, re-analyses the same panel data for Indian states used by advocates of labour market reform to argue that the growth-enhancing effects of India's economic reforms are not predicated on lax labour laws. In contrast to the standard 'race-to-the-bottom' narratives, which argue that to attract investment Indian states must retract protective labour legislation, Teitelbaum (2006) finds that the positive effects of India's economic reforms on investment, productivity, and wages depend neither on poor labour laws nor the level of restriction on labour mobility in particular states. Similarly, Piore and Schrank (2005) find that countries like the Dominican Republic have gained rather than lost apparel trade share by ratcheting up their labour standards and boosting their labour inspections regime in ways that have helped non-compliant firms meet higher labour standards rather than simply penalize them or look the other way. Tendler (2005) similarly recounts several instances in Brazil and Argentina where improved economic performance and sectoral growth were associated with—and a generator of—improved labour standards.

This chapter presents evidence emerging from my ongoing field research in the Indian apparel industry to illustrate some of the conditions under which new intermediaries are creating the conditions for improved labour practices and better working conditions, in labour intensive industries. To do so, the chapter tells the story of how these new organizations in the labour market have come about, and the novel ways in which they engage with firms, workers, government agencies, and NGOs to shape labour-friendly processes of industrial adjustment in the garment sector. The emergence of these new intermediaries is as much an outcome of shifts in global value chains, that are transforming the geography of apparel production and trade, as of institutional histories, legacies, and choice at the local level. Not surprisingly, the pro-labour processes that these intermediaries are forging co-exist with a series of challenges that firms face—price pressures, competition for skills and resources, distribution and financial bottlenecks—that are pitting producers against producers and workers against workers, producing the contentious and outcomes that we see on the ground. The purpose of highlighting the ability of more progressive processes to survive and thrive in such contradictory environments is to argue that these processes are not unique to particular locations, and can offer insights and lessons for diffusing decent work and labour-supportive experiences more broadly. Equally, this body of evidence suggests how labour, which is often treated as a residual or derivative category in global value chain (GVC) debates, can mould and re-shape the supply chain, and through it, shape the processes of globalization and industrial restructuring, rather than be passively shaped by them.

The findings reported in this essay are based on fieldwork carried out in seven Indian cities: Tirupur, Chennai, Bengaluru (earlier Bangalore), Delhi, Mumbai, Ahmedabad, and Ludhiana, between 2000 and 2007. During 2005 and 2006, fieldwork was supported by the Indian Council for Research on International Economic Relations in New Delhi. Over this period, open-ended, face-to-face interviews were conducted with 60 firms and supplemented by a survey of 85 textile and apparel firms (out of 206 firms contacted). In addition, interviews were conducted with over 45 officials in ministries at the Central level and in state governments, in regional research and development institutions, training institutions, industry associations, and unions.

The chapter is organized in two main sections. The first section sets the stage for the context within which the emerging innovations in the Indian labour movement are occurring by highlighting five key surprises that emerged from the fieldwork. The second section elaborates on the emerging labour market organizations and presents the case study of the New Trade Union Initiative. The final section concludes.

SETTING THE STAGE: FIVE SURPRISES FROM THE FIELD

Changing Product Mix

First, in spite of the widespread national rhetoric among government bureaucrats, the press, industry representatives, and business associations about the urgent need to alter India's purportedly rigid labour laws to make hiring and firing easier[2] and to allow the use of contract labour in seasonal industries such as apparel, the practices on the ground are far more mixed. In many cases the very firms that say they want liberal labour laws are working with a series of local actors to change their organization of work to reduce labour turnover and absenteeism and improve work quality. These efforts involve improving working conditions (such as by providing cleaner, airier workspaces, child care, and health facilities), providing better training and improving wages in some circumstances. But they also include attempts by firms to change their own business strategies. For example, several small- and medium-sized firms (with the assistance of state actors, new labour organizations, and workers) are trying to change their product mix so that seasonality—the very condition that makes them vulnerable to shifts in labour demand and hence fuels the desire for flexible hiring and firing laws—can be eliminated by combining product lines that will make year round production possible.

Where these efforts have been successful, firms are finding that they not only have lower turnover rates, lower absenteeism, and better worker productivity, but their unit values, profitability, and business (export) performance as a whole have improved. For example, one large exporter in Gurgaon, near Delhi, that had long produced high-end,[3] extensively embellished women's blouses, skirts, and dresses introduced home furnishings, jackets, winter clothing, and men's wear to smoothen out the seasonality cycle, especially between the months of May and August. To maintain productivity levels in this multi-product setting, the company needed to build up and retain even more skilled workers than it had previously. This required a restructuring of its training and human resources (HR) strategy, pushed in part by its overseas buyers and in part by the growing competition for skilled workers in the local labour market as exports expanded generally throughout the late 1990s and 2000s. The company eliminated all vestiges of its old piece-rate system and moved to a system of direct employment at regular wages, benefits, and bonuses for all workers. It expanded its training facilities in each of its plants and strengthened its design department. Apart from expanding its in-house training programmes, the company is launching a non-profit training school in collaboration with the National Institute of Fashion Technology (NIFT) that will train all interested workers in the locality, not just its own employees. The company expanded its worker welfare policy, taking it beyond the factory floor to the neighbourhoods where workers live. Apart from crèches, cafeterias, and health care facilities in each plant (which are mandated by the government), the company pays in full for the schooling of the children of its employees and has set up community welfare centres in neighbourhoods where its workers are concentrated. These welfare hubs provide subsidized medial care, a primary school, a training centre, and a garment sewing and embroidery unit where workers can work closer to their homes. Overall, labour turnover is down from double digits to low single digits, rejection rates have fallen, and productivity has improved (Interview, 2006).

In another example, a medium-sized apparel exporter in Bengaluru chose to specialize in a range of related products to gain control over scheduling, work pace, and the production cycle on the factory floor. Until 2002, the company, which has 1,500 machines in 10 units, followed what it called a 'turnover' based model—low prices, substantial runs per style, but with neither the massive scales needed to make the 'high turnover-low margins' model profitable nor the work organization to deal with variable designs. This led to long and unpredictable down time between orders contrasted with sudden demand for intense overtime during spikes in delivery schedules. It was also difficult for managers to schedule and allocate labour efficiently because different items required different skills. The firm's margins were too slim for it to be able to afford multi-skilled workers. At the same time, a reliance on relatively low-skilled workers led to high rejection rates and wastage and placed heavy demands on the manager's time and attention. Feeling the pressure on prices and a squeeze on margins (which were about 5 per cent), the company changed strategies in 2003. It decided to move out of the turnover business, and into a product niche where large-volume producers from countries like China and Bangladesh were not a threat. It chose fashion-based women's and girls' tops and clothing that had a predominance of hand-crafted finishes and complex operations (embroidery, sequins, and other labour-intensive processes).

While it modernized and automated some of its production process (button holing, hemming), it intensified the use of skilled workers overall.

The company now produces small batches (500–5,000 per order) of women's fashion wear for retailers and specialty stores in the European Union (EU) and the US. In 2006, the company's profits had risen to over 35 per cent from 5 per cent, and sales increased each year since 2003. Its biggest worries now are shortages of skilled workers and labour turnover (about 10–15 per cent), which puts pressure on turn-around times, quality, and consistency (author interview, 2005; also see Tiwari, 2006). As a result, the firm has increased worker compensation and is working with local NGOs and public sector support institutions to train and retain workers. Specialization and a changing product mix have thus imposed new demands on company performance, which in turn have translated into productivity-driven improvements in working conditions, benefits, and skill formation. Nonetheless, buyer pressure and the growing competition for skilled labour are important additional factors that have pushed the firm to develop—and deepen—its institutional supports for worker welfare and human capital development. The next point highlights the importance of these tight labour markets as an organizing moment.

Tight Labour Markets amidst Surplus Labour

It was surprising to find, in city after city, the problem of tight labour markets in the garment industry—even as unemployment in related sectors and rural areas continued to persist. The tight labour markets were for skilled workers. As export-oriented and domestic firms adopted new technologies that required special skills to operate, and as a growing number of medium and large firms turned towards design-intensive exports, they faced shortages of skilled labour. Consequently, fastest growing industry support institutions being provided by state governments, by the Ministry of Textiles, by private firms, and non-profit organizations were design and training centres—organized in a variety of ways and run by a variety of actors.

The tight labour markets and the joint vulnerability of producers and workers to delivery time pressures, quality, and consistency have been sources of substantial improvement in wages and working conditions in garment firms in many cities. For example, in the booming knitwear clusters of Tirupur and Ludhiana, skilled wages are more than double the market rate, and labour organizations, local governments, and the exporters' association have had to come together to prevent poaching of skilled labour (author interview, Tirupur, 2006). Even so, skilled wages now exceed unskilled wages by significant orders of magnitude. Whereas average unskilled wages are between $30 and $50 a month depending on the region, skilled wages can range six or seven times and be as high as

$300–$450 or even $600 per month depending on the region, gender, and nature of the task.[4] Thus, while tight labour markets have improved the lot of a subset of workers, they have also deepened inequality within the sector. Informal sector firms are the most vulnerable to losing their skilled craft workers to larger, formal sector firms, and as a result, one comes across the surprising phenomenon of a growing number of informal firms turning towards unions to help organize their shops (Centre of Indian Trade Unions [CITU] interview with local representative, 2005). The tightness of labour markets thus cuts both ways.

Cheap Labour versus Cheap Land

The Indian government is responding to the growing demand for labour market reforms (and the dismantling of labour protections) by launching a number of industrial 'clusters' and special economic zones (SEZs or apparel parks) with serviced land and public infrastructure where labour laws may be relaxed. But based on the author's discussions with representatives of some firms, for firms this seems to be more about getting access to subsidized land and clustered layouts where input suppliers, designers, key intermediaries such as processing firms, export assistance agencies, testing labs, and in some cases government-subsidized environmental infrastructure (such as centrally designed common treatment plants) can be co-located, than it is about carving out zones with relaxed labour laws. The rise and proliferation of private 'apparel parks' in each of the country's six key apparel-making regions over the past five years—where the labour laws remain unchanged—are a testimony to the growing interest of apparel producers in getting access to serviced land and sector-related infrastructure and services.

With growing pressure from global buyers for supplier compliance with company codes of conduct and norms of corporate social responsibility (CSR), wages and benefits are much less of a source of cost-cutting than the general rhetoric over 'labour market flexibility' would lead one to believe. Indeed, in some instances old loss-making collective institutions such as handloom cooperatives have experienced a revival on the basis of precisely the 'expensive' wage, welfare, and benefits packages that critics have long complained about as being responsible for their poor performance and low productivity.[5] Data and interviews from the Handloom Board (Interview, Director of Handlooms, Chennai, 2000) show that apart from the growing demand for fine handloom fabrics for home furnishing, since the late 1900s, the decent worker-welfare package has been a major draw for overseas buyers wary of adverse publicity over use of child labour and sweatshop practices. Buyers and agents of several European retailers talk of being 'impressed with the possibility to maintaining good working conditions', the willingness of the government agencies to offer training to the weavers based on buyer needs, and the weavers' capacity to learn new ways to doing things (Interview, Director of Handlooms, Chennai, 2000). By the early 2000s, handloom exports had grown over 45 times—from $0.22 million in 1997 to $10 million in the first quarter of 2000. Similarly, rejection rates had fallen dramatically: from a high of 50 per cent in 1997 to less than 3 per cent in 2000 (Davidar Interview, Chennai, 2000). The welfare package is not the only reason for this turnaround: the Handloom Board undertook several institutional reforms that improved the performance of the handloom cooperatives. Nonetheless, buyer interest in sourcing from a place where good labour conditions were at least assured, underscores the fact that good labour conditions can also be good for trade.

Productivity-driven Improvements in Labour Conditions

In contrast to the general sense that firms are more likely to improve their working conditions in the face of external pressures from foreign buyers, codes of conduct, or export competition, it was surprising to find better or equally good working conditions and work organization in several plants producing for the domestic market. Henrietta Lake (2006) has reported parallel findings. As she reports, in some cases the improved labour conditions—such as better lighting, ventilation, temperature control, less noise, the presence of a canteen, crèche, or health clinic, and/or health insurance and benefits began in the export units of firms that also produced for the domestic market. The positive effect that these conditions had on improving retention and productivity, and lowering labour turnover and absenteeism led many companies to voluntarily transfer similar conditions to their domestic units (Firm interview, Chennai, 2002, 2005). Other firms spoke of setting up community centres, schools, and clinics along with training centres in the residential clusters where their workers lived as a way of retaining them, upskilling them, and earning their loyalty (Firm interview, Gurgaon, 2006).

In other cases, improvements in the work organization of domestic units have resulted from the rapid growth and transformation of the large domestic Indian market. For example, in the past decade, as malls have sprung up across large and small towns, and as demand for readymade, designer clothing has grown, especially among a younger generation of workers employed in the nation's booming information technology (IT) and business process outsourcing (BPO) sectors, so has the competition among domestic chains to corner market share in this newly organized retail space. Domestic branded wear is fast becoming the new battleground for garment producers. Indeed, some of the largest, best-known firms in the country cater exclusively to the domestic market (for example, Pantaloon, and major exporters are launching brands exclusively for the home market (Tewari, 2006). Quasi-hyper markets such as Big Bazaar and Shoppers Stop have put in place extremely intricate and tight domestic supply chains for the production of these goods. Given the importance of cost and timeliness in the workings of these new supply chains, domestic firms are as likely as exporters to strive to retain their workforce. This has led to the upgrading of a large number of domestic enterprises despite the absence of export pressures (Mukherjee, 2005; Lake, 2006).

This suggests that despite an emphasis on a standard set of labour rights—for example, International Labour Organization's (ILOs) core labour rights—emanating from external sources, innovative pro-labour practices on the ground can take a wide variety of shapes. It is the unearthing, recognition, and validation of these diverse and ongoing practices that is key to diffusing decent work and supporting labour market transformation more widely, than passively expecting global forces to transform local workplaces. Indeed, dichotomizing external drivers from internal drivers of decent work is to perpetuate a false choice; all sources of good labour conditions are important to valorize, including their interaction, mutual constitution, as well as co-existence.

Shifts in Labour Organizing

Finally, another unexpected finding was that even as the public rhetoric surrounding the labour issue is focused on loosening labour protections, garment-sector unions are reporting an increase in recruitment for the first time in years. They are reporting the fastest increases in the organization of informal sector firms on the one hand and of workers in large and medium firms on the other (Interviews, CITU, 2005; New Trade Union Initiative [NTUI], 2006). But these successes do not track old union expectations of labour behaviour as being primarily confrontational with management or traditional forms of labour organizing. As one labour activist put it, worker behaviour (in labour-intensive sectors such as the garment and leather industries) is hard to predict these days. 'Workers don't seem to agitate when you would normally expect them to; and they do when you don't expect them to' (Interview, Chennai, 2003). Indeed, the most successful organizing efforts have been spurred by new and innovative labour market actors and unions that have themselves emerged or adopted new roles in India's post-liberalization years. These new unions represent new arrangements and alliances among long-standing local actors in the labour market. We will examine them in greater detail in the rest of the chapter against the backdrop of the industry-level differences and variations discussed earlier.

ORGANIZING FROM THE OUTSIDE-IN: THE CASE OF THE NEW TRADE UNION INITIATIVE AND THE GARMENT AND TEXTILE WORKERS UNION (INDIA)

It is in this context, and in these contradictory spaces that new labour organizations are beginning to deal with the issue of labour rights in new ways. This section traces the emergence of one of the most prominent of these experimental organizations, the NTUI—an alliance and federation of independent trade unions in India that arose in the mid-1990s and became formally constituted as a—federation in early 2005. Unlike many national unions that have faced stagnation or atrophy in membership in recent years, NTUI has had some striking successes, organizing workers in a variety of sectors including apparel, services, and agriculture. With over 200 constituent independent unions under its umbrella, NTUI has a membership base of 500,000 workers in the formal sector and another 300,000 in the unorganized sector (NTUI Interview with a local representative, 2006).

Three Distinctive Traits

Three traits set NTUI apart from other Indian trade unions. First, in an environment where traditional trade unions are usually affiliated with particular political parties or are company unions, NTUI is a federation of *independent* unions. It is not apolitical, but is not associated with any single political party. That it is a federation is equally significant. While the real work (and power) lies at the industry (sectoral) and state (and local) levels—or, at the level of the independent unions—NTUI's federated structure gives it significant national voice, clout, and visibility.

Second, unlike the typical union stance on trade, NTUI rejects protectionism as a response to globalization and intensifying international competition. It holds the view that given the internationalization of work and cross-border movements of labour and capital, the industry supply chain, rather than the nation-state, is the appropriate arena for organizing labour rights in a globalizing world. 'When supply chains are proliferating across the globe how do you enforce labor rights on the basis of the nation state? To organize effectively there has to be a fundamental realingnment [of labour] to the global supply chain, and not only the nation state' (NTUI interview, 2006). Third, the NTUI focuses simultaneously at two levels—at the worksite where workers labour and at the places or communities where workers live. Its organizational strategy, therefore, extends beyond the workplace to the community, and it is one of only a few Indian unions to embrace area- and 'place'-based organizing strategies. The community, and not just the factory floor are its organizing locus.

Together these traits have shaped NTUI's organizing strategy and embedded it both, within ongoing shifts in the global economy and the grounded adjustment practices of firms and workers at the local level (which it in turn helps mediate). For example, NTUI's interest in focusing on the global supply chain arose out of its misgivings about the way in which the debate on labour rights was being framed at the WTO (specifically at the 1996 Singapore Ministerial) and among global buyers. The mainstream emphasis at the macro level was on core labour standards. For example, on the elimination of child labour in the garment sector (following the Tom Harkin bill). Unconvinced that centralized standards were sufficient to improve labour conditions, NTUI viewed industrial sectors as linked and rejected the notion that core labour standards could be enforced by limiting one's view to particular sectors. In the case of child labour, for example, it wondered where the children who were eliminated from the garment sector would go? To answer this question, it carried out two studies on how standards such as those associated with child labour and voluntary codes of conduct played out on the ground among firms and buyers.

Microfoundations of a Cross-sectoral Focus on Global Supply Chains

The first case study that NTUI conducted was of the Bangladesh garment industry where child labour had been an endemic problem, but where, in a very short period of time after buyer pressure forced the introduction of core labour standards, child labour seemed to disappear (NTUI interview with Delhi Representative, 2006). Where had these children gone? NTUI researchers found that when garment firms stopped hiring children in fear of losing export orders, the children switched to more dangerous work in even less protected industries—stone cutting, quarrying, construction, chemicals, and human trafficking. This finding was central to NTUI's decision to work cross-sectorally and to focus on livelihood issues—spanning the workers' families and communities—in addition to workplace organizing. It also highlighted for NTUI the importance of partnering with sub-national institutions in shaping place-based production networks and eliciting bottleneck-breaking investments.

NTUI's second study was of Carrefour, the giant French retailer, and its sourcing patterns within Asia (NTUI interview with Delhi representative, 2006). The Union's central finding was that within a span of 10 years, the company had virtually eliminated all its sourcing intermediaries. In 1995, there were five to six layers, mostly of agents, that linked the vendor to the buyer. The buyer (Carrefour) often did not know who they were buying from. By 2005, Carrefour had used CSR agreements and corporate codes of conduct to eliminate all but two to three layers of intermediaries. What changed in the interim? NTUI's argument was that Carrefour used the labour rights debate especially CSR agreements and the enforcement of labour standards to eliminate the layers in order to streamline profitability and wrest control over what was an opaque chain. 'Carrefour created the Asia Sourcing Company in Hong Kong as a separate profit centre and began mapping the entire regional supply chain. Meanwhile, Carrefour set up a partnership (in Bangladesh) with a local union, a business association, and its own purchasing office spread some of the gains of eliminating the intermediaries to the vendor and workers' (NTUI interview, 2006). This partnership eventually failed, but by making orders contingent upon suppliers' compliance with certain conditions and labour standards, Carrefour, according to NTUI, forced disclosures which led to the elimination of layers of intermediaries. This streamlining of the supply chain raised Carrefour's profitability, even as the prices, which suppliers got, went down. As documented by several studies on GVCs, the gains of restructuring within buyer-driven chains such as apparel and retail mainly accrue at the retail end—not at the production end. In this case as well, Carrefour enlarged its profits—even as the responsibility for enforcing labour rights was shifted to vendors at the site of production without any increases in prices. (Indeed, if shirts cost $15 a dozen in 1995, they cost $12 per dozen in 2006).

This led NTUI to two insights about organizing—one related to the method of analysis and the other about the point of leverage where organizing could be most effective. As a senior official of the Federation said in an interview (2006):

> Our understanding is: let's look at it from the buyer's perspective. How does the global buyer make the decision to buy from Malaysia versus Indonesia? Is it about relative prices? Not really. That is where the real issue lies—the buyer is looking at how the garment's FOB [free on board] price translates into dollars (or PPP[purchasing power parity]). How has the movement of FOB prices [in different supplier countries] moved in dollar terms? At least ten percent of FOB cost is what they were interested in as profits. (NTUI interview, 2006)

In other words, *absolute price* is not the issue, but *price mediated by differences in productivity and variations in national price levels* (inflation and interest rates and exchange rates) makes a key difference for the buyers and their sourcing strategy. That, in other words, was the point of leverage that a labour advocate must target.

This analysis pointed directly at how NTUI interpreted its wider organizing strategy. In a world of complicated subcontracting and tiered supply, suppliers lower down the chain—say tier 4—are sites where workers and small firms' owners are socially the closest. Ideologically, this may be a good place to build alliances between workers and employers, but it would not be strategic. If, as NTUI's analysis revealed, the key linkage is between tier 1 suppliers and global buyers, then the top suppliers must be the union's organizing focus. This has two advantages: First, tier 1 suppliers are closest to the buyer; targeting them will enable the organizers to get closest to the global supply chain. Second, this focus on the largest suppliers is more pragmatic: 'We need to monitor only 50–60 companies, not 200 companies. It is an organizing strategy' (Interview, 2006).

Finally, the focus on the first tier of suppliers is driven by NTUI's end goal. The goal is to improve *livelihoods* of workers across the industry, and not just wage a fight for raising minimum wages. By targeting tier 1 companies *for a living wage* (which these companies are large enough to give), NTUI hopes to engender a cascading effect down the supply chain where suppliers lower down will at least be compliant with the minimum wage. 'If you leave Tier 1 to be minimum wage compliant, you can forget about getting Tier 4 to comply with the minimum' (NTUI interview, 2006). Second, to prevent buyers from jumping ship to other lower wage countries in Asia, NTUI is working with international NGOs such as, Jobs for Justice and others like it—to create an *Asian floor wage* based on purchasing power parity calculations. The union is confident that even if some jobs go to smaller Asian suppliers such as in Vietnam, who may not sign on to the idea of a wage floor, the sheer dominance of the workforce in South Asian countries make such fears less relevant in the long term. 'Even if all orders shift to Vietnam, they just don't have the labour force to sustain the shift long term' (NTUI interview, 2006).

How have these lessons from studying and understanding the workings of global supply chains in clothing translated into NTUI's ground-level organizing practices within the garment industry in India? How is it reinforcing the diverse trends we saw in the first section, where productivity-driven interests are leading some firms to adopt improved working conditions as a business strategy? Currently, multiple political unions can organize a single plant. NTUI's vision is to reform plant level collective bargaining in such a way that there is a single union in a plant and a single federation in an industry. This, in its view, would stop the fragmentation that has militated against union's ability to effectively organize the industry. Second, it has sought to target the fastest growing areas in the country—such as Karnataka, Gujarat, Maharashtra, and Tamil Nadu—and within these states has focused on the fastest growing regions and sectors, including garments in the manufacturing sector, and also agriculture and construction. Most of these targeted states have a relatively educated labour pool, relatively cordial business–state relations, are not lax in supporting labour laws, and have a strategic rather than an adversarial bargaining culture, and where both industry and government (and workers' associations) want a stable workforce.

Within these states, NTUI began its garment sector work in Bengaluru, where the Garment and Textile Workers Union (GATWU) was launched in 2006. By 2007, GATWU had over a thousand members. NTUI chose Bengaluru because 'Bangalore has scale' in the garment industry. In the last nine years (since 2000), a lot of new investment has concentrated in Bengaluru, on its outskirts and in semi-greenfield sites in the hinterland. Bengaluru also has one of the most feminized garment workforces in the country, and while this workforce can be skilled, it is also exploited with low wages and poor working conditions. At the same time, the region has numerous support institutions, a rich network of NGOs, and a history of successful social movements. 'Bangalore represents a new model [in garment production] and [we] wanted to engage with the industry' (Interview, NTUI, 2006).

What is striking in NTUI's work in Bengaluru is the path it took towards shop-floor organizing. NTUI first began its work at the level of the community, outside the shop floor. It built a working-women's organization in the garment clusters around Bengaluru. Though based in the community, the membership of this non-profit organization was sectoral—it focused exclusively on women who worked in the garment and textile industry. The idea was to build institutional capacity and develop leadership among women workers outside the garment factories first and then move to the shop floor, allowing the already organized cadre of women who had emerged as leaders to spearhead the organizing drive within the factories.

Over a two-year period, a strong leadership base of women developed that gradually began to successfully organize the garment factories and recruit members in the GATWU. Meanwhile, NTUI worked closely with local government officials, researchers, and several local non-profit organizations to understand and support the needs of the women garment workers in the community, beyond the workplace. For example, based on a study of women's work time, conducted by researchers from a university-affiliated institute, NTUI found that most of the garment workers work long hours—over 16 hours a day—at the factory and at home. Their most time-consuming chores outside the workplace were (*i*) laundry, (*ii*) cooking, (*iii*) childcare, and (*iv*) commuting. NTUI and GATWU picked laundry—the dreariest of the chores—and partnered with a non-profit organization to centralize this chore for all women in the community. The plan was to procure four washing machines as soon as funding was available and provide a central facility in the village where a local NGO will provide laundry services to everyone in the community. Since the task is water-intensive, the NGO will first provide free service on a trial basis, and then charge for it. This has earned the support of the garment firms where the women are employed because the expectation is that removing this burden (especially when water supply is erratic) will reduce absenteeism and improve productivity.

In future programmes, NTUI—through GATWU—plans to take on the task of brokering training services that government and private institutions provide but customize them to the plant-specific needs of the firms that employ its members. Unions such as NTUI are not alone in bridging the work and family demands facing garment workers, and helping mediate between workers and employers to improve working conditions. The emerging landscape has several other organizations that are starting to play similar roles. One example is of collaborations between small-firm associations and NGOs, such as between a non-profit organization funded by the German Foundation Frederich Naumann Stiftung and Tamil Nadu's most prominent small and medium firms' association, Tamil Nadu Small and Tiny Industries Association (TANSTIA). This partnership has provided collective crèches for women working in several different small firms in garment clusters around Chennai;[6] it has run a joint marketing web portal for local small firms, supported a design centre, and helped to collectively pool input procurement for its small member firms (Tewari and Goebel, 2002).

Other examples are of firm-centred approaches, where large buyers such as IKEA are developing innovative, place-based strategies to build up the skill, health, and education base not just of their suppliers and their workers but of the whole regional belt from where they hope to cull their long-term supply base for carpets, rugs, home furnishings, and shawls (IKEA Gurgaon interview, 2005). In a departure from the usual practice in firms where procurement and sourcing decisions are made separately from sections of the firm that enforce and CSR, IKEA has merged these functions: its purchasing department is simultaneously responsible for compliance. As a result, IKEA has developed an intricate set of ties with the ILO, World Health Organization (WHO), district commissioners (district-level government officials), and a university to re-combine existing government programmes or solicit multilateral support for more customized programmes that have led to the improvement of the health, schooling, training, and nutrition in the cluster of villages it draws its suppliers from—both in north and southern India. Its university partners use students to independently monitor suppliers' compliance with labour and environmental standards on a regular basis.

Finally, some government agencies, such as the Textiles Committee—an independent, but government-funded support institution for the garment and textile industry has reinvented itself in the past decade to serve as a one point source for disseminating information about quality standards, testing, compliance with international standards, certification (for chemical tests for dyes), and the provision of training to support small and medium garment firms in meeting labour and environmental standards. The Textiles Committee was set up in the late 1960s as an inspection agency charged with the inspection and certification of India's textile and apparel exports to the former Soviet Union and Eastern Europe. After the fall of the Soviet Union, the agency lost its raison d'etre and was nearly shut down. In the wake of a series of stringent bans on wet processing chemicals (such as PCPs [Pentachlorophenol] and Azo types) in the early 1990s by major importing countries such as Germany the Textiles Committee reinvented itself. With its skilled personnel, funding from the Department of Science and Technology, and from donors like GTZ (Gesellschaft für Technische Zusammenarbeit) and Danida it began to provide environmental testing and training to small firms on compliance, as well as certification, at a third of the cost of private sector consultants (author interview, Mumbai, 2003). As a result, in contrast to the time when 'we ran after firms, today, these firms run after us an official reported. Its work on diffusing good environmental and CSR practices among small and medium garment firms and dyeing and bleaching units has been central to enabling many smaller producers in the industry to improve their working conditions. The agency also conducts annual consumer surveys that provide demand information to producers which in turn helps improve their work planning and hiring decisions.

This collectivity of institutions in the labour movement, in civil society, and in the public and private sectors are evidence, then, that improved labour conditions are institutionally and socially constituted, crafted, and defended through a set of contested but deliberative practices. These practices have intended and unintended consequences and they do elicit resistance, but they also move forward the agenda of fostering more humane as well as productive workplaces. This calls for a key role for agency and choice, reflection, and learning in bringing these processes about and supporting them rather than presumptions that market discipline and subjecting firms and workers to external pressures of competition will automatically generate them.

CONCLUSIONS

The story about the globalization of work has so far been told mostly from the point of view of (multinational) capital, nation-states, buyer- and producer-driven value chains, and changing global regulatory regimes. Labour's role in shaping the trajectories of these ongoing transformations is largely absent from most accounts, not the least because of the 'market triumphalism' that has dominated neo-liberal discourses of development over the past two decades (Hart, 2006; and others). This chapter chronicled some of the ways in which labour processes are shaping and being shaped—on the ground—by global shifts in the apparel industry, as seen through an Indian lens. Much of the literature on labour rights and multinational production continues to speak in a macro tone of centralized labour rights, codes of conduct, and links between market access and labour standards. This literature has played a central role in advancing our understanding of how labour and the labour process are incorporated into processes of industrial transformation and upgrading.

However, while looking at centralized conceptions of labour rights as a set of core standards is useful, it remains an incomplete lens with which to understand the diverse practices on the ground, and the tremendous variation in the way in which improved labour conditions are actually obtained and sustained. For example, in the first section of this chapter we saw how, even in a footloose and deeply globalized industry such as apparel, where global buyers seek ever cheaper producers and improved wages and working conditions are often seen as adding to a supplier's costs, we find a number of instances when supplier firms have themselves sought to improve labour standards and working conditions, often driven by the productivity gains of improvements, such as, reduced turnover, greater retention, and the resulting benefits of timely delivery and good quality. We saw, therefore, that improved working conditions are not always inimical to growth and expanded trade. However, we also saw the fragility and fragmentation of these firm-driven gains. In some cases, gains were sustained, and in some cases they were not. As a result, the main argument of the chapter was that the link between improved business performance and improved labour conditions is real, but not inevitable or automatic even when firms see improved labour standards as a source of competitive advantage. For these gains to be sustained and diffused widely, we need to foster intermediation by a rich set of institutions in the public sector, private sector, and especially in the labour movement. The examples of NTUI, GATWU, and novel forms of hybrid institutions in the second section of the chapter provides some evidence of the kinds of institutions that are playing this role on the ground. Not only do mediating institutions such as these play a critical role in shaping and sustaining these labour-friendly employment relations, but they have the potential to diffuse them more widely across sectors. The linkages between place or community-based interventions and work-place strategies show that the trajectories of reform in industrial relations can be multifacted. They can emanate from a variety of sources and yet be synergistic.

In conclusion, therefore, a much more specific, detailed, and micro-institutional, historical approach is needed to make sense of these fledgling processes. Why are these progressive practices emerging in some places and not others; in some sectors and not in others; and how and under what circumstances can improved working conditions be compatible with competitiveness and upgrading than be growth-inhibiting as is often presumed.

A final, related insight from the cases discussed in the chapter is that posing the story of globalization and industrial restructuring as one of capital versus labour, state versus society, or global versus local, reinvents dualistic and polarizing categories that deflect our attention from precisely those connections between these categories that define the new spaces for progressive action and developmental practices that are both inclusive and transformative. A chronicling and analysis of actual labour practices and the in-between spaces where they take root is critical if we are to shed light on how work can be made more inclusive and humane even when it is shot through with persistent conflicts.

NOTES

1. This title borrows from the work of Thomas Bailey and Annette Bernhardt (1997), where they examine the prospects of high performance work systems in low-wage service jobs in the retail industry. This article focuses on improvements in labour conditions in labour-intensive manufacturing jobs.

2. Currently, firms with more than 100 workers cannot fire workers without government consent and a lengthy bureaucratic review process.
3. The company, for example, would not take a Wal-Mart order because of the low prices they offer. Recently, they made one skirt for Polo Blue that will retail at $119 (Interview, 2006; Mirza, 2006).
4. The exchange rate here is $1 = Rs 45.
5. The distinctive feature of the government-run handloom cooperatives was that workers and weavers could not be arbitrarily struck off the rolls—they were government employees. Wages and benefits conformed to regular government standards, subject to annual increases like in other government jobs. Over the past 25 years, the government has supported the handloom sector to preserve jobs and crafted welfare/benefits packages that include housing subsidies, work-shed subsidies, training programmes, savings schemes, and retirement funds. These initiatives taken together have improved working conditions for the weavers, but led to bitter complaints by private mills that the government was coddling inefficient weavers and indirectly raising labour costs for the entire industry. That said, it is important to note that there are differences between retrenchment and the firing of workers. As one anonymous reviewer pointed out, 'retrenchment rules do not apply at all when workers are fired for misconduct. It is also well known that even firms with 10,000 workers set up multiple units of less than 100 workers to side-step the retrenchment procedures applicable to large units'.
6. On-site crèches are mandated by government law for firms beyond a certain threshold of employees.

REFERENCES

Badrinarayan, G. (2005), 'A Note on Labor Market Flexibility in India', *Economic and Political Weekly*, 40(39): 4290–91.

Bailey, T.R. and A. Bernhardt (1997), 'In Search of the High Road in a Low Wage Industry', *Politics and Society*, 25(2): 179–201.

Besley, T. and R. Burgess (2004), 'Can Labor Regulation Hinder Economic Performance? Evidence from India', *Quarterly Journal of Economics*, 119(1): 91–134.

Flanagen, R.J. (2003), 'Labour Standards and International Competitive Advantage', in R. J. Flanagan and W.B. Gould (eds), *International Labour Standards: Global Trade and Public Policy*. Stanford: Stanford University Press.

Harrison, A. and J. Scorse (2004), 'The Nike Effect: Anti-Sweatshop Activists and Labor Market Outcomes in Indonesia', Unpublished Mimeo, University of California, Berkeley and NBER.

Hart, Gillian (2006), 'Post-Apartheid Developments in Comparative and Historical Perspective', in V. Padayachee (ed.), *The First Decade of Development and Democracy in South Africa*. Pretoria: HSRC Press.

Lake, Henrietta (2006), *Learning to Compete: The Performance Effect of Work Organization and Human Resource Management in the South Indian Garment Industry*, Unpublished doctoral dissertation, The Fletcher School, Tufts University.

Ministry of Commerce (2006), Mimeo on the Meeting of Chief Ministers, Ministry of Commerce, New Delhi, India.

Mirza, Salma (2006), Interview notes from the field. Mimeo, University of North Carolina at Chapel Hill.

Mukherjee, Arpita (2005), *FDI in Retail in India*. New Delhi: Academic Publishers.

Piore, M.J. and A. Schrank (2006), 'Trading Up: An Embryonic Model for Easing the Human Cost of the Free Market', *Boston Review*, September–October, 31(5): 1–11.

Rodrik, D. (1997), *Has Globalization Gone too Far?* Washington D.C: Institute for International Economics.

Sachs, J., N. Bajpai, and A. Ramiah (2002), 'Understanding Regional Economic Growth in India', Working Paper No. 88. Cambridge, MA: Center for International Development, Harvard University.

Teitelbaum, Emmanuel (2006), 'Does Successful Reform Require a Race to the Bottom? Evidence from the Indian States', Paper presented at the conference on Multinational and Labor Rights, University of North Carolina at Chapel Hill, 23 September.

Tendler, J. (2005), '"Under the Radar": Workers, Worker Protections, and Labor Unions', and 'Undoing the Poverty Agenda and Putting It Back Together: Social Policy, Economic Development, or What?' (2 chapters), in William R. Eastly (ed.), *Reinventing Foreign Aid*. Cambridge, MA: The MIT Press.

Tewari, M. (2006), 'Adjustments in India's Textile and Apparel Industry: Reworking Historical Legacies in a Post-MFA World', *Environment and Planning A*, 38(12): 2325–44.

Tewari, M. and G. Goebel (2002), 'Sources of Small Firm Competitiveness in a Trade Liberalized World: Lessons from Tamil Nadu, India', Prepared for the India Program, Center for International Development, Harvard University.

7 LABOUR MARKET ADJUSTMENT AND FEMALE WORKERS
Global Production and Expiry of Quotas in India's Textile and Garments Industry

Indira Hirway

INTRODUCTION

The process of globalization has opened up developing countries to global production networks (GPNs), which have now emerged as key players in world trade. The transnational corporations (TNCs) that control GPNs now account for around two-thirds of the world trade. The widespread use of international outsourcing in GPNs allows global producers to shed their non-core activities and focus on higher value-added activities like design, branding, and marketing. Developing countries compete with each other for outsourced production and, under the pressure to meet the cost, quality, and delivery requirements of their clients, as well as to handle fluctuating orders, they use different methods of hiring workers. These methods seem to have made an adverse impact on the terms of employment of different categories of workers, leading to their low wages and poor working conditions without adequate social protection. Being less equipped than men to demand a fair deal in the labour market, women seem to suffer more from the adverse impact on the labour market. A big challenge before policymakers is to ensure quality employment to workers and to reduce gender inequalities in the labour market to enable both male and female workers to access benefits from increasing trade.

This chapter examines the recent developments in the textile and garments (T&G) industry in India in this context, and attempts to draw policy inferences to promote decent work as well as gender equality in the face of expanding trade in the industry. The T&G industry, which is one of the important industries in the global economy as well as in the Indian economy, has shown a rapid growth in the global market (from US$ 212 billion in 1990 to US$ 396 billion in 2003, and to the projected US$ 600 billion by 2010) (GoI, 2006). It is one of the largest industries in India. At the turn of the century, India's T&G industry produced 18 per cent of total industrial production, earned 20 per cent of total export earnings, and employed about 38 million persons directly. India ranked seventh among the world exporters, with 3.8 per cent share in world exports. In terms of employment generation, this industry is still second in India after agriculture. The T&G industry typifies the development of global production networks in the world economy. The European Union (EU) and the United States together accounted for 70–80 per cent of the world textile trade and 73–75 per cent of the world clothing trade in the same time period (ibid.). Retailers in the EU and USA enjoy a powerful position in the global market that empowers them to allocate total activities, from design to raw materials to final products and distribution, across differnt countries as per the comparative advantages of countries.

India has embarked on the policy of liberalizing its internal economy as well as foreign trade since 1991. Accession to the World Trade Organization (WTO), phasing out of the Multi-fibre Agreement (MFA), and liberalization of capital and commodity flows characterize the environment facing India as well as many other countries in Asia at present. The expiry of the MFA and the Agreement on Textile and Clothing (ATC) in January 2005 has had a particularly significant impact on the region. The expiry is providing an opportunity to restructure the industry, to increase exports of products, and thereby promote growth of employment in the manufacturing sector in these economies. The actual impact, however, will be different in the future in different countries, depending on the specific situation of the country. While some countries are now facing challenges in sustaining production, some other countries like China, India, Indonesia, and Pakistan seem to have increased their exports to the US and Europe (UNDP, 2005a, 2005b).

The Indian textile industry is diverse and complex, with the organized formal sector operating on the one hand and the decentralized sector and down-the-line weavers and artisans operating in the informal sector on the other hand. The formal mill sector produces nearly 3 per cent of the cloth, power looms produce 63 per cent, handlooms 13 per cent, and the relatively new hosiery sector produces 21 per cent of the total textiles (Textile Commissioner's Office, 2007). The garments industry is again a relatively new phenomenon. With a modest beginning in the 1970s, it has grown into a gigantic industry spread over the country. The garments industry produces about 8,000 million pieces with the market value of US$ 28 billion (CMIE, 2007).

This chapter studies the impact of recent changes in the textile policy, particularly the phasing out of the MFA, on the Indian textile industry and on labour and gender inequalities in the labour market. The section that follows discusses the emergence of the MFA and the expiry of T&G quotas, and how the government and the industry have responded to the expiry of the quotas; the next section discusses how the industry has restructured and analyses the trends in employment and labour in the different segments of the industry; and the section following it makes recommendations for promoting improved sharing of the benefits of the growth in the industry.

MFA AND EXPIRY OF QUOTAS

The MFA came into existence in 1974 as a trade agreement between the US, Europe, and Canada, on the one hand, and about 65 developing countries, on the other, to protect jobs in the T&G industry in the former from cheaper imports from the latter countries. It was meant to be a temporary arrangement but was extended five times and continued till 1995. Since the MFA was seen as a protectionist measure in the 1990s, it was replaced in 1995 by ATC, under which a programme was designed for dismantling of the quota in a phased manner by 1 January 2005. It needs to be noted that the dismantling does not mean free trade in the industry, as trade remedy laws on anti-dumping and countervailing duties and safeguards, bilateral and regional agreements, generalized system of preferences (GSP), most favoured nation (MFN), as well as tariffs on imports of textile products, still continue after the quotas are gone (MFA Forum, 2005).

Under the competitive environment after the quotas, countries have tried to cut costs in multiple ways. For example, the Philippines has excluded the garment sector from the purview of the Minimum Wages Act; the Dominican Republic and El Salvador have exempted the wages of T&G workers from the cost of living index; Mauritius has increased working days to seven days a week without additional remuneration, etc. China has clear advantages in the competition due to its low labour standards, as Chinese textile workers reportedly work for 12–14 hours a day, seven days a week for low wages without any labour rights. The Chinese government declared the textile industry as 'a pillar of the nation' and invested US$ 21 billion during 2002–5 to increase the production capacity, backed by reducing the labour cost by different means, on the one hand, and under-cutting prices of export goods, on the other hand (ITGLWF, 2005). It is argued that the other countries are forced to reduce their own labour standards to face the competition from China.

HOW HAS INDIA RESPONDED TO THE NEW CHALLENGES?

The Government of India's main response has been to help the industry to take advantage of the new opportunities. The government had adopted an inward-looking strategy (Import Substitution Industrial Policy) for industrial development till 1985 based on licensing, reservation, and controls of different kinds. The textile industry, therefore, had a domestic focus till then. The National Policy on Textiles (1985) made a turnaround and started the process of deregulation of the industry. In 1991, after the economic reforms were adopted, several other policy reforms, like de-licensing of some sectors, removal of export barriers and slashing of import duties, de-reservation (also for garment industry), and allowing cent per cent foreign direct investment (FDI) in the garment industry without export obligations were introduced. The National Textile Policy 2000 has the vision to produce cloth of good quality at acceptable prices to meet the growing needs of the people and to contribute towards growth of sustainable employment and economic growth of the country (Government of India, 2000). The major objectives of the policy are to facilitate the textile industry to attain a pre-eminent standing in the manufacture and export of clothing; to equip the industry to stand in a competitive environment at home and in the global market; to enable the industry to build world-class manufacturing capabilities and to encourage FDI as well as research and development (R&D) for the purpose; to sustain traditional knowledge, skills, and capabilities of weavers and crafts of people; and to expand productive employment by promoting growth of the industry. The thrust areas of the policy are technological upgrading, enhancement of productivity, quality consciousness, strengthening of the raw material base, product diversification, export expansion, maximization of employment, and integrated human resource development. A major target for exports is to raise T&G exports to US$ 50 billion in 2010 from the present US$ 11 billion.

The Ministry of Textiles, along with its three statutory bodies—the Textile Committee, Central Silk Board, and Jute Development Council—is working for the promotion of production, exports, R&D, market research, etc. There are export promotion councils, research associations, and advisory bodies to cater to the needs of the different sub-sectors of the industry. The ministry has designed many schemes for the purpose, such as technology upgradation fund scheme (TUFS), a flagship scheme that offers soft loans for 20 years at 5 per cent interest with capital subsidy at 10 per cent; technology mission on cotton (TMC); integrated textile parks; and schemes for power looms.

Industry associations and federations also responded positively to the aggressive government policies and schemes and to the opportunities opened up after the expiry of the MFA. The Confederation of Indian Industries (CII) got a study done on prospects for the industry (Hindu, 2004); and its regional centres worked out plans to take advantage of the new opportunities. Textile associations, Federation of Indian Chambers of Commerce and Industry (FICCI), and many regional industrial bodies followed suit. One also observes public–private partnerships (PPPs) in the tasks of modernization, technology transfer, organizing trade fairs and exhibitions, export promotion, and accessing assistance from global organizations and advocacy with these organizations.

In short, the industry started expanding, innovating, and diversifying to take advantage of the new liberalized environment in general and the expiry of the quotas in particular. About Rs 500,000 million were invested during the first five years of the new century. According to Nayan Parikh, Chairman of Textile Committee, India will surpass the target of exports of US$ 50 billion by 2010.[1]

COMPETITIVENESS OF INDIAN T&G INDUSTRY IN THE GLOBAL MARKET AND TRADE PERFORMANCE

The T&G industry in India has several advantages in the global market. It has a strong multi-fibre base in cotton, jute, and man-made fibre; it has the largest loomage and the second-largest spindlage in the world; a wide range of products, with a wide range of production technology, ranging from hand spun–hand woven khadi to highly sophisticated IT-based technology (Singh and Kundu, 2005); and a vast pool of skilled labour, dynamic entrepreneurship, and vibrant design capacity. It also has a flexible production system, huge domestic market, and a wide production base within the country. In short, India has a good supply chain to enable it to take advantage of the new environment.

India had already acquired export markets, particularly in the EU and the US, when the quotas expired. Though India started late due to its inward-looking policy, the textile exports increased very rapidly, from US$ 1 billion in 1980 to US$ 6.8 billion in 2003. The exports of garments also increased from US$ 1 billion in 1990 to US$ 6.6 billion in 2003. Taken together,

India's T&G exports accounted for 21 per cent of merchandise exports in 2003 (Ministry of Textiles, 2005). Eighty-three per cent of India's clothing exports and 52 per cent of India's textile exports at present are for the US and the EU (CMIE, 2007). Unlike other countries, however, growth of exports in India took place without any significant presence of FDI, mainly through domestic capital and efforts/technology (in the case of China, one-third of export of apparel was by foreign-invested firms while the top 10 companies exporting textiles and apparels are all Indian companies).[2] Also, exports preceded entry of global buyers like Walmart and Nike, who entered much later; and the rapid progress in the integration of the textile industry in the global market came about without India entering into any Regional Trade Agreement (RTA) or Free Trade Agreement (FTA) with other countries (Tewari, 2005).

The inward-looking policy in the past that allowed growth of domestic industry seems to be responsible for this performance. The small-scale dominated and segmented structure of the T&G industry, a consequence of the inward-looking strategy, has inadvertently helped the industry in acquiring export market in the post-liberalization and post-quota period (Tewari, 2005). The T&G industry developed due to the protectionist policies; the large and diversified base of the industry emerged because of the inward policy that enabled the industry to grow to meet the large local market; the textile machinery industry developed to meet the local needs; and a sound technology has been created within the country. The segmentation and decentralization arising from the pressure in the past to remain in the small scale industry (SSI) sector forced firms to learn how to manage batch products and variability in orders. It made them efficient and flexible in the global markets, particularly for small EU buyers. This prevented 'Walmartization' of the Indian T&G industry. Again, it helped in developing designing, as many small and medium units had their own designing.[3] India's public and private fashion institutions are a great strength in the garment industry, which is capable of catering to the changing trends and demands (BERIC, 2004). And finally, India's small batch production has offered an opportunity for firms to capture the high-end value added, higher quality, automated apparel of complex and variable design.

On the other hand, the segmented structure is also a major constraint in the global market after the expiry of the quotas. As Nathan (2007) observes, the government restrictions that did not allow the industry to grow led to its segmented character and prevented it from emerging as a labour-intensive industry. India missed the bus of low-technology labour-intensive production.[4] According to him, India's competitiveness in the post-quota period is adversely affected by the predominance of small-scale units and fragmented structure. First, India is not in a position to meet demand from large global buyers like Walmart and Nike who account for 40 per cent of the US and EU retail markets. Second, India's response would be mainly in high value-added upper-end market and not much in low-end low value-added market that is more labour-intensive in nature and that can provide massive employment to less skilled workers. Third, small units, with their relatively high costs (compared to the costs of large-scale units abroad) find it difficult to survive in the domestic market due to the increased competition from outside. In short, the relatively more labour-intensive small and medium enterprises (SME) sector in the country finds it difficult to compete with the large-scale units in the global market. As Nathan (2007) puts it, it is not labour laws but the historical legacy of reservation to SSIs that is a constraint for the T&G industry in the expanding global markets.

In short, due to the past policies, India has advantages in high-end value-added products, but has problems (these problems can be addressed through proper policy measures) in low-end value-added products, manufacturing of which could employ semi-skilled workers on a large scale. However, as seen earlier, the industry has responded to this constraint by trying to increase the size of its units.

As pointed out by the United Nations Development Programme (UNDP) tracking report (2006) and BERIC (2004), the Indian T&G industry faces several other constraints like low skills/productivity of labour in the SSI and household segments, absence of technological upgrading, poor infrastructure, cumbersome trade procedures, poor market information to producers and potential exporters, lack of adequate financers, and poor R&D efforts. Again, the government and industry associations are trying to address these constraints through several programmes and measures.

To sum up, the Indian textile industry has clear advantages in the competitive global market. Though there are some problems, they are not insurmountable.

As regards the performance of exports in the post-reform and post-quota period, one observes an increasing trend in the export of cotton and man-made textiles as well as in garments since 1991. Exports of textiles and garments have increased continuously during 1992/3–2006/7. The compound annual rate of increase is 12.91, 12.77, and 16.08 per cent for readymade garments, cotton textiles, and man-made textiles respectively, during the period 1992–93 to 2006–07 (CMIE, 2007). Exports of handicrafts have, however, declined in recent years. Though appreciation of the Indian rupee against the US dollar resulted in a temporary setback, the exports show a rising trend in the post-quota period.

RESTRUCTURING OF T&G INDUSTRY AND LABOUR AND EMPLOYMENT

Restructuring of units became necessary in the liberalized environment, first, because the global market is change-oriented and unstable due to changing demand, particularly in this fashion-oriented industry. Units have to be flexible to adjust to this changing demand. Second, due to the high level of competitiveness, there is a need to keep production costs at the minimum, which calls for restructuring. As it is relatively easy to reduce labour costs, there is a tendency to restructure to reduce the same.

Though limited data are available to measure how the units in the industry have restructured in the new environment, there is some evidence from the available studies. Broadly, two ways have been adopted by the industry to face the global competition. One way is to integrate at the lower end of the market by producing low and medium value-added products. This has been done largely by reducing labour cost (wages) and lowering labour and environmental standards, that is, race to the bottom. The other way is to increase value of products by technological improvements and by product differentiation, and thus advancing from comparative advantage–based resource endowments to what M. Porter (1994) calls competitive advantage, which can be achieved through innovations and upgrading. Under this approach, units are producing high value-added products to enter the high end of the market.

In other words, there is a large segment of the industry that is producing low/medium value-added products through subcontracting, outsourcing, and informalizing; there is another segment that is getting into high value-added products. The former is dominated by contract workers, casual workers, and homeworkers with relatively low skills and low productivity; the latter is increasing the size of production units because high value-added products need capital-intensive technology and skilled and stable workforce. Since global retailers would like to deal with a smaller number of large producers in the post-quota regime, large producers have raised their size through vertical integration while small producers have raised their size by forming umbrella organizations of producers to meet the huge demands of large retailers (discussion with Chairman, Textile Committee). The increasing size is also facilitated by the de-reservation of garment industry from the SSI reservation list. The average size of unit of production in the T&G industry is already observed to be increasing in the post-quota period (Tewari, 2005). Large units are observed to be increasing their size by forward integration, that is, integration of yarn makers and spinning mills with garments manufacturing,[5] while small and medium knitwear and garment exporters are using backward integration to increase the size to take advantage of the new global opportunity. For example, a vibrant small firm-based knitwear export cluster in Tirupur has several small-scale units adopting aggressive modernization with backward linkages to turn into medium and large units (Singh and Sipra, 2007). The Apparel Export Promotion Council (AEPC) has also observed that the number of exporters of garments has declined drastically after the expiry of the quotas (2006).

What is interesting to note, however, is that along with increasing the size, large units are opting for a thin core and 'permanent' employment. The rest of the workers are employed as contract workers on the factory premises or in outsourced small and household units as informal workers. There is, therefore, a wide and widening gap between the skilled and professional workers (who are core workers enjoying high salaries and secured employment) and semi-skilled and unskilled workers (who work mainly as casual, contractual, and temporary workers; earn low wages; and have low social protection).

As we shall see later, women's share is disproportionately high and also increasing in the low end of the workforce but declining in the high end, as they are getting crowded in the low-skilled, low-wage employment.

Another mode through which a few units in the industry are getting integrated with the global economy is diversification into non-clothing application of textiles, known as 'technical textiles'; that is, non-woven textiles that are used in specialized products in industries. Since India has the capability to produce these textiles, the Government of India, in collaboration with the private sector, has decided to specialize in technical textiles. The plan is to raise the Indian share in the global market from the present 6 per cent (US$ 107 million) to 10 per cent by 2010 (EPW Editorial, 2002). This segment, which requires highly sophisticated machinery and highly skilled labour, will raise employment of skilled workers, mainly male workers. The low level of literacy and skills of women, on the one hand, and low mobility and domestic constraints on them, on the other hand, will act as major restrictions to women's entry into this new area of development in the T&G industry.

EMPLOYMENT AND WAGES IN T&G INDUSTRY

Table 7.1 presents data on employment generated in the T&G industry in India. It shows that the industry employed 34.42 million persons in 2001 and 40.15 million persons in 2006–7. The table also shows that the handloom sector, a highly decentralized sector with a wide range of products that combine traditions and heritage of Indian culture, is most employment intensive. The employment in this segment has declined because this sector, which was protected and subsidized for heritage and employment, is now opened to competitive markets (Textile Policy, 1985; and Government of India, 2000).

About 88.77 per cent workers in the textile industry and 92.91 per cent workers in the garments industry are in the unorganized sector (NSSO, 2005). This implies that only 10 per cent workers in this industry are entitled to regulated working conditions and full social security benefits. The share of women in the unorganized workers is much bigger, for both textiles and garments, than that of male workers.

One observes large gender inequalities in all labour market outcomes of the industry. Gender inequalities are reflected in employment and unemployment, industrial and occupational segregations, wages and related benefits, and access to improved skills, productivity, and upward mobility. The following paragraphs discuss these.

Working Conditions in the Organized T&G Sector

Employers in the organized sector are less inclined to employ women as 'permanent' workers due to the financial obligations of providing maternity benefits, crèches, separate toilets and rest rooms on the factory premises, and special provisions like nursing breaks and facilities to pregnant women. Women are also perceived as less mobile, more absent from work (due to domestic responsibilities), and less willing and less qualified/capable of taking up responsible jobs. Employers, therefore, tend to employ women mainly as temporary, casual, or contract workers, who are either young unmarried girls (without domestic responsibilities) or elderly women who have completed the task of raising a family. In the relatively new garments factories, young unmarried women are hired as temporary workers. The net result is that the share of women workers in the total 'permanent' workers is very small.

This marginalization of women workers in the organized sector is likely to be intensified in the post-quota period because of the increased demand for skilled labour in the sector. Since the overall literacy and skill levels of women are low in the country, they will fail to take advantage of 'permanent' jobs in the organized sector.

An additional source of insecurity for organized workers, including women workers, is the poor support in the event of downsizing and loss of employment in the process of restructuring of units (which has increased in the competitive environment). Even if the T&G industry as a whole is likely to gain in the country, there will be some units that will be downsizing or closing down. It is necessary to protect the affected workers during the period of frictional unemployment and help them in moving from one employment to another. The former requires unemployment insurance, while the latter requires employment services that provide counselling, information on available jobs (labour market information), training/re-training, and redeployment. Since these facilities are not provided by the present employment exchanges, workers who lose their jobs are left to fend for themselves. The studies by Patel (1999) and Breman (2004) have documented this vulnerability of organized textile workers very accurately. The studies have shown that in the wake of large-scale closure of textile mills in the 1980s and 1990s, workers suffered not only in terms of loss of jobs, but also in terms of non-payment of their dues including social security payments. These workers were forced to fall back on precarious low-paid unorganized sector jobs (Berman, 2004).

Working Conditions in the Unorganized Sector

In the case of unorganized workers, the working and living conditions are much worse than that of organized sector workers, whose conditions have been discussed above. Employers prefer to employ workers outside their premises in subcontracted units and as home-based workers because it reduces the overheads of employing workers, gives employers the freedom of using or not using workers as and when needed, scattered workers prevents from unionizing easily and bargaining for better terms, and saves on payment of social security benefits to workers.

Several micro studies have given accounts of the living and working conditions of unorganized workers in the T&G industry in India, showing how hard pressed and exploited these workers are and to what extent they are insecure and vulnerable. Neetha's (2002) study of knitwear workers in Tirupur, a major garment centre that exports more than 80 per cent of the total exports of cotton knitwear from India, shows that production in this centre is organized in such a way that most of the processes are contracted out to smaller units and to home-based workers. As a result, these workers, 70–80 per cent of whom are women, work seven days a week, in unhealthy environments, and without any social protection. According to the author, this industrial cluster is a classic case of feminization of labour and segmentation of labour market brought out through subcontracting. Though the fragmentation and dispersion of the industry has increased women's employment, disorganization and informalization have reduced women workers to production machines without any benefits (Roy Chowdhury, 2005).

Jeemil Unni's study, which has documented the insecurities of informal T&G workers in Gujarat (Unni and Rani, 2002), shows that these workers suffer from income insecurity (due to the irregular and uncertain nature of their work as well as low wages), employment insecurity (due to lack of ensured work), and skill insecurity (arising from their low skills and poor scope for skill upgrading). These workers also suffer from insecurity of food, health, education, shelter, etc. In short, informal workers in this industry, in the almost total absence of any provisions for social protection, including unemployment insurance, are left to fend for themselves.

Homeworkers, who operate in the household sector, are not fully wage workers as there is no guarantee that the employer will buy all their products. Products are rejected on quality grounds or simply not bought due to fluctuations in the market. Many of these workers need support in terms of technology upgrading, credit, marketing, and other infrastructure to upgrade their units into healthy ventures. Organization of such workers/self-employed people on a large scale can help in improving their position in the labour market. Non-governmental organizations (NGOs) like SEWA, Fabindia, and DESI have produced such models by organizing garment workers around production systems that successfully combine livelihood enhancement, heritage, and modern professionalism.

Employment in EPZ/SEZ Apparel Parks

In order to promote exports of T&G, the government has introduced several schemes, like textile parks, export promotion zones (EPZs), and special economic zones (SEZs), by creating excellent infrastructure and conducive business environment to encourage FDI, technical transfer, and knowledge spillover—to attract Indian and multinational companies to invest, to promote employment generation and increase in productivity and earnings of workers, and to promote rapid industrial growth in the economy. Though no well-researched studies are available on the working and living conditions of T&G workers in textile parks/EPZs, similar surveys in other industries have indicated that labour standards are given a back seat in these parks. Workers, particularly women workers, are forced to work long hours, earn low wages, and suffer from repressive conditions in general (Diwan, 2003). It is observed that employers are supported by officials, even from the department of labour, to reduce cost of production by reducing wages and other labour costs (Diwan, 2001).

To sum up, conditions of workers, particularly women, are far from satisfactory in the organized sector, unorganized sector, as well as in specially designed parks and EPZs. Clearly, labour in general and women in particular have been used for globalization of the industry but have been by-passed by its benefits.

EMPLOYMENT AND WAGES IN T&G INDUSTRIES

According to an estimate by the Textile Committee (2006), the increase in employment is expected to be 25 million by 2010, bringing the total employment in the industry to about 60 million. Of the additional 25 million, 12–15 million will be needed in the apparel sector (11 million skilled labourers, as estimated by AEPC [2005]). Though this projection may fall short slightly, thanks to the appreciation of the rupee against the US dollar, it is certain that this sector has and will experience a large increase in employment.

The employment, however, has not kept pace with the rapid growth of the industry in the post-liberalization period, particularly in the organized sector. In spite of the capital growing at more than 13 per cent per year in the organized sector, the employment growth rate was 0.21 for textiles and 3.73 per cent for garments during 1989–94. As against this, growth rates of employment are much higher in the unorganized sector, particularly in the 1990s, when the rate of growth of employment was 14.44 per cent per year (Unni and Rani, 2005). This indicates that the organized sector is becoming more capital intensive while the unorganized sector is becoming more labour intensive. The labour productivity is growing much faster in the organized sector than in the unorganized sector. A study by K.P. Kannan and G. Ravindran observes that this trend of very low growth of employment in the organized sector has continued during the recent period also (Kannan and Ravindran, 2009).

A striking feature of the table is that both the T&G industries have shown a rapid growth in capital investment and in output since 1989–90. The growth of the organized sector is particularly phenomenal where capital has grown by 13–15 per cent per year (Reports of the NSSO Rounds on Employment and Unemployment, 1993–94, 1999–2000, and 2004–05). The growth in the unorganized sector is much lower, and there has been a decline in the growth rate particularly in the case of the garment industry.

Again, the employment of women has increased at a much faster rate than that of men, in the textile as well as garment industry. In the case of textiles, the employment of women increased at an annual rate of 1.5 per cent during 1994–2001, as against a mere 0.1 per cent for men. The corresponding rates for the garments industry were 33.1 and 8.2 per cent for women and men respectively. As seen earlier, the increase in employment of men, and particularly women, is largely in the unorganized informal sector.

Table 7.1a shows that after 1994–5, the T&G industry shows a rapid growth of unorganized and home-based work for women. Table 7.1b indicates that women predominate as home-based workers, as compared to men. It is to be noted that women's share as home workers in the garments industry increased dramatically from 58.9 in 1994–95 to 93.1 in 2000–1.

The share of home-based workers in the textiles industry, however, declined during 1994/5–2000/1. This indicates that textiles are shifting to non–home based venues gradually, may be because the need is felt to raise the size of production units to produce high value-added textiles for the global market. Table 7.1b also shows that women's share in the home-based workers in the textiles industry is declining. Though there is a decline in the share of home-based male workers, the overall share of home-based workers in the garments industry does show an increase from 48.8 per cent in 1994–5 to 53.7 per cent in 2000–1.

Table 7.1a: Share of Women Workers in Unorganized Work and Home-based Work (in %)

	Unorganized			Home-based		
	1989–90	1994–5	2000–1	1989–90	1994–5	2000–1
Textiles	49.26	45.70	43.24	–	47.2	49.3
Apparel	33.69	15.65	31.09		18.2	49.8
T&G (Total)	40.35	34.60	33.73		43.2	46.3

Source: National Sample Survey Organisation (NSSO) Rounds.

Table 7.1b: Growth of Home-based Workers from 1993–4 to 2000–1 (in %)

	Share of Home-based Workers (1994–5)			Share of Home-based Workers (2000–1)		
	Male	Female	Total	Male	Female	Total
Textiles	72.1	87.4	80.6	70.1	64.3	78.5
Garments	45.7	58.9	48.8	39.1	93.1	53.7
T&G (total)	56.5	83.4	66.9	49.7	83.3	61.2

Source: National Sample Survey Organisation (NSSO) Rounds.

EMPLOYMENT, VALUE ADDED, AND LABOUR PRODUCTIVITY IN UNORGANIZED T&G INDUSTRY

Significant changes have taken place in the value added and labour productivity of workers in the T&G industry, in both organized and unorganized segments. Both textiles and garments show a higher growth rate in the value added in the post-reform period as compared to the pre-reforms period. In the case of textiles, the increase has been from –2.88 per cent in the pre-reform period (1993–94) to 6.26 in the post-reform period (1999–2000). The increase has been from 6.24 to 14.40 per cent in the case of garments (from 1994–2000). However, the employment in textiles has actually declined at a rate of –0.16 per cent. In the case the of textile industry, the increase in labour productivity has been much higher, that is, 6.42 per cent during 1994–2000 (NSSO, 1993–94, 1999–2000; Unni and Rani, 2005). This once again indicates that the textile industry has acquired higher capital intensity. It also indicates that industrial upgrading has taken place with limited social upgrading.

In the case of the garment industry, however, there is an increase in the growth rate of the value added and employment, but the labour productivity has declined by 0.05 per cent per year (NSSO, 1993–94, 1999–2000; Unni and Rani, 2005). This indicates deskilling or declining labour productivity in the garment sector. This implies that unorganized workers in the garment sector are experiencing decline in their productivity in the post-reforms period.

WAGE RATES AND GENDER WAGE GAP

Gender wage gap is an important indicator of the gender inequalities in the labour market. It is frequently calculated as a raw *gender* wage gap using the ratio of average wage rate of women (annual, monthly, weekly, or daily) to that of men. The measure for occupational segregation is an index of dissimilarity which explains the occupational wage gap between men and women, while unexplained wage gap refers to gender-based discrimination, which is measured through a residual technique, also called Oaxaca decomposition.

There are several theoretical presentations that explain the gender wage gaps. Under the neo-classical framework, the major explanations are presented in the human capital theory, the tastes and preference theory, and in the statistical discrimination theory. The *human capital theory*, based on supply-side explanations (for occupational segregation), argues that women possess low human capital as compared to men because (*i*) they invest less in education and skills due to their domestic responsibilities; (*ii*) they are more likely to work as part-time and intermittent workers due to their domestic responsibilities and, therefore, likely to acquire low human capital; and (*iii*) they are likely to get crowded in low productivity occupations due to their low mobility and low human capital (Becker, 1985). Consequently, women are likely to remain in the industries and occupations with low productivity and wages.

The *taste for discrimination theory* argues that earnings of women who are equally productive are likely to differ because employees and employers have irrational preferences (Seguino, 1997). Employers may prefer men for no apparent rational reason. It is argued by Becker (1985), however, that such irrational behaviour may not continue in a highly competitive environment as employers may not be able to afford this luxury when the competition is very high.

The *statistical discrimination theory*, a demand-side explanation of the gender gap, argues that the gender wage gap exists because of the market failure (Berik et al., 2004). Since market information is not perfect, group stereotypes exist. Using these stereotypes, employers discriminate against women workers.

According to the neo-classical theory, gender wage gaps decline with time, as competition in the market removes the information gap, irrational tastes, and preferences. The theory also argues for beneficial impact of trade expansion on workers, as trade expansion will increase the demand for abundant low-skilled workers and reduce large disparities among groups of workers. Trade expansion also changes the skill demand (the demand for skills required for exports increases), as a result of which workers specialize in the skills demanded. This again reduces wage inequalities.

In reality, however, wage discrimination is feasible even under neo-classical framework if it is possible to segment the labour market based on some of the characteristics of workers. For example, women workers are flexible (they prefer to work part time, at home), docile, and less likely to unionize, as well as peculiar in their supply behaviour. It is possible to treat them differently by providing them temporary, part time, or casual employment at low wages. That is, it is possible to employ more women than men to reduce costs to export in a competitive market. This raises the wage gap.

Another factor that leads to increased wage gap is the shift of the industry to high value-added products. Though labour productivity and wages are likely to be higher in this segment of the industry, women are likely to be fewer in this segment due to their low education/skill levels, on the one hand, and their domestic responsibilities, on the other. However, the neo-classical theory is unable to explain this wage gap, as it fails to underscore the roots of discrimination, that is, women's unpaid work. Neo-classical analysis, which assumes unpaid work as 'consumption' or 'not important for labour market' and also assumes unlimited capacity of women to undertake unpaid work, is inadequate to explain why women do not get into higher productivity occupations and why they do not share higher wages with men. In other words, the neo-classical approach ignores the real sources of discrimination that have a significant impact on gender inequality in the labour market (Berik et al., 2004; Young and Wallace, 2009). It ignores the fact that inequalities within household and inequalities in the labour market perpetuate each other. It also ignores the fact that discrimination cannot be isolated as only a labour market issue but there are feedback effects between macroeconomic and global economic developments and discrimination in the labour market. In short, the explanations for the gender wage gap lies in alternative non–neo-classical theoretical frameworks. The roots of the gender wage gaps in the final analysis lie in highly unequal distribution of unpaid domestic work within households.

Table 7.2 shows that the gender wage gap is the highest in the garment sector (2002–5), followed by silk textiles. The gender wage gap has increased in all sectors of the T&G industry between 1974–9 to 2002–5 except for

Table 7.2: Trends in Average Daily Earnings by Gender in the T&G Industry (1974–9 to 2002–5)

Industry	1974–9		1985–92		2002–5		Gender Wage Gap, M/F		
	Male	Female	Male	Female	Male	Female	1974–9	1985–92	2002–5
Cotton Textiles	14.6	11.63	42.8	29.74	78.1	73.24	1.25	1.04	1.07
Woollen Textiles	13.8	8.22	35.8	35.96	69.3	59.24	1.67	1.00	1.17
Silk Textiles	10.4	7.1	30.6	25.15	64	39.56	1.47	1.22	1.62
Synthetic Textiles	0	0	40.6	42.28	62.4	40.86	0.00	0.96	1.53
Jute Textiles	14.7	15.59	42.2	42	89.7	85.99	0.94	1.01	1.04
Textile Garments	11.3	7.12	34	18.61	60.6	37.83	1.58	1.83	1.90
Coefficient of Variation	0.17	0.37	0.16	0.25	0.17	0.37	0.46	0.64	0.46

Source: Occupational Wage Survey, Labour Bureau, Government of India.
Note: Data in INR.

cotton textiles and woollen textiles, which needs careful investigation. However, the wage gaps also increased in these two sectors during the period 1985 to 2002–05. Micro studies have shown that women are largely employed in low levels of occupation, that is, in unskilled or semi-skilled production work, in low-level supervision work, etc. (Neetha, 2002). The studies also indicate gender discrimination reflected in unequal wages for the same or similar work. Since it is possible for employers to employ women at lower terms by segmenting the labour market, the average wage rate of women tends to become much lower than the male wage rate.

Wage Gaps in Organized and Unorganized Sectors

The average daily wage rates in the organized sector are higher than those in the unorganized sector (Table 7.3). However, the gender wage gap is also higher in the organized sector, 3.5 and 1.78 for textiles and garments respectively and 2.54 for the sector as a whole. The corresponding figures for the unorganized sector are 2.01, 1.79, and 1.94. This is perhaps due to the high level of occupation segregation in the organized sector, with women overcrowding in low level of occupations. On the other hand, the occupation-wise differences in wages are lower in the unorganized sector due to the small size of the units, less qualified/less paid management personnel, and predominance of relatively less skilled production workers. Once again, wages for men are higher in the non-home-based textile sector than in the non-home-based garment sector, largely emanating from the higher capital intensity in the textile sector.

Gender Wage Gap in Different Segments of Workers

Neither the organized sector nor the unorganized sector is homogeneous. Workers in the unorganized sector include casual and temporary workers,

Table 7.3: T&G Wage Rates by Gender and by Organized/Unorganized Sectors (1999–2000)

	Organized		Unorganized	
	Male	Female	Male	Female
Textiles	120.49	39.38	59.21	29.45
Ratio (M/F)	3.05		Ratio (M/F)	2.01
Garments	96.15	54.00	65.60	36.61
Ratio (M/F)	1.78		Ratio (M/F)	1.79
T&G (Total)	117.56	46.14	60.63	31.33
Ratio (M/F)	2.54		Ratio (M/F)	1.94

Source: NSSO 55th Round (1999–2000).
Note: Data in INR.

Table 7.4: Daily Wages of Home-based and Non-Home-based Workers in T&G Industry, 1999–2000 (in Rs)

Workers	Textiles			Garments			All Manufacturing		
	Male	Female	Ratio	Male	Female	Ratio	Male	Female	Ratio
Regular Workers									
Home-based	57.32	23.68	2.42	46.44	109.74	0.42	48.01	27.48	1.75
Non-home-based	87.18	33.12	2.63	82.17	51.57	1.59	116.05	58.45	1.99
Casual Workers									
Home-based	42.44	27.36	1.55	38.56	27.65	1.39	43.21	25.1	1.72
Non-home-based	55.53	32.72	1.70	45.86	35.03	1.31	56.78	37.04	1.53

Source: NSSO 55th Round.

job workers or subcontracted workers, homeworkers, part-time workers, and concealed workers such as illegal child labour. The organized sector workers are permanent, regular, temporary, or casual workers. Table 7.4 shows that within regular and casual workers, as well as within home-based and non-home-based workers,[6] there are significant gender-based wage differentials. An interesting finding of the table is that the highest wages are earned by regular non-home-based male workers, while the lowest wages are earned by regular non-home based female workers.

The gender wage gap is generally higher in the case of regular workers, both home-based and non-home-based, than in the case of casual workers. It is indeed worth noting that the gender wage inequalities are the highest at the top end of the labour market; that is, formal, organized, and supposed to be more professionally managed. The lowest gender wage gap is in the case of casual workers.

CONCLUDING OBSERVATIONS

This chapter, based on analysis of selected secondary data and available literature, brings out important developments that are taking place in the T&G industry in India in the context of the expiry of the quotas. The overall prospects for the textile industry are bright after the phasing out of the quotas in spite of the appreciation of the rupee against the US dollar. The industry is growing rapidly and is getting increasingly integrated with the global market in the low and medium value-added products and in the high value-added products. However, both organized and unorganized sector units that are getting integrated have adopted strategies that generate largely informal employment. The labour market outcomes of the growth of the industry are highly unfavourable for workers in general and women workers in particular (UNCTAD, 2001).

In spite of the increased employment, women are not empowered, as they do not enjoy decent work; the new work has not led to any reduction in their horizontal and vertical segregation; women are losing out against men workers with the increasing gender gaps in labour market outcomes; and they are not likely to improve their position within the household as in spite of increased market work, there is no relief in unpaid domestic work. In short, women are losing out in multiple ways, as they are not able to share the gains of the trade in an equal manner.

The major challenge, therefore, is how to pass on the benefits of increased prosperity in the industry to workers: How to ensure decent work to workers in the industry and how to make women workers equal partners with men in employment and wages? The following recommendations are made in this context.

The first major need is to bring unorganized workers under the purview of regulations—labour laws. That is, a comprehensive law should be designed to regulate working conditions, including wages of workers as well as a minimum package of social security for workers in the industry (and in the economy). Apart from careful design, these laws call for an innovative institutional mechanism for implementation.[7]

These laws may reduce competitiveness of the industry in the global market, as it will increase the cost of production. The answer to this argument is that the final goal of development should not be integration with the global market per se, but it should be decent work, gender equality, and justice in the labour market. Also, India should try to expand global markets through better and consistent quality of products, improved efficiency, and other innovative approaches.

There is also a need to integrate gender concerns into mainstream policy making, that is, in the trade policy, industrial policy, labour policy, etc. A coordination committee of all concerned ministries should be set up to plan and monitor labour policy, including conditions of work, social protection, etc.

Considering the fact that gender inequalities in the labour market are rooted in the gender inequalities within the household, the labour policies for gender equalities should address the following concerns of women:

1. Reduction in the burden of unpaid work of women through organizing universal child care, provision of basic infrastructure like water supply and energy, and to help women to achieve a level playing field with men in the labour market;

2. promotion of women's education and skills to enable them to get to the top end of jobs;
3. promotion to self-employed women workers by providing them better access to technology, training, credit, market, etc.; and
4. promotion of organization of women workers;

Labour standards are internal domestic issues and they should not be included in WTO negotiations because (*i*) this is against the national autonomy; (*ii*) external pressures do not help as their impact is limited to tradables only and such measures will be commodity-specific (carpets, garments) and country-specific; and (*iii*) such measures coming from outside will not be sustainable. However, the Indian government must insist on enforcement of the core labour standards.

There is an urgent need to upgrade the present employment exchanges to help workers affected by industrial restructuring by providing them the required services like labour market information, training and re-training facilities, and redeployment facilities. Unemployment insurance scheme to protect incomes of affected workers is very important here. In the competitive environment under globalization, particularly after MFA, these services are absolutely essential to enable workers to transit from one job to another. Employment services should also pay special attention to promoting re-entry of women workers, who leave the labour market temporarily to meet domestic responsibilities.

And finally, there is a need to promote organizations of workers to increase their bargaining strength in the labour market, on the one hand, and to create healthy self-employment ventures through forming cooperatives and federations of cooperatives, on the other. An explicit policy on this will help considerably.

NOTES

1. The author had a long discussion with the Chairman, Nayan C. Parikh, in October 2007.
2. These include Arvind Mills, Indian Rayon, Raymonds, Indo Rama Synthetics, Gokuldas, Alok Industries, Welspun, Abhishek Industries, Bombay Dyeing, and Mahavir Spinning Mills.
3. As has been pointed out by Nike, buyers today prefer India for new and complicated designs to other countries, including China (Hashim, 2004).
4. For example, the low-tech labour-intensive exports from India were US$ 13 billion in 1995, while the corresponding figure for China was US$ 72 billion (Hashim, 2005).

5. For example, Arvind Mills, which was the largest producer of blends and denims in India and the third-largest denim producer in the world, has integrated into jeans and T-shirts production with its own brand.
6. Homeworkers are wage workers who usually get piece-rated wages, while home-based workers include homeworkers as well as self-employed workers working at home.
7. The National Commission on Self Employed in Unorganized Sector has already designed draft bills on this.

REFERENCES

AEPC (The Apparel Export Promotion Council) (2005), *Garment Exports Imports, India*. New Delhi: Apparel Export Promotion Council.

――― (2006), *Statistics on Garment Exports-Imports*. New Delhi: Apparel Export Promotion Council.

Becker, Gary S. (1985), 'Human Capital, Effort, and the Sexual Division of Labor', *Journal of Labour Economics*, 3(1): S33–58.

BERIC (2004), BERIC Davis Companies International Ltd., website: http://www.bericdavis.com/.

Berik, G., Y. van der Meulen Rodgers and J.E. Zveglich Jr. (2004), 'International Trade and Gender Wage Discrimination: Evidence from East Asia', *Review of Development Economics*, 8(2): 237–54.

Breman, Jan (2004), *The Making and Inmaking of an Industrial Working Class*. New Delhi: Oxford University Press.

CMIE (Centre for Monitoring Indian Economy) (2007), *Foreign Trade and Balance of Payments*. Mumbai: Economic Intelligence Service.

Diwan, Ritu (2003), *Ethics of Employment and Exports: Societal Dialogue and Fish Processing Export Units in India*. Mumbai: University of Mumbai.

EPW Editorial (2002), 'Textiles: Preparing for 2005', *Economic and Political Weekly*, 37(3): 110.

Government of India (2000), *National Textile Policy*. New Delhi: Ministry of Textiles.

Government of India (2006), *Official Indian Textile Statistics 2005–2006*, New Delhi: Office of the Textile Commissioner, Ministry of Textiles.

Hashim, Danish A. (2004), 'Cost and Productivity in Indian Textiles: Post MFA Implications', Working paper no. 147. New Delhi: ICRIER.

Hashim, Danish A. (2005), 'Post-MFA: Making the Textile and Garment Industry Competitive', *Economic and Political Weekly*, 40(2): 117–27.

ITGLWF (2005), 'Avoiding Meltdown in the Post MFA World', press release.

Kannan, K.P., and G. Ravindran (2009), 'A Quarter Century of Jobless Growth in India's Organized Manufacturing', *Economic and Political Weekly*, 44(10): 80–91.

MFA (Multi-Fibre Arrangement) Forum (2005), *Unpacking the Phase Out of MFA and Other Research Studies on MFA Phase Out*. London: MFA Forum.

Ministry of Textiles (2005), 'Apparel Park Schemes One and Two'. New Delhi: Government of India.
Nathan, D. (2007), 'Globalization of Labour', *Economic and Political Weekly*, 42(39): 3095–4001.
Neetha, N. (2002), 'Flexible Production, Feminization and Disorganization: Evidence from Tirupur Knitwear Industry', *Economic and Political Weekly*, 37(21): 2045–52.
NSSO (2005), *Report of Employment and Underemployment Survey*. New Delhi: Department of Statistics, Government of India.
Patel B.B. (2002), *Workers of Closed Textile Mills: A Study in Ahmedabad*. New Delhi: Oxford & IBH.
Porter, M (1994), 'Developing Competitive Advantage in India', Publication based on a special talk given to the Confederation of Indian Industy, New Delhi.
Roy Chowdhury, S. (2005), 'Labour Activism and Women in the Unorganized Sector: Garment Export Industry in Bangalore', *Economic and Political Weekly*, 40(22), 28 May–4 June.
Seguino, Stephanie (1997), 'Gender Wage Inequality and Export-led Growth in South Korea', *Journal of Development Studies*, 34: 102–32.
Singh, N. and S.S. Kundu (2005), 'An Analysis of the Competitive Dimensions of Indian Cotton Textile Industry', *India Development Report 2005*. Mumbai: Indira Gandhi Institute for Development Research.
Singh Navsharan and Mrinalini Sipra (2007), 'Liberalization of Trade and Finance: India's Garment Sector in Trade Liberalization and India's Informal Economy', in Barbara Harriss-White and Anushree Sinha (eds), *Trade Liberalization and India's Informal Economy*, pp. 42–128. New Delhi: Oxford University Press.
Tewari (2005), 'Post MFA Adjustments in India's Textile and Apparel Industry: Emerging Issues and Trends', ICRIER Working Paper No. 167. New Delhi: ICRIER.
Textile Committee (2006), *National Household Survey 2006: Market for Textiles and Clothing*. Mumbai: Ministry of Textiles, Government of India.
Textile Commissioner's Office (2007), *Compendium of Textile Statistics*. New Delhi: Ministry of Textiles, Government of India.
The Hindu (2004), 'Prospects for Textile Industry in India in the Post-quota Period', 21 November, Chennai.
Transnationals Information Exchange-Asia (TIE-Asia) (2005), *The Multi Fibre Agreement and Phasing Out of Quotas*. Amsterdam: TIE-Asia.
UNCTAD (2001), 'Globalization and Labour Market', paper presented at the meeting of the ILO on Social Dimension of Globalization.
UNDP (United Nations Development Programme) (2005a), 'Concept Notes for Programme Development on Trade and Human Development Issues in Selected Asia-Pacific Countries', Policy Advisory Support for Country Offices, Trade and Investment Cluster, April. Colombo: UNDP Regional Centre.
―― (2005b), 'Trade Flows and Recent Developments in T&G in Asia-Pacific', Tracking Report. Colombo: UNDP Regional Centre.

UNDP (2006), *Sewing Thoughts: How to Realize Human Development Gains in the Post-quota World: Tracking Report*. Colombo: UNDP Regional Centre.

Unni, J. and U. Rani (2002), *Insecurities of Informal Workers in Gujarat, India*. Geneva: International Labour Office.

——— (2005), 'Impact of Recent Policies on Home-based Work in India', Discussion Paper Series 10, April, UNDP, India.

Young, M.C. and J.E. Wallace (2009), 'Family Responsibilities, Productivity, and Earnings: A Study of Gender Differences Among Canadian Lawyers', *Journal of Family and Economic Issues,* 30(3): 305–19.

8 GLOBAL AGRIBUSINESS VALUE CHAINS, SMALL PRODUCERS, AND WORKERS IN INDIA
Governance, Upgrading Opportunities, Policies, and Strategies

Sukhpal Singh

INTRODUCTION

The analysis of global value chains (GVCs) helps to examine their impacts on upgrading possibilities and strategies by developing country firms. Upgrading involves enhancing the relative position of a firm, which can be achieved through improvements in processes (doing things better), products (making better things), or functional upgrading (moving into higher stages of value addition along the chain like design or marketing) (Schmitz and Knorringa, 2000). The type of chain (buyer- or supplier-driven) and the nature of its governance affect the nature and degree of upgrading. A bulk of the physical parts of most GVCs is located in the developing countries while more significant value-adding parts are in the developed countries. In global markets, whether or not local producers can gain access to GVCs and at which point, is likely to be an important factor in determining whether they will benefit from trade liberalization (Eapen et al., 2003). The issue is not whether to participate in the global commodity chain, but how to do it in a manner that leads to sustainable and equitable income growth. If those who lost from globalization have been those confined to the non-participants in the chains, then the policy implication is to take every step to make them active participants in global production and trade (Kaplinsky, 2000). But there are others who caution about this 'getting on board' approach in general, as there are differences across sectors and within a sector in the organization and governance of the chain, which determine upgrading possibilities and their sustainability (Gibbon, 2003b).

This chapter examines the issue of governance in food chains with a view to locate primary producers and workers in these chains. It analyses the functioning of these chains with special focus on implications for small and marginal producers, and workers in developing countries, including India. The second section examines the context in which governance of these chains has acquired importance, and profiles the governance mechanisms and the issues involved, including upgrading opportunities. The third section profiles the state of primary producers and workers involved in the food and the fibre chains, including supermarkets, in India. The fourth section outlines some of the ways through which the chains can be made more affordable for the small and the marginal producers and farm workers in the developing world, including India. The chapter concludes in the fifth section with broad policy issues and research suggestions.

AGRIBUSINESS VALUE CHAINS AND THEIR GOVERNANCE

The collapse of public trust in government regulatory capacity provided the global buyers in value chains with the opportunity to project themselves as the new and more effective gatekeepers of the food chain. In fact, the retailer acts as a gatekeeper between the producers and the buyers of food products and decides and filters what is to be sold and how. But, simultaneously, the near monopoly power of many retail chain buyers or supermarkets has made these buyers vulnerable to criticism (Freidberg, 2003).

Governance, which is central to value-chain analysis, can be defined as non-market coordination of economic activities. It is nothing but the ability of a firm in the chain to influence or determine the activities of other firms in the chain, which can include defining the products to be produced by suppliers and specified processes and standards to be used (Gibbon, 2001a). The issue of governance refers to the key actors in the chain that determine the inter-firm division of labour and shape the capacities of participants to upgrade their activities (Gereffi, 2001). Chains differ significantly with respect to how strongly governance is exercised, its concentration in the hands of a single firm, and the role of the lead firm (Gereffi et al., 2001).

Governance matters because market access does not automatically follow the dismantling of trade barriers, as the chains that developing-country producers feed into are often controlled by a limited number of buyers. Governance is also needed because the buyer has a better understanding of the demands of the market and of the risks associated with non-compliance with standards (Eapen et al., 2003) and the supplier lacks technical competence or market knowledge. The positioning of a product in the chain—which involves quality, consistency, variety, processing, packing, reliability, and price—requires governance. The need for external or internal governance in a chain also arises due to product differentiation; difficulty for the developing-country producers to meet developed-country market standards; and increased concern with labour, environmental, and product safety standards either due to legal obligations or consumer, government, or non-governmental organization (NGO) pressures (Dolan and Humphrey, 2000). The global chains can be producer-driven or buyer-driven in terms of their internal governance (Gibbon, 2001b). The issue of governance in value chains assumes importance due to reasons of market access for developing countries in the new trade regime, fast track to acquisition of production technologies, distribution of gains, leverage points for policy initiatives, and a funnel for technical assistance.

The important questions in agro-value chains are how to devise a mechanism of regulation that can make upgrading opportunities more socially broad-based and how to devise a way to ensure that the rewards from meeting these opportunities become more predictable (Gibbon, 2001a), as it has been found that upgrading of the local suppliers is affected by the type/mode of governance exercised in the chain (Giuliani et al., 2005). The important questions outside the chain are about the role of government agencies and other external forms of regulation in determining both product and process parameters in value chains, extent of trade-off between coordination and control within the chain, and use of external agencies to certify and regulate firms. Even the question of power relationships within a chain has not been given enough prominence in the discussion on chain dynamics (Gereffi et al., 2001). The division of labour within value chains and the nature of network linkage, which includes connection mechanism, governance style, and power dynamics, are also important research questions (Sturgeon, 2001).

The governance exercised by the global companies has consequences not only for the inclusion and exclusion of firms in the chain but also for the opportunities for upgrading (Opondo, 2000). Furthermore, possibility for upgrading depends on which stage the supplier is in—incipient or advanced; whether the chain is quality- or price-driven; and whether sourcing is direct or indirect. Though buyers keep supporting suppliers even in the advanced stage, the intensity may come down and the buyer may not assist in non-production skills. Similarly, quality-driven chains are more conducive to mutual learning and improvements, and loose sourcing chains have more gaps into which local producers can grow;

therefore, local upgrading is more likely, though direct sourcing can give more regular market access and support capability building for suppliers (Schmitz and Knorringa, 2000).

VALUE CHAINS AND PRIMARY PRODUCERS AND WORKERS

Global Production Networks (GPNs) have led to more of intra-industry trade and not inter-industry trade. Wages paid to labour and prices paid to small producers in the developing world are squeezed between the competition from new entrants in product and labour markets and the pressure from buyer-/retailer-dominated networks who can threaten to exit or relocate to suppress the prices paid to small producers (suppliers) and wages to their workers (Figure 8.1). There can be higher costs of compliance due to change in production and management practices as well as costly market access, and even loss of access to key markets due to global standards, thereby reducing potential competitive advantages like cheap labour (Barrientos and Kritzinger, 2004).

On the other hand, gains from global standards can be significant for labour and environment, improving efficiency and working conditions, raising competitiveness and market access, and providing a way out of the 'race to the bottom'. But there is only limited evidence that compliance leads to competitive advantage for local firms or opens new markets (IDS, 2003). Thus, though there can be larger gains from standards like environmental protection, working conditions' improvement, and efficiency, they may not always percolate down to producers and workers and value chain pressures

---

Shareholder pressure for high returns and consumer expectation of low price
↓
Retailers and brand owners push for lowers prices from producers, flexible and fast production, high technical and quality standards, and better social codes of conduct like labour conditions, wages, or environment; and offload costs and risks down the chain
↓
Chain suppliers and subcontractors seek low cost producers
↓
Factories and farms hire women/migrants/children on short-term contracts, demand extra work, and violate labour rights; and pass the pressure on to farm producers and workers

---

Figure 8.1: Value Chain Pressures Create Precarious Employment and Livelihoods

Source: Andreas et al., 2006.

in competitive markets could rather lead to negative impact on employment and livelihoods of primary producers and workers.

Three major issues of impact of food and fibre supermarkets on local producers include: market concentration and, therefore, producer and consumer interest; downward pressure on producer prices with higher costs and responsibilities; and exclusion of small producers and impact on small local retailers. The procurement practices of supermarkets and large processors have a big impact on, and are an important challenge for, farmers. The downstream segments of the chain (supermarkets and large processors), through their coordinating institutions and organizations such as contracts, private standards, sourcing networks, and distribution centres, are reformulating the rules of the game for farmers and first-stage processors (Reardon and Berdegue, 2002).

The implications of the rise of supermarkets for farmers do not come from the type of store but from the methods of procurement used and the quality standards applied (Shepherd, 2005). The imposition of new rules of the game in food retailing by supermarkets is made possible by their bargaining power with suppliers, based on their sheer scale of buying, their access to financial capital, and the speed of investment capital rotation. A retailer's market share and the exercise of buyer power are highly co-related. The UK supermarket chain Tesco consistently paid its suppliers 4 per cent below the average price paid by retailers due to its buying power (Stichele et al., 2006). These savings due to buyer power may not even be passed on to or shared with the customers in the form of lower prices. Due to the low prices paid, producers cannot attend to many investments which may be necessary for environmental and social reasons. The objectives of these chains are simultaneously financial and logistic; that is, to increase commercial margins by reducing the cost of the product from the supplier and the cost of the transactions (which are achieved by working to reduce the procurement price using their bargaining power), to lengthen the payment period, and to increase the turnover speed of products in the store by reducing inventories and increasing frequency of deliveries from suppliers to achieve zero inventories and just-in-time operations, thus transferring the management of inventories to the suppliers (Gutman, 2002). Though supermarkets initially offered prices to producers which were higher than those offered by traditional channels, but such farmers incurred extra costs like processing and packaging, marketing, transport, and other transaction costs unlike their counterparts in traditional channels (Cadilhon et al., 2006).

In general, supermarkets purchase larger volumes and create new systems of procurement; that is, they deal directly with individual growers, or specialized wholesalers or suppliers. Most of the time, they work with multiple channels of supplies and insist both on lower price and higher quality, meaning that only efficient and large growers would be able to work with them in the long run. They used both fixed and variable pricing methods and delayed payments up to as long as 60–90 days despite regulations to pay within week in some countries like Malaysia. Furthermore, farmers need to make a large investment in order to be able to supply to supermarkets successfully despite credit constraint and lack of production or marketing associations in the absence of any targeted government policy. This leads to their exclusion from value chains (Ghezan et al., 2002). Supermarket practices in fresh-produce supply chains which undermine labour standards are: placing same-day orders, pressuring workers to do unplanned overtime in pack houses; demanding complex packaging and labelling standards without additional payments to producers; using online auctions, putting producers on price competition; last minute breaking of agreed orders without alternative markets for producers; and using price-cutting promotions to hit sales targets, leaving producers to bear the cost of lower prices (Oxfam, 2004).

Though competition from supermarkets improves quality standards in local markets, it creates problems for small producers, who lose this traditional market as well due to failure to meet higher standards. Further, those supplying to supermarkets do not have any benchmark to compare their prices, as there is no wholesale market. Rationalization of grower numbers is another implication of supermarket procurement. In 2002, GIANT had 200 vegetable suppliers in Malaysia which were only 30 in 2004 (Shepherd, 2005).

The more common supermarket malpractices include asking for payment to be on the supplier list; threats of de-listing if supplier price is not low enough; payment from producers for various promotions and opening of new stores; rebate from producers as a percentage of their supermarket sales; minus margins whereby suppliers are not allowed to supply at prices higher than the competitor price; delayed payments; penalties for failing to supply agreed quantities; lowering prices at the last minute when the supplier has no alternative; changing quantity and quality standards without notice and support; just-in-time systems to avoid storage and inventory costs; removing suppliers from lists without good reason; logistical conditions like form and frequency of product delivery, ex-post discounts at the time of payment without previous notification, slotting fees for shelf space, fees for risk sharing of new product launch, manufacture of private label products for retailer as a condition for supply, charging high interest on credit, and using contracts that cannot be enforced by suppliers (Gutman, 2002; Shepherd, 2005; Stichele et al., 2006). These practices hamper upgrading of suppliers into better producers and into processing and marketing.

In 2005, Carrefour was fined in South Korea for unfair business practices; that is, forcing suppliers to cut prices to save 1.737 billion won on supply order for 10 months. It was also accused of intentionally delaying signing of contracts with suppliers (*The Hindu Business Line*, 5 July 2006). It was also fined US$ 170,000 in Indonesia by the Indonesian Business Competition Authority (KPPU) in 2005 for not sourcing goods from a listed supplier who then went bankrupt, which was considered an unfair competition practice. It was also asked to stop minus margin practices. Its agreement was found to include listing fees, fixed rebate, minus margin, terms of payment, regular discount, common assortment cost, opening cost/new store, fees for bi-weekly advertisements, and penalties. Its listing fee was significantly higher than competitors and was applied before the suppliers could sell in its supermarkets (Stichele et al., 2006). Tesco and Asda in the UK have been charged with sending threatening e-mails to suppliers, farmers, and dairy producers to keep their prices low. The low prices have led many producers out of business (*Down to Earth*, 15 September 2007, p. 17).

Agribusiness companies working with farmers are driven by the profit motive alone most of the time and, therefore, tend to ignore the social dimensions of their operations. The examples of such behaviour include abandoning an area if not profitable to continue and exclusion of small and marginal growers from their operations (Andreas et al., 2006). Besides reneging on contracts and hold-up problems in the guise of quality-based rejection of produce, agribusiness firms may also make farmers dependent on their technology; for example, an animal feed supplied may be formulated to delay the growth cycle or decrease the daily weight gain, resulting in lower productivity and final prices paid to farmers. Also, delayed delivery schedules can lead to farmers receiving lower prices as the quality of produce deteriorates. Firms avoiding transparency in pricing and agribusiness normalization are other problems in contract farming, besides ecological degradation and monoculture (da Silva, 2005). The contracting firms tend to aggravate the natural resource crisis as most of the contracts are short term (one or two crop cycles) and firms tend to move on to new growers and lands after exhausting the natural potential of the local resources, particularly land and water, or when productivity declines due to some other reason (Torres, 1997). The over-exploitation of groundwater, salination of soils, soil fertility decline, and pollution are typical examples of environmental degradation due to contract farming (Siddiqui, 1998). The firms do not care for this as the costs of such effects are externalized for them.

With regard to the impact on local retailers (neighbourhood stores), the spread of supermarkets did lead to 14 per cent reduction in the share of 'mom and pop' stores in Thailand within four years (Stichele et al., 2006). On the other hand, in stores, low wages, job cuts, long and irregular working hours, and non-contract workers are the abuses reported to be resorted to cut labour costs. In Vietnam, supermarket Metro Cash & Carry employed 1.2 workers per tonne of tomatoes sold as compared to 2.9 persons per tonne employed by traditional wholesale channels (Cadilhon et al., 2006). This meant loss of employment due to supermarket retail chains or higher efficiency of its workers as Metro produce was 'ready to retail' when it arrived from suppliers unlike the wholesale channel. Thus, whereas supermarket chains can lead to new and better employment generation, improvement in food quality, and lower consumer prices, and provide new avenues for agricultural development, the negative impacts include: exclusion and squeezing out of small producers from these chains due to high cost and risky investments needed, and decline of the traditional wholesale markets important for small producers (Cadilhon et al., 2006).

Even at the bottom of the value chains, that is, farms and pack houses, GVCs have led to casualization, feminization, flexiblization of work and gendering of tasks and wages, due to pressures of price competition which lead to squeezing of profits of exporters, just-in-time production aimed at reducing inventories, demand for new products, and category management at the supermarket level. This has meant low-skill jobs with low wages being given to women with no other benefits or social protection, and to which even codes of conduct do not apply (Dolan, 2004).

FOOD VALUE CHAINS IN INDIA: IMPACTS ON PRIMARY PRODUCERS AND WORKERS

Small producers have also been excluded from various value chains which operate with contract farming schemes at the producer level in India. It is mostly medium and large farmers who have been beneficiaries of such backwardly coordinated value chains (Singh, 2002). The exclusion of small and marginal farmers from high-value chains is because of lack of resources and high risk involved, with the exception of crops like gherkins which are labour intensive and require family labour. The enforcement of contracts, high transaction costs, quality standards, business attitudes and ethics like non/delayed/reduced payment and high rate of product rejection, and weak bargaining power of the small growers contribute to their exclusion from contract farming (Kirsten and Sartorius, 2002). Furthermore, lack of information about prices, markets, and lack of financial means hamper the bargaining position of the growers. There have been instances of lack of sustainability of contract arrangements and 'agribusiness normalization'; that is, supply chain driving firms reducing procurement prices over time in order to cut down their costs and resorting to open market procurement to weaken the bargaining power of the contract growers.

There are no formal written contracts with primary producers as the buyers do not want to share the risk of the growers. The system of no written contracts and consignments places the financial risks solely with the producers/suppliers. The supermarkets can eliminate all financial risk from their end of the chain due to this direct procurement from growers as they do not need to maintain stocks, carry no price risk, and have no commitment to buy. Furthermore, they have control over and traceability of production, reduced risk of low-quality produce, can impose standards and production requirements anytime, and lower prices as there are no intermediaries. This puts farming businesses under pressure, which is passed on to the workers on the farms, often women, resulting in deteriorating work conditions, very low pay, and casual employment (Stichele et al., 2006).

The chains give market-based prices to their farmer vendors. Is it fair, because market prices are highly volatile in India? Could prices be determined instead by calculating the cost of production, as contract farming is based on that? If market prices are efficient, why did the chain have to go to growers? This is a serious issue, as even a significant premium over market price may not help a farmer if open market prices go down significantly, which is not uncommon in India. Even in organic produce supply chains, this is the norm though organic prices are separately determined at the consumer end. Thus, the issue remains of what is a fair price for the primary grower in a chain, as there is little transparency in pricing and costing of operations (IFAD, 2005).

The firms also manipulate provisions of the contracts in practice, for example, in the case of broiler chickens in Tamil Nadu, where they picked up birds before the due date or delayed it depending on the demand, which resulted in losses for contract growers, besides delaying payments by up to 60 days. But growers were locked into these contracts due to the firm-specific fixed investments they had made (Singh and Asokan, 2005). The contracts protect company interest and pass costs to the farmer, without covering farmer's production risk (such as crop failure), and retain the right of the company to change price (Singh, 2002).

Several European supermarket chains such as Sainsbury's, Safeway, and Tesco have extended their procurement into India with GlobalGAP (Good Agricultural Practices) standards for local suppliers and farmers. Tesco alone procures greens worth Rs 250 million annually from India and has its own global standard for food called Nature's Choice (Srinivas, 2005). Some of the local companies involved with these chains are Mahindras and Bharti-Rothschild. There are more than 400 farmers in Maharashtra, Andhra Pradesh, and Uttarakhand supplying to these chains. The crops include litchi, mango, grape, potato, and gherkin. Supermarkets in India presently account for a very small share of fresh produce retail sales unlike South-east Asian countries. There are many Indian supermarket chains like Food World, Nilgiris, Spencer's, Reliance Fresh, Birlas' 'More', ITC Fresh, Future Group's Food Bazaar, Tata's Star India Bazaar, and Subhiksha which are procuring fruits and vegetables either from wholesale markets (Agricultural Produce Marketing Committee [APMC] markets) or from growers without any formal contracts and at prices which are linked to market prices. Besides, there are fast food chains like McDonald's, Pizza Hut, and Nirula's which procure from large suppliers like Radhakrishna Foodland, Trikaya Agriculture, and Adani Fresh which have emerged as dedicated wholesale suppliers to these food retail chains.

Thus, supermarkets in India presently use a wide variety of fresh fruit and vegetable procurement practices. At present, the following channels can be seen:

1. direct, uncontracted purchases from farmers at individual supermarkets or their collection centres;
2. purchases from wholesalers, who either work directly with farmers or buy from wholesale markets;
3. direct purchase from *mandi* (wholesale market) or through commission agents;
4. purchases through independent procurement companies (dedicated suppliers) who often work with farmers approved by the supermarkets chains (preferred suppliers);
5. purchases through informal farmer groups, farmer associations, or cooperatives;

6. purchases through large individual contract farmers, who often subcontract part of the supply to smaller farmers; and
7. multiple channels.

But many of the supermarkets in India may not go for direct linkages with producers as there are a large number of contracting agencies/companies which can cater to their needs. Even when they procure from growers directly, it is non-contract procurement without any support being provided to the growers.

Contract farming has led to increased incidence of the practice of reverse tenancy in India as the returns from farming have increased for those who can invest in it and take the risk of crop failure, and these are mostly the large landholders or those who have other non-farm sources of income. This is certainly leading to higher orders of economic differentiation in the region (Singh, 2002).

The newly emergent organic produce supply chains in India have also been found to exclude small producers due to reasons of high certification costs, smaller volumes they produce, and tighter control by the chain leaders in the absence of any local market outlets for the organic products (Raynolds, 2004; Singh, 2009). The important issues in organic produce chains are the exclusion and inclusion of primary producers by the buyers, product and production standards, and timelines for produce delivery. The farmers are the weakest link in the chain. They are not ensured of sustainable incomes in these chains which function in the absence of the state and the presence of increasingly globalized markets.

The question of who owns the organic certificate is crucial. The growers are locked into the contract due to the firm-specific fixed investments they make by going organic and are not able to sell elsewhere without certification. This raises a governance issue as it limits the market options for growers to those dictated by the certificate owner and, thus, diminishes their interest and commitment to organics. Though the organizer pays certification fees, they are not so high as to not give any right to the grower over his/her farm's certification (IFAD, 2005).

The fair trade players are also attempting mainstreaming strategy for rapid growth in market share by encouraging corporations, governments, major retailers, and other large economic actors to support fair trade. In fact, by mainstreaming fair trade products, there may be a risk of including the original targets of fair trade criticism, that is, powerful global corporations, among fair trade's key participants. Furthermore, even in fair trade channel, it has been seen that the agencies find it difficult to pass on the fair trade premium to non-producer stakeholders like farm workers for whom they are meant, and there is lack of fair trade standards due to resistance from farmers (Singh, 2009).

In contracted farms, there is use of low-paid female adult and child labour for reasons of 'nimble fingers'; that is, it is docile, low wage, and quality labour, besides existence of poor working conditions for such labour. Girls were preferred in cottonseed production because their wages were lower than those of adults, they worked longer hours and more intensively, and were generally easier to control. Though the agreement obliged these female children to work for only one season (six–nine months), in practice, they tended to work for several years for the same farmer. In some cases, girls were brought in from outside the local area and made to stay in the employer's house or cattle sheds throughout the season (Singh, 2003).

The employment of female children in cottonseed farms had many impacts on gender relations at the household level. For example, girls had more responsibility for household provisioning, and with more money coming in, men might withdraw from work and often resort to drinking. There were health implications, including menstrual problems, for girls involved in cottonseed work due to higher levels of pesticides used in this crop than in ordinary cotton cultivation (Singh, 2003). This was similar to the conditions of grape-farm workers in Maharashtra where major problems faced by women grape workers included lower-backache, neck pain, headaches, and menstrual problems. The women working on grape farms had the highest morbidity rate among all groups of women agricultural workers (Rath, 2003). There is a similar practice in Gujarat where migrant female child labour is used and abused in cotton seed production, especially Bt cotton seed (Singh, 2008).

Contract farms under company supervision were little more than 'factories in the fields' from the point of view of labour. Their labour system resembled that of the industrial sector because of timing, quality, and standardization requirements which could not be met by mechanical methods. This required 'quality labour', that is, efficient, timely, and paced; 'flexible labour', that was readily available and cheap; and 'docile labour', in other words, politically trouble-free labour. These conditions were met more easily by women, who were perceived to be homemakers and, therefore, low cost, sincere, and more obedient workers. This amounted to manipulation of the cultural understanding of gender. Women and girls mostly transplanted and harvested tomatoes and harvested and graded potatoes in the Indian Punjab as such workers were more easily available, cost less, were more honest, and better suited to picking and transplanting jobs. Mothers with infants also worked in contract farms, and infants and children remained on the farm throughout the day, with implications for their health and nutrition. There was a piece-rate system of wages linked to output. But wages soon became depressed with large seasonal inflow of migrant male labour. In fact, migrant agricultural labour accounted for 25 per cent of the total agricultural labour force in Punjab. The daily wage rate for female workers was only two-thirds of that received by men. In tomato harvesting, half-day wages were also common as harvesting should be completed before noon (Singh, 2003).

Organic farming is suggested to have more equitable gender distribution of farm labour and power by challenging large-scale business agriculture and its associated ideologies through its focus on small-scale, less mechanized, and more labour-intensive farm processes, less reliance on commercial inputs, increased diversity and emphasis on local markets and local farmer knowledge; though higher labour intensity is not really due to organic practices but due to the nature of crops grown (Hall and Mogyorody, 2007). The organic food chains also do not show any differences in gender division of labour and treatment of labour on the farms (Hall and Mogyorody, 2007; Singh, 2009). In fact, this is the result of the dominance of organic produce markets in the West by supermarkets, for which organic produce is targeted, and the 'mainstreaming' of organic by supermarkets is leading to most of the ills of conventional supply chains ('conventionalization') into the organic sector as well (Raynolds, 2004; Hall and Mogyorody, 2007).

STRATEGIES AND POLICIES FOR BETTER GOVERNANCE, SMALL PRODUCER PARTICIPATION, AND UPGRADING

Market access for small producers depends on (*i*) understanding the markets, (*ii*) organization of the firm or operations, (*iii*) communication and transport links, and (*iv*) an appropriate policy environment. There are a large number of interventions which attempt market access for small producers, but, on various parameters of ensuring market access, multinational corporations (MNCs) and alternative trade companies and large direct private buyers seem to be better placed (Page and Slater, 2003). Though it is important to be a part of a global value chain to gain access to competitive export markets, there is a danger that too much reliance on those at the head of the buyer-driven chain for design, technical, and marketing assistance may trap exporters and producers into low-level production roles (Tewari, 1999).

Small Producer Inclusion

The exclusion of small farmers from participating in food chains does not appear to be, in any way, automatic (Reardon and Berdegue, 2002). There have been cases of success when public or private assistance to the growers in terms of technical assistance and supply of input credit was made available. Fabindia, an upmarket textile chain in India which has 106 stores across 40 Indian cities and procures from 750 locations, has achieved supply-chain efficiency in textiles and organic food through NGOs, small companies, and individual growers/grower groups (Singh, 2009). The chains should also experiment with different ways of including small growers into their fold.

There is a need to reduce the vulnerability of organic growers due to fluctuations in market prices by offering minimum purchase prices, not market-based premiums as is being done by the chains/contracting companies now. The essence of contract farming, among other things, is a pre-agreed price which reduces farmers' market risk. NGOs and development agencies need to be vigilant about declining organic premiums due to increasing competition and need to plan their responses or alternative market propositions, including cultivating domestic market, more local-level value addition, and local capacity building.

The problem of financing the small organic producers needs to be tackled by finding innovative ways to provide finance and enabling policies like availability of credit that is friendly (or at least neutral) towards organic cultivation, crop insurance and other supportive measures, and subsidies that are friendly (or at least neutral) towards organic farming. For example, in Benin in Africa, the yield of organic cotton per hectare was lower, but this was compensated by waiver of input credit loans (30 percent of gross conventional cotton income) and premium of 20 per cent over the local conventional produce price. The producer price was set at the start of the season and purchase of the entire organic cotton crop was guaranteed. Furthermore, to help the producers of organic cotton—most of whom were illiterate—to organize themselves, a great deal of attention was spent on developing education methods and training programmes (Farmer Field Schools) (Verhagen, 2004).

To overcome the organic certificate ownership malpractice, either farmer or farmers' groups should pay 100 per cent of the cost of certification or share it with some government or development agency where the certificate will be with the farmer or the group, not the agency or the chain organizer. The government agencies should not share the cost of certification with private agencies operating in the organic sector if the purpose is to empower the growers.

Role of Chain Drivers

The standards need to be flexible and interwoven with local conditions if they have to benefit poor workers. They must also involve local stakeholders who reflect the interests of workers in the process of standards setting and monitoring. The policy challenges on standards include standard setting, monitoring compliance, providing assistance to achieve compliance, and sanctions on non-compliance. Much depends on how standards are implemented, monitored, and verified (IDS, 2003). The value chains drivers should promote workers' empowerment throughout the chains by respecting labour standards and conducting joint workplace inspections; make respect for women's rights integral to the company's vision by in-house expertise on ethical issues and incentives for ethical sourcing and business transparency; and integrate these commitments into purchase practices through making labour standards a key sourcing criterion, setting adequate delivery lead times, negotiating fair prices, and working with producers to improve labour standards with financial and technical support (Oxfam, 2004).

Group contracting is another way out. The groups or farmers' organizations like cooperatives not only lower transaction costs of the firms but also lower input costs for the farmers and give them better bargaining power. In contract arrangements with small producers in west African countries, the cotton companies started transferring some of the operational or functional responsibilities, like distribution of inputs, equipment orders, and credit repayment management, to the village associations in the 1970s itself, by making provision of management skills for these tasks. The companies relied on traditional village authority structures for organizing the associations but limited the associations to one per village to simplify company purchasing, delivery, and marketing procedures. This arrangement accounted for a significant part of each cotton company's success (Bingen et al., 2003). Only Spencer's in India delegates post-harvest activity to contract farmers, helping to create capability at the local level. But, unfortunately, contracting companies and supermarket chains have not been very keen to organize or support cooperatives in India. Only recently, a company has organized fruits and vegetable growers into producer companies in Punjab.

Regulation of Value Chains

Regulation of supermarket chains to control or mitigate their market power can be an effective tool to ensure the presence of small growers in value chains, as seen in the case of banana trade regime in the pre-WTO (World Trade Organization) period in the European Union (EU) policy, single channel (monopoly) exports by producer bodies in some exporting countries like South Africa, and regulation of domestic import markets in France (Gibbon, 2003a). Some of the ways to mitigate the ill effects of supermarkets on the primary producers are: ban buying of products below cost and selling below cost; improve local traditional markets for small growers; delay the pace of supermarket expansion; establish mutli-stakeholder initiatives in the chains; support by state/development agencies for small producers; encourage use of fair trade, SA 8000, and ethical trade standard to protect the grower and the labour interest; market orientation of small producers by state and development agencies; and group contracts with the intermediation of local NGOs and other organizations and institutions.

So far as impact on local retailers (neighbourhood stores) is concerned, there is need for a zoning regulation on the pattern of Indonesia (Stichele et al., 2006). Also, provisions for legally binding and clearly worded rules for fair treatment of suppliers, an independent authority like retail commission to supervise and regulate supermarkets for supplier, consumer, and labour interest protection, and support to local retailers are required.

Role of the State

So far as the role of government in value chains is concerned, it can proactively help the stakeholders in the chain to identify opportunities and threats in global value chains. It can also assist producers to enter the chains. Various policy instruments can be used to reposition the key players within the value chain so that they can derive a greater share of the gains (Kaplinsky, 2000).

Above all, the state needs to correct the anti–small producer bias in its public policies. For example, the Government of Punjab, through the Punjab Agri Foodgrains Corporation (PAFC), was reimbursing extension cost to the contract farming agencies/facilitators at the rate of Rs 100 per acre. But doing it irrespective of the size of holding of the contract growers defeated the purpose as it did not ensure that small and marginal farmers, who could afford to pay for extension and needed to be brought into the contract system, were included. The government should also play an enabling role by legal provisions and institutional mechanisms, like helping farmer cooperatives and groups, to facilitate smooth functioning of the contract system, and not intervene in contract farming directly. Besides, there could be enabling policies like availability of credit that is friendly (or at least neutral) towards new crops, crop insurance, and other supportive measures.

Legal protection to growers, like that to subcontracting companies under the Fair Trade Commission (FTC) in Japan, can also be helpful (Sako, 1992). If contract farming is the only flexible production system prevalent in industry applied to farm production, then it is only logical to extend such legal provisions with necessary modifications to farming contracts. The Indian model contract farming agreement is quite fair in terms of sharing of costs and risks between the sponsor and the grower (GoI, 2003). But it leaves out many aspects of farmer interest protection like delayed payments and deliveries, contract cancellation damages if producer made firm-specific heavy investments, inducement/force/intimidation to enter a contract, disclosure of material risks, competitive performance-based payments, and sharing production risks. It is not known how far the model contract agreement will be adopted by the agencies unless it is a conditionality to avail of certain other incentives or policies. In Thailand, even after three years of its notification, the standard agreement was used only by two companies (Singh, 2005).

Role of Producer Organizations and NGOs

The farmers' organizations and NGOs are also needed to monitor and negotiate more equitable contracts with dominant organizers of the chains. These types of organizations have been able to secure the standardization of contracts and their scrutiny by a government agency in the US (Wilson, 1986), and the bargaining groups have negotiated input purchase and output sale collectively (Welsh, 1990). In Japan as well, farmers have managed their relationships with companies well through cooperatives (Asano-Tamanoi, 1988). In Bangladesh, many NGOs like Bangladesh Rural Advancement Committee (BRAC) and Proshika have got into contract farming to supply to domestic supermarkets as well as those abroad. Producers' organizations amplify the political voice of smallholder producers, reduce the costs of marketing of inputs and outputs, and provide a forum for members to share information, coordinate activities, and make collective decisions. Producers' organizations create opportunities for producers to get more involved in value-adding activities such as input supply, credit, processing, marketing, and distribution. On the other hand, they also lower the transaction costs for the processing/marketing agencies working with growers under contracts.

CONCLUSION

The value chains approach can contribute to reducing poverty if it is used strategically and targeted towards poverty reduction. However, this requires a focus on options to support the poor, such as fostering associations, skill development and learning, facilitating contract arrangements, and supporting information and service delivery. Often, it is necessary to combine value chains promotion with a livelihood perspective to enable the poor to enter into and stay in commercial markets. Choosing the right markets and market development strategies is essential to scale up and avoid the 'race to the bottom', which can come only by innovation of products and business models. In this, partnerships with the private sector can come in handy as they can provide technology and help upgrade quality and social standards. The role of policies can be leveraged by pro-poor approaches for sectors where poor producers predominate and facilitating supportive policies as well as social and ecological standards (GTZ, 2007).

The main requirements of small farmers in this changing environment are better access to capital and education. Management capacity is as important as physical capital, and very difficult to provide. Furthermore, collective action to deal with scale requirements must be designed to satisfy new product and process standards or to avoid exclusion from the chain. Collective action through cooperatives or associations is important not only to be able to buy and sell at a better price, but also to help small farmers adapt to new patterns and much greater levels of competition (Farina, 2002). It has been found that collective efficiency also makes a difference to enterprise upgrading, especially in natural resource–based value chains, although this differs across sectors and takes different routes. Strengthening of small farmer organizations is also required, by providing them with technical assistance to increase productivity for the cost-competitive market, providing help in improving quality of produce, and encouraging them to participate more actively in the marketing of their produce (thereby capturing greater value-added from the chain). Finally, the problem of financing small producers needs to be tackled by finding innovative ways to provide finance (Schwentesium and Gomez, 2002).

The labour issues which need to be addressed with a gender perspective are those of skills transfer, choice of technology, working conditions, and terms of work. The organization of labour is another important measure to prevent or eliminate some of the ills of value chains for labour. The associations of contract farm/small factory labour can also be used for monitoring wages and work conditions. In fact, there could be legal provisions to involve labour representatives when companies and growers/growers' groups decide on labour and wage issues. As a civil society intervention, there could be codes of conduct for farmers as regards labour use, which could be enforced by contracting agribusiness firms that should also constantly work towards more ethical and human labour standards.

REFERENCES

Andreas, S., C. Jost, C. Kreiss, K. Meier, M. Pfister, P. Schukat, and H.A. Speck (2006), *Strengthening Value Chains in Sri Lanka's Agribusiness: A Way to Reconcile Competitiveness with Socially Inclusive Growth?* The German Development Institute (DIE) Studies No. 15, March. Bonn: DIE.

Asano-Tamanoi, M. (1988), 'Farmers, Industries, and the State: The Culture of Contrast Farming in Spain and Japan', *Comparative Studies in Society and History*, 30(3): 432–52.

Barrientos, S. and A. Kritzinger (2004), 'Squaring the Circle: Global Production and the Informalisation of Work in South African Fruit Exports', *Journal of International Development*, 16: 81–92.

Bingen, J., A. Serrano, and J. Howard (2003), 'Linking Farmers to Markets: Different Approaches to Human Capital Development', *Food Policy*, 28: 405–19.

Cadilhon J-J., P. Moustier, N.D. Poole, P.T.G. Tam, and A.P. Fearne (2006), 'Traditional vs. Modern Food Systems? Insights from Vegetable Supply Chains to Ho Chi Minh City (Vietnam)', *Development Policy Review*, 24(1): 31–49.

da Silva, C.A.B. (2005), 'The Growing Role of Contract Farming in Agri-Food Systems Development: Drivers, Theory and Practice', Draft Paper, July. Rome: Food and Agriculture Organization.

Dolan, C.S. (2004), 'On Farm and Packhouse: Employment at the Bottom of a Global Value Chain', *Rural Sociology*, 69(10): 99–126.

Dolan, C.S. and J. Humphrey (2000), 'Governance and Trade in Fresh Vegetables: The Impact of UK Supermarkets on the African Horticulture Industry', *Journal of Development Studies*, 37(2): 147–76.

Eapen, M., J. Jeyaranjan, K.N. Harilal, P. Swaminathan, and N. Kanji (2003), 'Liberalisation, Gender and Livelihoods: The Cashew Nut Case: India', Phase-1, Revisiting the Cashew Industry, IIED Working Paper 3. London: International Institute for Environment and Development (IIED).

Farina, E.M.M.Q. (2002), 'Consolidation, Multinationalisation, and Competition in Brazil: Impacts on Horticulture and Dairy Products Systems', *Development Policy Review*, 20(4): 441–57.

Freidberg, S. (2003), *The Contradictions of Clean: Supermarket Ethical Trade and African Horticulture*, IIED Gatekeeper Series No. 109. London: International Institute for Environment and Development (IIED).

Gereffi, G. (2001), 'Beyond the Producer-driven/Buyer-driven Dichotomy: The Evolution of Global Value Chains in the Internet Era', *IDS Bulletin*, 32(3): 30–40.

Gereffi, G., J. Humphrey, R. Kaplinsky, and T.J. Sturgeon (2001), 'Introduction: Globalization, Value Chains and Development', *IDS Bulletin*, 32(3): 1–8.

Ghezan, G., M. Mateos, and L. Viteri (2002), 'Impact of Supermarkets and Fast-Food Chains on Horticulture Supply Chains in Argentina', *Development Policy Review*, 20(4): 389–408.

Gibbon, P. (2001a), 'Agro-Commodity Chains: An Introduction', *IDS Bulletin*, 32(3): 60–8.

—— (2001b), 'Upgrading Primary Production: A Global Commodity Chain Approach', *World Development*, 29(2): 345–63.

—— (2003a), 'Value Chain Governance, Public Regulation and Entry Barriers in the Global Fresh Fruit and Vegetable Chain into the EU', *Development Policy Review*, 21(5–6): 615–25.

—— (2003b), 'The African Growth and Opportunity Act and the Global Commodity Chain for Clothing', *World Development*, 31(11): 1809–27.

Giuliani, E., C. Pietrobelli, and R. Rabellotti (2005), 'Upgrading in Global Value Chains: Lessons from Latin American Clusters', *World Development*, 33(4): 549–73.

GoI (Government of India) (2003), *Contract Farming Agreement and its Model Specifications*. New Delhi: Ministry of Agriculture, Department of Agriculture and Co-operation, 17 September.

GTZ (Deutsche Gesellschaft für Technische Zusammenarbeit) (2007), Conference Report, International Conference: Value Chains for Broad Based Development, 30–31 May, Berlin.

Gutman, G.E. (2002), 'Impact of the Rapid Rise of Supermarkets on Dairy Products Systems in Argentina', *Development Policy Review*, 20(4): 409–27.

Hall, A. and V. Mogyorody (2007), 'Organic Farming, Gender, and the Labour Process', *Rural Sociology*, 72(2): 289–316.

IDS (Institute of Development Studies) (2003), *The Cost of Compliance—Global Standards for Small Scale Firms and Workers*, IDS Policy Briefing 18, May. Brighton: IDS, University of Sussex.

International Fund for Agricultural Development (IFAD) (2005), *Organic Agriculture and Poverty Reduction in Asia—China and India Focus*, Thematic Evaluation, IFAD Report No. 1664, July. Rome: IFAD.

Kaplinsky, R. (2000), 'Globalization and Unequalisation: What can be Learned from Value Chain Analysis?', *Journal of Development Studies*, 37(2): 117–46.

Kirsten, J. and K. Sartorius (2002), 'Linking Agribusiness and Small-Scale Farmers in Developing Countries: Is There a New Role for Contract Farming?', *Development Southern Africa*, 19(4): 503–29.

Opondo, M.M. (2000), 'The Socio-economic and Ecological Impacts of the Agro-industrial Food Chain on the Rural Economy in Kenya', *Ambio*, 29(1): 35–41.

Oxfam (2004), 'Trading Away Our Rights—Women Working in Global Supply Chains', *Oxford Campaign Reports*, Oxford, 4 February.

Page, S. and R. Slater (2003), 'Small Producer Participation in Global Food Systems: Policy Opportunities and Constraints', *Development Policy Review*, 21(5–6): 641–54.

Rath, S. (2003), 'Grape Cultivation for Exports—Impact on Vineyard Workers', *Economic and Political Weekly*, 38(5): 480–9.
Raynolds, L.T. (2004), 'The Globalisation of Organic Agro-Food Networks', *World Development*, 32(5): 725–43.
Reardon, T. and J.A. Berdegue (2002), 'The Rapid Rise of Supermarkets in Latin America: Challenges and Opportunities for Development', *Development Policy Review*, 20(4): 371–88.
Sako, M. (1992), *Prices, Quality and Trust—Inter-firm Relations in Britain and Japan*. Cambridge: Cambridge University Press.
Schmitz, H. and P. Knorringa (2000), 'Learning from Global Buyers', Institute of Development Studies Working Paper No. 100. Brighton: IDS, University of Sussex.
Schwentesium, R. and M.A. Gomez (2002), 'Supermarkets in Mexico: Impacts on Horticulture Systems', *Development Policy Review*, 20(4): 487–502.
Shepherd, A.W. (2005), 'The Implications of Supermarket Development for Horticultural Farmers and Traditional Marketing Systems in Asia', Revised Version of the Paper Presented at the FAO/AFMA/FAMA Regional Workshop on 'Growth of Supermarkets as Retailers of Fresh Produce', Kuala Lumpur, 4–7 October, 2004, Rome: Food and Agriculture Organization.
Siddiqui, K. (1998), 'Agricultural Exports, Poverty and Ecological Crisis—Case Study of Central American Countries', *Economic and Political Weekly*, 33(39): A128–36.
Singh, G. and S.R. Asokan (2005), *Contract Farming in India: Text and Case Studies*. New Delhi: Oxford & IBH.
Singh, S. (2002), 'Contracting Out Solutions: Political Economy of Contract Farming in the Indian Punjab', *World Development*, 30(9): 1621–38.
―――― (2003), 'Contract Farming in India: Impacts on Women and Child Workers', Gatekeeper Series Paper No. 111. London: International Institute for Environment and Development (IIED).
―――― (2005), 'Role of the State in Contract Farming in Thailand: Experience and Lessons', *ASEAN Economic Bulletin*, 22(2): 217–28.
―――― (2008), 'Gender and Child Labour in Cottonseed Production in India—A Case Study of Gujarat', *Indian Journal of Labour Economics*, 51(3): 445–58.
―――― (2009), *Organic Produce Supply Chains in India—Organization and Governance*. New Delhi: Allied Publishers.
Srinivas, N.N (2005), 'Field Test: You Reap What You Sow', *The Economic Times*, Ahmedabad, 30 March.
Stichele, M.V., S.V. Wal, and J. Oldenziel (2006), *Who Reaps the Fruit? Critical Issues in the Fresh Fruit and Vegetable Chain*. Amsterdam: Centre for Research on Multinational Corporations (SOMO).
Sturgeon, T.J. (2001), 'How do We Define Value Chains and Production Networks?' *IDS Bulletin*, 32(3): 9–18.
Tewari, M. (1999), 'Successful Adjustment in Indian Industry: The Case of Ludhiana's Woollen Knitwear Cluster', *World Development*, 27(9): 1651–71.

Torres, Gabriel (1997), *The Force of Irony: Power in the Everyday Life of Mexican Tomato Workers*. Oxford: Berg.

Verhagen, H. (2004), *International Sustainable Chain Management—Lessons from the Netherlands, Benin, Bhutan and Costa Rica*, Royal Tropical Institute (RTI) Bulletin 360. Amsterdam: KIT Publishers.

Welsh, R. (1997), 'Vertical Coordination, Producer Response, and the Locus of Control over Agricultural Production Decisions', *Rural Sociology*, 62(4), Winter: 491–507.

Wilson, J. (1986), 'The Political Economy of Contract Farming', *Review of Radical Political Economics*, 18(4): 47–70.

9 GENDER, LABOUR, AND GLOBAL PRODUCTION NETWORKS

Indigenous Women and NTFP-based Livelihoods

Govind Kelkar, Meenakshi Ahluwalia, and Meenakshi Kumar

GLOBAL VALUE CHAIN: GENDERED TRADE IN THE MARKET

The global production network (GPN) is a complex network of producers and agents in which large corporate buyers and retailers operate across international borders, feeding into global value chains (GVCs). Any role in retaining value at the top of the chain is transferred to the suppliers who in turn offset risks onto agents and subcontractors at the lower tiers within the GPN (Barrientos and Kritzinger, 2004).

Within these mystified conditions of production, GPNs are also challenging socially embedded norms of the division of labour and generating new employment opportunities for rural and indigenous peoples. However, these job openings are based on informal employment relations, making it difficult for the workers to access their rights to decent work and equality in employment benefits.

As documented by the United Nations Conference on Trade and Development (UNCTAD) (2004), trade liberalization has created jobs for women in non-traditional agriculture exports, such as fruit, vegetables, and cut flowers, in many developing countries. However, rural women face socially embedded multiple disadvantages within the home and outside and often lack access to credit, new technologies, and knowledge on marketing. As a result, they are more likely than men to be employed in low-wage seasonal jobs, with neither social protection nor decent work opportunities in GPNs; hence 'women are a source of competitive advantage for producers using labour-intensive production methods because of gender gaps in power in households and labour markets' (Elson et al., 2007: 45). If production is expanded as a result of women's links to GPNs, the household may receive greater income and women's voice in the household may increase, but the effect for women may be limited because the 'competitive advantage of the local subcontracting firms that employ them depends greatly on women's lower pay and poorer conditions, compared to men' (Elson et al., 2007: 46).

Importantly, the GVC does not necessarily include the poor or indigenous people. A pioneering work on domestic and export markets in Ghana clearly demonstrates that 'without developing the necessary physical and institutional infrastructure and human capacities at the micro level, value chain support activities at meso and macro levels are not only likely to bypass the poor, but to widen the gap between the poor and non-poor' (Berg et al., 2006: 16). The poor were left out from the GVC of mangoes in Ghana as production costs were very high and product quality was difficult to achieve. The domestic market for *gari* (fermented and roasted cassava) production in contract involved thousands of women microprocessors and had a ready market in schools, prisons, and hospitals. The poor can only enter the mango value chain if they receive financial support during the first five years of plantation. Similarly, the poor women involved in gari production can increase their efficiency if they use better processing equipment and invest in storage facilities—but they have neither the finance nor the skill required to carry out these changes.

Many of the indigenous communities in the state of Andhra Pradesh, India, combine gathering with some form of agriculture. Some indigenous communities, such as the Chenchu, carry on very little agriculture. The one non-timber forest product (NTFP) they have collected and sold over a long period of time is *gum karaya*, used in dentistry and as a food additive. Over the last two decades or so, however, as the market for various NTFPs has grown and the opportunities for direct gathering and hunting of foods have declined, collecting and selling NTFPs has emerged as a major source of income.

However, there is one major problem that collectors face. Due to the very precarious nature of their livelihoods, they are often forced into distress sales or transactions in interlinked markets—transactions that reduce the prices they get for their products. If they take a loan, it is given only on the condition that they will give nuts or other NTFPs in exchange. Nobody is willing to give them loans on cash repayment with interest, which is otherwise 5 per cent per month. But the indigenous women who directly exchange NTFPs for loans in effect pay an interest rate of more than 100 per cent for a three-month period; that is, at least 33 per cent per month. The precarious food security position of the indigenous peoples forces them into interlinked transactions (linking the market loans with the market for products), rather than separate transactions in the loan and product markets.

In the market, many NTFPs are purchased by parastatals, such as the Girijan Cooperative Corporation (GCC) in Andhra Pradesh. But this does not necessarily mean a higher income for the producers. Until recently, the GCC staff refused to pay them even the price fixed by the government, arguing that the product had not been sufficiently dried, and so on. The traders and GCC staff reportedly often insulted the collectors, and abused and harassed the women (Kelkar interview with Chenchu women, October 2006).

There is another problem in price realization, that of grades. Gum karaya has three grades. The staff of the parastatal GCC, however, usually refused to buy graded gum from the collectors. They bought it all as Grade 3, taking advantage of the weak market position of the collectors. They obviously subsequently graded the gum and pocketed the difference. Even weighing was not done accurately. Rather than a table balance, the staff used very large scales more appropriate for something like firewood, sold in tens of kilograms, rather than gum karaya, where even half a kilogram needs to be weighed accurately (Kelkar interview with Chenchu women, October 2006).

The price realized from the sale of gum karaya and other NTFPs was very low. The situation was made worse in that what reached the household for meeting its food and other requirements was even less, often not even half of the amount of the sales income. Since the markets and GCC centres are located at a distance from the forest villages, men usually went to sell the products. Even if a couple would go together, it was the man who controlled the money. Men would use a lot of the money in drinking alcohol and bring back only a small amount, if any at all, for food and other household needs. Some traders took advantage of men's drinking habits and gave part of the sales price directly in the form of alcohol.

Thus, women in their interaction with the GVC of NTFP faced two problems. One, they (or rather, men of their households) received very low prices for their products. Two, much of this income did not go towards meeting household well-being needs.

SELF-HELP GROUPS AND COLLECTIVE MARKETING

The United Nations Development Fund for Women (UNIFEM)/Society for the Elimination of Rural Poverty (SERP)/Kovel Foundation project,

'Women's Empowerment in the Market Place: India Gum Karaya Project' (2003–2006), covering more than 2,500 NTFP-dependent households in the districts of Mahboobnagar and Vishakapatnam in Andhra Pradesh, India, was designed to provide twin solutions to two problems: increase collectors' incomes and empower women in the marketplace.

A value chain analysis[1] of the incomes currently earned at different stages of NTFP collection, processing, and sale showed that (*i*) there could be substantial gains even through simple post-collection processing like drying and grading; (*ii*) collective sale by women could yield higher prices than sale by individuals; and (*iii*) higher incomes could be earned by moving up the value chain through processing the raw NTFPs.

Individual women on their own would be unable to deal with problems in the market, even in the household. Thus, women were organized into self-help groups (SHGs), which are also savings and credit organizations, by the Kovel Foundation and SERP. The role of these SHGs, or Sangams as they are called locally, went much beyond that of savings and credit. They provided a forum where women came together and discussed their problems. They provided collective strength in dealing with traders or GCC officials in the market, and even with men in the community and households.

These SHGs set up procurement centres in villages. These procurement centres had a number of effects. First, there was a reduction in transport cost. With reduced transport costs, some NTFPs that were formerly not collected for sale also began to be collected and sold. More important, women were now able to sell NTFPs at the procurement centres and did not have to leave marketing to men in distant weekly markets (*shandies*). Through the procurement centres, there has been a change in gender relations and power relations between NTFP collectors and buyers; women have emerged as the sellers of NTFP, have secured higher prices for the products, and also gained household-level control of the resulting income. Furthermore, women NTFP collectors could sell both to GCC and directly to buyers, such as Natural Remedies, a pharmaceutical company in Bangalore.

VALUE-ADDED PROCESSING

NTFP collectors sell their products as raw material. In the case of gum karaya, the drying had to be carried out by the collectors, as otherwise the resin would spoil. But most other NTFPs are sold as raw material. Value-added processes are carried out by the buyers. For instance, adda leaves are sold in bulk. The buyers then prepare leaf plates. Amla, a rich source of vitamin C and often used in dietary supplements, is also sold as raw material by the collectors. The traders then organize its processing into semi-processed dried amla or into finished products, such as amla preserve (*murabba*). Some portions of the processed amla are exported to be used in dietary supplements.

Many aspects of value-added processing are relatively simple, do not require large amounts of investment, and can be carried out in the house. As in the case of gum karaya, even simple measures such as sorting can lead to a substantial increase in income. In the case of amla, it can be steamed and dried. The resultant dry amla can get a price of Rs 25 (or even Rs 30) per kg, while the price of green amla is Rs 2 or even Re 1 per kg. Steaming and drying produce 1 kg dried amla out of 5 kg green amla. The net income is more than doubled by this process.

All these processes were introduced in the areas covered by the project started by SERP and UNIFEM; the Kovel Foundation (a partner of UNIFEM) acted as a facilitator and intermediary. Besides training, it also established contact with the buyers and carried out quality control. What this shows is that an outside intervention helps the informal sector producers in moving to a higher level of production and income. Such a role of non-informal sector actors is well-known in the case of non-governmental organization (NGOs) such as Self-Employed Womens' Association (SEWA) in India and Bangladesh Rural Advancement Committee (BRAC) in Bangladesh. Various such organizations have played a role in taking up scale-sensitive functions of upgrading such as design, standardization, and marketing.

BARGAINING IN GPNS

Is there space for women and other small producers to improve their positions within GPNs? Given the strong monopsony of the buyers and the competition among small producers, it might seem that there cannot be any scope for manoeuvre within GPNs. But the UNIFEM project shows two specific ways in which women small producers can improve their position within GPNs.

The first is to organize women producers in groups such as SHGs and take up collective marketing. With some capacity-building support, women's groups can capture part of the share earlier taken by traders. They can then sell directly to the GCC or to exporting firms, such as Natural Remedies, and other private traders and individuals. In the latter instance, they might even get a better price (Rs 31/kg) than that given by the parastatal GCC

(Rs 25/kg). Of course, it remains important for the women's groups to retain some space for bargaining between the two organizations. A monopoly of any one organization would work to the disadvantage of the women producers, while competition among buyers is obviously an advantage for the sellers.

The second step is for the small producers to undertake some of the value-added processing of raw materials. As with other commodities, more income is earned in value-added activities than in the mere collection and sale of raw materials. By moving up the value chain in undertaking some parts of processing, those which can be easily done at the household level and do not require much investment, it has been possible for indigenous women NTFP producers to increase their share of income within the GPNs.

Of course, both these measures are taken by small producers at the expense of traders and processors and the advance is within the confines of the domestic production chain (as against the global production chain). It is not a change in the distribution of value between the Indian section of the chain and its non-Indian or global section. That is not something that a group or few groups of small producers could hope or even think of tackling. But it is important to note that contrary to many sceptical analyses, which do not see any opportunity for small producers to increase their share of income within global production chains, the UNIFEM project of indigenous women has been able to do just that. What they have achieved may seem very little—the elimination of various elementary frauds in trading and undertaking simple forms of processing. But these measures are quite substantial from the point of view of the livelihoods of indigenous women.

The example we have studied—indigenous women's role in marketing and processing of NTFP in Andhra Pradesh, India—however, is not the only instance of women small-scale producers increasing their share of income in the GVC. In the following, we give some other examples of such upward movements by women.

The example of shea butter in the Bassila region of Benin in West Africa has received international attention. Shea butter is used in margarine, chocolate, and the cosmetic industry. It is mainly women who are involved in collecting shea kernel. Shea kernel collection requires no investment by women and has significant gains for them. Importantly, a very large number of women are also bulk buyers or agents or suppliers to GPNs. (Schreckenberg, 2004). However, it was noted that the increase in demand for shea butter in Europe did not benefit the shea-kernel collectors, largely because they continued with the sale of the kernels through middle merchants at the marginal price. The unionization of workers benefited women in some cases, without much impact on the social well-being and economic agency (Carr and Chen, 2004).

A UNIFEM analysis concluded that there was greater potential in the production and marketing of shea butter, rather than raw kernel (UNIFEM analysis of projects in West Africa, reported in Schreckenberg, 2004). Contacts were also made with some large buyers, such as Body Shop, L'Oreal, and L'Occitaine. Some of them preferred to purchase directly from the women producers' unions and even provided training in quality control. All this has increased the income from shea butter and made it regular.

Likewise, we noted a marginal change in women's economic agency in the case of producers of lac (Kerria lacca, a natural polymer) in the districts of Ranchi and Khuti in the state of Jharkhand, India. Under the International Fund for Agricultural Development's (IFAD) Jharkhand Tribal Development Programme, a number of SHGs (more than 90 per cent women's groups) and *mahila mandals* (rural women's organizations) were trained by scientists on how to grow lac on the best available trees in the village and neighbouring forests. The impact assessment report of 2007–8 by IFAD's Jharkhand project office noted that a large number of women were able to return the overdue personal loans in the range of Rs 20,000–25,000 within a period of six months from the sale of lac. Further, the lac-producing households were investing money in different income-generation activities like fishery, agriculture, forestry, and watershed development. They were able to provide higher education for their children (IFAD, 2008). However, much of the decision-making with regard to household management and marketing of lac and other NTFPs remained with men, who have the traditional power of decision-making in the home and community.

In the Munger district of Bihar, SEWA Bharat has set up centres to help increase the livelihood of women by involving them in the making of *agarbattis* (incense sticks) (Ramesh, 2007). Agarbattis are in great demand all over the world and the market is rapidly growing. SEWA linked up with International Trade Centre (ITC). This initiative has helped rural women to enhance their agarbatti-rolling skills; this accompanied with the ITC buy-back assurance has made a substantial difference in the lives of many rural women.

The Assistance in Social Habilitation through Agarbattis (ASHA) was started by ITC to provide training to women to make high-quality agarbattis to match international standards recommended by the International

Fragrance Regulatory Association. The Mangaldeep agarbatti brand of the ITC has about 2–3 per cent of the Rs 1,200-crore market that is growing at 7 per cent a year. But the importance of the venture lies in the fact that it provides livelihood to some 7,000 rural women in the country (Ramesh, 2007).

The International Fair Trade Organization (IFAT) certification has already been acquired for the Mangaldeep brand. This is a major breakthrough in agarbatti exports for ITC. With the help of Exim Bank and ITC's initiative, the Mangaldeep brand is now available in Singapore, Malaysia, Nepal, the United Arab Emirates (UAE), Bahrain, South Africa, and the US (*The Hindu Business Line*, 17 August 2007).

A high demand for gum in the global market has made it a possible livelihood source for indigenous women in many parts of India. Andhra Pradesh, Chhattisgarh, Madhya Pradesh, Maharashtra, and Orissa are the main contributors of gum karaya, kendu leaf, and sal seed in India; more than 75 per cent of NTFPs are collected in these states (Kovel Foundation and International Resources Group, 2005: 1). In 1991, SEWA decided to organize women gum-collectors to ensure fair and regular income to them. With the assistance of SEWA, cooperatives were established in 11 villages in the Radhapur block of Gujarat. The women were taught about forest laws, market rates, and variations in gum quality. SEWA also helped these women to obtain licences from the State Forest Development Corporation. Currently, over 1,000 women gum-collectors are members of SEWA Cooperative. Eighty per cent of the village residents in Radhapur block are engaged in gum collection led by its 200 women, who became the primary breadwinners. The major advantage of this trade is that it comes without any capital investment; that is, the babul trees scattered throughout the desert ooze gum naturally. Gum collection is limited to the dry period from July to October. Every woman earns around Rs 1,200 per month through gum collection (Centre for Science and Environment, 2008).

What these various experiences show is that women small-scale producers of various forest- or tree-based products have been able to increase their incomes from the gathering and sale of NTFPs. Four points are common in these experiences: (*i*) the elimination of middlemen from the trading chain; (*ii*) upgrading to some forms of processing; (*iii*) facilitating intermediary such as a development agency or an NGO; and (*iv*) the women were organized in groups, unions, or cooperatives. These groups were important in enabling the women to undertake higher-order functions, such as marketing.

HOUSEHOLD–MARKET RELATIONS

Gender relations are complex, dynamic, and socially embedded with many interlocked dimensions. Cultural traditions of women's exclusion from community management confer authority and prestige on men. Men hold virtually all formal positions of power and decision-making in villages in both patrilineal and matrilineal systems, though women often exercise considerable influence in certain areas of village life. What this also means is that household and market outcomes are not independent of each other—positions within the household (gender relations) influence market outcomes, and market outcomes in turn influence household positions.

While economic growth is considered the most powerful instrument for reducing poverty, the power of social and cultural institutions still helps to determine the extent to which women are included in the market development or allowed economic independence, improve their lives free of violence, attain better health and education, and achieve greater control over their lives.

Many of the feminist economist analyses have further demonstrated that household and individual well-being are not necessarily the same; that individuals living in the same household may have very different control over the household income and assets (Deere and Doss, 2006; Rao, 2006). Women's lower status at home is mirrored in their lower status in the labour market, because it is determined by their duties for unpaid domestic work, such as washing; cleaning; cooking; collection of basic goods like fuel wood, water, vegetables, fodder for cattle; home management; and caring of children, the old, and the sick. These responsibilities deprive women of level playing fields in the labour market. Further, women experience limited opportunity for technical education and health care due to the patriarchal values at home, which in turn limits them to access opportunities for skills in the labour market. It is also noted that 'women are less mobile in their job due to domestic responsibilities and women tend to be subordinate to men and tend to become much meek and docile as workers' (Hirway, 2008: 13) The gendered distribution of assets and resulting vulnerability of women substantially limit development efforts at overcoming poverty, thus indicating the need for policy attention to address persistent gender discrimination and the weaker starting point of women in ownership and control of assets.

As pointed out earlier, the low price realized from the sale of gum karaya and other NTFPs was made worse as what reached the household for meeting its food and other requirements was even less, often not even half of the amount of the sales income. Men who undertook and controlled the money from marketing used a major part of this income for buying alcohol and for their other personal needs. Thus, it is not sufficient to confine attention to just increasing household income. If this increase in income remains under the control of men, then its impact on household well-being will be limited. To the extent that women are able to get control over a portion of household income, there will be a greater impact on household well-being.

In Andhra Pradesh, there were clear impacts of the UNIFEM/SERP/Kovel Foundation project on improved well-being of the household, including children. Everywhere in the project areas, women were firm in saying that since they now carried out the selling at the procurement centre, they now had effective control over that income. But the change in gender relations—who controls household income—was not just, so to say, an automatic effect of the economic change. The economic change strengthened the hands of women, so that they could take up the struggle against men's drunkenness. This struggle was not just carried out individually by each woman in her own home, but also, and importantly so, collectively. This success of the project in changing gender relations in controlling household income is of great importance in building secure livelihoods for the NTFP collectors and thus improving the well-being of women and their households.

IMPROVEMENTS IN WELL-BEING AND SELF-ESTEEM

Women in the areas covered by the UNIFEM/SERP/Kovel Foundation project are able to use more of household income to buy food and other household necessities. Many more children are going to school. The diet is more varied. Earlier, the staple grain was jowar (sorghum), but now they also include rice and more vegetables in their diet. In Vishakapatnam district, women said that they were also able to consume eggs and *dal* a few times each week and even chicken once a week. Men too appreciate the fact that there is now more food in the house. School attendance of children has improved. Girls, however, are still asked to help with household work after they return from school, while boys are allowed to play.

This impact on well-being, however, is not confined to the other members of the household. Being the earners of the additional income, women are also able to improve their own well-being. As members of organizations, as community leaders, and even trainers in the use of new technologies, they gather a greater social respect. The terms of social recognition of indigenous women, both within their communities and within the broader society, have changed.

A similar change was noticed with producers of shea butter in Burkina Faso. '[R]egular and certain source of income to women engaged in shea butter production has imparted a certain sense of self-respect among the workers. It has also helped the women producers earn the respect of their family and the right to speak out in the community' (UNIFEM, 2008).

Again not in any automatic manner, but through organization and struggle, women are also able to achieve a reduction in domestic violence against women in their homes and even some redrawing of boundaries in domestic responsibilities. The change in their conditions of material well-being, women's greater say in the use of household income, and their expanded horizons and knowledge, all contribute to an increase in their capacity to aspire, not as mere dreams but for goals that they can plan to achieve.

Women too spend more on their own consumption, not only of food but also of other things that increased their own self-esteem, such as improving their diet, along with that of their children and men, and spending money on their grooming and appearance, something they now pay more attention to. This is due not just to their ability to use more of household income for consumption but through the social interaction in regular Sangam (group) meetings. In an Oxfam Australia study on wages and living costs of sportswear workers in Indonesia, women workers reported that 'if they had more money they would buy herbal tonic to drink during menstruation' (Oxfam, 2006: 16). This seemed achievable for these NTFP-collectors and processors in the UNIFEM/SERP/Kovel Foundation project.

Indigenous women are at the bottom of the social ladder. Traditionally unkempt and illiterate, they have been looked down upon by their agriculturist and other neighbours. As some women themselves said, 'We did not know how to carry ourselves or know where a bus was going' (Kelkar interview with Chenchu women, October 2006). They deeply felt this humiliation. 'Earlier people looked down on us, saying you don't know where the bus is going and where to go...Now people talk to us with respect. People from neighbouring villages admire us for our work and our ability to do these things [dealing with the bank and GCC Centre]', women said in a village meeting in Petralchenu (Kelkar's interview, 2006). Their ability to get loans, spread information in the village about new things, and the reduction of men's violence—all this has contributed to women's increased social prestige both in the village and in the area around. In Vishakapatnam district, the added factor is that some women have become known for their knowledge of NTFP processing and have been invited as trainers by women and men from other villages.

INCENTIVES AND WORK

The problem of women doing the labour but men controlling the resulting income is not confined to indigenous women in India. With the increasing feminization of agricultural labour in Asia, but ownership of land and other productive assets remaining in the hands of men, there is a similar problem of a disjunct between the performance of labour and control over the proceeds of labour. Although it has been recognized that rural women have an important role in livestock rearing (such as animal care, grazing, fodder collection, cleaning of animal sheds, processing of milk, and sale of livestock products), their control over livestock and livestock products is minimal. With some regional variations, women account for 93 per cent of employment in dairy production in India. But 75 per cent of dairy cooperative membership is male (Sujaya, 2006). Cheng Fang Lui, in her recent study questioning the managerial feminization of agriculture in China, noted, 'Where as women contributed 64 percent of production work in livestock, men control 59 percent of the marketing work. This is a sign that as far as the traditional female-dominated livestock sector is concerned, the feminization is more labour feminization, and not, according to earning control measure, managerial feminization' (2007: 14).

This lack of control over earnings is not confined to agriculture. This is a feature of the manufacturing sector too. In the Bangalore garments industry, it was reported that since men, who gather at factory gates on pay day, take away women's wages, there is a high level of attrition among women garment workers (Daljit Kaur, presentation at IILS/ICSSR/IHD seminar in Bangalore 2007). In Asia, 'a large proportion of women are not able to retain their earned income—over 40 per cent in Bangladesh, over 40 per cent in Gujarat and over 70 per cent in Indonesia' (ILO, 2004: 54). With regard to control over the way their income is spent, in China, 57 per cent of women reported that they have 'greater control than their husband on daily expenditure items. However, on bigger items, only 7 percent of the wives have the greater control of the decisions' (Bao, 2002, quoted in MacPhail and Dong, 2006: 33). In South Asia, far fewer women could make decisions. Furthermore, discriminatory barriers and socio-cultural rigidities remain the major reasons restricting women from obtaining effective control of property, assets, and resources.

Does women's control or lack of control over the earnings from their labour have an incentive or disincentive effect in terms of the amount and quality of work that she would put in? In other words, does gender inequality in the household affect production and productivity? This question has not been researched very much. Our study of Chenchu women and some others, however, does provide some pointers in this matter.

With regard to the indigenous women in Andhra Pradesh, there clearly was an incentive effect of their securing control over income from their labour and the resultant positive effects on their well-being and of their households. They were much more enthusiastic about the work than earlier and reported putting in greater effort. Such an effect is intuitively obvious. When the net income goes up, one can expect a greater effort in labour—unless the labour were being performed in hunter–gatherer style for fulfilling very limited needs. For those who attempt to maximize income, an increase in net return can be expected to result in increased labour.

Is there also a disincentive effect on women's labour of men gaining control of what was formerly under women's own control? This counter-case could not be observed in Andhra Pradesh, but there is an analysis of women's labour in export-oriented cultivation of French beans in Kenya. These plots are given to women (wife or co-wife) by the men; and the woman is expected to work on both her own land and the husband's land, a common practice in many African countries. Women, of course, perform the labour on all plots, but women and men control the use of income from their respective plots. But when production of French beans for export became an important source of income, men redrew the plot line and reduced the spaces for women. This created an incentive problem that limited the application of women's labour and led to quality problems (Dolan, 2001; Nathan, 2004).

What these examples show is that the disjunction between ownership and control from the performance of labour can create incentive problems in the performance of labour. This could affect both productivity and the quality of production. Further, the effect is not confined to own-account production, as in agriculture or production of NTFP. It can even extend to the garment factory. Gender relations within the household cannot be kept out of the analysis of the factors in decent work.

ECONOMIC SECURITY AND DECENT WORK

The cases in this study are instances of women's control over income from sale of NTFP, etc. We have argued that women's control over their own income affects the well-being outcomes from this income and is thus a necessary condition for moving towards the achievement of decent work. But the issue of economic security is also pertinent for agriculture as such, an agriculture that is being increasingly feminized across much of Asia. Secure and inalienable use rights, with full control, if not full ownership, are necessary for investment. In the absence of this security of use rights, women clearly would not invest their own money in improving the land.

A recent study by the International Labour Organization (ILO) observes that economic security is worsened by the fact that policies and institutions do not realize that promoting women's control rights to incomes and resources would help boost growth and development. This is one of the 'main forms of gender inequality across the world' (ILO, 2004: 86) and systematically neglected in social policy and income statistics.

Not being landowners is at least part of the reason why women are not perceived as 'farmers' even when they do much of the farm work. As a result, agricultural extension and information on new technologies are almost exclusively directed to men, even when traditionally women are responsible. Although vegetable growing is almost universally women's work, projects that aim to diversify agricultural production by promoting commercial vegetable growing (as in Bangladesh) often train, or used to train, men. Something is inevitably lost when the knowledge is passed on to women. If women were accepted as owners and hence as farmers, it is more likely that they would be targeted for training as farm managers, and not only as home managers. With the increasing feminization of agricultural work in China and India, contemporary rural–urban inequality in these countries is a matter of gender inequality.

In the midst of increasing feminization of agricultural labour, women lack title to land, which is one of the causes for the persistent gender inequality. A recent analysis of the state of Indian farmers by the National Commission on Farmers (NCF) emphasizes that lack of title to land makes it difficult for women farmers to access institutional credit.

For example, hardly 5 percent of women seem to have been issued with Kisan [farmer] credit cards out of the many millions to whom such cards have been issued...Extension and input supply services also do not reach women at the right time and place. Therefore, as stressed by the NCF, there is need for a new deal for women in agriculture (Swaminathan, 2005).

A new deal for women in agriculture, along with necessary inputs and credit support, could increase the efficiency of resource use and thus contribute to increasing production. This is borne out in an IFAD project in Bangladesh—the Aquaculture Development Project. In this project, women were exclusively trained in fish aquaculture and provided credit for commercial fish culture in ponds owned by the male members of their families. With this knowledge and credit, women were able to transform pond aquaculture from a semi-subsistence mode to a regular commercial mode, with an increase in productivity of more than 50 per cent (Nathan and Jahan, 2004). Women in Andhra Pradesh, India, also used micro-credit to take on lease lands that were being fitfully cultivated and develop them into regular cultivation with higher productivity than earlier.

Women's ownership and control rights to income and land can not only lead to higher and better quality production. They can also enable them to control the use of household income for their well-being and of other members of the household. It can also benefit women by being associated with a reduction in violence. Recent studies in India and other countries have estimated the costs of domestic violence against women. This cost includes the direct economic loss experienced by the individual (such as through absence from paid work and/or lost productivity, expenses related to physical and mental health care, and lost lifetime earnings due to disability), government's costs through its health and social sector expenses, the criminal justice system, employer and third-party expenses. The India study showed that domestic violence against women can push economically fragile households into economic crisis (UNIFEM, 2005). An earlier study in India (UNIFEM, 2003) estimated that women lost, on average, five working days after an incident of violence. Violence against women also has personal and social effects, besides the calculable economic costs. It is a question of women's agency, very much needed for better outcomes from international trade. Some new studies in the region point that there exists a positive correlation between women's ownership of specific assets (that is, land and/or house) and reduced vulnerability to experiencing inter-spousal violence (Bhatla, 2006).

If women have access to more highly paid market work, they are likely to spend lesser number of hours for house work. As observed in the case of China and India, women with a higher share of household income are less likely to take the major responsibility for house work (Kelkar, 2005; MacPhail and Dong, 2006). It is not surprising, therefore, that despite exhaustion due to longer working days and lower wages, women value market work highly. The earnings from market work are seen as important by women as they raise their standing to that of an economic contributor to the household.

CHALLENGES AND STRATEGIES

Our concern in this study is two-fold: valuing women's contribution to the export sector, and challenging gender inequality by drawing attention to women's inequality in access to earnings and productive assets. Through an analysis of gendered distribution of employment and productive assets, it is possible to propose policy recognition of women's contribution to the economy and to tackle their experience of disadvantage, discrimination, and violence in a wider context at home, in the community, and in the market, as well as state institutions. The intra-household gender-based power dynamics, coupled with erosion of the state provisioning of education, health care, sanitation, water, and other services, also constrain women of the poorer households from taking advantage of market opportunities (Beneria and Floro, 2005).

In the end, we suggest four overarching themes that should inform the alternative framework for development of gender equality and decent livelihoods in Asia:

1. Creating decent employment opportunities with attention to rural poor and indigenous women: These will allow the state, the civil society, and women's organizations in particular, to assess and address the questions of gender segmentation of labour force and inequalities in remunerative employment.
2. Gender responsive terms of trade: It is important to understand the interaction between market and non-market (unpaid housework and caring) work. Policies for 'the social sector' and for 'the productive sector' are an artificial divide. To improve gender-based gains from trade, it may be necessary that development policy interventions concede the crucial importance of non-market work and strengthen measures that support the provision of caring, child care facilities, as well as education of the male employees to undertake non-market activities. Particular schemes need to be instituted in the export industries for transport and infrastructure to facilitate women's mobility, such as those introduced to facilitate work in the information technology 'call centres'.
3. Distribution/Redistribution of Assets: Women's efficiency as skilled workers in the process of trade liberalization is closely linked to reducing their dependency in the household. This can be mainly achieved by providing women with an unmediated (independent of the household and the head) access/ownership/control of productive assets and management rights over property and self-earned income. Such asset distribution and redistribution provide the basis for overcoming distortion in the functioning of the trade institutions, which can be geared to restructure gender equality through an enabling environment to make use of economic opportunities to work outside the home. At the international labour conference in June 2002, six major organizations

of women workers—Committee for Asian Women, HomeNet(Asia), International Federation of Workers' Education Associations in Zambia and England, StreetNet (South Africa), International Restructuring Education Network, Netherlands (IRENE), and Women in Informal Employment Globalizing and Organizing (WIEGO) at Harvard, USA—suggested that governments at local and national levels should introduce measures that can enable the informal economy workers to have effective access to and control over productive assets and resources, such as land, credit, capital, marketing, and technology (ILO, 2003).

4. Individualization of Capabilities: The distribution of capabilities within a household is subject to variation, depending on the way in which income and household assets are controlled and used within the household. Such relations are structured on the basis of power and hierarchy in the household. Thus, in order to improve the capabilities of women workers in the export industries (currently constituting the majority of basic skilled workers), it is necessary to invest in development of technological and knowledge capabilities of women as individuals, as against the household head- and community-based strategies for poverty reduction.

Technological change and economic development policies need to be supported by programmes for equality-based gender and social relations and necessary institutions at micro, meso, and macro levels. As widely recognized in development literature, equality in social and economic relations and effective institutions are the two main factors for facilitating conditions for economic growth and human development. Such an approach will enable poor rural women and men to have greater access to institutional credit, promote greater bargaining power against unjust practices in the market, improve well-being outcomes in the household, and facilitate implementation of development policies.

NOTES

1. This was carried out by UNIFEM in consultation with Govind Kelkar and UNIFEM project coordinator, Meenakshi Ahluwalia.

REFERENCES

Bao, X. (2002), 'More Women Wear the Pants', *China Daily*, 10 September.
Barrientos, S. and A. Kritzinger (2004), 'Squaring the Circle—Global Production and the Informalization of Work in South African Fruit Exports', *Journal of International Development*, 16: 81–92.

Berg, C., S. Bercher-Hiss, M. Fell, A. Hobinka, U. Muller, and S. Prakash (2006), *Poverty Orientation of Value Chains for Domestic and Export Markets in Ghana*. Ghana: SLE Publication Series.

Benerìa, Lourdes and Maria Floro (2005), 'Labor Market Informalization, Gender, and Social Protection: Reflections on Poor Urban Households in Bolivia, Ecuador, and Thailand', Mimeo, Paper prepared for the UNRISD Research Programme on Gender and Social Policy.

Bhatla, Nandita (ed.) (2006), *Property and Inheritance Rights of Women for Social Protection—South Asian Experience*. New Delhi: International Centre for Research on Women.

Carr, M. and M. Chen (2004), 'Globalization, Social Exclusion and Work: With Special Reference to Informal Employment and Gender', Working Paper No. 20. Geneva: International Labour Organization.

Centre for Science and Environment (2008), 'Global Demand Makes Gum Collection Viable Livelihood Source' (available at http://www.cseindia.org/programme/pov-env/livelihood20050228.htm, accessed on 1 March 2008).

Deere, Carmen Diana and Cheryl R. Doss (2006), 'The Gender Asset Gap: What do We Know and Why does It Matter?', *Feminist Economics*, Special Issue on Women and Wealth, 12(1&2): 3–69.

Dolan, Catherine S. (2001), 'The "Good Wife": Struggles over Resources in the Kenyan Horticultural Sector', *Journal of Development Studies*, 37(3): 39–70.

Elson, D., C. Grown, and N. Cagatay (2007), 'Mainstream, Heterodox and Feminist Trade Theory', in I. van Staveren, D. Elson, C. Grown, and N. Cagatay (eds), *Feminist Economics of Trade*. London and New York: Routledge.

Hirway, Indira (2008), 'NREGA: A Component of Full Employment Strategy for India, An Assessment', Paper presented at International Seminar on National Rural Employment Guarantee Scheme in India, 16–17 September, New Delhi.

International Fund for Agricultural Development (2008), 'Tribal Development Project for Jharkhand', Mimeo. Rome: IFAD.

International Institute for Labour Studies (IILS), Geneva/ Indian Council for Social Science Research (ICSSR), New Delhi/Institute for Human Development (IHD), New Delhi, (2007), 'Global Production Networks and Decent Work: Recent Experience in India and Global Trends", Research Workshop, 18–20 November, Bangalore.

International Labour Organization (ILO) (2003), *Key Indicators of the Labour Market*. Geneva: ILO.

—— (2004), *Economic Security for a Better World*. Geneva: ILO.

Kelkar, Govind (2005), 'Development Effectiveness through Gender Mainstreaming: Gender Equality and Poverty Reduction in Asia', *Economic and Political Weekly*, XL(44&45): 4690–9.

Kovel Foundation and International Resources Group (2005), *Report on the Gum Karaya Sub-Sector in Andhra Pradesh, India*, November. Washington D.C.: United States Agency for International Development.

Liu, Cheng Fang (2007), 'Is Feminization of Agriculture Occurring in China? Debunking the Myth and Measuring the Consequences of Women's Participation in Agriculture', Unpublished Draft Paper.

MacPhail, Fiona and Xiao-Yuan Dong (2006), 'Women's Status in the Household in Rural China: Does Market Labour Matter?', in Shunfeng Song and Aimin Chen (eds), *China's Rural Economy after WTO: Problems and Strategies*, pp. 29–58. USA: Ashgate.

Nathan, Dev (2004), 'Micro Credit in East Africa: Creation of Women's Space, Transition from Subsistence Accumulation', Working Paper 20. New Delhi: IFAD and Institute of Human Development.

Nathan, Dev and Rownok Jahan (2004), *Women as Fish Managers*, Aquaculture Development Project, Bangladesh, Supervision Mission Report. Rome: UNOPS, Kuala Lumpur and IFAD, June.

Oxfam (2006), *Offside! Labour Rights and Sportswear Production in Asia*. London: Oxfam International.

Ramesh, M. (2007), 'There is Lot More in Agarbattis than Just Good Smell' (available at http://www.thehindubusinessline.com/2007/06/18/stories/2007061801061800.htm, accessed on 10 March 2008).

Rao, Nitya (2006), 'Women Access and Rights to Land: Gender Relations in Tenure, A Scoping Study in the Indian Context', IFAD-UNIFEM Working Paper No. 6. New Delhi: UNIFEM South Asia Regional Office.

Schreckenberg, Kathrin (2004), 'The Contribution of Shea Butter (Vitellaria paradoxa C.F. Gaertner) to Local Livelihoods in Benin', in Miguel N. Alexiades and Patricia Shanley (eds), *Forest Products, Livelihoods and Conservation: Case Studies of Non Timber Forest Product Systems*. Bogor (Indonesia): Center for International Forestry Research (CIFOR).

Sujaya, C.P. (2006), *Climbing a Long Road: Women in Agriculture in India, Ten Years after Beijing*. Chennai: M.S. Swaminathan Research Foundation.

Swaminathan, M.S. (2005), 'The Sons of the Soil', *The Hindu*, 19 April.

The Hindu Business Line (2007), 'ITC Agarbattis to Find New Markets through "Fair Trade"', 17 August (available at http://www.thehindubusinessline.com/2007/06/18/stories2007061801061800.htm, accessed on 10 March 2008).

UNCTAD (2004), Conference on Trade and Development, Eleventh Session (UNCTAD XI), June, Sao Paulo Brazil.

UNIFEM (2003), *Not a Minute More: Ending Violence against Women*. New Delhi: UNIFEM South Asia Office.

—— (2005), *Progress of South Asian Women*. New Delhi: UNIFEM South Asia Office.

—— (2008), 'Wild Shea Tree Benefiting Burkina Faso: Women Engaged in Shea Sector Gain from Trade' (available at http://www.thecommonwealth.org/gtinformation/, accessed on 17 June 2008).

10 UPGRADATION OR FLEXIBLE CASUALIZATION?

Exploring the Dynamics of Global Value Chain Incorporation in the Indian Leather Industry

Sumangala Damodaran

INTRODUCTION

The idea of global value chains (GVCs) has been a crucial one in the analysis of international production and trading systems for about a couple of decades.[1] Recognizing the importance of globally dispersed production and trading systems that are networked and coordinated through the dominance of some 'leading actors', a vast volume of analysis and research has revealed several typical patterns of such networks across very diverse contexts.[2] It has lent new dimensions to work on networks of small enterprises in developing countries which are found to play key roles in many types of GVCs by focusing on issues of control and governance within international chains, the role of drivers of chains in relation to firm-level and industry-level upgrading, the possibility of setting standards at the global and local levels, and so on.

In developing countries, the linkages with global manufacturing value chains are seen prominently for labour-intensive industries organized in industrial clusters. The literature on industrial clusters analysed the fact that industrial clusters[3] offer a form of organization for small firms that allow them, in specific production and institutional contexts, to overcome constraints associated with isolated existence and achieve growth and efficiency. However, many actual experiences of clustering showed that export-oriented clusters particularly saw a great deal of dynamism, giving rise to a vast literature that argues that export orientation offers a viable development path for industrial clusters in different sectors. Given that export orientation, in most contexts, involved incorporation into GVCs, it was further argued that the GVC route can be advocated as a sustainable developmental path for developing-country industries because such incorporation requires constant firm-level upgrading in order to remain competitive.[4]

This chapter looks at an important labour-intensive industry in India, the leather industry, which is organized in the form of clusters and has been incorporated into the GVC from the early 1970s onwards.

The leather and leather products industry was chosen because it is a traditional export-oriented industry, on the one hand,[5] and is organized primarily in the form of small-firm dominated industrial clusters, on the other. Almost half [6] of this sector's output is exported. It is also a sector where social factors have played a major role in shaping economic organization. A large number of people engaged in the industry (entrepreneurs as well as workers) are even today from the traditional leather-working castes (belonging to the lower castes in the caste hierarchy) and the Muslim community.[7] State intervention has been crucial in this sector with government policies emphasizing export-orientation and value-added production primarily geared towards exports.[8] The industry is concentrated in several leather clusters in four or five distinct locations in the country, with each cluster containing a wide variety of enterprise forms and organizational structures. Each of these clusters, even though dominated by small-scale firms, has a wide spectrum of firms, varying from tiny firms at one end to large, integrated firms at the other, with a large variety of intermediate size firms in between, leading to the variety in enterprise forms and organizational structures mentioned earlier.

Despite the leather industry being export-oriented from colonial times and a thrust sector for exports from India from the 1960s onwards, followed by conscious value-chain incorporation from the early 1970s, it has progressively lost share in important segments in the international market. Conscious GVC incorporation has, therefore, not resulted in increasing and sustained shares in the international market. The Indian leather industry is thus a classic case of the opportunities presented as well as the limitations imposed by particular kinds of incorporation into GVCs.

The essay thus looks at the structural changes in the leather industry that resulted from GVC incorporation and particularly considers the issue of upgrading. It specifically looks at changes in the structure of production, the nature of industrial organization, and the conditions of employment and work in examining whether upgrading took place or not. Keeping in mind the agenda of 'decent work', the essay considers the question of whether the leather industry saw development of the 'high road' or 'low road' type. In the former, increase in exports and structural transformation in industries result in major gains to labour in terms of conditions of work and employment while in the latter, industrial organizational changes take place without upgrading labour.

These issues are examined by studying economic organization in three major Indian leather clusters: Chennai, Kolkata, and Agra.[9] These three clusters have different histories and degrees of export orientation. Chennai and Kolkata are clusters that have been part of international trade from colonial times onwards, and Agra turned into a significant exporting cluster only from the 1990s. Between them, Chennai is exclusively export-oriented whereas Agra and Kolkata also cater to the domestic market. Chennai and other clusters in the south Indian state of Tamil Nadu have become major centres of footwear components and larger scale footwear production that exclusively cater to exports, having begun as tanning centres and integrated forward systematically following policy changes relating to GVC incorporation.

Similarly, Kolkata began with tanning and integrated forward successively to specialize in production of leather goods. Agra has always been a footwear production cluster, which made the transition from being almost exclusively domestic market–oriented to exports. In the analysis of the leather industry in India that has been done by one of the very few studies available on the subject (Banerjee and Nihila, 1999) as well as similar views expressed by some policymakers and organisations involved in the industry, it is argued that this industry in India has faced vastly changed market conditions since 1991. These conditions are extremely favourable, characterized by the increasing opportunities provided by the western European and American markets along with the collapse of the large markets in the former Soviet Union and Eastern Europe. Given the right institutional conditions, the leather industry in India can take advantage of vastly expanding international markets for its products.

The abovementioned study (Banerjee and Nihila, 1999) compares the Chennai and Kolkata leather clusters and argues that the growth of each presents an interesting contrast of the way in which it has dealt with institutional constraints hampering modernization and growth. In Kolkata, agent behaviour (ranging from entrepreneurs to workers) is influenced substantially by historical factors and social embeddedness in terms of caste and community identities being paramount. This has been manifest in a resistance to change, reflected in an unwillingness to upgrade technology and to introduce a modern work culture that is essential to produce for highly discerning international markets. In Chennai (and Tamil Nadu in general), by contrast, the leather industry was able to respond immediately to the crisis imposed by the disappearance of the Soviet market by tapping the more lucrative Western markets due to the more favourable institutional structure in the city that allowed it to shake off the stranglehold of retrograde institutions such as caste and community. Agents as well as production systems are seen to be significantly more modern with attitudes suitable to quality upgrading and production for discerning international markets.

While this argument has been dealt with in detail elsewhere (Damodaran, 2004), what is important from this chapter's point of view is the fact that Kolkata and Chennai are assumed to have completely different structures of production and labour markets, with the latter being more modern and capable of dealing with international markets, whereas the former is seen to be bogged down by informal networks and outmoded production structures and also having to, therefore, rely on lower quality domestic markets. This chapter attempts to bring out aspects of organization that are common to both these clusters and Agra, which made the transition from domestic market to export orientation.

The rest of the chapter is divided into two major sections: the next section explores the relationship between value chain incorporation, organizational structure, and export performance in the industry. The section following it brings out the links between the organization of production, the structure of the labour market, and conditions of employment. The final section presents the major conclusions of the chapter.

VALUE CHAIN INCORPORATION, POLICY FRAMEWORK, AND ORGANIZATIONAL STRUCTURE

The Global Value Chain in Leather and the Policy Framework for the Indian Leather Industry

The leather and leather products industry is a typical case of a buyer-driven commodity chain (Gereffi, 1994). Production and trade of leather and leather products span a wide range of countries, with a large number of developing countries having joined the fray from the late 1970s or so, apart from the traditional producers.[10] Till the end of the 1960s, the leading meat-producing countries of the West were the major producers of tanned leather as well as of finished products, and developing countries such as India were suppliers of raw material for the leather industry in these countries. From the late 1960s onwards, structural changes that took place in the international economy influenced the structure of India's exports of leather and leather products, as well as policies.

The first among these was relocation in the international leather industry in two major stages that have been referred to as the first and second 'migrations' of the industry (Sinha and Sinha, 1992; CLRI, 1994). In the late 1960s, the developing countries of the world were major exporters of hides and skins, and advanced countries such as USA, Germany, UK, France, and Italy were the manufacturing nations. Developed countries started to close down their tanneries due to stringent pollution measures, on the one hand, and the rise in labour costs, on the other. From the 1970s, a migration of the tannery segment to countries such as Korea and Taiwan was witnessed, as also to countries such as India that had a raw-material base and where pollution norms were not a major consideration. It became possible for these countries to produce finished leather in a big way and also develop capacity for producing leather manufactures, although the major production centres for leather manufactures continued to be in the advanced countries mentioned earlier. In India, this was reflected in a major policy initiative in 1973, where the transition to production of finished leather was sought to be made. Until 1973, the pattern of exports and organization that was set in the colonial period continued.

A second migration of the industry took place in the 1980s, with some countries such as Korea and Taiwan becoming uncompetitive, partially due to rising labour costs and the relocation of labour-intensive processes within the production of leather and leather manufactures to other developing countries, particularly in South Asia and the less developed of the Southeast Asian countries. In India, the main policy changes in this period were in export policy, favouring production of labour-intensive value-added manufactures, including intermediate products. India thus came to play different roles in the international market for leather and leather products— as a supplier of raw material in the colonial and immediate post-colonial periods until 1973; as an intermediate product supplier (that is, supplier of finished leather, footwear components, etc.) from 1973 onwards; and also as a supplier of low-labour cost leather products in the lower ends of the international market from the 1980s.

The thrust on production for exports also resulted in a large number of institutions that were set up to cater to the industry, marking it out from other traditional industries. Further, the policy structure that came up for the industry reflected several assumptions: that the domestic market should not act as a barrier in the expansion of exports; that expansion of scales in a big way is the only way to tap the international market effectively, especially in the footwear segment; that low labour costs would give India a competitive edge over other countries that have higher labour costs, and an export structure that takes advantage of this is a preferred strategy for India.

The next sub-section unravels the structure of production organization that came up in response to this GVC incorporation.

Export Orientation and Organizational Structure in Three Leather Clusters—Markets vs Hierarchy

The conscious incorporation into the GVC for leather resulted in several changes in the Indian leather industry. First, the structure that developed to cater to the international market through successive value addition resulted in a complete transformation of the production chain in the leather industry. Second, in the clusters that thrived, the organization of production came to be characterized by a hierarchical structure of enterprises. Third, the structure that emerged happened because of the nature of GVC incorporation, involving an exclusive and disproportionate emphasis on exports, the nature of demand for Indian leather and leather products in the international market, and the nature of transactions with buyers, indicating purely hierarchical power dynamics characteristic of particular segments in GVCs. Each of these is summarized in the following.

To begin with, what was a scattered industry with tanning as well as leather product-making spread across the country, came to be concentrated towards production in major clusters that focused on exports, with this tendency accelerating from the 1970s. There was a systematic decline in small clusters that were tanning centres, and this reflected in general the thrust of the policy of orienting production and channelling raw material supplies towards the major clusters.

In the field study that this chapter is based on, one such centre—Warangal, in the state of Andhra Pradesh—was studied. The tanning industry in Warangal existed as small-scale and home-based units through the nineteenth century, during which tanning operations were performed manually using vegetable dyes. The cluster switched to chrome tanning sometime in the 1970s. In 1981, there were about 33 tanneries in Warangal. The finished leather produced in these tanneries was being exported to the international market through agents and fairs. The nature of the industry started undergoing a change in about the mid-1980s. Competition among the various units increased and the existing tanneries started doing jobwork for exporting units in Chennai. By about the late 1990s the number of tanneries declined to 18, and further to eight by 2006. This process, in turn, resulted in large-scale unemployment among leather workers in these areas; it will be discussed in the next section. Further, even clusters that catered primarily to the domestic market came to be increasingly focused on exports, the Agra cluster being one such prominent one.

What the aforementioned meant was that a large part of the production chain that consisted, in addition to the activities of carcass collection and flaying centres, of centres for tanning and leather product-making, came to be transformed into a structure to permit the transfer of raw material to the large clusters and even within that to production for exports.[11] Further, across different segments of the industry, it became possible for the production process to be split up into many component processes with the possibility of production being done under a wide variety of production organization forms. The specific organizational form depended on how many processes are being undertaken by an enterprise, how mechanised the operations at each stage are, and how employment intensive and skill intensive they are, with all these determining how large or small the enterprise is, what kind of employment takes place, and what the conditions of production are.

Coming next to the organizational structure that emerged in Kolkata, Chennai, and Agra, the fieldwork showed the existence of complex organizational forms that have developed to cater to the export market. All the three locations studied are typical small scale clusters, with a wide range as well as depth. Thus, in addition to the main production units, there are a large number of raw material dealers, machinery and chemical suppliers, and repair workshops in all three clusters.[12] However, there are significant differences between them with regard to their market orientation and histories.

In Agra, what appears to have happened is that in what was primarily a domestic market-oriented cluster with some segments of exporting units, as earlier studies (Knorringa, 1996)) showed, there was a clear emergence of a very significant segment to cater to the export market and a commensurate rise in the contribution of the city to leather exports.[13] Further, Agra is a cluster that specializes only in footwear production, with a clear segmentation in the areas that produce footwear for the domestic and export markets. It has been a relatively later entrant in a significant way to the GVC for leather,[14] and the exporting segment exhibits the same hierarchy of enterprises that will be described later.

In Kolkata, the exporting units have been exporting finished leather for a long time and entered the market for leather goods in the 1980s, when the policy to encourage value added production was adopted. Being major exporters of finished leather to Eastern Europe and the erstwhile Soviet

Union, the fall in exports as a result of the break-up of the Soviet bloc in the early 1990s was countered through a greater supply of finished leather to exporters in other clusters and an increased focus on producing leather goods for the international market. Further, many firms also retained the option to sell leather goods in the domestic market through leather fairs and the like.

In Tamil Nadu, the clusters have always been almost exclusively export-oriented, with the state's contribution to exports being the highest among all regions.

In spite of these differences in being relatively export-oriented or domestic market–oriented, the fieldwork found that the organizational forms that exist in all three locations are similar in terms of the layers of activities. All three clusters contain the whole range of organizational forms, from vertically integrated enterprises with the whole production process internal to the firm to a large number of units doing part processes and linked to each other vertically or horizontally, with a wide range of intermediate structures in between. In industrial organization terms, there are a large number of forms between the traditional extremes of market and hierarchy, but analytically we can distinguish three levels of enterprises (see Figure 10.1).

Level III		
Medium and Large Tanneries	Medium and Large Product Manufacturers	Medium and Large Tannery -cum-Product Manufacturer
Level II		
Small Scale Independent Tanneries	Small Scale Independent Product Manufacturers	Small Scale Tanneries/ Product Manufacturers who are part of Groups
Level I		
Jobwork Tanneries	Product Fabricators	

Figure 10.1: Hierarchy of Enterprises in Chennai and Kolkata

At the lowest level, designated Level I, there are large numbers of jobwork tanneries and leather product fabricators involved in hierarchical, vertical relationships with firms that place orders with them. These have come into existence in response to the export thrust and represent the response to fragmented, highly volatile demand in the international market. These enterprises belong entirely to the informal sector, that is, the unorganized or unregistered sector. As far as the system is concerned, they exist in order to provide the major cushion against the adverse impact of fluctuations in demand. These enterprises aim to grow into larger enterprises as independent producers and exporters, in keeping with the trajectory of growth seen in the sector as a whole. While there are fabricators who undertake able production of full products in some cases, in the majority of cases these units specialize in particular parts of the production process in the tannery as well as the product-making segments, and undertake the operations that are considered less skilled or those that warrant less supervision. Raw materials, when they have to be purchased, are obtained from areas within their state in the case of these firms;[15] it was reported in all three clusters that there is great uncertainty in raw material supplies, with firms being unable to establish long-term relationships with any specific suppliers. Exporters reported that the relationship with subcontractors is not long-standing and they give the orders to whoever agrees to do the work at the given price. Exporters as a strategy keep changing their subcontractors.

At the next level, Level II, there are a large number of small-scale producers of finished leather and leather products who are either independent producers or produce for a group consisting of many small-scale enterprises in different stages of the production process. The small-scale independent enterprises are involved in vertical hierarchical relations with jobwork units or fabricators (depending on what they produce), who either supply specific products to them or undertake specific processes regularly, or in times when demand is buoyant. They are also involved in relatively stable vertical relations with one another, in complementary parts of the production process, and these are more or less independent, equal relationships with little hierarchy. Many of these small-scale firms in all three clusters have established export contacts on their own, although these are not very stable, long-term relationships. These firms have relatively more stable suppliers of raw material in their home states as well as from other clusters. In many cases, they also import finished leather from different countries.

The top level, that is, Level III, consists of medium- and large-scale enterprises that are independent, as well as those that form part of groups. In many cases, they have grown from small scales, sometimes even from fabricator levels. Vertical integration within the same firm does not necessarily mean the absence of vertical relationships with other firms, and this goes side by side with extensive relations with jobwork or fabricating units. They use imported finished leather and accessories quite extensively.

The structure that has emerged is one that allows for maximum flexibility. Thus, for a typical firm in the industry, the choice is not between whether to make or buy but to retain the capacity to do either or both through a combination of internal capacity and arms-length relationships with smaller firms, depending on the situation. The situation can be characterized by one of extreme flexibility given the conditions for profitable production in the conjecture that the industry is faced with.

What can be said with regard to the degree of upgrading that the industry has seen from the experience of these three clusters; that is, whether the clusters have facilitated endogenous innovation by firms and whether the nature of technological upgrading has been sufficient to cater to the needs of discerning buyers? In general, production for export markets, particularly for footwear production on a large scale, has meant an increase in mechanization in all three clusters. Within this, the Tamil Nadu clusters, because they have a higher number of large firms, appear more mechanized and more 'technologically upgraded'. However, it was seen that the majority of firms take decisions on modernization or the degree of mechanization on the basis of whether and how they can link up with other firms or whether they can achieve maximum flexibility in the hiring of labour. Thus, while machinery acquisition has been determined to a large extent by liberal imports of capital goods as well as the emphasis on value-added exports in the export policies for the sector, actual decisions with regard to the nature of technology upgrading have been circumscribed by the need for flexibility in production and labour processes. This is a major feature in all three clusters and constitutes the nature of the link between clustering and technological upgrading in the leather industry.

Coming to the link between the organizational structure described earlier and the value chain, the structure described earlier has emerged because of the nature of GVC incorporation, involving an exclusive and disproportionate emphasis on exports, the highly volatile and unpredictable nature of demand for Indian leather and leather products in the international market, and the nature of transactions with buyers. The disproportionate emphasis on exports has resulted in major incentives for export production and the urge seen in the majority of firms to become exporting enterprises. However, the segment of demand that India caters to is one where price is the dominant determinant of competitive advantage.

This brings us to the issue of control in the value chain from the point of view of inter-firm linkages within the global economy for this segment of demand. Humphrey and Schmitz (2001) stress the critical parameters—what is to be produced, how it is to be produced, when it is to be produced, and how much is to be produced. The ability to govern and have control in a chain rests in intangible competencies (research and development [R&D], design, branding, and marketing) that are characterized by high barriers to entry and command high returns, usually reaped by the developed-country firms. In contrast, developing-country firms tend to be 'locked into' tangible production activities, producing to parameters set by 'governors', suffering from low barriers to entry, and reaping low returns. In this context, even the large firms in the clusters reported that a large proportion of their products were sold in the cheaper ranges of supermarkets or of brands. While exporters have direct relations with some buyers, most of the contacts are through agents of brands, retail houses, and supermarket chains which have regular offices in the clusters. These agents help exporters get in touch with new buyers and in marketing their own designs. Participation in international fairs is another key strategy of the exporters as this also helps them establish direct relations with the buyers. Only the largest firms in the clusters have some long-standing contracts with their buyers, which might be standard brands like Reebok and Hush Puppies. The parameters of how, what, when, and how much to produce are exclusively set by buyers in all the three clusters. In the field study, all the exporters interviewed reported that designs are developed by buyers. Indigenous designs are developed only occasionally and are subject to the approval of the buyers. In fact, in many cases, exporters expressed that strict adherence to buyer specifications becomes an area of their own core competence and constituting their 'primary competitive advantage'. Buyer specifications include not only the product design but also the raw material, depending on the quality and colour of the final product. This sometimes also implies that the buyers specify the country from which the raw material should be sourced. In fact, some buyers insist on the use of imported leather for their products. Even the accessories to be used and packaging boxes are specified by buyers. These are in the case of products of quality higher than the rock-bottom segment. In the rock-bottom segment, the emphasis is purely on price, that is, the ability to provide the cheapest product.

The field study also found that quality control regulations in the case of standardized products are strictly directed by brands and maintained by exporters, and there is no negotiation possible in delivery schedules fixed by the buyer. The brands conduct regular inspection of the products. In case of the orders acquired through an agent, the agent conducts regular inspection of the products. The field study also indicated that despite thin margins, cut-throat competition among each other often compels exporters to further reduce their profit margin per piece in case they get a greater quantity of the order. For the same order, exporters in the study stress that sample price fixed once cannot be changed even if the prices of raw materials fluctuate.

This is true even for product ranges where quality control is essential. In fact, the study found that the premium range in the domestic market fetched a higher price than what it fetched in the international market. The leather industry's case, therefore, substantiates arguments by Humphrey and Schmitz (2001) that while non-price factors (like quality, brand, and speed) have come to play an increasing role for competing in global markets, price competition continues to be unrelenting, leading to a downward pressure on prices, particularly in labour-intensive products. The resulting profit squeeze leads buyers to scout continuously for new producers who offer lower labour costs.

The nature of the international market for leather in the range that India caters to and the kind of policy structure that exists to cater to this have thus resulted in a highly flexible production structure in terms of organizational forms. This flexibility is not only in the structure of production but in labour processes as well. The following section looks at the link between the organizational structure and the labour market.

LABOUR MARKET DYNAMICS AND OUTCOMES IN THE LEATHER CLUSTERS: SOCIAL UPGRADING OR FLEXIBLE CASUALIZATION?

The question that we address in this section is whether GVC incorporation resulted in social upgrading, reflected in an increase in labour welfare. In other words, has the path of the Indian leather industry been a 'high road' one?

It has been argued, as mentioned in the introduction, in the case of the Indian leather industry (Banerjee and Nihila, 1999) that the clusters of Tamil Nadu are more modern and forward-looking than the others because, among other aspects, the state has a relatively better organized labour market and a 'disciplined' labour force unlike in other clusters such as Kolkata. One of the arguments put across to substantiate such a stance is that the Tamil Nadu clusters are relatively unaffected by militant and 'destructive' trade unionism. Further, it is argued that the industry in Tamil Nadu treats its workforce much better than other places because of its forward-looking nature. In the critical area of labour relations and the functioning of the labour market, it is held up as an example.

Our fieldwork found that in the industry as a whole and specifically the three clusters studied, the extent of social upgrading has been very minimal, although GVC incorporation resulted in several structural changes in labour markets and labour processes. First, a very large segment of the labour in the leather industry that is engaged in the process of raw material collection and processing, or carcass collection and flaying of the hide or skin off dead animals, has strong links to traditional caste structures. Most of these tasks are performed by people belonging to lower castes in rural areas, as part of caste-determined occupational structures. Although the traditional system of disposing carcasses to the traditional flayers by farmers has been undergoing changes,[16] it was estimated that even in the mid-1980s, on an average, 55 per cent of carcasses were being disposed of in this manner all over the country (CLRI, 1987). The activities of carcass collection and flaying are still linked to customary obligations and to caste; as a result, those engaged in them are part of a large informal workforce that earns very little from these tasks. There has been no social upgrading at all at this backwardly linked level in the industry, although the necessity of this is well recognized for generating higher quality.

Second, informalization is a major feature of the labour market, although it manifests itself in different ways, irrespective of the nature of the enterprise. In the clustering literature, the leather industry is a classic case of the 'low road to flexible specialization', and this is equally applicable to the modern units that cater to the medium range in the international market. This is because informal methods of recruitment and remuneration are a guaranteed system of exerting control over the labour process; even in the segments such as footwear manufacture and finished leather production where production conditions can favour vertical integration and the growth of large firms, flexibility is attained through control over labour and informal labour processes. The availability of cheap labour presents the possibility of adjusting instantly to changes in demand, and control over the labour process constitutes the most certain element in the production process for an entrepreneur. In a situation where entrepreneurs consider production conditions to be vulnerable, informal labour processes are used and are widespread.

How is this control over the labour process established without threatening the basis of production? It takes place through the working of the labour market in ways that appear formal to a certain extent, but in actual terms are based on norms of informal employment which also effectively use the conditions of 'social embeddedness' in the leather industry. To be more specific, the use of informal labour processes is possible due to employment based on caste in Agra and Kolkata, and that segregated by gender in Tamil Nadu.

There are stark differences and striking similarities between Chennai, Agra, and Kolkata as far as the nature of the labour market, the nature of the workforce, the degree of mobility of the workforce, their wages, benefits, and working conditions are concerned. The labour markets in Kolkata and Agra are based mostly on caste and are largely informal in nature. In Kolkata, the workforce in the tannery as well as the product-making segments consists of traditional Chamar labour from Bihar.[17] This is an institutional characteristic that de facto admits only Chamars into the industry and determines the division between the workers on the basis of region.[18] On an average, only about 35 per cent of the tannery workforce has regular employment (very often referred to as having 'permanent jobs') and the remaining workforce is employed on casual basis, with no guarantee of employment (author's fieldwork). In leather product-making units, the scenario is quite the same, except that it was more difficult to find even informal estimates for the percentage of casual to regular workers.

'Regular' or 'permanent' are terms that only mean that the labourers continue working with the same unit without being retrenched arbitrarily subject to demand. On the other hand, a casual worker is uncertain about his job on a day-to-day basis, although he might have long stints of uninterrupted casual employment when demand is buoyant. Having regular employment does not imply the existence of a long-term employment contract or the existence of records with any administrative authority, as would be necessary in the organized sector, even when the units clearly belong to the organized sector. This employment takes place through labour contractors who most often belong to the same caste and region as the workers in the specific segments. Even in the regular workforce, wages are paid only for specific operations, with piece-rates for most machine operations dominating as against time wages. Piece-rates vary across different machine operations and sometimes piece-rated workers earn almost as much as the workers who earn wages in times when demand is buoyant and plenty of work is available. No benefits—except dearness allowance for regular workers—are available for any worker in the industry in Kolkata.

In Agra, it is mostly low-caste Jatav workers who are employed in the leather industry, and the labour market functions exactly in the same way as in Kolkata (Knorringa 1996). Here again, caste-based employment ensures a regular pool of workers, larger numbers of whom are employed on a 'regular' basis than in Kolkata, resulting in a much smaller proportion of casual workers. The majority of workers interviewed earned an average wage of less than Rs 3,000 per month, similar to the average wage in Kolkata. No benefits, even in terms of wage-related benefits such as increments and dearness allowance to compensate for inflation, are available to most workers in Agra.[19]

Kolkata and Agra are thus classic cases of informalization in the labour market, with minimum wages not being adhered to and hardly any benefits being provided even in enterprises that belong to the formal sector. The case of Chennai is a little different, although, as we shall see later, the informal sector's norms set the benchmark there too. In Chennai, the labour market is relatively 'formal' in large part. Most of the workers in the larger units, leaving aside the jobwork units and the fabricating units, are employed on a regular basis, with the proportion of casual workforce much lower, probably at less than 10 per cent. All workers in regular employment get some benefits they are entitled to under the Factories Act, such as provident fund (PF) and Employees' State Insurance (ESI). Enterprises maintain regular records of workers employed and there is an office of the Labour Commissioner outside the cluster, which is expected to look into the workers' grievances and regulate conditions of work. However, while some benefits might be available, which becomes necessary when enterprises in the organized sector reveal their employment profiles, hardly any worker reported possessing an employment contract clearly stating the length and terms of employment. Retiring employees just left the employment they were in and did not get any retirement benefits from the companies. Similarly, no provisions exist for compensation of employees in the case of lay off or lockouts, although by law these would be applicable to firms that employ more than 10 workers.[20]

While most tannery workers in Chennai are male,[21] most of the leather product segment workforce consists of women in the age group of 16–30 years and the rate of turnover of this workforce is very high, with most of the women leaving their jobs after marriage, having worked for five or six years. This is a feature of the labour market for many industries in Tamil Nadu, where levels of feminization of the manufacturing workforce have been quite high. Employers reported that women tended to create less trouble, were more docile and disciplined than men, and tended to unionize less—which is why they were preferred. Also, they did not develop long-term stakes in the industry as they left after a few years and, therefore, firms did not have to provide long-term benefits of various kinds. Males are employed mostly in supervisory and decision-making positions, with only a few operating machines in the product-making segment.

In the late 1990s, for the same operations, there was a clear difference between wages of the male and female workers, with the former earning wages similar to those in Kolkata and the female workers earning between Rs 600 and Rs 1,000 on an average. Very few women got absorbed into higher positions with higher wages, and even when they did, they earned less than their male counterparts. However, when the fieldwork was repeated in 2006, this obvious gender difference in wages seems to have disappeared, although average wages were still low with the majority of workers earning the same average wage of less than Rs 3,000. While the labour market in Chennai is formal and regulated, there is a feminization of the labour force, and this possibly helps to keep average wages low across the sector. Further, what is interesting is that even those who considered themselves 'permanent' did not possess any employment contracts and were not entitled to retirement benefits.

In the larger enterprises in Chennai, adjustments to demand take place not through layoffs, but through the system of 'retention wage'. This wage is paid to workers in slack times or when there is no demand, which ensures that they remain in the employment of the firm concerned. The retention wage is significantly lower than the monthly wage that is paid when demand is buoyant; the workers are required to 'compensate' for the retention wage received with longer working hours at the regular monthly wage when demand surges again. Overtime rates are not paid in such a case. What is guaranteed here, therefore, is regular employment, but with adjustment to demand volatility taking place by adjusting wages in the aforementioned manner and maintaining flexibility. This system came into existence when India entered the leather product segment after the mid-1980s, with this segment facing the most volatile demand conditions. At the same time, firms did not want to deal with high turnover in the workforce but desired a stable manpower. Now, in all kinds of units in Kolkata and Agra, as well as in the smaller units in Chennai, adjustments to a fall in demand take place through a reduction in the working hours or by laying off workers in proportion to the reduction in demand.

A major difference between workers in Agra, on the one hand, and in Kolkata and Chennai, on the other hand, is in the degree of unionization, with the history of worker organization beginning from the 1930s. In Kolkata, although trade unions have not managed to change conditions of employment in any substantial manner, they negotiate whatever minimal increases have taken place in the wages and the dearness allowance. There is a long history of strikes in the leather industry in Kolkata, and many of the settlements that exist and determine the terms of employment have been arrived at as a result of threats of strikes or actual strikes.

In Chennai, too, trade unions have existed in the leather industry from the 1930s and have been instrumental in pressuring the industry to confer some minimum benefits for workers such as PF and ESI. However, over time they have become less effective due to a variety of reasons (such as changes in the organization of firms, the labour process, and the feminization of the workforce), and the possibilities for labour militancy have become limited in the sector as a whole. For example, in Chennai, firms have systematically replaced the right of labour to link up with industry-level unions with the setting up of plant-level committees, diluting the potential for effective action by labour in the case of violations. Further, with the objective of both government policy as well as of firms being to minimize labour costs in the interest of maximizing exports, the potential for labour militancy being able to achieve concrete gains for labour has been eroded significantly. There is no attempt on the part of the Labour Commissioner's offices outside the Tamil Nadu leather clusters to enforce minimum wage legislation in spite of blatant violation. The employment of women in very large numbers is also to ostensibly depend on their 'docility and obedience' to not challenge violations. We found, however, that women workers did keep contact with the industry-level unions and even got them to take up cases of violations in PF and ESI payments by companies in both instances when fieldwork was done. Further, the unions were consciously raising the issue of gender discrimination in wages, which has possibly played a role in the narrowing of the gender gap.

It is clear that the way the sector has developed gives very little gains to labour, and in this sense the leather industry is a classic case of the low road to flexible specialization. However, what is interesting is that the low labour standards seen come with a combination of modernization and growth in the larger enterprises in the industry. There appears to be no contradiction between perpetuating low labour standards and embarking upon modernization in an effort to cater to the GVC for leather.

CONCLUSION—FLEXIBLE CASUALIZATION: COINCIDENCE OR CONSCIOUS STRATEGY?

Our fieldwork in the three clusters of Agra, Chennai, and Kolkata showed that the strategy of linking up to the GVC for leather, constituting a crucial element of government policy for the leather industry, effected substantial transformation in the indigenous leather industry in India. However, the strategy's main focus has been on capitalizing on the low-cost advantage that India has, which translates to a low labour-cost advantage. The flexibilization of the production as well as labour processes has taken advantage of the artisanal origins of the industry, its links with the social structure, and the flexibility afforded by feminization, and has taken the form of cut-throat competition and undercutting by producers to compete on the basis of price.

However, in spite of the structure and organization of the industry as well as policy being primarily tailored towards production for the international market, India has been progressively losing share in various segments in the international market for leather and leather products. Its export performance in terms of rates of growth has declined in the 1990s and it has been steadily losing out to competitors in all segments. Damodaran (2004) found that in dollar terms, leather and leather product exports grew at rates averaging 15 per cent per annum between 1973–74 and 1990–91, whereas this fell drastically to just about 3 per cent per annum between 1991–92 and 2000–01. The industry as a whole has been unable to either maintain its position in existing segments or reach out to higher value-added segments in the international market in any significant manner (the latter, where it has taken place, is limited to a few firms in the industry). In a crucial sense, government policies favouring export orientation, in the context of India's position in the international market for leather and leather products, set limits to the possibilities for sustained development of the industry.

NOTES

1. The term may be said to owe its origins to Gereffi's (1994) idea of global commodity chains, which consisted of tracing products at different levels of value addition across space, along with the unravelling of networks around the organization of activities that constitute backward and forward linkages in the production of these products.
2. Ranging from the extremes of markets and arm's length transactions, on the one hand, to hierarchy or complete vertical integration, on the other, other patterns—described as modular, relational, and captive chains—consist of networks (Gereffi, Humphrey, and Sturgeon, 2005) that are organized in intermediate forms.
3. Cadene and Holmstrom (1998) and Nadvi and Schmitz (1998) are two representative works from a huge corpus of literature.
4. The United Nations Industrial Development Organization's (UNIDO) *Industrial Development Report 2002/2003*, representing this 'positive view' on GVCs, stated that this would provide developing country enterprises with opportunities to upgrade their capabilities. For such enterprises, or clusters of enterprises, it was argued that the task is to insert themselves into the GVCs.
5. India's leather industry has been export-oriented from the nineteenth century onwards, and research (Swaminathan, 1992; Roy, 1999) has shown that the major impetus to change in the industry from a traditional dispersed craft activity to workshop and factory forms took place as a result of international demand becoming significant.
6. There are no actual estimates of the size of the domestic market and this is

the figure that is provided by the industry's representative organizations, such as the Council for Leather Exports.
7. This is considered a typical feature of classic industrial clusters, with 'social embeddedness' constituting a crucial condition that allows for cooperation.
8. This constituted one of the major aspects of GVC incorporation, with state policies being tailored to changes in the international market.
9. This is based on work done in the Kolkata and Chennai clusters for the author's doctoral dissertation in 1999–2000 and a study undertaken for the Centre for Education and Communication (CEC) in Chennai and Agra in 2006–7.
10. Who the traditional producers are and who joined later will become clear later in the chapter.
11. A major part of policy changes consisted of various duty exemptions and other incentives for exports for firms that were located in the main clusters. Firms in smaller clusters like Warangal found raw material prices high and were also unable to access enough raw material and also orders for production, which came to be concentrated in the major clusters.
12. They are all typical industrial clusters, as the literature sets out.
13. In 2006, Agra accounted for 22.71 per cent of India's footwear export and 7.25 per cent of export of leather and leather products (Sankar, 2006). This occurred through an increase of 25 per cent every year over the preceding two years.
14. Before this phase, which began from the mid-1990s or so, Agra's export presence was overshadowed by its identity as a cluster producing primarily for the domestic market, with exports being limited to cheap shoes to the erstwhile Soviet Union and Eastern Europe.
15. In the case of Chennai, firms procure their raw material from Erode or Trichy; in Agra, they are procured from Kanpur and Unnao.
16. The changes as well as the continuities in methods of carcass procurement and flaying can be traced historically.
17. The Chamars are low-caste workers who were brought into the leather tanneries in Kolkata in large numbers when the industry started undergoing market-induced changes in the early nineteenth century and clusters for tanned leather production were set up in Kolkata, Kanpur, and Tamil Nadu.
18. It has been seen how the only outsiders who have managed to break this de facto entry barrier into the labour market is a group of Nepali workers who might constitute around 5 per cent of the tannery workforce and are employed on higher wages.
19. About 10 per cent of interviewed workers in Agra received ESI and PF benefits, but this was not seen in Kolkata.
20. Enterprises covered by the Factories Act are those that have 10 or more workers (with power) or 20 or more workers (without power).

21. This is true only in Chennai. In other clusters in Tamil Nadu, women are employed for specific operations, as an earlier section showed.

REFERENCES

Banerjee, N. and M. Nihila (1999), 'Business Organisation in the Leather Industries of Calcutta and Chennai', in A.K. Bagchi (ed.), *Economy and Organisation: Indian Institutions under the Neoliberal Regime*, pp. 115–36. New Delhi: Sage Publications.

Cadene, P. and M. Holmstrom (eds) (1998), *Decentralised Production in India*. New Delhi: Sage Publications.

Central Leather Research Institute (CLRI) (1987), *Report of All India Survey on Raw Hides and Skins*. Madras: CLRI.

⸻ (1994), *Indian Leather 2010: A Technology, Industry and Trade Forecast*. Madras: CLRI.

Damodaran, S. (2004), *Export Orientation and Industrial Clustering—An Analysis of Organisational Structure and Performance of the Leather and Leather Products Industry in India*, Unpublished Ph.D. thesis, Jawaharlal Nehru University, New Delhi.

Gereffi, G. (1994), 'Capitalism, Development and Global Commodity Chains', in Leslie Sklair (ed.), *Capitalism and Development*, pp. 95–122. Westport, CT: Routledge.

Gereffi, G., H. Schmitz, and T.J. Sturgeon (2005), 'The Governance of Global Value Chains', *Review of International Political Economy*, 12(1): 78–104.

Humphrey, J. and H. Schmitz (2001), 'Governance in Global Value Chains', Paper presented at a Workshop on Global Value Chains held at the Rockefeller Foundation's Bellagio Conference Centre, September.

Knorringa, P. (1996), *Economics of Collaboration: Indian Shoemakers between Market and Hierarchy*. New Delhi: Sage Publications.

Nadvi, K. and H. Schmitz (1998), 'Industrial Clusters in Less Developed Countries: Review of Experiences and Research Agenda', in P. Cadene and M. Holmstrom (eds), *Decentralised Production in India*, pp. 60–138. New Delhi: Sage Publications.

Piore, M. and C. Sabel (1984), *The Second Industrial Divide*. New York: Basic Books.

Roy, T. (1999), *Traditional Industry in the Economy of Colonial India*. Cambridge: Cambridge University Press.

Sankar, U. (2006), 'Trade Liberalization and Environmental Protection: Responses of Leather Industry in Brazil, China and India', *Economic and Political Weekly*, 41(24): 2470–77.

Sinha, S. and S. Sinha (1992), *Indian Leather Industry: The Challenge of Modernisation*. New Delhi: Sage Publications.

Swaminathan, P. (1992), 'State Intervention in Industrialisation: A Case Study of the Madras Presidency', *Indian Economic and Social History Review*, 29(4): 479–506.

United Nations Industrial Development Organization (UNIDO) (2002), *Competing through Innovation and Learning: Industrial Development Report 2002–03*. Vienna: UNIDO.

11 COST CUTTING PRESSURES AND LABOUR RELATIONS IN TAMIL NADU'S AUTOMOBILE COMPONENTS SUPPLY CHAIN

T.G. Suresh

INTRODUCTION

This chapter attempts an empirically grounded analysis of the globalization-induced trends in the automotive components sector in Tamil Nadu. It focuses on a cluster of variables that are differentially located in the supply chain to explain their varying outcomes. This entails an inquiry into the ways in which the local components sector was restructured and how it impinged upon the labour as well as the small firms. The main concern here is to understand how the driving trends in the global automobile industry produce flexible labour regimes that help the large firms to achieve cost advantage which cause adverse consequences for employment and wages. This aspect has been explained by investigating the mode through which labour has been incorporated into the automotive supply chain in Tamil Nadu in the context of the shift from local to global.

The main questions of this study are organized around five interrelated concerns that try to provide a thematic sequence. It opens with an introductory discussion on the rise of a new industrial development model in Tamil Nadu and the growth trajectory of the automobile industry. The following section will look at how globalization has transformed the local components supply base by examining the way it was restructured and the trends that it has set in motion across the supply chain. How these processes have adversely affected the automobile workers is examined in the fourth section by focusing on the rise of flexible labour regimes. The last section will try to show how the cost-down trends have created new barriers and challenges to the small enterprises in the light engineering sector and their consequences on the wages.

This study draws from two rounds of field studies carried out in the Chennai region in December 2006 and in October 2007. The first round focused on the labour institutions in Tamil Nadu and tried to investigate how the reforms-induced adjustments have affected the labour regulations mechanism in the state. The sector-specific data on the automobile components supply base was collected during the second round. The field interviews covered respondents from nearly all constitutive segments of this integrated industry including the components manufacturing firms of different sizes and capacities, the workers of different employment statuses, industry associations of varying sub-sectors and strength, and the trade unions.

THE RISE OF A NEW INDUSTRIAL DEVELOPMENT MODEL IN POST-REFORM TAMIL NADU

Tamil Nadu is one of the most industrialized states in India. Since the mid-1990s, it has emerged as one of the most favoured investment destinations in the country. This impressive turnaround in the growth trajectory for well over a decade seems to have been an outcome of a rather complex blend of factors and circumstances. At the core of this process lies Tamil Nadu's rather trouble-free transition to a reform-oriented economy. When it was introduced in the early 1990s, the rationale for reforms won instant political support, and has catapulted into a popular theme widely shared by a cross-section of the society in the urban areas. This marks a sharp contrast when compared to the experiences of other southern states such as Kerala where the reform policies deeply polarized the political classes as well as the popular mood. And when the political contestations in the state largely focused on identity-based aspirations, a new industrial development model was in the making without being subjected to any serious public debate.

A series of public policies that were announced in post-reform Tamil Nadu pertaining to investment, employment, and regulation signalled the coming of a new industrial policy in the state. A key element in this shift was redefining the role of the government with respect to industrial development where it assigned itself a new role of an active facilitator of capital investment and guarantor of stable industrial relations in the state. The hallmark of this policy was institutional synchronization of various administrative departments to execute investment projects which require official approval, land acquisition, infrastructural support, fiscal incentives, and so on. This was achieved mainly by rolling back the procedural hurdles that characterized the earlier system. But a corollary of the same policies was the weakening of a number of public institutions, particularly those involved in labour regulations. The new industrial development model that has come to dominate Tamil Nadu in the last decade has set in motion a process that has today seriously eroded the capacities of labour institutions in the state. Although they still exist as formal legal institutions bearing their earlier insignia and structure, they hardly have any capacity to deliver their mandate. The functions of the institutions of labour protection such as labour commissioner, labour inspectorate, and arbitration are now redefined in effect, if not officially stated, in conformity with the new development model that rests upon the government's eagerness to project industrial peace and the 'excellent' work culture in the state.

The new model was built around the core objective of bringing foreign investment into the state. In bringing foreign firms into the state, the Tamil Nadu government pursued a proactive investment policy. This approach received a strong fillip in the milieu of an increasing trend of competitive federalism among Indian states as they vied with each other to attract global capital. In the mid-1990s, the state government started a concerted campaign to attract foreign investment by showcasing the main advantages that the state possesses in infrastructure, human resources, and policy framework.[1] The main thrust of this campaign was an argument about the low-cost advantage that the state possesses and that makes it an ideal destination for foreign investment. This idea of low-cost advantage is premised on two factors: the abundant availability of trained human resources and what is called an 'excellent work culture' in the state.[2] The second point was well elaborated by pointing out a generally peaceful industrial climate in the state characterized by relative absence of trade unionism and workers' strike. These factors, including the greater availability of skilled labour, lower wage rates, peaceful labour and industrial relations, and strong government support, formed the centrepieces in the government's campaign for making Tamil Nadu the ideal choice for investments.[3]

AUTOMOBILE INDUSTRY IN TAMIL NADU: THE RECENT GROWTH PHASE

Fuelled by significant income rise in urban areas and increasing demand for passenger cars, the automobile industry in India has been on a robust growth track since the early 1990s. This generated considerable rise in the annual auto components production. According to the Automotive Components

Manufacturers Association (ACMA), in about seven years since 1997, the annual components production in India has more than doubled from an aggregate value of US$ 3,008 billion to US$ 6,730 million in 2003–4. It recorded an impressive growth of 18–20 per cent per year, and by 2006, registered a turnover of US$ 12,000 million.[4] This growth phase witnessed a range of tendencies as well as movements across the sector that have redefined the previous profile of the industry. The most dramatic of all was the consolidation and rise of a number of leading domestic firms.

In the backdrop of an expanding passenger-car market nationally, the automobile industry in Tamil Nadu is set for a momentous revival. Since the mid-1990s, attracted by the large pool of skilled labour, the strong presence of local components producers, and of the proactive political dispensations, a number of global car assemblers began to set up their assembling centres in the state (see the next section for a detailed discussion). Their arrival into the city suburbs of Chennai has brought about a significant turnaround in the automotive components industry in Tamil Nadu. Until then, the local components sector was mainly catering to after-market services. There were very few original equipment manufacturers (OEM) who could sustain stable components production. Nevertheless, it was the presence of Ashok Leyland that greatly helped Chennai's auto components sector to sustain itself. For decades it was supplying Ashok Leyland, and the after-market services were the main drive of components manufacturing in the Chennai region.

The starting of car production by Hyundai Motors India in 1996 in a 500 acre plot in Iringattukottai near Chennai with an installed capacity to make 120,000 units was one of the significant developments that contributed to the revival of the local components sector. The company's integrated plant in Sriperumbadur acquires nearly 85 per cent of its components locally. This was followed by Ford Motors commencing production in Maraimalainagar in 1999 with more than 90 per cent of its requirements met by locally produced components. The arrival of large firms with long-term plans and significant investments instilled a strong drive in the local components manufacturing sector. Since then the auto components industry in the state has been on a robust growth path. By 2005, Tamil Nadu had achieved a 35 per cent share of installed capacity of auto components in the country. The state's automotive sector is estimated to be around US$ 3 billion, contributing to 7–8 per cent of the gross state domestic product (GSDP) (CII, 2005: 22). The state today controls a significant share in India's total output in various automotive segments. Tamil Nadu accounts for 21 per cent of the passenger cars, 33 per cent of commercial vehicles, and more than 35 per cent of the total automobile components produced in the country (CII, 2007: 23). In the components manufacturing sector in particular, the local firms have become the leading producers of high-quality electrical, braking/suspension, and engine parts. Well over 100 large components manufacturing firms are based in the state, mainly concentrated around the Chennai region, Coimbatore, and Hosur. Altogether, they provide employment to about 45,000 people.

The present competitive advantage that the Tami Nadu-based components firms are enjoying is in fact derived from certain historical conditions and factors. Well before the recent turnaround in the industry, the state established itself as one of the leading automotive centres in the country. The state had gained an early lead in the components sector as some of the local-based companies such as TVS, Rane Group, and MRF had a pioneering presence in the region.

These factors, such as a strong commitment of the state and its prominent role in the early industrialization during the planning era, created some of the best industrial estates in the country like the Guindy Industrial Estate that synergized the resources of the state, local entrepreneurship, and skilled manpower. The existence of focused state policies to promote industrial growth and the direct involvement of the government in providing necessary institutional conditions as well as facilities gave strong impetus to engineering-based manufacturing in the state. During the planning decades, the state specially encouraged and promoted the small-scale enterprises. This factor had significantly contributed to the growth of vastly dispersed small engineering units in the state. The existence of thousands of small and micro units has played a critical role in making Tamil Nadu a major automotive hub in the country.

THE COMING OF THE GLOBAL ASSEMBLERS AND THE RESTRUCTURING OF THE LOCAL COMPONENTS SUPPLY BASE

The coming of global assemblers into the Chennai region has stimulated a new phase of industrial transformation in the local automobile components manufacturing in Tamil Nadu. Tewari (2001) has observed an energizing effect of the arrival of large auto assemblers on the local components suppliers. The global firms have infused a new dynamism into the region's components manufacturing industry, especially among medium firms. With appropriate responses and strategizing, these firms were able to innovate new production technologies and have emerged as the most potent mechanisms of new technological diffusion. Since then, the sector has undergone significant structural reorganization. The way the industry has evolved in the recent growth phase and new system that has come to dominate are different from what had existed earlier. Until the late 1980s, the sector was composed of a large number of medium and small firms that were scattered and mainly catered to the after-market services. The supplier base that existed then was quite broad and the comparative advantage that the leading firms enjoyed in terms of technological capabilities was only relative to other medium firms. It was their stronger capital base, industrial facilities, and organizational stability that enabled them to remain in their leading positions. The small firms operating on low capital base, limited production capacities, and often with five–six workers were able to sustain as viable business units. They confronted only relative barriers within the industry and enjoyed a certain degree of autonomy in strategizing their growth path. These firms used to account for a substantial portion of the components produced then.

The deregulation of the automobile industry in 1991, the arrival of the global assemblers, and the subsequent expansion of the components sector have drastically transformed the structure of the supplier base. First, some of the old leading firms were able to achieve impressive industrial transformations through technological upgrading, increasing capacities, diversification of production, effective marketing, and increasing export share. With the upgraded capacities and enhanced brand value, they were able to capitalize on the new market opportunities that opened up after the deregulation. Since the early 1990s, these firms have been steadily consolidating their leadership position in the sector. Second, these processes have impelled centralizing tendencies within the supply chains. The rise of the large firms with greatly enhanced technological capabilities, increasing volume of turnover, and strong capital base helped them to create new brand identities in terms of efficiency, reliability, and quality control. They became direct vendors to an increasing number of foreign assemblers and domestic vehicle manufacturers and developed long-term partnerships with them. This created a new kind of supplier–buyer relationship that is very different from what existed earlier. Third, this centralizing process has created new barriers for the small and tiny firms.

The structure of the automotive components manufacturing sector in Tamil Nadu as it has come to evolve during the recent growth phase (late 1990s) has drastically altered the supplier–buyer relationship that existed until then. The transformations that the driving forces of the growth brought about were such that they nearly reconfigured the sector along a completely different set of priorities and drives that propelled the industry. The incorporation of the local components supply chain into the global automotive industry has induced a complex range of movements down the line. As a sub-sector governed by the requirements of the automotive assemblers, the components supply firms have always been subject to various kinds of pressures. However, the present global integration has generated a new set of pressures which are structurally different from those that existed during the planning era (see the next section for further elaboration).

The sector today has formed into a vertically integrated pyramid in which around a hundred large and medium firms dominate the supply chain. They vary in terms of ownership, size, and management and include wholly local-based firms, joint and collaborative ventures, and wholly owned subsidiaries. Among them, some are conglomerations such as the TVS Group.[5] Started as a motor company in 1911, it has evolved into one of India's major industrial conglomerations of 19 companies. The group has a number of foreign collaboration subsidiaries such as Lucas–TVS established in 1960, India Nippon Electricals Ltd since 1985, and TVS Cherry Ltd which started production in 1994. Sundaram Fasteners, one of the group's firms, has emerged into a globally competitive supplier source. Established in 1966, it manufactures a range of products from high tensile fasteners, radiator caps, and powder metal parts to gear shifters. Sundaram Fasteners has around 1,650 regular workers.

Another leading player, The Rane Group, is a conglomeration of components firms. Rane Engine Valves, the company's flagship firm, started in 1959. It manufactures valves, guides, and tappets for internal combustion engines and has more than 1,400 regular employees. Some of the other large firms from Tamil Nadu include Ennore Foundaries established in 1961, which today employs around 2,396 workers engaged in the production of grey iron casting, transmission cases, and axles housings. India Pistons, a company from the early planning era, manufactures a range of products from pistons, cylinder liners, and air compressors, and has 1,200 regular employees. The Pricol Ltd commenced production in 1974 and over the years became a firm with much greater products' diversity, covering 53 components from decompression units to vacuum switches. The company has an employee strength of 4,615 and a number of foreign collaborations. Other large players in the supply chain are the UCAL conglomeration led by UCAL Fuel System Ltd, Amalgamation, and Devendra Exports. The Tamil Nadu supply base also has the presence of foreign components firms such as the Visteon Corporation. In 1999, the company started production in two projects in Maraimalainagar near Chennai, which comprises Visteon Automotive Systems India Pvt Ltd (VASI) located in Keelakarai village and Visteon Powertrain Control Systems India Pvt Ltd.

At the lowest tier of the industrial structure lie the small and tiny enterprises numbering around 8,000 units. Located mostly in the outskirts of the industrial estates such as Perungudi, Ekkattuthangal, and Ambattur, they form slum-like clusters. These small and micro enterprises suffer from a number of structural disadvantages in the entire supply chain. As such, they are entirely dependent on the subcontract work from other medium firms. A recent study conducted by the state-run Micro, Small and Medium Enterprises Development Institute (MSME-DI) has identified the following factors crippling the small and micro firms (Government of India, 2007: 47). First, started mainly by the workers-turned-entrepreneurs, these units have very poor capital base. According to the existing lending guidelines, they are often not eligible for loans and, therefore, have no access to institutional credit. Second, small firms have very a limited product range. The job contract that they receive is mainly restricted to products that are reserved for small industries. In this too, specialization is taking place. For instance, there are welding units in Ekkattuthangal engaged in grilling and fabrication works. Third, the profit margins of these firms from the subcontract work are very low.

The structural position of the small firms subjects them to various kinds of exploitation. At present, they are simply restricted from direct access to the market as all contracts are originally won by the leading firms. A recent trend within the OEMs is to reduce their supplier base from a large number of widely dispersed vendors to a limited compact supply base. This has directly contributed to the increasing elimination of smaller firms from getting direct contracts. The subcontracting firm, usually a second-tier or a third-tier firm that works as an intermediary dealer, appropriates large profits from the small firms. We will return to this issue in the next section.

GLOBALIZATION, COST-CUTTING PRESSURES, AND LABOUR RELATIONS

By the late 1990s, the auto components manufacturing in Tamil Nadu had integrated with the global automobile industry. Although the state's export share is marginal, the industry has been reorganized along the drives and pulls of the global automotive industry. The larger context of this transition from a locally determined and domestic market-driven sector to that propelled by global market imperatives is worth noting here. This transition cannot be adequately explained by only referring to the local institutional initiative such as the state government's new policy regime or the local components firms' technology alliance with foreign firms. The main factor that set off this transition was the tendency of transnational firms to relocate their manufacturing plants to low-cost regions in the developing countries.

But above all, it was the cost-cutting pressures that the global automobile industry has been subjected to since the early 1980s that forced the large firms to relocate to the developing countries. Pertinent to note here is that competitive pricing has been the trend in the global automobile market in the recent times. Kaplinsky (2005) has pointed out that the key characteristic of the components sector is the cost-down pressure in which suppliers throughout the chain are expected to reduce prices every year. This progressive reduction of prices has to be achieved through improvements in product specifications (ibid.: 149). In their analysis of global value chains (GVCs), Nathan and Kalpana (2006) have pointed out that to retain or increase competitiveness, cost-cutting has become a driving tendency. This observation seems very relevant in the case of the components manufacturing sector in Tamil Nadu during the recent growth phase.

With globalization, the sector was increasingly exposed to a broad range of market pressures. Cost reduction became the industry rationale and the principle around which the sector was reorganized since then. In a hierarchically organized industrial structure, the pressure to reduce cost worked in a series of chain reactions down the line. It sets off from the transnational vehicle assemblers triggering a downward impact on the components suppliers. The vehicle assemblers, large components supply firms, and medium suppliers have evolved their own production strategies to reduce costs.

The discussion that follows about the recent industrial trends in Tamil Nadu's automotive components sector brings forth how assemblers have introduced an overall propensity towards cost reduction. The main trend that is fast getting entrenched in components manufacturing is the movement towards just-in-time production. The range of processes and transactions involved in the delivery of supply has been greatly shortened, and more and more responsibilities and risks are passed on to the suppliers. Posthuma (2005) has noted that in the case of the Brazilian automotive industry during the 1990s, the rapid insertion into international flows of production, distribution, and sales has significantly increased the competitive pressure on firms throughout the domestic supply chain. We will see a similar trend in the present case. Earlier, the product specifications and their quality standards were examined by the assembler firms before they were sent to the assembly line. But today, quality control is the full responsibility of the supplier firms, and the delivered products go to the assembly line without being stored for long periods. To meet the desired levels of quality standards and on-time delivery requires strong firm-level capacity. The present trends are gravitating towards just-in-time production method where components will be supplied straight to the assembly line.[6]

This new context has compelled many firms to upgrade their technological levels and capacities. Large firms such as Sundaram Fasteners and MRF had been upgrading their technologies through foreign collaborations even earlier and were in a position to adapt to the new production system that was fast evolving in the sector. However, this posed complex challenges for the medium firms. The upgrading was generally aimed at introducing more automation in the production process that can replace labour input. Industrial upgradation normally involves increased costs in the form of capital investment in new machines. But the outcome in this instance is cost reduction as it helps the firms to offload skilled labour. In particular, in recent years many medium firms imported computer numerical control (CNC) machines for a variety of purposes including drilling, cutting, etc. For instance, the SAV Autocomp, a medium-size firm and a long-time supplier to Ashok Leyland, bought a CNC machine from Thailand which the company says will help to replace at least 20 workers.[7]

Second, the assembler firms are increasingly contracting their supplier base to achieve better efficiency. Earlier, a multitude of components firms of all size and product specializations had been contracted by the OEMs for a wide and complex range of components that are used in the production of a vehicle. A large number of these firms were the small enterprises of the light engineering industries. As the assemblers embrace more cost-effective methods, the practice of procuring components from a large number of small firms has been gradually replaced with a new system under which a select number of firms will be given contracts to deliver components of vast range. This trend within the OEMs to reduce their supplier base from a large number of widely dispersed vendors to a limited compact supply base has directly contributed to this increasing elimination of smaller firms from getting direct contracts.

Third, the aforementioned has led to the rise of subcontracting in the supply chains in a big way. In the components sector not all firms are manufacturing the components that they are supplying to the assemblers. They subcontract the production work of those components to lower-tier firms. The Confederation of Indian Industry (CII) sources have conceded that subcontracting accounts for a significant share of products, roughly estimated at around 50–60 per cent of the industrial production.[8] It is very difficult to trace the chain of subcontracting as it is often conducted through informal mechanisms. Many tier-one firms such as Sundaram Clayton, Lucas–TVS, and Brakes India Ltd avoid high fixed investments in manufacturing non-critical and even precision components, and outsource their manufactures to lower-tier firms. A trend that has been pointed out by small enterprises' sources is the rise of intermediary firms in recent years which are capitalizing on the subcontracting business. The subcontract work is typically given to the small and tiny enterprises of light engineering industries concentrated in Perungudi, Ikkattukotttai, and Ambattur. Such work has become the lifeline of these enterprises and they have extremely weak bargaining power. Although they are the real producers of those components, they do not receive the price that OEMs pay for these products. The intermediary firms appropriate a large share of profit through a variety of methods.[9] First, they fix a very low price for the work outsourced. Sometimes, the price diminishes in value from the time of contract to that of delivery. This fluctuation is often created artificially by using a variety of unfair practices. The intermediate firms regularly create long time gaps between delivery from and cash payments to the small firms. These delayed payments severely affect the functioning of the micro units as their capital base is too weak to offset such crises arising from delayed money flows.

The globalization-induced cost-cutting trends have generated a range of pressures in the industry, seriously affecting labour relations in the components supply chain in Tamil Nadu. It seems that there has been a general weakening of the position of labour in the automobile industry across the board. The recent growth phase has been symptomatic for its disciplinary conditioning of labour in Tamil Nadu. Be it in the transnational assembler firms, leading components firms, and in the small industries, labour has been brought under harshly restrictive conditions. Since the advent of the global car assemblers, we see the spread of a number of new labour management models that greatly help the firms to achieve cost advantage. The creation of multiple labour markets within firms is a model that the transnational car assemblers have evolved. Lansbury et al. (2006: 142) have demonstrated how the human resource policies of the Hyundai Motor Company, which combine a strict dual labour market within, and flexibility-linked wage policies have helped it to achieve a cost-effective approach. The majority of workers in the Hyundai Motors India's (HMI) Chennai plant are hired at the trainee level for the initial three years.[10] The HMI expects a segment of them to leave the company during the trainee period under a variety of circumstances. The trainee workers, contrary to this misleading designation, are inducted into core production processes and are paid very low wages. In effect, the trainee position is a de facto short-term contract job and helps Hyundai Motors to keep the wages down and retain a low-paid workforce. It also enables the company to achieve greater flexibility in labour management as they could provide a 'buffer' if a situation arises where there is a need to reduce the workforce. This practice of employing disproportionately large irregular workers has now become the norm in the automobile industry in the state.

This chapter argues that the automotive components sector in Tamil Nadu today is manifest with a striking incongruity between faster industrial growth on the one hand and decelerating employment and lowering of wages on the other. In the absence of firm-wise and time series data, it is difficult to ascertain the actual employment that the industry has generated during the growth phase. However, estimation based on available sources suggests that there has not been any significant increase in regular employment in the components manufacturing sector over the years. According to the Tamil Nadu government, the sector provides direct employment to 45,000 people. But this figure apparently excludes employment in the small enterprises. The current strength of the workforce in the entire supply chain is approximately 90,000. The basis of this estimate is the data provided by the ACMA on large and medium firms and an aggregate calculation of employment in small and tiny enterprises. The ACMA has provided the employee status of 77 Tamil Nadu-based companies which totals around 51,000.[11] But from this it is unclear how much of this number was actually created during the growth phase as more than 50 per cent of the firms were established much earlier. And the majority of them started production well before the recent boom transformed the industry. It is possible that some of these firms may have expanded their workforce in recent years. But the actual share of that expansion is difficult to ascertain in the absence of a firm-level and time-wise data.

But there is another significant aspect that is indicative of the employment trends in recent years. Roughly 30 per cent of the firms are of recent origin, starting their operations around the mid-1990s, and a majority of them are lean in terms of the employment size as they provide work for less number of people compared to the older companies. Therefore, the employment growth in the large and medium firms does not seem to correlate with the increase in the volume of production and the earnings. Employment in small firms is estimated by multiplying the number of firms with their average size. There are around 8,000 small firms that are doing all kinds of light engineering works in the automobile components sector. Most of them are run with four to five workers operating various kinds of casting or dyeing works. From this, it was estimated that there will be around 40,000 workers in this sector. The discussion that follows in the subsequent sections has tried to explain the prevailing incongruity between increasing earnings for leading firms and diminishing wages for production level workers across the supply chains as well as the declining profit margin for small firms.

FLEXIBLE LABOUR REGIMES AND INDUSTRIAL DISTURBANCES IN THE SUPPLY CHAINS: SOME RECENT TRENDS

The term flexible labour regime is used here to suggest the historical formation of a mode of labour mobilization characteristic of the present age of globalization. The rise and spread of flexible labour relationships across the low-income economies have been well documented and there exist substantial literature on the subject. Guy Standing (1999) has examined the global spread of flexibility and its diverse forms and manifestations in the context of the weakening of the labour institutions and regulatory mechanism under welfare capitalism. Much of the discussion is centred around specific forms of flexibility and is explained as a labour market trend induced by the process of globalization.[12] While this explanation helps us to understand the core process involved in the labour market exchanges, it misses the point about the institutional externalities that make such relationships possible on a large scale as we are currently witnessing in the Asian region. It is pertinent to note here that flexibility has acquired a certain degree of institutional stability. I have taken the idea of labour regime from Bernstein's discussion on the colonial labour regimes.[13] Drawing from his concept, this chapter uses flexibility to define the characteristic feature of the way labour is mobilized, inducted into any given industrial sector, and the way it is utilized in the industrial movements driven by cost-cutting pressures.

The new system targets the production-level workers and is designed to ensure their incorporation into the production process while at the same time reducing their scope for bargaining. At the outset of this system is a labour mobilization strategy that creates arbitrary categories of employment for largely similar labour inputs. The workers are recruited from a group of people who possess more or less the same skill levels into greatly varying employment categories such as regular employee, temporary workers, trainee workers, apprentices, and contract workers. Their wages and employment conditions vary significantly from one another. However, in an integrated production system on the shop floor, they perform largely similar tasks. As noted earlier, vehicle assemblers and large components firms typically employ a disproportionately large segment of irregular workers. Trainees and contract workers constitute the bulk of the workforce in many firms. The hiring of fresh Industrial Training Institute (ITI) diploma holders as trainee recruits and employing them for longer periods is a common practice institutionalized by these firms. Although recruited as trainees, these young men perform all production related works after a brief in-house training session and are given very low wages that are calculated as stipends during that period.

Similar employment terms are applied to apprentices who constitute another category of irregular workers in large and medium firms. The existing standing orders of the Government of India concerning the trainee recruits and apprentices have restricted such employment to a maximum period of three years. But most companies, especially the foreign firms, engage them for five to seven years. The use of temporary workers and contract workers is another mode of labour mobilization that helps the vehicle assemblers and large components firms to reduce costs. The actual percentage of these categories of irregular labour in the automobile industry and the extent to which they are inducted into production processes are to be examined further. At present, no relevant source provides any detailed and complete data on the nature of firm-level employment, and only an extensive survey can generate detailed statistical data.

The irregular workers under the aforementioned categories of employment are generally subjected to severe performance pressures. At all levels of the works, they are expected to provide labour inputs far exceeding the value of their wages, which are calculated on a daily basis. Overtime is not calculated on the basis of their basic wages but linked to their shifts so that a worker will be eligible to get the benefit of overtime only when he completes an additional full shift and there is compulsory overtime to meet urgent production requirements.

The rise of flexible labour regimes has had an adverse impact on the Tamil Nadu workers as a social group. The political consequence of this division was that it fractionalized the collective interests of workers. Their segmentation into different categories of employment such as regular, temporary, casual, and trainee recruits seems to have induced a sense of competing group interests among them. The workers of each of these categories are driven by concerns and anxieties relating to their terms of employment such as tenure, wages, and prospects of mobility. These exogenously induced competing group interests have seriously weakened their bargaining position and have given greater leverage to the management. For instance, the huge reserve of casual labour force readily available within the firms will potently restrain the regular workers from collective bargaining, and the threat of strike will become less of an effective bargaining course as the casual labour reserve will ensure uninterrupted production to a large extent.

The new labour regimes have provoked different kinds of responses from the workers. In recent years, the supply chain has witnessed two sets of trends. On the one hand, flexible labour regimes have intensified the narrow group interests between and among different categories of workers. At times, the anxieties arising out of such labour regimes can intensify fractional interests between different categories of workers and provoke group-based conflicts. In July 2007, clashes broke out between permanent workers and casual labourers in the Coimbatore factory of Pricol Ltd, a leading components manufacturing firm. The clashes left 28 workers injured on both sides and forced the company to seek police protection inside the factory premises.[14] This incident points to the growing industrial tensions that arise from flexible labour regimes across the supply chain.

But at the same time, there is also growing realization about the need to have collective action and effective trade unions. The brief discussion that follows is an illustrative case of this trend. In 2005, the workers of the Visteon Power Train Control Systems's manufacturing unit in Keezhakkarani village in Kancheepuram district formed an independent union. The company has 130 regular employees and 450 workers on temporary basis. The union raised a wage revision demand. The management refused to recognize the union and did not respond to the issues raised by the workers. At the same time, it adopted a directly hostile approach and set up a workmen committee handpicked by the managerial leadership. While refusing to negotiate with the union, the Visteon management arrived at a wage revision settlement with the committee. In an attempt to co-opt a section of the workers, the settlement awarded promotion and salary increase to the members in the workmen committee. According to the Visteon workers' union, the draft of the agreement was prepared by the management and the workmen committee was simply asked to sign. The trade union sources termed the wage revision between the management and the workmen committee as a clear violation of the existing labour legislations, in particular, provision 18–1 of the Industrial Disputes Act which provides for bipartisan settlement involving the workers' union and the management to be reached after negotiation. Hence, they refused to accept it as a negotiated settlement. The workers' union then raised these issues as an industrial dispute before the Conciliatory authority. However, the Conciliatory authority declined to consider the points raised by the union and decided in favour of the Visteon management. Having been dismissed at this stage, the union demanded that their petition be referred to the industrial tribunal for adjudication.

Understandably, the Tamil Nadu government did not want to drag a foreign firm to adjudication procedures as it would be sending a 'wrong' signal to investors. At this stage, the Centre of Indian Trade Unions' (CITU) Tamil Nadu branch took up the issue and got itself involved directly and mobilized its various organizational branches across the districts in support of the striking workers of the Visteon's Keezhakkarani village plant. The CITU later organized a state-wide picketing in taluk and district headquarters raising the Visteon issue and demanded that the dispute be referred to the tribunal. It was only after such state-level trade union protests and political pressure that the government decided to refer the matter for adjudication. The tribunal accepted the contentions of the workers and passed a favourable judgement directing the Visteon management to revise wages for the regular workers.[15] The sequence of events that followed since the workers raised the wage revision issue points to the nature of challenges that they confront in the present context. It also brings to light the weakening of the institutional system that is available to the workers to get access to their basic entitlements.

WAGES AND LABOUR CONDITIONS IN THE SMALL ENTERPRISES

The experience of the small and micro enterprises in the light engineering industries in the automobile components sector in Tamil Nadu during the growth phase has been strikingly different from that of the large and medium firms. When the industry recorded a high growth in terms of production, turnover, and exports, the small enterprises experienced an overall decline in their earnings. The cost-down pressures of globalization have been severely felt by these last-tier components manufacturers. The coming of the global assemblers and the subsequent restructuring of the local components base have spread a set of restrictive regimes and new barriers around the small enterprises. The contraction of the supply base by vehicle manufacturers and car assemblers led to their institutional exclusion from direct access to the market. The rise of subcontracting and the role of intermediary firms further weakened their position. But at the same time, they have been well integrated into the industry under a new division of labour that takes advantage of their structural weakness. Today, their lifeline for survival precariously hangs on the 'job work' that they get from third-tier firms. The light engineering industries in Tamil Nadu, which were earlier flaunted as one of the mainstays of the state's industrial base, are today facing a serious crisis, at a time when the automobile industry is on a growth trajectory.

This trend marks a serious paradox in the 'success story' of the automobile components industry in Tamil Nadu.

Typically, these firms are run with an extremely limited capital base, technology levels, and work area, and operate from residential backyards, industrial slums, or pavements. A vast majority of them are started and managed by workers-turned-entrepreneurs, often pooling labour force from familiar social networks such as castes and kinship, neighbourhoods, and peer groups. Such employment usually comes as an opportunity to acquire skills, experience, and earnings. And their employer is a senior relative, a respected elder, an adolescent friend, a resourceful neighbour, or a co-worker in the earlier company. The employer–worker relations that come into form under these conditions are vastly different from those in the larger firms where a series of hierarchies separate the latter from the former. In small enterprises, a worker is well aware from the very outset of the social bonds that link him and his employer and the common economic prospects they share. The knowledge that they are both subjected to the same factors of exploitation weighs above all other considerations in the worker's attitude towards their employer.

Workers in the small enterprises engaged in light engineering manufacturing receive very low wages. The average daily wage of a worker is around Rs 60 per day.[16] To earn this small amount, they have to endure extremely demanding conditions. The workplace does not provide the workers with even a little extra space where they can rest during breaks or meals as most of these units function from a build-up area of around 400 square feet or even less. The work area is crammed with machines and tools, and in some units this lack of adequate space has constrained the physical movements of the workers within the unit premises. Since the low capital base and low earnings have inhibited these firms from upgrading, they are still operating with the older machines, which require more human craftsmanship and skill. And errors and casual handling can easily lead to accidents.

Low wages and harsh work conditions are forcing many workers to leave the sector. The pressure of rising living expenses on these male workers is enormous as many of them are expected to bring home a decent income. With increasing wages in other sectors such as garments, the workers in components manufacturing find it difficult to continue in their jobs with the prevailing wages. In search of better wages, many have been leaving their jobs in the small units. This trend of labour mobility in terms of shifting their occupation has today become a serious problem in this sector. It not only reduces the available skill in the sector but, above all, impinges on the human capital resources. The extremely inhibiting conditions that the workers are enduring in the small engineering firms cannot be understood in relation to these firms alone. It appears that these conditions are produced by a number of factors external to these firms and their sectors. The workers and the proprietors of these firms are subjected to the same institutional pressures brought on them by the large firms and the intermediaries. The declining earnings for the small enterprises and low wages for workers arise from their structural subordination within the industry that denies them any direct participation in the supply chain.

CONCLUSION

Globalization of the automobile industry in Tamil Nadu has produced strikingly varied experiences for large components firms, automobile workers, and small enterprises. The arrival of transnational car assemblers has set off a process of restructuring across the supply chain. This process has propelled a strong centralizing tendency among the supply firms in which some of the large firms became globally competitive suppliers while creating new barriers for the chunk of small enterprises. The globalization of the automobile industry in Tamil Nadu was strongly driven by the logic of cost advantage and it introduced a new model for production as well as labour management. The policies that most large firms have adopted are aimed at achieving better cost advantage that brought the workers across the supply chain under increasingly restrictive labour relations. The growth phase of the automobile industry has impelled the rise and spread of flexible labour regimes across the supply chains. The institutionalization of this labour system that has come to dominate the components sector has greatly weakened the position of labour in a range of areas. The irregular workers in the leading firms and the workers in the small and micro enterprises are subjected to the most exploitative conditions in terms of employment, wages, conditions of work, and managerial arbitrariness. But workers in the small and tiny firms encounter problems that are completely different from those of the workers in larger firms; the problems of the former arise mainly from the structural disadvantages suffered by the small and tiny firms in terms of their position as part of a dependent sector that survives entirely on subcontracted job works. The robust economic performance accompanied by declining regular employment and wages across the supply chain has come to form a serious incongruity in the context of the global integration of the local components manufacturing sector. The rise of flexible labour regimes has provoked different kinds of responses from the workers. While it has seriously disrupted the social characteristics of the production workers and triggered competing group interests among themselves, there is also a growing tendency towards collective intervention to secure their rapidly dissipating labour rights.

NOTES

1. Tamil Nadu had a high literacy rate of 73.5 per cent in 2001 and ranked first among Indian states in terms of the annual turnout of skilled technical manpower. This is mainly because of the greater concentration of technical and professional educational institutions in the state. According to the *Statistical Handbook of Tamil Nadu for 2006–07*, the state has 263 engineering colleges, 226 polytechnics, 56 ITIs (Industrial Training Institutes), and 613 ITCs (Industrial Training Centres). See Government of Tamil Nadu (2008).
2. The CII study on Tamil Nadu's human resources has identifies the state as the largest source of technical manpower in the country with around 80,000 engineers and 60,000 diploma holders graduating annually. Based on 2001 statistics, the study projected that Tamil Nadu's existing educational infrastructure consisting of the engineering colleges, polytechnics, arts, science and commerce colleges have the combined potential of turning out around 400,000 skilled manpower every year (CII, 2006).
3. The state government provided substantive support to foreign investors. Its commitments in this regard include immediate land allotment in industrial parks, infrastructural support including power, water supply, and access to roads, and a range of fiscal incentives. In addition, the vast pool of apprentices and the fresh degree and diploma holders from the ITIs and engineering colleges is a major incentive for the investors in Tamil Nadu. In 2006, the state had a total of 681 ITIs with a seating capacity of 85,307 students. The excess of engineering graduates is evident from the fact that in 2001 the percentage of graduates absorbed into the automobile sector was much lower than that of the preceding years. While in 1994, about 82 per cent of the graduates were absorbed in this sector, in 2001 that percentage dropped to a mere 13. See Institute of Applied Manpower Research (2008: 91, 307).
4. See ACMA's *Status of Indian Automotive and Auto-components Industry: Status Report* (2008).
5. The details relating to the different firms are compiled from ACMA (2007).

6. Interview, SAS Autocom, Sidco Industrial Estate, Ambattur, Chennai, October 2007.
7. Interview, SAS Autocom, Sidco Industrial Estate, Ambattur, Chennai, October 2007.
8. Interview CII Southern Regional Headquarters, Velacherry Main Road, Chennai, October 2007.
9. Interview with N. Arumugam, Perungudi Engineering Cluster, Perungudi, Chennai, October 2007. However, according to the trade union sources and Hyundai workers, this period often extends to more years, sometimes even up to six years. Interview, 2007.
10. Compiled from ACMA (2007).
11. For a detailed elaboration, see Guy Standing (1999: Chapter 4).
12. Bernstein, H., (1998), 'Labour Regimes and Social Change Under Colonialism', in Ben Crow, and Mary Thorpe (eds), *Survival and Change in the Third World*. London: Oxford University Press.
13. See *The Hindu Business Line*, 15 July 2007.
14. Interview with K. Palanivelu, Assistant Genereal Secretary, Tamil Nadu State Committee, Centre of Indian Trade Unions (CITU), 'A. Nallasivan Ninavagam', Chennai, October 2007.
15. Interview, Perungudi, Chennai, 2007. According to the Labour Bureau statistics, the minimum wage rate in Tamil Nadu in the relevant employment listed as automobile engineering is well above this. As on 2004, the minimum wage was Rs 92.60, which had increased marginally from Rs 82.55 since 2001. See Labour Bureau (2008).
16. Interview with N. Arumugam, Perungudi Engineering Cluster, Perungudi, Chennai, October 2007.

REFERENCES

ACMA (Automotive Components Manufacturers Association of India) (2007), *The Indian Automotive Industry Buyers Guide 2007*. New Delhi: ACMA.

―――― (2008), *Status of Indian Automotive and Auto-components Industry: Status Report*. New Delhi: ACMA.

Bernstein, H., David Wield, L. Harris, Ben Crow, and Mary Thorpe (eds) (1988), *Survival and Change in the Third World* (pp. 30–49). London: Oxford University Press.

Confederation of Indian Industry (CII) (2005), *Vision for the Tamil Nadu Auto Industry*, Report. Chennai: CII.

Confederation of Indian Industry (CII) (2006), *Study on Mapping of Human Resources and Skills for Tamil Nadu-2015*. Chennai: CII.

―――― (2007), *A Vision for Tamil Nadu Automotive Industry*. Chennai: CII.

Micro, Small and Medium Enterprises Development Institute (MSME-DI) (2007), *Diagnostic Study on Engineering Cluster*, Chennai: MSME-DI.

Government of Tamil Nadu (2008), *Statistical Handbook of Tamil Nadu 2007*. Department of Economics and Statistics. Chennai: Government Central Press.

Institute of Applied Manpower Research (2008), *Manpower Profile India Year Book 2008*. Delhi: Institute of Applied Manpower Research.

Kaplinsky, Raphael (2005), *Globalization, Poverty and Inequality*. Cambridge: Polity Press.

Labour Bureau (2008), *Labour Statistics Minimum Wages, New Delhi: Ministry of Employment, Government of India* (available at http://labourbureau.nic.in, last accessed on 10 October 2009).

Lansbury, R.D., S. Kwon, and C. Suh (2006), 'Globalization and Employment Relations in the Korean Auto Industry: The Case of the Hyundai Motor Company in Korea, Canada and India', *Asia Pacific Business Review*, 12(2): 131–47.

Nathan, Dev and V. Kalpana (2007), 'Issues in the Analysis of Global Value Chains and Their Impact on Employment and Incomes in India', Discussion Paper. Geneva: International Institute for Labour Studies.

Posthuma, Anne Caroline (2005), 'Industrial Renewal and Inter-firm Relations in the Supply Chain of the Brazilian Automotive Industry', SEED Working Paper No. 46. Geneva: International Labour Office.

Standing, Guy (1999), *Global Labour Flexibility: Seeking Distributive Justice*. London: Macmillan.

Tewari, Meenu (2001), 'Engaging the New Global Interlocutors: Foreign Direct Investment and the Transformation of Tamil Nadu's Automotive Supply Base' (available at http://www.cid.harvard.edu/archive/india/papers.html, last accessed on 2 January 2007).

12 SMALL PRODUCERS AND LABOUR CONDITIONS IN AUTO PARTS AND COMPONENTS INDUSTRY IN NORTH INDIA

Dinesh Awasthi, Sanjay Pal, and Jignasu Yagnik

INTRODUCTION

The economic reforms ushered in during the 1990s in India have brought into their fold a mixed bag of challenges, mainly due to increased global competition, as well as new opportunities. The overall response, notwithstanding the differential performance of the various sub-sectors, has been noteworthy. The manufacturing sector, particularly the small-industry sector, has contributed to the overall 8+ per cent growth of the Indian economy. However, the benefit of such growth has not percolated equitably across the various stakeholders. The process of this growth has, to a great extent, bypassed workers engaged in the micro, small, and medium enterprise (MSME) sector. The MSMEs are facing severe competition because of their following the 'low road of growth', which is characterized by lowering of wages and poor environmental and labour standards. One would expect that with increasing markets the share of workers would improve, and there would be more focus on innovation, skill formation, higher productivity and improved working conditions, including higher wages; the process usually known in the literature on clusters as 'high road to growth' (Kaplinsky, 1998). However, by and large, the MSME sector did not experience such a phenomenon in India, like in most developing economies.

A new dimension, that is, 'value chains', has been added to the fast emerging literature on clusters. It is argued that it is not only the collective efficiency of the cluster stakeholders (collective actions within the cluster) that leads to higher competitiveness; the external linkages also play an equally important role in the processes of growth and competitiveness of industry, particularly MSMEs (Bell and Albu, 1999; Schmitz and Nadvi, 1999; Guerrieri et al., 2001). The most debated issue in this stream is the role of value chains, particularly global value chains (GVC). It is argued that if a cluster/firm becomes a part of the GVC, its overall efficiency and competitiveness improve because of the information, knowledge, and technology flows (Gereffi and Korzeniewicz, 1994; Schmitz, 2004; Giuliani et al., 2005). It may also transform a cluster from a 'low road' to a 'high road' of competitiveness, through process upgrading, product upgrading, functional upgrading, and inter-sectoral upgrading (Humphrey and Schmitz, 2000).

The process of upgrading is likely to be significantly influenced by the governance of the cluster/value chain (Bazan and Navas-Aleman, 2005). Governance is usually considered in terms of the relationship between the supplier and the buyer code of conduct that sometimes extends to inter-firm code of conduct. It includes 'what should be produced', 'how should it be produced', and sometimes even 'when', 'how much', and 'at what price' (Humphrey and Schmitz, 2000). However, in our view, the overall governance must also address the issues related to workers who are major stakeholders in the production process. When one talks about how much and what price and margins, one must take into consideration how the fruits of surplus are shared across the board. And the working conditions in the industry must form a part of the agenda.

The value chains could be local, regional, or global and could co-exist in a cluster. The functioning of these value chains might differ significantly with each other, especially in terms of their governance (Artola and Parrilli, 2003; Giuliani et al. 2005). Moreover, not only might different value chains have different implications for different stakeholders, a majority of micro enterprises might not even be a part of any organized regional or GVC. The cluster governance will mean little to them.

This chapter attempts to map the value chains that operate in auto parts and components clusters at Jalandhar, Ludhiana, and Phagwara (JLP), and gauge the differences in the labour standards in enterprises located across such value chains. It also makes an attempt to compare labour standards across the original equipment manufacturers (OEMs) supplier and exporting firms on the one hand, and with the unorganized sectors on the other, to understand if some differences in labour standards exist between these two segments.

WHY AUTO PARTS AND COMPONENTS INDUSTRY?

The global auto component industry was valued at US$ 1 trillion in 2005 (Cygnus, January 2007). It is growing at a compounded annual growth rate

(CAGR) of 6.63 per cent and reached US$ 1 trillion in 2005, from US$ 725 billion in 2000. Keeping pace with the global trend, the Indian automobile industry grew at CAGR 18.31 per cent during 2001–2 and 2006–7; the auto components industry in India also witnessed an excellent growth touching CAGR of 20.32 per cent during the same period and reached Rs 12.03 billion (US$ 0.30 billion) in 2006–7. It is expected to touch Rs 52.86 billion (US$ 1.32 billion) by 2014–15. Export of auto parts grew at CAGR 23.56 per cent during 2001–2 and 2006–7 (Cygnus, August 2007). Also, the share of exports in total production has risen from 12.93 per cent in 2001–2 to 18.48 per cent in 2006–7, accounting for the exports worth Rs 2.22 billion (US$ 0.06 billion) in 2006–7. More importantly, the ratio of OEMs to 'after market' or 'spares market' has changed from 35:65 in 1990 to 75:25 in 2006 (Cygnus: January 2007). The Indian auto components industry is in the midst of transition from being low-quality, low-tech, and heavily dependent on the domestic market to a global industry driven by quality, delivery, and reliability. As per Cygnus (January 2007), its major exports destinations are Europe (34 per cent) and USA (26 per cent).

As reported in Cygnus (August 2007), there are 400 large firms in the organized sector which mostly cater to OEMs; another 10,000 firms are operating in the unorganized sector, manufacturing low-tech auto parts and components. The entire industry is organized in about 10 major clusters in the country—Aurangabad, Belgaum, Chennai, Gurgaon, Jalandhar, Jamshedpur, Ludhiana, Phagwara, Pithampur, and Pune—accounting for over 93 per cent of the output. Its high growth performance and potential, high presence of the unorganized sector, and clustered growth make it an interesting case to study.

DATABASE AND METHODOLOGY

This chapter is based on a field survey of 183 MSMEs and about 125 workers operating in the auto parts and components industry in Ludhiana, Phagwara, and Jalandhar (Punjab). These are the three important auto components manufacturing centres in northern India. While Ludhiana, with 3,454 (14.57 per cent) small scale industry units and Rs 18,319 million (US$ 366.4 million), that is, 37.50 per cent of output of auto-parts industry in India, tops the country, Jalandhar is at number seven with 293 units and an output of Rs 935 million (US$ 18.7 million or 1.91 per cent). Phagwara ranks number 32 at the all India level with 158 units and Rs 188 million (US$ 3.7 million; 0.39 per cent) output, as per the estimates of the Third

Census of Small Scale Industries conducted by DCSSI (Development Commissioner Small Scale Industries, 2002).

Of the 183 sample units, 101 firms are located in Ludhiana, 52 in Jalandhar, and 30 in Phagwara. The enterprises were selected in a manner that signifies the basic tenets of the clusters. A structured but open-ended schedule was administered to collect information on enterprises. The interviews of entrepreneurs and/or their managers were conducted to get their perception on various issues related to the production process, governance, networks, value chains, and marketing channels. The visits were also used to observe labour conditions and the work environment in those units.

One cannot claim the study to be inclusive unless opinion of the workers, who constitute the prime focus of the study, is sought. The focus group discussion (FGD) method was employed to collect information from the workers. In all, nine FGDs were conducted during the course of the study: four in Ludhiana, three in Jalandhar, and two in Phagwara. These FGDs were conducted in their habitat to provide them a free environment so that they do not hesitate to 'open up'. In all, 124 workers participated in the FGDs (usually, 12–15 workers were present in each FGD).

To compare the statistical significance of the difference between the two categories of firms, that is, (*i*) OEM suppliers and exporters, and (*ii*) unorganized firms, z test of difference in proportions based on normal approximation of the binomial distribution was used.

SAMPLE PROFILE: ENTERPRISES

Of the 183 sample firms, 11 (6 per cent) are global OEM suppliers and exporters, six are domestic OEM suppliers, 32 (17.49 per cent) are only exporters, and the remaining 134 (73.23 per cent) are non-OEM and non-exporters, catering to the domestic spares market (see Table 12.1). The 11 global OEM suppliers are part of the GVC as they supply to companies like Mercedes Benz, Ford, Chrysler, Iveko of Turkey, Arvin Motors and Piaggio of Italy, Audi Motors, Renault, Komatsu, and Fiat. The domestic OEMs supply their products to companies like Tata Motors, Bajaj Auto, Sonalika Tractors, Punjab Tractors, Maruti Udyog, and Mahindra and Mahindra.

In terms of investment (in plant and machinery as of 2006), only 19 (10.38 per cent) firms have investments exceeding Rs 5 million (US$ 0.12 million), while as many as 79 firms have investments of less than Rs 0.5 million (US$ 0.01 million). Of these 183 firms, 76 (41.53

Table 12.1: Sample Profile of Respondents

Sample Profile of Entrepreneurs			Sample Profile of Workers		
Cluster			**Participation in FGD by Clusters**		
	No.	percentage		No.	percentage
Ludhiana	101	55.2	Ludhiana (4 FGDs)	58	46.8
Jalandhar	52	28.4	Jalandhar (3 FGDs)	42	33.9
Phagwara	30	16.4	Phagwara (2 FGDs)	24	19.4
Total	183		Total	124	
Type of Enterprise			**State of Origin**		
	No.	percentage		No.	percentage
			Uttar Pradesh	52	41.9
Global OEM	11	6.0	Bihar	50	40.3
Domestic OEM	6	3.3	Punjab	19	15.3
Export but not OEM	32	17.5	Others	3	2.4
Non-OEM/ Non-Export	134	73.2	Total	124	
Total	183				
Type of Organization			**Age Distribution**		
	No.	percentage		No.	percentage
Registered (under Factories Act, 1948)	76	41.5	17–25	28	22.6
Unregistered/ Unorganized	107	58.5	25–30	29	23.4
Total	183		30–35	30	24.2
			35–40	22	17.7
			Above 40	15	12.1
			Total	124	
Target Market			**Qualification**		
	No.	percentage		No.	percentage
OEM/Export	49	26.8	Upto Class 4	17	13.7
Non-OEM/ Non-Export	134	73.2	Class 4–8	20	16.1
Total	183		Up to Higher Secondary	38	30.6
			ITI	35	28.2
			Technical Diploma	10	8.1
Size of Enterprise (Investment 2006★)			Graduate	4	3.2
	No.	percentage	Total	124	
< 0.5	79	43.2	**Experience**		
0.5–2.5	63	34.4		No.	percentage
2.5–5.0	22	12.0			
5.0 +	19	10.4	Less than 1 Year	6	4.8
Total	183		1 Year–2 Years	10	8.1
			2–5 Years	30	24.2

Sample Profile of Entrepreneurs			Sample Profile of Workers		
Size of Enterprise (Sales Turnover 2006*)			5–10 Years	36	29.0
	No.	percentage	More than 10 Years	42	33.9
< 0.5	45	24.6	Total	124	
0.5–1.0	1	0.5	Skill Level		
1.0–2.5	21	11.5		No.	percentage
2.5–7.5	64	35.0	Unskilled	15	12.1
7.5–10	18	9.8	Semi-Skilled	63	50.8
10 +	34	18.6	Skilled	46	37.1
Total	183		Total	124	
Size of Enterprise (Employment)			Monthly Wage (Rs/Month)		
	No.	percentage	No.	No.	percentage
01–05	39	21.3	Up to 2,000	14	11.3
06–09	68	37.2	2,000–2,500	17	13.7
10–20	46	25.1	2,500–3,000	38	30.6
21–50	25	13.7	3,000–3,500	24	19.4
51+	5	2.7	3,500–4,000	19	15.3
Total	183		Above 4,000	12	9.7
			Total	124	
Size of Enterprise (Export*)			Amount of Remittances (Rs/Month)		
	No.	percentage		No.	percentage
< 2.0	26	60.5	Up to 500	19	15.3
2–4	3	17.0	500–1,000	35	28.2
4–8	6	14.0	1,000–1,500	44	35.5
8+	8	18.6	1,500–2,000	15	12.1
Total	43		Above 2,000	11	8.9
			Total	124	

Source: Field Survey.
Note: *Rs in millions.

per cent), including 49 OEM suppliers and exporters and 27 non-OEM non-exporting firms, are registered under the Factories Act, 1948. However, only five firms have number of workers exceeding 51 (see Table 12.1). In terms of sales turnover, 34 firms have an annual turnover of more than Rs 10 million (US$ 0.25 million), whereas 45 (24.59 per cent) firms have on an average less than Rs 0.5 million (US$ 0.01 million) turnover.

It may also be mentioned that while most of the OEM suppliers have graduated from small unorganized units to the larger ones, a few started 'big' from day one. In fact, in the view of these 'graduated' entrepreneurs, there are several advantages of starting small. The learning they acquire while operating (as small units) for a couple of years equips them better to graduate to the category of OEM suppliers.

SAMPLE PROFILE: WORKERS

As can be seen from Table 12.1, most of the 124 workers belong to Uttar Pradesh and Bihar, followed by Punjab. A majority of the workers who participated in the FGD were semi-skilled, had work experience ranging from six months to 20 years, and were living without their families. In terms of education, about 36 per cent had technical education and another 30 per cent had studied up to higher secondary. A large segment of workers was comprised of school dropouts. Most of them had acquired skills on-the-job. Very few sample workers had undergone some formal technical training in Industrial Training Institutes (ITIs). In the majority (50 per cent) of the cases, their wages ranged between Rs 2,500 and 3,500 per month. Only about 10 per cent, most working in the organized sector, earned over Rs 4,000 per month, whereas a quarter of them earned less than Rs. 2,500 per month. The remittances ranged between Rs 1,500 and 2,000 per month.

THE SURVEY RESULTS

Value Chains, Share of Wages, and Working Conditions

It was envisaged that as the workers move up the value chain and become part of the global production networks (GPNs), their overall standards will also go up, commensurate with their changing work profile and firms' profits. However, the workers who fail to achieve upward mobility, due to the firms they are engaged in, will not enjoy this benefit. To assess the validity of this postulation, we plotted two value chains, one for the firm that was a part of the GPN and the other that was confined to the domestic market (see Figures 12.1 and 12.2). Both the firms, located at Ludhiana, manufactured 'shackle pins'. The GPN firm was an OEM supplier-cum-exporter firm. The turnover of the GPN firm was about Rs 138 million (US$ 3.45 million) while that of the other firm was about Rs 4.5 million (US$ 0.11 million) per annum. The GPN firm employed 30 workers whereas the domestic market firm employed nine workers (officially). The investment of the GPN firm in plant and machinery was to the tune of 100 million (US$ 2.50 million), whereas the domestic market firm had an investment of barely Rs 1.2 million (US$ 0.03 million). However, there was a sea difference in the technology used by them. This difference in capital intensity reflected the difference in the level of technological sophistication and quality of the product between the two firms. While the GPN firm was hi-tech, using computer aided designs, the domestic firm was using quite archaic machines.

Product: Shackle Pin   Material used: EN 8D

Process	Cost per kg(Rs.)
Raw Material	35.00
↓ Bar drawing	0.40
↓ Cutting	1.50
↓ Rough grinding	2.00
↓ Facing	1.90
↓ Chamfering	2.00
↓ Milling	5.40
↓ Thread step drilling	2.15
↓ Long drilling	2.35
↓ Cotter slotting	4.50
↓ Grinding hole milling	3.50
↓ Grease outlet holes	1.40
↓ Induction hardening	5.20
↓ Final grinding	2.10
↓ Rust preventing oil	1.60
↓ Packaging	7.80
Total Cost of Production	**74.90**

S. No.	Source of Value Addition	Cost at Source (CS)	Value Added (VA)*	Total (CS+VA)*	Profit Margin (P)	Total Cost (CS+VA+P)
1.	Manufacturing	35.00	34.90	74.90	6.00 (8%)	80.90
2.	Distribution	80.90	4.00 (5 %)	84.90	5.50 (6.5 %)	90.40
3.	Trading/Retailing	90.40	6.30 (7%)	96.70	8.70 (9 %)	105.40
4.	Workers' Intake				7.59%**	

Figure 12.1 Value Chain Analysis★
(Firm catering to global supply chain)

Source: Field Survey.
Notes: ★ Includes entire cost of production (e.g., raw material cost, wage component, utilities, taxes, transportation, etc.). It may be noted that it is not value added in the classical sense, but assumed to be value added due to lack of disaggregated information.
★★ Average Wage, 6,000 p.m. x 30 workers = Rs 180,000 p.m.
- Per day wage payment 180,000/25 (working days) = Rs 7,200
- Total production cost per day, 900 kg. @ Rs. 105.40 per kg = Rs 94,860

Product: Shackle Pin   Material used: EN 8D
       Process   Cost per kg(Rs.)

Process	Cost per kg (Rs.)
Raw Material	30.00
↓ Bar drawing	0.40
↓ Cutting	1.20
↓ Rough grinding	1.75
↓ Facing	1.50
↓ Chamfering	1.85
↓ Milling	4.00
↓ Thread step drilling	1.60
↓ Long drilling	1.75
↓ Cotter slotting	3.00
↓ Grinding hole milling	2.80
↓ Grease outlet holes	1.30
↓ Induction hardening	4.00
↓ Final grinding	1.70
↓ Rust preventing oil	1.30
↓ Packaging	6.00
Total Cost of Production	**64.15**

S. No.	Source of Value Addition	Cost at Source (CS)	Value Added (VA)*	Total (CS+VA)*	Profit Margin (P)	Total Cost (CS+VA+P)
1.	Manufacturing	30.00	34.15	64.15	5.13 (8%)	69.28
2.	Distribution	69.28	2.77 (4 %)	72.05	4.68 (6.5 %)	76.73
3.	Trading/Retailing	76.73	5.37 (7%)	82.10	7.39 (9 %)	89.49
4.	Workers' Share/ Wage Component				(10.34%)**	

Figure 12.2 Value Chain Analysis*
(Firm catering to domestic spares' market)

Source: Field Survey.
Notes: *Includes entire cost of production (e.g., raw material cost, wage component, utilities, taxes, transportation, etc.). It may be noted that it is not value added in classical sense, but assumed to be value added due to lack of disaggregated information.
** Average Wage, 4,500 p.m. x 9 workers = Rs 40,500 p.m.
- Per day wage payment, 40,500/25 (working day) = Rs 1,620
- Total production cost per day, 175 kg @ Rs 89.50 per kg = Rs 15,663
- Contribution of wage in the total cost, 1,620 x 100/15663 = 10.34 %

The cost of production per kilogram is somewhat higher in the GPN firm as compared to the firm catering to the domestic market. The cost difference starts in the cost of raw material itself and follows through the packaging. Most of the process is automatic in the GPN firm, using more electricity, skilled workers (thus higher wages), and upgraded production process. Therefore, the final product stands the test of every possible quality parameter. On the other hand, the firm which caters to the domestic market manufactures product which ranks low on quality parameters. There is a significant difference in the technical features of the final product manufactured by these two types of firms. While the rejection rate in the GNP firm is just 0.35 per cent, the rate in the other firm is over 10.5 per cent due to lack of consistency.

The wage component as a proportion of cost in both the firms is significantly different. The wage component in the GNP firm is lower (7.59 per cent) as compared to the 10.34 per cent in the domestic market firm. It is quite understandable as it is the labour component that plays a vital role in the production process rather than technology. However, the average wage rates are far higher (Rs 6,000 per month per worker) in the GPN firm as compared to Rs 4,500 in the case of the other firm. This is also because of the difference between the levels of skill employed by these firms.

We also visited both the factories to get a feel of the working conditions and also talked to a few workers. There was a marked difference in both the factories. The GPN firm looked quite organized, neat and clean, with adequate lighting, due safety measures, and various quality control systems like ISO 9000, QS 9000, OHSAS 18001, and ISO 14001, and practiced TQM, 6-Sigma, and Lean Manufacturing, as demanded by their Germany-based buyers. The factory also had a small canteen-cum-card room that served tea and biscuits and also boasted of table tennis facility (which we did not see). They had a clean toilet and water purifier facilities for clean and safe drinking water.

The condition of the other factory was just short of a junkyard. There was no proper layout of machines, quality control was being done only by visual inspection, raw material and scrap were littered all over, and the firm had a 'hellish' toilet with broken doors for workers. For drinking, they had an earthen pot with a steel tumbler and two glasses welded with iron chains. Ventilation was aplenty as the broken tin roof allowed enough sunlight to seep in during the day. We did come across gloves and other safety measures that were being used sparingly.

We checked with the owner of the GPN firm as to who enforced all these systems. He said that before he was finally approved as the OEM supplier/

vendor, he was invited to the company's head office in Germany for an exposure visit. Subsequently, the buyers helped the firm in obtaining various quality certifications and helped them introduce various good manufacturing practice (GMP) measures. Besides, they also sent two engineers to train the workers in various production processes. The German company also provides designs besides the purchase orders.

The owner claimed that the quality measures are strictly enforced in the factory. They denied any insistence on enforcement of labour standards by the German company. However, the labour standards are enforced by various Central and state regulatory authorities of the government. The only concern of the OEM was the use of 'child labour'. However, given the nature of the industry (engineering), an entrepreneur hardly employs any child labour. We also did not witness any case of child labour in the 183 factories that we surveyed.

LABOUR STANDARDS IN LUDHIANA, JALANDHAR, AND PHAGWARA AUTO PARTS AND COMPONENTS INDUSTRY CLUSTERS

For the purpose of analysis, the sample firms have been segmented into three categories, that is, OEM Suppliers and/or exporters that are a part of the GPN (all of which are registered under the Factories Act, 1948), registered but non-OEM, and non exporters firms and unregistered/unorganized firms. As expected, labour standards and conditions of work were found to be better in the first category and to an extent in the second category. Such was not the case of unregistered firms that are, by and large, out of the regulatory framework. Workers in the first two categories of firms enjoy better wages as compared to the third category.

The labour standards, to a great extent, also depend on the kind of workforce employed in a firm. Working conditions are far better in OEMs and exporters as compared to an unorganized small factory. The former category of firms follow a somewhat more systematic recruitment process and better criteria, the process of skill formation and induction, nature of employment (contract or regular), process of wage negotiations, and the incentive structure. Such firms also have better working conditions, including safely measures, social security measures, and welfare measures. They employ skilled worker force and focus on skill formation and upgrading on a continuous basis.

The aforementioned analysis indicates that the GPN firms have performed far better than the non-GPN firms. Therefore, it would be prudent for a local firm to move up the value chain/value addition ladder that would lead to benefits for both the employers and the employees in terms of better profits and better working conditions, respectively. Customers will also benefit in the process because they would be assured of the quality as well as timely delivery. Moreover, this upward mobility would also indicate their better competitiveness, which is a necessity in the era of globalization.

Another dimension that needs to be explored is: do the small firms, upon their graduation to the larger OEM category firms, retain their old workers or do they recruit a fresh workforce to meet new challenges? Interviews with such entrepreneurs indicate that most of the firms, upon graduating to the status of OEM units, prefer to recruit afresh rather than continue with the old workers. In fact, when they graduate to higher investment-size firms, they also shift to a higher level of technological sophistication that the old workers are not able to handle.

Nevertheless, in a few cases, it was also observed that some of the experienced and proactive workers were not only retained but also facilitated in sharpening their skills and move upwards to the position of supervisors. The experience and loyalty to the company does matter, after all. There is also a category of workers who are retained because of their sincerity and work devotion, but are downgraded to perform low-end tasks.

Recruitment Process and Criteria

Four major modes of recruitment of workers, that is, direct recruitment through advertisement, following standard procedures; personal contacts; through labour contractor; and referral are in vogue in the JLP auto parts

Table 12.2: Recruitment Process in the Sample Firms

S. No.	Question	OEM/Export		Non-OEM/Non-Export				Sig.[#]	Total	
				Registered		Unregistered				
		No.	Percentage	No.	percentage	No.	percentage		No.	percentage
1	Direct	48	98.0	13	48.1	27	25.2	★	88	48.1
2	Contact	10	20.4	5	18.5	30	28.0		45	24.6
3	Labour Contractor	4	8.2	2	7.4	11	10.3		17	9.3
4	Referral	2	4.1	3	11.1	90	84.1	★	95	51.9
	Total	49		27		107			183	

Source: Field Survey.
Notes: [#] OEM/Export vs Unregistered Non-OEM/Non-Export.
★ in columns titled 'Sig.' indicates significant differences at 1%.

and components clusters. While all the segments use all the four modes of recruitment, most OEM suppliers and a few registered units use the direct recruitment mode. The unregistered units bank heavily upon referrals. In such units, the old workers help the owners in recruiting new workers, as and when there is a requirement. Similar is the case of referrals as a mode of recruitment (Table 12.2). The major criteria used for recruiting workers by the OEMs are their technical qualifications (89.8 per cent) and skill base (81.6 per cent), whereas wages also play an important role in the case of unorganized firms (30.8 per cent) while recruiting workers.

CRITERIA FOR WAGE FIXATION

Firms in JLP clusters use multiple criteria for fixing wages. However, skill base, as reflected in technical qualifications of the candidates, and their work experience emerge as the major parameters for fixing wages. About 92 per cent OEMs fix wages using skill base, and over 83 per cent of these firms also use experience as a criterion. Reliance of unorganized sector firms on these two parameters is much less (57.7 per cent and 49 per cent respectively) as compared to the OEMs. The other parameters include fixation of wages on piece rate and norms of the company (see Table 12.3).

Table 12.3: Base for Fixing Wages in the Sample Firms

S. No.	Question	OEM/Export		Non-OEM/Non-Export				Sig.#	Total	
				Registered		Unregistered				
		No.	Percentage	No.	percentage	No.	percentage		No.	percentage
1	Skill Base/ Technical Qualification	44	91.7	8	33.3	60	57.7	★	112	63.6
2	Experience	40	83.3	6	25.0	51	49.0	★	97	55.1
3	As per company norm	7	14.6	7	29.2	22	21.2		36	20.5
4	Per piece production	9	18.8	2	8.3	25	24.0		36	20.5
	Total	48		24		104			176	

Source: Field Survey.
Notes: #OEM/Export vs Unregistered Non-OEM/Non-Export.
★in columns titled 'Sig.' indicates significant differences at 1%.

NATURE OF EMPLOYMENT, MODE OF WAGE PAYMENT, AND INCENTIVE STRUCTURE

The nature of employment appears to be reasonably fair in the JLP. Over 80 per cent firms prefer to engage workers on a regular basis, as there is an acute shortage of skilled workers in the clusters. There is no formal training institute where workers can get training in manufacturing auto parts and components. Most of the learning is on the job and persons who have spent years in the industry are in demand from the local firms. Head hunting is rampant. Workers do not hesitate to change firms for even as small a raise as Rs 200–300 per month, The problem is more acute with smaller firms who are not able to pay wages attractive enough to retain their workforce. The proportion of unorganized domestic firms engaging regular workers is much lower (69.8 per cent) than the OEMs (97.9 per cent). However, almost all the factories, irrespective of their category, did employ temporary/contractual workers depending upon the exigencies and short-term needs, though the magnitude was much higher among the unorganized units (see Table 12.4).

Table 12.4: Nature of Employment in the Sample Firms

S. No.	Question	OEM/Export No.	OEM/Export Percentage	Non-OEM/Non-Export Registered No.	Non-OEM/Non-Export Registered percentage	Non-OEM/Non-Export Unregistered No.	Non-OEM/Non-Export Unregistered percentage	Sig.[#]	Total No.	Total percentage
1	Regular Employment	47	97.9	22	84.6	74	69.8	*	143	79.4
2	Temporary/ Contractual	17	35.4	6	23.1	57	53.8	**	80	44.4
	Total	48		26		106			180	

Source: Field Survey.
Notes: [#] OEM/Export vs Unregistered Non-OEM/Non-Export.
* in columns titled 'Sig.' indicates significant differences at 1%.
** in columns titled 'Sig.' indicate differences at 5%.

The terms of payment of wages also showed a similar trend as observed in the case of nature of employment. While the OEMs and the registered firms paid fixed wages (following the minimum wages fixed by the government), only 59.6 per cent of the unorganized firms followed the suit. In fact, 51 per cent of these firms paid wages based on the piece

Table 12.5: Payment Terms in the Sample Firms

S. No.	Question	OEM/Export		Non-OEM/Non-Export				Sig.#	Total	
				Registered		Unregistered				
		No.	Percentage	No.	percentage	No.	percentage		No.	percentage
1	Fixed wages	47	100.0	26	100.0	62	59.6	*	135	76.3
2	Per piece production	13	27.7	2	7.7	53	51.0	*	68	38.4
	Total	47		26		104			177	

Source: Field Survey.
Notes: # OEM/Export vs Unregistered Non-OEM/Non-Export.
* in columns titled 'Sig.' indicates significant differences at 1%.

Table 12.6: Incentive Structure in the Sample Firms

S. No.	Question	OEM/Export		Non-OEM/Non-Export				Sig.#	Total	
				Registered		Unregistered				
		No.	Percentage	No.	percentage	No.	percentage		No.	percentage
1	Based on Performance/ production record	39	100.0	22	100.0	72	100.0		133	100.0
2	Based on leave record	1	2.6	0	0.0	1	1.4		2	1.5
3	Based on overtime track record	1	2.6	0	0.0	1	1.4		2	1.5
	Total	39		22		72			133	

Source: Field Survey.
Note: # OEM/Export vs Unregistered Non-OEM/Non-Export.

rate (see Table 12.5). Most of the firms claimed to be giving various incentives like bonus, overtime, interest-free loan, and vacation gifts (when regular workers go on their annual vacations, the owners, particularly small-firm owners, give some ad hoc amount to their workers as 'family gift'). However, while the OEMs and registered factories paid overtime and bonus, etc., as a part of the statutory compliance, the unorganized sector firms also did not lag behind, though voluntarily. It is probably the shortage of workers that has led to better incentive payments by the owners. However, the incentives, by and large, are determined on the basis of performance, regularity of attendance, and overtime track record (see Table 12.6).

WORKING HOURS AND OVERTIME FACILITIES

In close to 92 per cent of the firms surveyed, working eight hours is a norm. However, whenever there are more orders to be executed and deadlines to be met, the producers negotiate longer hours of work. In the case of only about 8 per cent firms, the working hours were stated to be between 9 and 12 hours (see Table 12.7). The producers were also asked about the overtime provisions in their firms. Surprisingly, all the OEMs and exporting firms, about 89 per cent registered non-OEM and non-exporting firms, and over 79 per cent small producers stated that they do have a provision for overtime in case they have to engage workers beyond the normal eight hours.

Table 12.7: Working Hours in the Sample Firms

S. No.	Question	OEM/Export		Non-OEM/Non-Export				Sig.#	Total	
				Registered		Unregistered				
		No.	Percentage	No.	percentage	No.	percentage		No.	percentage
1	8 hrs	40	81.6	25	92.6	103	96.3	★	168	91.8
2	9–12 hrs	9	18.4	2	7.4	4	3.7	★	15	8.2
	Total	49		27		107			183	

Source: Field Survey.
Notes: # OEM/Export vs Unregistered Non-OEM/Non-Export.
★ in columns titled 'Sig.' indicates significant differences at 1%.
★★ in columns titled 'Sig.' indicates significant differences at 5%.

HEALTH AND SAFETY MEASURES

Given the nature of the industry, a number of health and safety measures are required to be put in place. The fieldwork brought to the fore some stark facts. While OEMs and exporting firms are complying with almost all safety measures, it is just the opposite in the case of registered non-OEM, non-exporting firms and unregistered firms. There is a significant difference in the safety measures adhered to by these two sets of firms. Depending on the requirements, hand gloves, fire safety measures, first-aid facility, and masks are the key safety devices being used in the JLP clusters. All the OEMs and exporting firms have made adequate provisions for these measures. The unorganized sector enterprises fail miserably on this front. Only 28.4 per cent firms provide gloves, 13.5 per cent have installed fire safety devices, only 9.5 per cent firms have first-aid provisions, and 20.3 per cent of the firms provide masks to their workers. The situation is no different in the case of registered non-OEM, non-exporting firms (see Table 12.8).

Table 12.8: Health and Safety Practices in the Sample Firms

S. No.	Question	OEM/Export		Non-OEM/Non-Export				Sig.#	Total	
				Registered		Unregistered				
		No.	Percentage	No.	percentage	No.	percentage		No.	percentage
1	Gloves	49	100.0	9	33.3	21	28.4	★	79	52.7
2	Fire safety devices, Fire extinguisher	49	100.0	3	11.1	10	13.5	★	62	41.3
3	First aid	49	100.0	5	18.5	7	9.5	★	61	40.7
4	Mask	21	42.9	1	3.7	15	20.3	★	37	24.7
5	Others	3	6.1	1	3.7	4	5.4		8	5.3
	Total	49		27		74			150	

Source: Field Survey.
Notes: Others include: finger protection, eye glasses, shoes, helmets, etc.
OEM/Export vs Unregistered Non-OEM/Non-Export.
★ in columns titled 'Sig.' indicates significant differences at 1%.
★★ in columns titled 'Sig.' indicates significant differences at 5%.

WELFARE MEASURES

An attempt was made to assess the extent of welfare measures in vogue in the clusters. The situation is somewhat better in this regard as compared to health and safety measures. The first two categories of firms have adequate provisions for safe drinking water and toilets. A few factories in this segment also have provision of some recreation facilities like volleyball, carrom board, cards, and television. Of the 49 OEMs and exporting units, 13 have their own canteens (all OEMs, global and domestic). In a few cases, the canteen itself is converted into a recreation hall (small room), making it a 'canteen-cum-recreation centre', as it is fitted with a TV (see Table 12.9). The situation is not very encouraging in the unorganized-sector firms. Almost one-third of firms do not have adequate provision even for safe drinking water and toilets, what to talk of other facilities. The condition of toilets was horrible even in the small factories that had a toilet constructed within their premises.

SOCIAL SECURITY MEASURES

Since some of the social security measures like provident fund (PF) and Employees' State Insurance (ESI) are mandatory under the Factories Act, all the registered factories surveyed complied with these provisions. All

Table 12.9: Welfare Measures in the Sample Firms

S. No.	Question	OEM/Export		Non-OEM/Non-Export				Sig.[#]	Total	
				Registered		Unregistered				
		No.	Percentage	No.	percentage	No.	percentage		No.	percentage
1	Drinking water	49	100.0	27	100.0	69	67.6	★	145	81.5
2	Toilet	49	100.0	27	100.0	66	64.7	★	142	79.8
3	Recreation facility	10	20.4	2	7.4	5	4.9	★	17	9.6
4	Canteen	13	26.5	0	0.0	2	2.0	★	15	8.4
	Total	49		27		102			178	

Source: Field Survey.
Notes: [#] OEM/Export vs Unregistered Non-OEM/Non-Export.
★ in columns titled 'Sig.' indicates significant differences at 1%.

Table 12.10: Social Security Measures in the Sample Firms

S. No.	Question	OEM/Export		Non-OEM/Non-Export				Sig.[#]	Total	
				Registered		Unregistered				
		No.	Percentage	No.	percentage	No.	percentage		No.	percentage
1	PF	35	100.0	25	100.0	14	63.6	★	74	90.2
2	ESI	35	100.0	25	100.0	0	0.0	★	60	73.2
3	Insurance	35	100.0	12	48.0	1	4.5	★	48	58.5
4	Gratuity	35	100.0	20	80.0	1	4.5	★	56	68.3
	Total	35		25		22			82	

Source: Field Survey.
Notes: [#] OEM/Export vs Unregistered Non-OEM/Non-Export.
★ in columns titled 'Sig.' indicates significant differences at 1%.

the 35 OEMs and exporting firms that responded on this issue had made provision for insurance and gratuity as well. None of the unorganized small producers had made provision for ESI, and only 14 (63.6 per cent) firms were paying PF (see Table 12.10). Social security remains a major issue in the unorganized micro and small enterprises.

FGDS: THE WORKERS' PERSPECTIVE

As mentioned earlier, in all nine FGDs were conducted during the course of the study: four in Ludhiana, three in Jalandhar, and two in Phagwara, covering 124 workers. The FGDs for select groups of workers were conducted in industrial areas, their place of habitat, tea/*paan* shops, etc., so that they open up without any hesitation. Since disclosure of names was not mandatory, all the workers participated in a free and congenial environment. Initially, the groups (of 12–15 workers each) were briefed about the objective of the FGD and how they could contribute in understanding the labour conditions in the JPL auto parts clusters. Most of the workers were initially amused by the methodology of probing. However, as the proceedings moved ahead, they started understanding the seriousness of the purpose and discussed the issues intensively.

Social Background

During the course of discussion it was found that majority (51 per cent) of the respondents came from Uttar Pradesh and about 30 per cent came from Bihar. The discussion processes revealed that they have, on an average, a five-to-six member family including two to three children, back home. In majority of the families there is only one earning member. But some workers said that they have two earning members in the family. The other member, mostly working as an agricultural labourer in their native places or working on daily wages, earns Rs 1,000 per month.

A very high proportion realized the importance of education as they were sending their children to schools. Children of a few participants were undergoing higher and technical education as well. However, in a few cases, their children were found to be working in tea and cigarette stalls, mostly operated by their close relatives, and supplementing the family income. When asked about saving habits, the participants mentioned that they manage to save Rs 700–800 per month, which is generally remitted to their native place through money order, drafts, or personal contacts (persons known to them are often approached to carry money at the time of their visits to their native places).

Initiation to Work

Most of the workers used referrals/contacts of their village peers or relatives to get their first job, as persons from different rural and semi-urban areas have been working in this cluster for several decades. Local industry also uses these contacts (mostly their own senior workers) to recruit workers at the time of labour shortage, particularly during festivals and the harvesting season. Lack of opportunity was cited as one of the major reasons for migrating to these places, to find some source of livelihood. Initially, most of them come as unskilled workers and learn the tricks of the trade through apprenticeship or on-the-job training. However, these greenhorns are paid extremely low wages (in the region of Rs 35–40 per day), as they are not able to handle technical jobs. They are engaged on daily wages and paid without signing any document. In fact, such workers are not even put on record and asked not to come from the next day if there is no work.

Skills, Earnings, and Social Security

Interestingly, the majority (90 per cent) of the participants claimed to be skilled workers. However, at the end of the month their earnings (including overtime) hardly exceeded Rs 3,000 or in some cases Rs 4,000, depending on the skill levels and norm of their employers/firms, taking the total family earnings to Rs 3,000–5,000 per month. There are even discrepancies in the actual wage they get and the amount mentioned in the salary slip that regular workers sign. A very common practice (only in non-GPN firms) is that a person getting a wage of Rs 2,050 per month would sigh on a receipt of Rs 3,275 per month.

The major route to acquiring skills is to assist a skilled worker and observe him working. In the initial (recruitment) phase, they get some informal training tips from supervisors or experienced fellow workers, but instances of formal skill upgrading training are minimal. Of course, a few workers did mention in-house training as a part of the induction programme in some larger factories. However, in micro enterprises, without any exception, there is only an informal route to acquiring skills. Learning on the job and learning by observing others are the two most commonly cited skill upgrading processes. After acquiring skills, they do get incentives in terms of enhanced income, but this enhancement is considered to be on the lower side. It was pointed out that for an average worker it takes two to three years to source a regular rather than an ad hoc position in some factory. However, it works both ways. During the course of discussions it was also found that, on an average, a worker changes two to three jobs in three years' time, and in most of the cases, it is due to better wages offered by the prospective employer. However, since the industry is growing fast and needs workers to execute its expansion plans, an increasing number of factories have started offering regular employment in view of the shortage of skilled workers over the last few years.

The groups were somewhat divided while talking about available social security measures like ESI, PF, and gratuity. A good number of participants said that they do get PF and ESI facilities that are statutory in nature. But all those working in the unorganized sector did not have these privileges. For a majority of the participants, benefits like pension, insurance, mediclaim, and gratuity were almost non-existent.

Working Conditions

As the discussion proceeded, an attempt was made to understand the in-factory facilities available to them during working hours. Sufficient time was devoted to understating the welfare measures/facilities available to them while working. So far as working environment was concerned, the response was quite positive. Everybody indicated that they have good lighting arrangements, ventilation, and workplace cleanliness. As they represented different firms, we could draw a conclusion that they consider their general work environment to be conducive.

Among the health and safety measures, first-aid boxes and fire safety devices are omnipresent in large factories. It is beyond the capacity of the smaller of the small factories. Though, usually, workers do not use gloves, masks, etc., while working, these are available and are used whenever required. The finger cover to protect the skin is also provided by the employers. Clean drinking water is generally made available to the workers. Toilet facilities are provided but the toilets are usually very dirty and are almost unusable. The canteen and recreation facilities are said to be 'non-available' in most of the factories. However, they did not see any utility of such measures as a large number of tea stalls and food hawkers were always available within walking distance from the factory.

Living Conditions

Most of the workers live in unauthorized shanties, *chawls*, and slums. Nevertheless, a few of them also live in rented premises (one-room half constructed structure/house) by paying a monthly rent in the range of Rs 400–500 a month. While a majority of the workers inhabit slums and shanties, sometimes a few do boast of living in a rented premise (proper house), just to show off. Generally there are three to four occupants in a room who live either with their co-workers or with their village mates. There are light and water facilities in their residence but provisioning of toilets is generally absent. They spend leisure hours by gossiping, roaming, chatting. About 20 per cent of the participants possess a radio and 15 per cent have access to TV (may be a common TV purchased with joint financing or watching TV programmes in the house of a better-off neighbour under the pretext of social visit). A good number of workers were observed to possess mobile phones.

Most of the participants denied indulging in drinking habits; however, an insider's observation would lead one to conclude that there are more drinkers than non-drinkers. For example, when asked about their drinking habits, 99 per cent of the workers responded in the negative. However, when one of the self-confessed drinkers stated that 'everybody drinks', there was only a confirmatory 'laugh'. But it appears that a majority of them are casual drinkers as their pockets hardly permit such a luxury.

Level of Workers' Satisfaction with Labour Standards

The workers' satisfaction level, with respect to six parameters—working conditions, working hours, income, incentive structure, behaviour of the manager/owner, and living conditions—was also discussed in the FGDs. They were asked to rate these parameters on a 5-point scale ('1' indicating 'highly dissatisfied' and '5' indicating 'highly satisfied'). As far as working conditions were concerned, the groups, without any significant variation across the towns, rated it to be '4'. The working hours got a rating of '5'. It appears that the workers are satisfied with the working conditions and working hours. Their major source of dissatisfaction emanates from low wages and earnings. They strongly feel that their income level is not commensurate with the labour/effort put in by them. They felt that with the eroding value of the rupee, their wages must be at least doubled. The incentive structure is considered to be okay at '3'. Behaviour of the employers in these auto parts clusters was rated as 'good' but the group rated the behaviour of the managers as 'bad', as they often create enough pressure and use 'bad' language to get the job done. The living conditions got a rating of '3', indicating somewhat satisfactory status.

Their Future as the Workers See It

The future plans of the participants were also discussed at length. All of them were interested in upgrading their existing skill base. Their expected salary ranged from Rs 5,000 to Rs 8,000 per month, and it is believed that the skill upgrading process will help them in this endeavour. They also opined that with enhanced salary, they will be in a position to purchase a bike, send more money to their homes, afford better education for their children, and stay in better rented premises.

Overall Impression of the Investigators

An overall impression that one gets is not too pessimistic, if one goes by the workers' ratings. Plausibly, they do not have any idea of good working conditions as they see only the next-door factory, which provides similar working conditions. If judged by the normal standards of decent living and decent working conditions, all the three auto parts and components clusters fall far below the acceptable standards. However, while discussing the labour standards, one should also look at the overall structure of the industry, size of operation, and affordability. While registered factories, willingly or unwillingly, are complying with the usual statutory norms, the issue of decent work is with reference to the informal sector, micro enterprises.

NATURE OF INTER-FIRM LINKAGES IN THE CLUSTERS

There is no major link between firms catering to OEM and unorganized units. While the unorganized units mostly cater to the domestic replacement market and manufacture low quality, second-hand spare parts, the firms catering to OEM—domestic as well as overseas—manufacture products as per the design and technical specification of the original equipment manufacturers. Manufacturing these products necessitates modern facilities, latest plants and machinery, technical acumen, and a skilled workforce. These facilities are available in the firms catering to OEM (see Figure 12.3 for the inter-firm linkages).

There are several OEMs in Punjab like Sonalika Tractors Ltd, Punjab Tractors Ltd, and Eicher Ltd. These companies manufacture different categories of tractors. The ownership of the design of various tractor parts lies with their parent OEMs. First, the OEMs decide which parts to manufacture on their own and which are to be outsourced. They supply drawing, design, and process manufacturing of outsourced parts to the firms manufacturing auto components. The manufacturing takes place under the stringent technical parameters decided by OEMs. They even send their engineers and technical personnel to oversee the quality parameter. For example, the suspension system needed by Punjab Tractors Ltd is supplied by M/s Acme Udyog, Jalandhar. Similarly, other reputed national OEMs like Tata Motors, Ashok Leyland, and international OEMs (having operations in India) like Hyundai and General Motors source axles for their cars from local firms in Punjab.

The job-work units operate in a different manufacturing domain. They have limited facilities and thus can only take up limited type of work. They, by and large, do not have 'own-marketing' infrastructure and access to markets and thus always remain dependant on 'job work providers'. They mostly cater to the requirements of both registered and unregistered (and unorganized) units. Nevertheless, there are few job-work units that have developed specialized expertise over time. Such units do get job-work from tier-one firms, that is, firms catering to OEMs and exporters. However, a majority of the OEM suppliers have integrated manufacturing facilities which enable them to deliver 'quality' and adhere to the supply schedules.

JOB-WORKING UNITS IN A VICIOUS CIRCLE

The job-working units in the auto parts clusters, that is, JLP, are somehow managing their livelihood. Majority of them are operating with two to three machines and doing jobs like chamfering, facing, cotter slotting, stamping, heat treatment, induction hardening, plating, etc. On an average, they employ two to three workers, mostly on a contractual basis. The duration of the labour contract depends on the number of days of job work they have in hand. As the job work of a particular company gets over, the workers are relieved till the next order materializes. There is no formal contract and wage payment; contract days are decided on verbal terms. There are few job working units who get regular orders from the companies and, therefore, are able to employ workers for a longer duration.

The workers' loyalty, especially in the job working units, is abysmally low. If another unit provides Rs 100–200 more per month, they do not hesitate to switch over. As a typical worker clarifies, 'We came here all the way from Bihar to earn, therefore we change jobs if better remuneration is offered.' Therefore, retention of workers is a major issue in the job working units in JLP.

The intermittent nature of the work order does not allow the owner to settle in business. At times, one could find the owner operating a machine and thus trying to save the cost of a worker. This happens specially when there is no continuity of work and the owner prefers to do the job on his own instead of hiring a worker. The short-term nature of the work neither interests a skilled worker nor removes suspicion of the owner about a new recruit's work commitment. They make themselves conversant with all the machines, which helps them in overcoming problems emanating from absenteeism, turnover, etc. Interestingly, many a time the opportunity cost of the owner is not considered while calculating the total cost of manufacturing/job working. The 'wage' component in the total production cost is generally 8–10 per cent. However, units in the higher echelons can afford to pay better wages, and share of wage in the total cost comes to around 10 per cent.

There is an interesting angle in the profitability/income distribution. Suppose a unit takes up job work like drilling, cutting, or chamfering. He is given, say, 100 kg of raw material. He will process the same and return the final products without building-in the job work charges. The scrap generated in the manufacturing process (which varies between 25 and 50 per cent, depending on the job) remains with the job work unit as the processing charges. He then sells the scrap in the market (chips at Rs 18 per kg and dead ends at Rs 22 per kg) and thus recovers the cost of manufacturing and 'manages' the surplus. Their monthly earning could vary between Rs 4,000 and 8,000; an earning certainly not remunerative, considering the time and energy spent in the units. Moreover, there is no certainty factor; good 'orders' in a particular month do not ensure 'orders' in the next month. In fact, they are 'self-exploited worker entrepreneurs'. Their monthly remuneration hardly exceeds that of an organized-sector worker.

Pressure on the productivity, quality, and cost fronts always keeps them under tension. Due to intense competition, there is always a possibility that other job workers would offer a better deal (less job-work charges) to the job-work providers. The suppliers/providers would thus cite the example of others while negotiating a lesser rate per piece of job work. However, quality is never compromised, leaving the only option of maintaining income (per day) by working late in the evening. Thus, the following would delineate the status of job working units in the auto parts clusters, JLP:

1. uncertainty of getting regular job work;
2. large number of job working units signifying intense competition;
3. pressure on the quality and cost fronts;
4. non-remunerative income; and
5. problems of workers turnover, absenteeism.

As a long-term strategy, proactive job working units should think of moving upwards in the value chain. If they can graduate to 'own manufacturing' at least to serve the replacement market, they would enjoy a better share in the profit margins. This is the point where they would be able to sustain themselves and provide decent work conditions to their workers. They would be in a position to increase their profitability further if they could cater to OEMs/export markets and then further move to become a GPN.

This upward mobility, however, is not an automatic process. Only visionary and proactive entrepreneurs, who are willing to invest and take calculated risks, would be able to make headway in their business fortunes. With every upward stage in the value chain, the entrepreneurs would meet different categories of customers whose quality requirements would become more and more stringent. Therefore, meeting the increasing demands of discerning customers is a challenge that a few of the entrepreneurs would prefer to accept while the others would prefer to avoid.

Thus, cost-investment, risk-incentive, and capability factor would determine whether a firm would make any progress in the value chain or

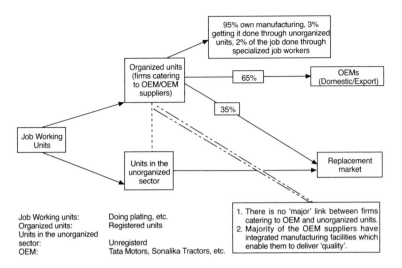

Figure 12.3: Auto Parts and Components Supply Chain

not. The ability to comprehend these three factors would vary from person to person. One could argue that at any given point in time, there would be different categories of firms doing job work, own manufacturing, catering to replacement market, OEM/export supply, and GPN. Proactive firms would make progress and others would continue to operate on the margins. As mentioned earlier, the empirical findings suggest that this progress (of firms) is accompanied by improvement in labour welfare measures as well. But the shortage of skilled labour needs to be sorted out by taking strategic measures like establishing/linking up with skill development centres like ITIs and organizing periodic training programmes.

CONCLUDING OBSERVATIONS

With ever-increasing demand for automobiles in the country, the auto parts and components industry in India is one of the fastest growing segments in the Indian manufacturing sector. With this burgeoning demand, a large number of small and medium enterprises engaged in manufacturing of auto parts and components are emerging on the scene. However, the structure of this segment of industry is highly fragmented. On the one hand, OEMs, which are a part of GPNs, are emerging at a fast rate; on the other hand, there are a large number of micro and small enterprises that produce and cater to the domestic and spares market. Labour conditions in OEMs are observed to be reasonably good. They provide decent work conditions to their workers, though, more often than not, enforced by the OEM buyers and the regulatory authorities. The working conditions in micro and small enterprises are far from satisfactory, as measured on various parameters of 'decent work'. There is a need to improve governance of the clusters through upgrading value chains at all levels to give the workers their due. Therefore, the segmented marketing strategies lead to segmented labour practices. On the one hand, there are firms at the higher end of the value proposition (catering to OEMs) where labour practices would fall in the category of 'decent work'; on the other hand, labour practices in the firms offering lower value proposition were found to be far from satisfactory.

The issue of decent work must also be discussed with reference to the job working units. An academic argument could demand that every job should be a decent job. However, in practice one could hardly find a decent work environment in the job work units. One would like to raise questions like: Is it a matter of choice that these self-employed do not offer decent work conditions to their workers? Does affordability prevail over intentions? Is it possible and feasible for a job work unit to be competitive and still provide a decent work environment? Is it possible for them to achieve upward mobility in the value chain? Will it be advisable and feasible to impose labour standards and decent work conditions in such units? Can one create a situation where affordability and willingness go hand in hand? Is it possible to create a win–win situation? If so, what are the ways? These are difficult questions to answer. But the answers must be found, in view of the size of this sector.

REFERENCES

Artola, N and M. Parrilli (2006), 'The Development of a Diary Cluster in Boaco and Chontales, Nicaragua', in C. Pietrobelli and R. Rabellotti (eds), *Upgrading to Compete: Global Value Chains, Clusters, and SMEs in Latin America*. Washington, D.C.: Inter-American Development Bank.

Bazan, L. and L. Navas-Aleman (2005), 'Making Value Chain Governance Work for the Implementation of Quality, Labour and Environmental Standards: Upgrading Challenges in the Footwear Industry', in E. Giuliani, R. Rabellotti, and M. Pieter van Dijk (eds), *Clusters Facing Competition: The Importance of External Linkages*. Hampshire: Ashgate.

Bell, M. and M. Albu (1999), 'Knowledge System and Technological Dynamism in Industrial Clusters in Developing Countries', *World Development*, 27: 1715–34.

Cygnus (2007), 'Industry Insight—Indian Auto Components', January, Cygnus Business Consulting and Research, Hyderabad.

——— (2007), 'Industry Insight—Indian Auto Logistics', August, Cygnus Business Consulting and Research, Hyderabad.

DCSSI (2004), *Final Results: Third All India Census of Small Scale Industries*. New Delhi: Government of India, Development Commissioner, SSI.

Gereffi, G. and M. Korzeniewicz (1994), *Commodity Chains and Global Capitalism*. Westport: Praeger.

Giuliani, E., C. Pietrobelli, and R. Rabellotti (2005), 'Upgrading in Global Value Chains: Lessons from Latin American Clusters', *World Development*, 33(4): 549–73.

Guerrieri, P., S. Iammarino, and C. Pietrobelli (2001), *The Global Challenge to Industrial Districts: Small and Medium-sized Enterprises in Italy and Taiwan*. Cheltenham: Edward Elgar.

Humphrey, J. and H. Schmitz (2000), 'Governance and Upgrading: Linking Industrial Cluster and Global Value Chain Research', IDS Working Paper, No. 120. Brighton: Institute of Development Studies, University of Sussex.

Kaplinsky, R. (1998), 'Globalization, Industrialization and Sustainable Growth: The Pursuit of the Nth. Rent. Brighton', IDS Discussion Paper 365. Brighton: Institute of Development Studies.

Schmitz, H. (2004), *Local Enterprises in the Global Economy: Issues of Governance and Upgrading*. Cheltenham: Edward Elgar.

Schmitz, H. and K. Nadvi (1999), 'Clustering and Industrialization: Introduction', *World Development*, 27: 1503–14.

13 TAKING THE HIGH ROAD?
Labour in the Indian Software Outsourcing Industry

Carol Upadhya

INTRODUCTION

The Indian software outsourcing industry is a prime example of how global production networks (GPNs) can create high-quality employment opportunities in developing countries. Employees of software companies—'information technology (IT) professionals'—are regarded as privileged due to their high salaries, comfortable working environments, the range of 'employee friendly' human resource (HR) policies and amenities that they enjoy, and the opportunities they have to work abroad. Moreover, with the rapid increase in demand for skilled software labour and high rates of employee turnover, software professionals apparently have substantial bargaining power in the workplace and labour market. While 'decent work' does not appear to be a relevant question for this industry, a closer look reveals a more complex picture—India's position in the global 'information economy' as a provider of primarily low-end software services has translated, for most employees, into long working hours and monotonous work. Moreover, because of the dependence of the Indian software industry on foreign clients and the consequent volatility of demand, most IT jobs are highly insecure.

This chapter attempts to provide a more nuanced picture of labour in the Indian software outsourcing industry by describing several significant features of work, the labour market, and employment practices. I also examine variations in skills required and acquired, employment and working conditions, and the nature of work across different segments of the industry.

Finally, arguing that the software outsourcing industry is creating mostly labour-intensive, low-skilled rather than skill- and knowledge-intensive jobs, I address the question of 'decent' work and labour regulation.[1]

INDIAN SOFTWARE SERVICES IN THE GLOBAL INFORMATION ECONOMY

The rise of the software outsourcing and IT-enabled services (ITES) industries in India is representative of the restructuring of the global economy that has been underway since the 1980s. The 'servitization' of the advanced economies and the spread of new information and communication technologies (ICTs) have led to the emergence of global networks of service provision, and a range of white and 'pink collar' jobs are being outsourced or offshored to places where cheap and malleable labour is available. India has achieved prominence as the 'back office' of the world, a prime destination for both 'hi-tech' work such as computer programming as well as ITES such as insurance claims processing and customer call centres. These processes have transformed local labour markets and created new 'knowledge' workforces.[2]

India's IT industry[3] has recorded impressive growth since the 1990s, reaching total earnings of US$ 39.6 billion in 2006–7, of which $31.4 billion were from exports.[4] Software services and development are provided by captive offshore software development centres set up by foreign multinationals as well as by Indian software services companies. According to the industry body NASSCOM (National Association of Software and Services Companies), the IT industry generated total direct employment of approximately 1.6 million by 2006–7.[5] The growth of the Indian IT industry can be attributed not only to liberalization policies and the push towards technological modernization, but also to the significant state support it has enjoyed (Heeks, 1996; Parthasarathy, 2005; Balakrishnan, 2006). In addition, the industry has benefited from the availability of the large pool of skilled manpower (especially engineering graduates) that was produced during the period of Nehruvian state-led development.

The Indian IT industry provides software services primarily to companies located in the advanced industrialized countries. This export orientation has significant implications for the kinds of work and employment that have been created. Despite frequent claims that it is 'moving up the value chain' towards providing end-to-end software solutions, consultancy, and 'knowledge process outsourcing', the Indian IT industry continues to rely mainly on labour cost arbitrage (Balakrishnan, 2006). Its profitability is based largely on the ability to marshal large numbers of well-qualified human resources, deploy them on projects as needed, maximize labour productivity, and keep costs down. These features structure the labour market and organization of the labour process in specific ways, elaborated later.

The following discussion draws on field research on the software industry and its employees that was carried out in Bangalore and three European countries during 2004–05. Research methods were primarily qualitative, including informal interviews and interactions with over 600 IT and ITES employees, managers, chief executive officers (CEOs), and other key persons connected with the industry, as well as observations at workplaces. While most of the fieldwork was ethnographic, in order to generate some amount of quantitative data, we also conducted semi-structured interviews with a purposively selected sample of IT employees. The final sample was drawn from two large Indian software services companies, two medium-size Indian companies (one product and one service), five multinational software development centres, and six small firms. Within each company, we interviewed a small number of employees (ranging from 20 to 40 each in the medium and large companies to around five each in the small ones), selected randomly to reflect the demographics of that company's workforce. Completed formal interviews of this type totalled 132—much too small a sample from which to make generalizations. However, insights gained from the quantitative analysis of interview responses are supported and fleshed out on the basis of more extensive information collected through unstructured interviews.

TYPES OF WORK AND SKILL REQUIREMENTS

The software services industry encompasses a wide range of jobs, types of work, and employment conditions, from 'high-end' research and development to 'low-end' services such as software testing, customization, and systems maintenance. In this section, I briefly outline the key features of the IT industry that shape the demand for different types of labour and describe the various kinds of IT work, jobs, and employers in India.

The software business is usually divided into three major categories: solutions, products, and services. However, most software engineers divide software work into two categories—'projects' (software services) and 'products' (development of a software package or product for sale). This distinction roughly corresponds to that between 'low-end' and 'high-end' work, terms that are also commonly used in the industry. This refers to the fact that as one moves down the steps of the software development process (the 'waterfall' or 'cascade' model)—from conceptualization, design, and analysis to coding, testing, delivery/installation, and maintenance—the level of skill and knowledge required becomes progressively lower. The tasks at the beginning of the cycle are regarded as 'high end' in contrast to relatively less skilled work of coding and maintenance. The various stages of software development can be undertaken as separate projects or modules, allowing the 'low-end' labour-intensive processes to be de-linked and outsourced. Indian software companies have specialized in the provision of low-end services (Rothboeck et al., 2001: 15–16). 'Products' companies (most of which are multinationals), on the other hand, provide more opportunities for 'high-end' work since they often engage in software development from scratch. For this reason, most computer programmers prefer to work in 'products' companies, which are considered to offer more challenging high-end work—opportunities that are relatively scarce in India.

With regard to the types of software companies operating in India, the official classification (by Software Technology Parks of India [STPI], the government agency that promotes the IT industry) contains three categories: small/medium enterprises (SMEs), major Indian companies (MICs), and multinationals or firms with foreign equity participation (MNCs/FEs). There are about five MICs with workforces of over 50,000 each(two now have more than 100,000 employees each) and these companies dominate the labour market. At the other end of the scale are the 1,000-plus SMEs, most of which have less than 50 employees (Parthasarathy, 2000). In addition, there are over 200 overseas development centres (ODCs) of foreign companies operating in India, with workforces of 200 to 1,000 or more.

Most of the large Indian companies focus on software services outsourcing, catering to customers located primarily in North America and Europe. The industry developed on the basis of 'bodyshopping', a system of contract labour in which software engineers are deployed to the customer site. Over time, however, an increasing proportion of work has been shifted to India as improvements in communication technologies have enabled many tasks to be performed remotely, 'offshore'. Offshoring has produced new forms of mobility as well as immobility—the mobility of 'knowledge work' minus the body of the worker, or what Aneesh (2001a, 2006) terms 'virtual migration'. In the offshore model, software engineers located in India are logged onto the computer networks of their customers abroad, working on projects as part of 'virtual teams' consisting of colleagues, managers, and customers spread across several geographical locations. The client is able to monitor progress, check the quality of the work, and communicate with programmers as if they were 'onsite'. In this case, globalization may lead not to increased international labour migration but to the immobilization of workers who are restricted to their national territories.[6] Indian software services companies have perfected the 'global services delivery model' (innovated by Infosys) in which the work is divided across several locations and carried out round the clock, taking advantage of timezone differences. These firms provide primarily 'generic' services, taking on a wide range of software development, customization, maintenance, testing, and other types of projects on many different platforms and in diverse 'domains'. As noted earlier, the Indian companies have concentrated on the 'low end' of the software development cycle, which is labour-intensive but relatively low-skilled work, the earlier stages of conceptualization and design usually being retained by the client or carried out by global consultancy companies. Although Indian companies now also execute more complex projects and engage in consultancy and some amount of design work, the software industry continues to be dominated by software services.[7] In contrast, most of the multinational software development centres in India work on software products for their parent companies, such as embedded software for non-computer products, communications systems, and so on.

Apart from these STPI registered firms, there is a large 'informal sector' consisting of small companies that take on subcontracted work and employment consultants who contract out software labour. Most studies of the IT workforce have ignored this segment, focusing instead on the more highly qualified engineers employed in the large Indian companies and MNCs.[8] As a result, data on the size, composition, and stratification of the IT workforce are inadequate. The National Sample Survey Organisation (NSSO) data for 1999–2000 show that 38 per cent of 'IT occupation workers' are employed in small, informal enterprises (proprietorships or partnership firms), 25 per cent in public limited companies, and 28 per cent in private limited companies, indicating that small firms participate in the labour market to a significant extent (Basant and Rani, 2004: 5324).

This diversity in types of employment and employer means that a wide range of skills are utilized by the industry, from relatively less skilled 'generic programmers' to highly qualified computer scientists and domain specialists. Despite this wide range of skill requirements, the IT workforce is quite homogeneous in composition, being dominated by engineering graduates, who are available in large numbers in India. Engineers are considered to have the educational background and broad skills needed for IT work, although their specific training is largely irrelevant to the software industry.[9] Some companies also hire graduates and postgraduates with non-engineering but computer-related degrees, especially science graduates with Master's in Computer Applications (MCA) degrees. The following sections describe the salient features of work, the labour market, and employment in the IT industry.

FLEXIBILIZATION OF LABOUR

Flexibilization is regarded as a key feature of work and employment in the post-industrial economy of the West (Harvey, 1989). Labour flexibilization actually refers to several distinct processes: (*i*) a shift to flexible forms of employment, such as part-time, temporary, and contract work; (*ii*) greater 'flexibility' in the work process and organizational forms; and (*iii*) flexibility of the workforce itself (Benner, 2002). All three processes can be observed in the context of the Indian software industry, but their specificities are somewhat different from those described for the advanced economies.

The emergence of a range of flexible forms of employment has eroded job security and created longer working hours and double shifts.[10] This trend is found in the Indian IT industry as well, where the labour market is highly fluid and employment relations are more flexible than what was typically found in India's 'old economy' (which was dominated by the public sector). Here, flexibilization is linked mainly to the fact that software services companies operate on the 'human resources (HR) augmentation mode', in which the revenue of an organization is directly related to the number of projects executed and number of people working in the project (Ilavarasan, 2008). These companies must be able to execute projects quickly, within tight timelines, which means being able to put engineers to work on projects as and when needed. Flexibilization is accomplished in several ways.

First, the Indian service companies prefer to hire and train 'generic' programmers who are 'flexible' in the sense of being able to work on multiple platforms and languages, rather than those who are highly specialized. This enables managers to tap sufficient 'resources' quickly for their projects, rather than having to wait for engineers with particular 'skill sets' to be assigned or hired. Indian software engineers are known in the global market for their 'flexibility' in terms of technical skills, that is, their ability to adapt to new platforms and learn new technologies quickly. In contrast to this, the American IT industry depends much more on the specific skills, deep domain knowledge, and long work experience of its employees.[11]

Second, the IT workforce is highly flexible in terms of the nature of employment contracts and conditions. Most companies follow a 'hire and fire' policy, expanding or downsizing their workforces depending on the market. Often, employees are given little or no notice before being given the 'pink slip'—a common practice in many American companies but which is very new in the Indian context. Jobs in the large Indian software service companies are considered by employees to offer more job security, while the multinational ODCs provide better salaries and working conditions but relatively less security. Employment in smaller companies is the most insecure due to the high level of instability in the industry, which sees several companies go under each year. However, job security has been an issue throughout the industry periodically, especially during periods of global economic downturn such as the post-dotcom phase, as well as more recently in 2008 when the industry saw many layoffs.[12] Because the Indian software industry is almost entirely dependent on business from the US and other developed countries, the job market is deeply affected by shifts in the global economic scenario. An additional source of insecurity is the fact that several companies annually 'churn out' the bottom 10 per cent of employees based on performance appraisals, a policy about which several informants bitterly complained.

Third, various types of contract labour prevail in the industry, depending on the type of company and the kind and location of work. At the lower end of the spectrum is the 'bodyshopping' system—by supplying software professionals temporarily and only for the length of time needed, bodyshops help clients reduce their costs by downsizing their permanent workforces (Xiang Biao, 2007). Bodyshopping is analogous to the 'just-in-time' techniques characteristic of post-industrial production (Aneesh, 2001a: 358). Although bodyshopping as a means of supplying software labour to customers outside India is in decline, the use of temporary contract labour is still prevalent in the IT industry *within* India. Almost all of the large software companies, Indian as well as multinational, hire as much as 10 to 20 per cent of their workforces on short-term contracts through employment agencies or consultants. This practice enables companies to respond quickly to shifts in demand and is cheaper than maintaining a large proportion of permanent employees 'on the bench' (on the payroll but not currently assigned to a project). Temporary jobs are by definition insecure, but those who work as contractors do so because they hope to get absorbed as regular employees. Temporary staffing is also used as a mode of recruitment by companies, which are able to try out contract workers before deciding to offer them regular positions. From the industry point of view, temporary staffing enhances flexibility in the deployment of human resources, but for employees it is a highly insecure form of employment.

Fourth, the physical mobility and youth of the IT labour force adds to its flexibility. Most software engineers travel abroad at intervals for 'onsite' assignments, for varying periods of time. They are also highly mobile within India because they are liable to be shifted between different centres of a company or may relocate when they change jobs. The high level of geographical mobility is reinforced by the young profile of the workforce, with a median age of about 27. The large proportion of IT professionals, who are young unmarried men with few family responsibilities (only about 20–25 per cent are women), contributes to the flexibility of the workforce—an advantage from the industry point of view.

LABOUR MARKET FLEXIBILITY AND INDIVIDUALIZATION

Another dimension of labour flexibility flows from the fluidity in the labour market. Added to the job insecurity caused by a volatile market and the hire-and-fire culture of the industry is the high employee 'attrition rate' that is a constant complaint of HR managers. According to them, one of their major difficulties is attracting and retaining skilled workers. This pattern of labour mobility is typical of the American IT industry and of the 'new economy' in general (Carnoy, 2000; Benner, 2002), but represents a new trend in the white collar/professional workforce in India. IT companies demand the freedom to expand or shrink their workforces according to their requirements, and in response employees too feel free to pursue their career goals without regard to their employers' needs, giving them a reputation as 'migratory birds'.

The process of individualization that marks this industry also contributes to high employee turnover rates. Employees tend to deal with managements as individuals, whether in registering complaints or negotiating salaries, and when they are not satisfied with their jobs they vote with their feet—at least when the job market is good. Job hopping as a career strategy is a rational response to job insecurity and software engineers often change jobs in pursuit of higher salaries or better positions.[13]

In contrast to this, the corporate tradition in India has always been closer to the European pattern of life-long employment. While this shift has been seen across all industries after liberalization, it is even more marked in the IT industry. It is somewhat ironic that companies complain about high attrition rates and attempt to nurture employee loyalty, for it is the IT industry itself that has ushered in a new culture in which it is considered normal to switch jobs every two or three years. As mentioned earlier, IT companies in India tend to replicate contemporary American corporate culture, which values labour flexibility and individual achievement over long-standing employment relationships.

The culture of individualism in the IT industry is manifested in other ways as well. For instance, salaries and promotions are based on individual performance appraisals and salary structures are non-transparent, while the organizational cultures of IT companies promote competition among employees for promotions and rewards. Individualization is also linked to the absence of collective identity among employees, one reason for which is the relatively fuzzy distinction between 'worker' and 'manager' in the 'knowledge industries'. Most Indian software engineers aspire to managerial roles rather than the 'technical path'; hence they tend to identify with management. Moreover, because they are highly educated and perform 'high tech' work, they do not see themselves as 'workers' in the classical sense, even though the structural position of 'individual contributors' in the organizational structure and production process is similar to that of factory floor workers in manufacturing industries. These factors explain the general lack of interest in unionization or collective action in this industry. This characteristic of the IT workforce represents a political shift in India, with its strong tradition of white-collar unionization (for example, bank and government employees). Thus, the industry's allergy to labour laws and other forms of state regulation, as well as to unionization, is largely shared by workers, who display little awareness of their rights.

A significant outcome of individualization is the displacement of responsibility for the shaping of careers and the management of risk away from the corporation or the state, onto employees. In this rapidly changing industry, software engineers must constantly upgrade their skills in order to compete in the labour market. Many respondents expressed the fear that they would be made redundant if they are unable to keep up with changing technologies. But, as noted earlier, Indian software engineers have excelled at 'flexibility' in terms of skill sets, and this ability, together with the expanding job market in India, means that the fear of obsolescence is not yet as acute here as it is in other countries. While IT professionals in the US and Europe face loss of jobs due to downsizing and outsourcing, in India the reverse situation has obtained in most years, with companies competing to hire the best talent.

ROUTINIZATION OF WORK AND JOB SATISFACTION

Indian software services companies have been successful in the global market mainly by perfecting a 'factory' approach to software development, through the application of rationalized processes such as those prescribed in the Capability Maturity Model (CMM) Level 5 model. In these 'software factories', work is divided into small portions and allocated among many engineers, the workflow is tightly controlled and coordinated, and work is carried out mainly through the use of modular programming and software engineering tools, reducing the scope of individual initiative or creativity. Clients retain control over projects by employing remote computer-based techniques to monitor the performance of offshore teams.

The rationalization of software production has turned software work into a largely mechanical activity, one that is constantly monitored through measurements of time, 'effort', productivity, and output. Indeed, many of the software engineers we interviewed complained about the routinization of their work, describing it as boring and unchallenging. They believe that their jobs require little technical expertise: 'We are doing trash jobs', said one respondent. In software testing or 'quality assurance' functions, the work process is especially routinized, governed by centralized software tools designed to automatically track workflow and output, similar to those employed in call centres. At this end of the software services industry, the distinction between IT and ITES work becomes fuzzy.

The advent of 'software factories' and the consequent fragmentation of the work process have given rise to a debate on the 'deskilling' of software engineers (Prasad, 1998; Aneesh, 2001b; Ilavarasan, 2008). Braverman (1975) argued that Taylorist strategies of dividing the work process into small parts—task fragmentation—is aimed not only at increasing productivity and profits but also at enhancing managerial control over the labour and tacit knowledge of workers. Similarly, these software factories' engineers simply carry out prescribed routines or put together pre-cast pieces of software, and are not the autonomous and creative agents usually associated with computer programming (Barrett, 2001). Moreover, in large software projects, the work is divided among many engineers so that no individual worker is aware of the scope or objective of the entire project or how his/her component fits into the whole. This is not just a project management strategy, but is also a tactic used by companies to retain control over intellectual property—a key issue in the context of high employee attrition rates. Software engineers frequently complain about this aspect of their work, for it reduces the scope for gaining in-depth knowledge of particular domains or programming languages.

Due to the rationalization of the labour process and the industry's preference for 'generic' programmers, managements tend to regard engineers as mutually replaceable units whose contribution or 'performance' is measured only in terms of the amount of time they put in, the number of lines of codes they can write in a day, or how many test cases they complete, rather than their specialized knowledge of a specific language, platform, or domain area. In this sense, Indian software engineers represent the ultimate flexible labour force. The large services companies encourage this flexibility by moving programmers frequently among different types of projects, platforms, and domains. A negative outcome of this practice is that engineers are unable to develop expertise in any one area and so are not qualified to seek higher-end jobs in MNCs or research centres, which require specialized skills. This 'flexibility' tends to keep workers at the low end of the software production chain through 'deskilling'. But the reduction of programmers to 'abstract labour' in this way is effectively masked by the ubiquitous use of terms such as 'knowledge worker' and 'IT professional', which imply that all IT employees are engaged in highly challenging and creative work that fully utilizes their intelligence and expertise.

The routinization of software work has created a high level of job dissatisfaction among software engineers, which is indicated by responses to several survey questions. When asked whether they would like to remain in the IT profession, only 54 per cent said yes, 5 per cent said no, and 35 per cent said that they would like to stay in the industry for some time and then try something entirely different (usually after saving enough money). One-third of the respondents said that the job they were doing did not meet their expectations in some respects, which included: personal life affected negatively (29 per cent), work not satisfying (23 per cent), not working in preferred domain area (23 per cent), and excessive work pressure (17 per cent). The most common reasons reported for job dissatisfaction were that 'the job is not interesting', 'work is monotonous', and 'I am stagnating'; and a major reason given for wanting to move to a new job was to get 'better work'. These responses suggest that frustration with work and the consequent tendency to change jobs frequently are linked in part to the routine nature of the work. Moreover, many software engineers believe that they are over-qualified for their jobs—a problem that stems from the preference of software companies for engineering graduates. Respondents in research, consultancy, and management jobs, and those in 'products' companies, were more likely to describe their work as 'challenging' or 'interesting' as compared to those working in software development or testing and in services companies. While many companies have devised strategies to enhance employee satisfaction and stem attrition, they cannot change the fact that much of the work is routine and monotonous.

The unchallenging nature of much of the technical work that is outsourced to India also explains why most Indian software professionals aspire to move into management positions as soon as possible, unlike their peers in the US and Europe, many of whom pursue technical careers. In most Indian companies, there is no clear 'technical path', or this track is open to very few employees, which means that the only way software engineers can develop their careers is by moving into management. Although more companies (especially the MNCs) are now receiving more design-related or high-end development work, the majority of Indian software engineers are consigned to routine jobs. This, together with high stress levels and long working hours, leads to frustration and burnout.

WORKING HOURS AND STRESS

One of the most remarked upon aspects of the Indian software outsourcing industry is the very long working hours. Most of the software engineers in our survey reported that they work for at least 10 hours a day on average, usually coming to office at 9.00 or 10.00 in the morning and staying till 7.00 or 8.00 in the evening. But they often work much longer hours or even stay overnight (known as a 'night out') or work on weekends when faced with a project deadline or a crisis.

There are several reasons for this pattern of overwork, which apply more to the services companies than to the MNCs and products companies. First, when companies bid for projects, the man-days required are almost always underestimated. Although the standard man-day is of eight hours, estimates are usually based on the assumption of longer working hours, forcing engineers to work beyond eight hours in order to meet project deadlines. Second, the project cycle involves up and down phases—during periods when deadlines are looming or problems crop up, everyone on the team is expected to work as long as required. A third important reason is the time difference between India and the client site. Outsourced projects require a fair amount of 'overlap time' in order to function effectively, and conference calls take place almost on a daily basis. For the Indian team these usually happen late in the evening, when it is morning in the US. Although, in theory, employees are allowed to come to the office later in the morning to compensate for the fact that they stay late in the evening, they usually come in by 9 am or 10 am and still have to remain in office till the conference calls are over, until 8 pm or 9 pm. Extended working hours are facilitated by the policy of 'flexi-time' followed by most companies, which is supposed to give employees the freedom to choose their working hours, but in practice means that they have to work as long as necessary to finish the tasks at hand. In addition, there are factors related to the culture of the software industry that reinforce the pattern of long hours, including peer pressure, competition for recognition (and hence for better performance ratings), and subtle pressure from managers. As an informant put it, 'Unlike in the manufacturing sector, the number of units produced is not definite. You can always do a little bit more.'

IT work also tends to be high-pressure, at least at certain points in the project cycle. The workflow is regulated by the tyranny of project timelines and software engineers are always struggling to meet unrealistic deadlines and 'fire fighting' last minute crises.[14] Most HR managers acknowledge that long working hours and deadline pressures lead to stress and adverse health effects, and a few companies have devised measures to limit working hours. But most organizations, rather than addressing the root causes of overwork, offer 'stress management' and 'time management' programmes, yoga or karate classes, and provide recreational facilities such as table tennis in the workplace. To participate in such activities, however, employees need time, which is their most scarce resource.[15]

Although software organizations recognize the problem of extended working hours and high stress levels, the pattern of overwork actually benefits them because their profit margins are linked to the maximum utilization of their 'resources'. Overwork is rationalized by managers who claim that software engineers are strongly motivated to perform and that they cannot limit their desire to work hard. They also argue that engineers are well compensated for their work, a contention with which many software engineers seem to agree. As one respondent put it, 'We are not being paid for eight hours of work a day.' This attitude again reflects the individualized culture of the 'new workplace', with its 'entrepreneurial' employees (Beck, 2000) who accept individual responsibility for completing work, even if it means working very long hours (Perlow, 1999). In the Indian software industry, the pressure to keep extended working hours, among other factors, adversely affects women's careers (Upadhya, 2006).

'DECENT WORK' AND LABOUR REGULATION

On the surface, there appears to be little need for labour regulation in the IT sector. The rapidly increasing demand for skilled labour and high rates of employee attrition mean that companies must compete with one another to hire the best. In this context, software engineers are supposed to enjoy substantial bargaining power in the workplace as they can credibly back up their demands with the threat of quitting. This, at least, is the consensus view that has been created, in part, due to the ideological power that the software industry and its leaders have garnered in the post-liberalization period. IT industry leaders have been at the forefront of industry attacks on 'rigid labour laws' that are blamed for stifling the growth of industry and employment. They argue that the IT industry has grown rapidly due to non-interference by the government; hence any sort of state intervention—including the enforcement of labour laws—will harm both industry and workers. Indeed, the government has followed a hands-off policy for the IT sector, especially with regard to labour regulations. But it must be pointed out that while the government has imposed only a minimum of regulation on the IT industry, it has also facilitated its growth through a variety of tax breaks, fiscal incentives, and other policies.

Although IT leaders agree in principle that they should comply with minimum labour standards, they contend that labour laws are not relevant to the IT industry because most labour-related issues are settled by 'market forces', due to which their labour standards already exceed international standards. Industry representatives have also argued that standards and policies should be formulated by the industry itself, which can regulate itself by voluntarily adhering to a code of 'best practices'. However, the discussion of employment and labour practices in this chapter suggests that there are at least four issues that are problematic from the perspective of 'decent work' as conceptualized by the International Labour Organization (ILO)—job security, social protection, working hours, and work-life balance.[16]

With regard to job security and social protection, it should be noted that labour market flexibility has not had the same negative social and economic outcomes in India as in the US. Indian IT employees do feel insecure knowing that they could lose their jobs at any time, but IT jobs are still desirable because of the high salaries they offer. The outsourcing of IT jobs to India has created an economic boom in several cities and led to upward economic mobility for employees. Nonetheless, the volatility of the labour market is a concern for many and industry spokespersons too acknowledge the need for some kind of safety net. Job security at the company level is considered to be unfeasible as a policy, but it has been suggested that a collective unemployment insurance scheme for software professionals could be created by the state and companies together. However, there is no such initiative on the anvil as yet.

On the issue of long working hours, most industry leaders maintain that high salaries compensate for this level of 'commitment' and that it is not possible to impose fixed working hours on software engineers. They also argue that the government should not enforce any restrictions that would undercut the main advantage that the country has in the global software market—its 'flexibility' (a code word for long working hours and relatively lower wages). At present, there is no regulation of working hours in this sector, even though IT companies presumably are governed by existing labour laws and India has subscribed to the ILO Core Standards.

Long and irregular working hours, frequent travel, and stress are the main factors that negatively impact the work–life balance of IT workers. A running theme in the narratives of most software engineers is the adverse effect of their work on their personal and family lives, the lack of time to pursue outside interests or have a fulfilling social life, and consequent frustration and burnout. Work–family balance is particularly problematic for women employees, many of whom leave the industry when they start a family (Upadhya, 2006). Again, while this problem is widely recognized by managements, few companies have taken concrete steps to address it.

CONCLUDING REMARKS

The IT industry has created a new global image for India and is regarded by many business leaders and political elites as a model for India's future development. However, this euphoria tends to ignore its specific location and role within the global information economy as an export-oriented enclave industry providing specific types of services. Despite the widespread celebration of IT, important questions about its impact on India's development trajectory need to be asked, especially about the nature of the work and employment opportunities that have been created and their wider social implications.

The employment outcomes of ICT-based development are largely dependent on the position of a country or industry in the global division of labour. Although India has become a significant 'global player', it remains at the low end of the software services market—a position that has only been enhanced by the recent emphasis on business process outsourcing. Although there has been a definite move up the value chain in the nature of IT work that is outsourced to India, it remains to be seen whether the Indian industry as a whole will make a decisive shift from 'projects' to 'products' and compete in the global IT market on the strength of its intellectual capital rather than labour cost arbitrage. There is some evidence that outsourcing to India is motivated as much by the easier availability of skilled software labour as its relatively lower cost, but the conceptualization and design elements of most outsourced projects are still retained with the client or parent company. There appears to be little effort from the industry or the state to move the industry towards social or economic upgrading in the future (unlike the Irish software industry, for instance; see O'Riain, 2004).

The salient features of employment relations and work in the IT industry—flexibilization and individualization—are inter-related and also linked to wider economic transformations. India's shift from a relatively closed, state-controlled economy to a more liberalized regime and its increasing integration with the global economy have led to a deterioration in employment security. Although average incomes have risen for a substantial proportion of the middle class, the earlier social contract between the state and the middle classes is breaking down. This transformation is most visible in the IT sector with its flexible labour market, individualistic labour relations, and mobile and flexible workforce. The high attrition rates bemoaned by HR managers are primarily a manifestation of the deeper structural changes in the labour market and employment relations towards a regime of flexible labour. A central feature of individualization is the fact that employees do not have a collective identity as workers or as employees, nor do they collectively negotiate with management on common issues. Under the new dispensation, workers are responsible for their own job security by continually re-skilling themselves in order to compete in the ever-changing job market. Flexibilization of labour is also apparent in the emergence of a variety of temporary and contract employment arrangements. Although many of these features of work and employment characterize the IT industry globally, flexibilization in this case is related more to India's position as a provider of low-skilled, low-cost IT services. Bangalore branding as the 'Silicon Plateau' is thus misleading, for it is not a replication of Silicon Valley but its 'back office'.

The software industry has provided lucrative job opportunities to many educated youth, but we must also note the sharp disjuncture between the working conditions and salaries of Indian software engineers and their counterparts in the West, even within the same companies. This asymmetry again stems from India's position in the global informational economy. The costs of being at the bottom of the 'value chain' in the global software production/services network are borne by Indian software workers. For instance, the need to maintain tight control over the deployment and output of large numbers of workers (both remote and local) has led to the extensive use of rationalized quality and control processes and long working hours. Routinization of software work increases efficiency and productivity but reduces the scope for individual growth or the acquisition of new skills. Long working hours are necessitated by stiff competition for projects based on the lowest bid and for workers they translate into stress, frustration, and poor work–life balance. However, the situation of IT employees is effectively masked by the industry's successful self-representation as progressive, employee-friendly, and socially responsible.

The IT industry's position as ideological leader of India's liberalization agenda has allowed it to escape from most forms of government regulation. For the present, the non-enforcement of labour regulations in this sector may not be an urgent issue, but it remains to be seen whether there will be pressure on the industry in the future to lower its labour standards in response to international competition. In the absence of universal and enforced labour standards and labour unions, Indian software workers are highly vulnerable to fluctuations in the global economy and have little voice or power in their workplaces.

NOTES

1. This chapter is based on a sociological study of the Indian IT/ITES workforce that was carried out by A.R. Vasavi and the author along with a research team at the National Institute of Advanced Studies (NIAS), Bangalore, between November 2003 and March 2006. The research project was funded by the Indo-Dutch Programme for Alternatives in Development (IDPAD), and was conducted in collaboration with Peter van der Veer of the University of Utrecht. Although the study covered both the IT and ITES sectors, this chapter is concerned only with the software industry. The essay draws on the final report of this study (Upadhya and Vasavi, 2006) and on Upadhya and Vasavi (2008).
2. India accounts for 65 per cent of the global market for offshore IT services. Summary of NASSCOM–McKinsey Report 2005, in *NASSCOM Newsline*, No. 50, December 2005 (available at www.nasscom.org, accessed on 22 May 2006).
3. The software and services industry is commonly referred to in India as the IT industry, and the term is often used to include ITES or business process outsourcing (BPO).
4. NASSCOM, *IT Industry Factsheet*, October 2007 (available at www.nasscom. org, accessed on 2 November 2007).
5. Of these, about 550,000 are in IT services and 140,000 in engineering services and software products, totalling 690,000 in the export sector; 553,000 are in the ITES–BPO sector, and the rest (378,000) are in the domestic sector or are 'in-house' IT professionals. NASSCOM, *IT*

Industry Factsheet, August 2007 (available at www.nasscom.in, accessed on 2 November 2007).
6. Aneesh (2006) suggests that online software services should be construed as flows of *labour* rather than movement of goods and services, as it is regarded under the current international trade regime.
7. Engineering services, research and development (R&D), and products together constituted only 15 per cent of total software and services exports in fiscal 2007. NASSCOM, *IT Industry Factsheet*, October 2007 (available at www.nasscom.org, accessed on 2 November 2007).
8. Our study also did not capture the entire range of software work, but concentrated on the organized and export-oriented sector of the industry.
9. This profile is also linked to the export-oriented and customer-driven nature of the industry—by hiring mainly engineers, Indian companies attempt to 'signal quality' to customers (Athreye, 2005: 159), and it is also easier to get H1B visas for them (required for onsite assignments in the US).
10. Beck (2000), Benner (2002), Carnoy (2000), Castells (1996), Sennett (1998), and others have described these changes in detail—especially in Silicon Valley, considered to be the heart of the 'new economy'—as well as their implications for workers, families, and communities.
11. In both cases, the IT labour market is fluid and flexible, but the reasons for this are very different, as are the modes of flexibility. In the US, 'flexibilization' has meant the detachment of work from institutions and the demise of the full-time secure job as well as the disintegration of collective identity among workers (Carnoy, 2000). At the same time, flexibilization has enabled highly qualified (and highly paid) IT professionals to sell their services in the market as independent agents (Benner, 2002). In India, there is little market for such consultants because of the type of work that is outsourced. Instead, most software engineers must be employed if they want to work, they have little choice of assignments within their organizations, and they are required to be 'flexible' or adaptable workers.
12. During the downturn of 2001–2, many software workers in India were laid off and many others came back from the US, swelling the pool of engineers looking for jobs. Although the job market was again buoyant between 2004 and 2007, and employment expanded rapidly, in early 2008–9, Bangalore again witnessed the 'pink slip' syndrome in response to the global economic meltdown.
13. Our survey data revealed that only 18 per cent of respondents aged 31 and above had worked in a single company; one-third were in their second companies; another one-third had worked in three or four companies; and the rest in five or more.

14. The pace of work in hi-tech companies of Silicon Valley is well described by Shih (2004), who argues that the notion of time itself has been altered by the new economy, from the 'clock time' that governs the industrial workplace to 'project time' that constructs a cyclical rhythm of work. Because work is organized through projects, it is infinitely extendable, cutting into personal and family time and causing a 'displacement and desynchronization of other spheres of time in individuals' lives' (Shih, 2004: 230).
15. One of India's premier software services companies has a basketball court, swimming pool, and a well-equipped gym on its campus. However, the company found that employees using these facilities during daytime disrupted work and so they are kept closed during the core working hours. Employees hardly get to use the sports facilities because of their work timings—by the time they finish work in the evening, it is late and they want to go home (especially if they are catching a company transport bus), or else they would have to come in very early in the morning. Thus, the purpose of providing such amenities appears to be mainly cosmetic.
16. I use here the dimensions of decent work and indicators suggested in Anker et al. (2003). This section also draws on a consultation with industry, government, and employee representatives on employment policies for the IT industry, organized as part of the NIAS–IDPAD project in December 2004.

REFERENCES

Aneesh, A. (2001a), 'Rethinking Migration: On-Line Labour Flows from India to the United States', in W.A. Cornelius, T.J Espenshade, and I. Salehyan (eds), *The International Migration of the Highly Skilled*, pp. 351–70. San Diego: La Jolla, Center for Comparative Immigration Studies, University of California.

——— (2001b), 'Skill Saturation: Rationalisation and Post-Industrial Work', *Theory and Society*, 30: 363–96.

——— (2006). *Virtual Migration: The Programming of Globalisation*. Durham: Duke University Press.

Anker, Richard, I. Chernyshev, P. Egger, F. Mehran, and J.A. Ritter (2003), 'Measuring Decent Work with Statistical Indicators', *International Labour Review*, 142(2): 147–76.

Athreye, Suma S. (2005), 'Human Capital, Labour Scarcity and Development of the Software Services Sector', in A. Saith and M. Vijayabaskar (eds), *ICTs and Indian Economic Development: Economy, Work, Regulation*, pp. 154–74. New Delhi: Sage Publications.

Balakrishnan, Pulapre (2006), 'Benign Neglect or Strategic Intent? Contested Lineage of Indian Software Industry', *Economic and Political Weekly*, 41: 3865–72.

Barrett, Rowena (2001), 'Labouring under an Illusion? The Labour Process of

Software Development in the Australian Information Industry', *New Technology, Work and Employment*, 16: 18–34.

Basant, Rakesh and Uma Rani (2004), 'Labour Market Deepening in India's IT: An Exploratory Analysis', *Economic and Political Weekly*, 39: 5317–26.

Beck, Ulrich (2000), *The Brave New World of Work*. Cambridge: Polity Press.

Benner, Chris (2002), *Work in the New Economy: Flexible Labour Markets in Silicon Valley*. Oxford: Blackwell.

Braverman, Harry (1975), *Labor and Monopoly Capital: The Degradation of Work in the Twentieth Century*. New York: Monthly Review Press.

Carnoy, Martin (2000), *Work, Family and Community in the Information Age*. New York: Russell Sage.

Castells, Manuel (1996), *The Information Age: Economy, Society and Culture. Vol. I: The Rise of the Network Society*. Oxford: Blackwell.

Harvey, David (1989), *The Condition of Postmodernity: An Enquiry into the Origins of Cultural Change*. Oxford: Basil Blackwell.

Heeks, R.B. (1996), *India's Software Industry: State Policy, Liberalization and Industrial Development*. New Delhi: Sage Publications.

Ilavarasan, P. Vigneswara (2008), 'Software Work in India: A Labour Process View', in Carol Upadhya and A.R. Vasavi (eds), *In an Outpost of the Global Economy: Work and Workers in India's Information Technology Industry*, pp. 162–89. New Delhi: Routledge.

O' Riain, Sean (2004), *The Politics of High-Tech Growth: Developmental Networks States in the Global Economy*. Cambridge: Cambridge University Press.

Parthasarathy, Balaji (2000), 'Globalisation and Agglomeration in Newly Industrialising Countries: The State and the Information Technology Industry in Bangalore, India', Ph.D. Dissertation, University of California, Berkeley.

——— (2005), 'The Political Economy of the Computer Software Industry in Bangalore, India', in A. Saith and M. Vijayabaskar (eds.), *ICTs and Indian Economic Development: Economy, Work, Regulation*, pp. 199–230. New Delhi: Sage Publications.

Perlow, Leslie (1999), 'The Time Famine: Toward a Sociology of Work Time', *Administrative Science Quarterly*, 44: 57–81.

Prasad, Monica (1998), 'International Capital on "Silicon Plateau": Work and Control in India's Computer Industry', *Social Forces*, 77(2): 429–52.

Rothboeck, S., M. Vijaybaskar, and V. Gayathri (2001), *Labour in the New Economy: The Case of the Indian Software Labour Market*. New Delhi: International Labour Organization.

Sennett, Richard (1998), *The Corrosion of Character: The Personal Consequences of Work in the New Capitalism*. New York: W.W. Norton & Co.

Shih, Johanna (2004), 'Project Time in Silicon Valley', *Qualitative Sociology*, 27(2): 223–45.

Upadhya, Carol (2006), 'Gender Issues in the Indian Software Industry', in Anita Gurumurthy, Parminder Jeet Singh, Anu Mundkur and Mridula Swamy (eds), *Gender in the Information Society: Emerging Issues*, pp. 74–84. Bangkok: UNDP-APDIP.

Upadhya, Carol and A.R. Vasavi (2006), *Work, Culture, and Sociality in the Indian IT Industry: A Sociological Study*. Final Report submitted to Indo-Dutch Program on Alternatives in Development. Bangalore: National Institute of Advanced Studies.

—— (2008), 'Outposts of the Global Information Economy: Work and Workers in India's Outsourcing Industry', in Carol Upadhya and A.R. Vasavi (eds), *In an Outpost of the Global Economy: Work and Workers in India's Information Technology Industry*, pp. 9–49. New Delhi: Routledge.

Xiang Biao (2007), *Global 'Body Shopping': An Indian Labour System in the Information Technology Industry*. Princeton: Princeton University Press.

14 GLOBAL PRODUCTION NETWORKS AND DECENT WORK
Recent Experience in India and Global Trends

Sandip Sarkar and Balwant Singh Mehta

INTRODUCTION

Economic liberalization has ushered in rapid changes in the service sector. Knowledge-based industry is emerging as an important component of the service sector. The knowledge economy creates, disseminates, and uses knowledge to enhance its growth and development. One of the major functional pillars of this economy is information and communication technology (ICT). ICT continues to be a dominant sector in the overall growth of the Indian economy. India has emerged as a major global provider of information technology (IT) software and services and even in the recent phenomenon of IT-enabled services–business processing outsourcing (ITES–BPO).

According to the National Association of Software and Services Companies (NASSCOM) estimates, ICT sectors were responsible for 5.4 per cent of gross domestic product (GDP) in 2007, rising from 1.2 per cent in 1998 (NASSCOM, 2007). The sustained annual compound growth rate of over 45 per cent during the last decade has been unprecedented in any of the sectors of the Indian economy since independence. As a result, the ICT sector is contributing about one-fifth of India's total export earnings and provides employment to over 2.75 million people. The workforce has increased more than eight fold (0.19 million to 1.63 million) in the IT-ITES sub-sector from 1998 to 2007 (NASSCOM, 2007). The IT sector continues to show a robust growth and the total value of IT exports was estimated at Rs 1,41,800 crore (US$ 31.3 billion) in 2006–7, as compared to Rs 1,04,100 crore (US$ 23.6 billion) in 2005–6, an increase of over 36 per cent in rupee terms. The ITES sector has emerged as a key driver of growth for the Indian IT-ITES industry. Export revenues from ITES grew from US$ 6.3 billion in 2005–6 to US$ 8.3 billion in 2006–7; a year-on-year growth of over 31 per cent was achieved (http://www.mit.gov.in).

In the past, a large number of studies have mainly focused on examining the different aspects of India's IT-ITES services (Schware, 1992; Sen, 1995; Heeks, 1996; Kumar, 2001; Joseph and Harilal, 2001; Parthasarathy and Joseph, 2002; Kumar and Joseph, 2005). A few recent articles (Basant and Rani, 2004; Biradar, 2005; Sarkar and Mehta, 2007) have also highlighted the employment and labour market characteristics of the ICT sector. These essays have revealed that there has been a rapid increase in the production and export of software and employment generated in the ICT sectors. It is also evident that the growth of ICT is not only contributing significantly to export earnings and gross domestic product (GDP) but is also emerging as a major source of increased quality/decent employment in the country. The Millennium Development Goals (MDGs) also highlight not only full and productive employment but also decent work for all.

In India, there is hardly any study on decent work, although at international level several distinguished authors have worked in the International Labour Organization (ILO) on a special issue of the *International Labour Review* on 'Measuring Decent Work'. The aim of this issue was to elaborate the range of approaches to demonstrate the multi-dimensional nature of decent work. Dharam Gai (2003) presented the first four distinct approaches of decent work with employment, social protection, workers' right, and social dialogue. Bescond et al. (2003) selected seven indicators—hourly pay, hours of work, unemployment, school enrolment, the youth share of employment, the male–female gap in labour force participation, and old age without pension. Bonnet et al. (2003) sought to establish a family of decent work indexes applicable at all three levels included in the macro (aggregate) and meso (workplace) levels and the micro (individual) level. Fields (2003) presented a simplified two-component model of decent work consisting of quantity and quality of employment (proxy of labour standard), and argued and empirically analysed how economic growth could contribute to the promotion of decent work.

The growth pattern of output in the Indian ICT sector not only generated a good number of new employment opportunities but also altered the demand pattern for educated, trained, and skilled manpower in the Indian labour market. Against this background, an attempt has been made in this chapter to explore how growth of the ICT sector is contributing to the promotion of decent work in this sector. A two-component model of a 'decent work frontier' consisting of both quantity and quality of employment approach has been used.

This chapter is divided into six sections. It begins with a brief discussion about database, methodology, and definition of ICT. The second section highlights quantitatively decent work by examining the pattern and trend with quality and nature of ICT employment. The next section also further undertakes the quantitative part of decent work by the analysis of wage and earning patterns of ICT workers by different enterprise type, quality of employment, and by level of education. The fourth section covers the issue of inequality of earnings of regular workers between ICT and non-ICT workers and differentials in return to education among them. The fifth section explores the qualitative part of decent work by covering social security, unionization, nature of job contract, reasons for job change, working hours, and conditions. The last section concludes.

DEFINITION, DATABASE, AND METHODOLOGY

The only data available and analysed so far on participation of workers with different skills, education, and quality in the ICT sector is from NASSCOM. Its estimates are essentially based on data collected from its members, which were over 1,200 in 2007. The members are ICT firms involved in IT service, ITES–BPO, product research and development (R&D), and other hardware services (NASSCOM, 2007).[1] These firms included 74.4 per cent of small companies, 10.1 per cent of medium companies, 7.4 per cent of large companies, and 8.1 per cent of institutional companies. The large companies are those that have gross revenue of $4.4 million, for medium companies it is $1.1 to $4.4 million, small have less than $1.1 million, and institutional companies in the ITES-BPO sector (these are training/support institutes and mostly non-profit institutes). NASSCOM does not cover manufacturing, telecommunication, and trade segments of ICT.

Further, the estimates may not adequately capture employment of ICT workers in ICT-using sectors. It is, therefore, desirable to explore other available data sets to analyse issues relating to the ICT labour market in India. So, in this chapter, National Sample Survey (NSS) data for 1999–2000 and 2004–5 have been used. Other sources such as NASSCOM and the Census are also incorporated wherever required.

The quality of employment/decent work can be measured by a two-component model consisting of both quantitative and qualitative employment. The employment indicators—employment pattern, trend, formal/informal employment, status of employment, and hours/daily wages—explain quantity of employment and are widely referred to in discussion of decent work but, in fact, they do not reveal the heterogeneity. Over the years, attempts have been made to compensate for some of the shortcomings of these indicators by developing additional qualitative indicators. The qualitative indicators like social security, unionization, nature of job contract, reasons for job change, working hours, and working conditions have been argued as better indicators for decent work in developing countries like India.

Different definitions have been used for the ICT sector by various organizations and authors. Still, there is no universally accepted definition of ICT, because the concepts, methods, and applications involved in ICT are constantly evolving. In India, the term 'ICT' has been predominantly used to denote one particular sub-sector—software and ITES, which accounts for a substantial proportion of total employment in the ICT sector in the country. In some other countries, the term also includes the communications and hardware sectors. In this chapter, the Organisation for Economic Co-operation and Development (OECD) definition approved in 1998 has been used, which includes the activity of manufacturing and services industries (OECD, 1998). Manufacturing industry includes hardware, central processing units (CPUs), communications equipment, electronic components, and industrial control and supervision equipment manufacturing (not including medical equipment). Service industry includes telecommunication services, computer and related services (IT and ITES), R&D services, and also start-up companies (Annexure 14.1). However, due to data constraints, some sections of the workforce involved in the ICT sector have remained out of the analysis.

EMPLOYMENT STRUCTURE

The following section deals with the quantitative part of decent work by analysing employment patterns, trends, and quality of employment in the ICT sector. The quality of employment is further analysed by formal and informal sector, enterprise type, and education level of ICT workers. A detailed analysis of the ICT sector by its major sub-sectors, manufacturing, trade, telecommunication, and IT–ITES has also been conducted to observe the diversity of employment.

Employment Patterns and Trends

The development of the ICT sector is providing employment to a large pool of educated and skilled manpower of India (NASSCOM, 2007). According

Table 14.1: Profile of Workers in ICT Sector in 1999–2000, 2004–5

Year	Rural	Urban	Total
Number (% share)			
1999–2000	284,491 (17.29)	1,290,883 (82.17)	1,575,374
2004–5	464,208 (16.90)	2,293,450 (83.50)	2,757,659
Share of total workers			
1999–2000	0.10	1.43	0.44
2004–5	0.15	2.08	0.65
Growth Rate of workers (2000–5)			
Annual Compound Growth Rate	10.29	12.18	11.85

Source: NSS, Unit Level Data, 55th Round (1999–2000) and 61st Round (2004–5).

to the National Sample Survey Organisation (NSSO), about 2.75 million employees were working in the ICT sector in 2004–5, which is 0.65 per cent of total employment in the country (see Table 14.1). About 1.04 million (40 per cent) of the ICT workers are involved in the IT–ITES segment (see Table 14.2). According to NASSCOM, this number rose to 1.63 million in 2007 (NASSCOM, 2008).

The ICT workforce has grown by 11.85 per cent annually from 1999–2000 (1.57 million) to 2004–5 (2.75 million), which is almost six times more than the total employment growth of the country during the same period (Table 14.1). The shares of ICT employment in rural and urban areas in the country are 0.15 per cent and 2.08 per cent respectively. This is a predominantly urban sector and urban workers constitute about 84 per cent of the total workers in the ICT sector. The share of urban workers had marginally increased (by 1.33 percentage point) from 1999–2000 to 2004–5.

Sector-wise Patterns and Trends

The composition of the ICT sector has changed significantly in recent years. These changes can be seen in terms of ICT sub-sector employment, which shows a shift from manufacturing to IT–ITES services and telecommunication sub-sector during 1999–2000 to 2004–5. The share of workers in IT–ITES (by 16 percentage points) and telecommunication (by 8 percentage points) has increased substantially, whereas the share of manufacturing has fallen substantially (by 24 percentage points) and marginally in case of trade (by 0.5 percentage points) during 1999–2000 to 2004–5 (Table 14.2). Break-up by rural and urban areas gives an interesting picture. In rural areas, telecommunication is the dominant sector and IT–ITES had negligible presence in 1999–2000. But by 2004–5, the share

Table 14.2: Pattern of Employment in ICT Sector and Sub-Sectors (in %)

Sub-Sector	Rural		Urban		Total	
	1999–2000	2004–5	1999–2000	2004–5	1999–2000	2004–5
Manufacturing	29.1	16.3	46.3	20.3	43.3	19.6
Trade	0.6	1.5	3.9	3.1	3.3	2.8
Telecommunication	63.0	68.1	22.1	31.3	29.2	37.6
IT–ITES Services	7.3	14.1	27.7	45.3	24.2	40.0
Total	284,491	464,208	1,290,883	2,293,450	1,575,374	2,757,659

Source: NSS, Unit Level Data, 55th Round (1999–2000) and 61st Round (2004–5).

of both these sectors has increased by 5 and 7 percentage points respectively, at the cost of the manufacturing sub-sector. In urban areas, however, the emergence of ITES services has been mainly responsible for the increase in the share of the service sub-sector, whereas manufacturing sub-sector employment was wiped out due to the huge decline in informal sector manufacturing, as people moved from assembling to bundling (branded companies) (Table 14.2).

The picture gets clearer when we analyse the growth of employment. Employment grew in IT–ITES, telecommunication, and trade sub-sectors by 19.5 per cent, 14.3 per cent, and 6.92 per cent respectively during 1999–2000 and 2004–5. On the contrary, the share of workers in manufacturing fell by 3.7 per cent during the same period. A similar trend had been observed in the rural and urban sectors. However, telecommunication in urban areas and trade in rural areas experienced substantially higher growth rates (Table 14.3).

Nature and Quality of Employment

As discussed, the ICT sector is overwhelmingly urban. Therefore, it is imperative to look at the nature of jobs created in this sector. On the basis

Table 14.3: Employment Growth in the ICT Sector during 1999–2000 and 2004–5 (Compound Annual Growth Rate in %)

Sector	Rural	Urban	Total
Manufacturing	–1.5	–4.1	–3.7
Trade	26.1	5.8	6.9
Telecommunication	9.9	16.6	14.3
IT–ITES Services	21.1	19.4	19.5

Source: NSS, Unit Level Data, 55th Round (1999–2000) and 61st Round (2004–5).

Table 14.4: Distribution of ICT by Formal and Informal Sectors (in %)

Sector	Formal		Informal	
	1999–2000	2004–5	1999–2000	2004–5
Manufacturing	77.5	59.0	22.5	41.0
Trade	73.1	89.3	26.9	10.7
Telecommunication	87.6	96.1	12.4	3.9
IT–ITES Services	82.7	87.6	17.3	12.4
Total	80.4	84.1	19.6	15.9

Source: NSS, Unit Level Data, 55th Round (1999–2000) and 61st Round (2004–5).
Note: Formal sector is defined as follows:
1. Includes all workers belonging to public and corporate sectors.
2. Includes all workers working in non-public and non-corporate enterprises employing 10 or more workers.
3. Excludes workers in manufacturing, in enterprises employing 10–19 workers without electricity.
4. Includes self-employed with degree higher secondary and above.
5. For basic telecom services (code 64201), we have included employees only belonging to public and corporate sectors. They all belong to the formal sector.

of some quality of employment indicators (see the note to Table 14.4), workers have been divided into formal and informal employment. In the ICT sector, the majority of workers (84.1 per cent) were working in the formal sector in 2004–5, with the highest share in telecommunication and lowest in manufacturing. The share of workers in the formal sector has increased by 3.6 points from 1999–2000 to 2004–5. The share of the formal sector within telecommunication, trade, and IT–ITES segments has also increased from 1999–2000 to 2004–5 (Table 14.4).

ICT sector employment is mainly in the formal sector and in some ways it can be considered to be quality employment. The quality of employment can be seen by NSS employment status category as regular, self-employment, and casual labour employment. Regular employment is the most secure form of employment and casual labour is the least secure. The ICT sector is completely dominated by regular workers; about 82 per cent ICT workers were employed as regular employees in 2004–5. Casual workers constituted a small proportion of employment, that is, 3.2 per cent in 2004–5. In this respect, it is quite different from any other sector in India. In accordance with overall employment trends, self-employment in both formal and informal ICT sectors has increased during 1999–2000 and 2004–5 (Table 14.5).

The quality of employment is also attributed to a great extent to the ownership structure of the ICT sector. Corporate and public sectors are known for better paid and quality jobs, while the non-corporate private

Table 14.5: Distribution of ICT Workers by Formal and Informal States of Employment Contract (%)

Status	Formal		Informal		Total	
	1999–2000	2004–5	1999–2000	2004–5	1999–2000	2004–5
Self-Employed	11.0	15.6	11.4	11.0	11.1	14.8
Regular Workers	86.2	81.1	80.7	86.5	85.1	82.0
Casual Workers	2.8	3.4	7.9	2.5	3.8	3.2
Total	100.0	100.0	100.0	100.0	100.0	100.0

Source: NSS, Unit Level Data, 55th Round (1999–2000) and 61st Round (2004–5).

Table 14.6: Distribution of ICT Workers by Enterprise Type (%)

Enterprise Type	Formal		Informal		Total	
	1999–2000	2004–5	1999–2000	2004–5	1999–2000	2004–5
Not mentioned	2.7	0.4	39.7	19.1	9.4	3.3
Public Sector	34.4	23.5	0.0	0.0	27.7	19.8
Private Sector	31.7	35.8	60.3	80.9	37.3	43.0
Corporate	31.2	40.3	0.0	0.0	25.6	33.9
Total	100.0	100.0	100.0	100.0	100.0	100.0

Source: NSS, Unit Level Data, 55th Round (1999–2000) and 61st Round (2004–5).

sector is considered to be dominated by low-paid and bad-quality jobs. By taking the ICT sector as a whole (formal and informal together), corporate and public sectors constituted more than one-third and one-fifth of total employment, respectively, in 2004–5. Together, they account for more than half of total employment. The presence of public, private, and corporate sectors differs substantially in various segments of the ICT sector. On the one hand, the presence of corporate and private sectors was rising, and on the other, public sector presence was shrinking over the period 1999–2000 to 2004–5 (Table 14.6).

EDUCATIONAL STATUS OF WORKERS

The ICT sector in India is largely a part of the knowledge economy, where education plays an important role in employment and its quality. In the overall employment in ICT, graduates and those with higher qualifications constituted 45 per cent of the ICT workforce in 2004–5 (Table 14.7). Those with secondary (19.5 per cent) and higher secondary (18.9 per cent) education were also a substantial proportion of the total ICT employment in

Table 14.7: Distribution of Workers by Educational Level and Status (%)

Educational Level	Self-Employed		Regular		Casual		Total	
	99–00	04–05	99–00	04–05	99–00	04–05	99–00	04–05
Up to Primary	2.9	0.8	9.2	5.7	46.1	9.2	9.4	5.3
Middle	2.8	5.7	7.0	12.4	30.2	21.7	7.2	12.0
Secondary	6.3	13.6	15.6	19.3	9.4	40.3	14.0	19.5
Higher Secondary	24.0	27.1	19.4	18.0	8.5	17.0	19.7	18.9
Graduate & above in other subjects	50.6	37.0	43.6	35.5	5.9	7.7	43.4	34.6
Graduate & above in engineering	13.5	15.8	5.2	9.2	0.0	4.1	6.3	9.7
Total	100.0	100.0	100.0	100.0	100.0	100.0	100.0	100.0

Source: NSS, Unit Level Data, 55th Round (1999–2000) and 61st Round (2004–5).

2004–5. Interestingly, self-employed personnel are relatively more qualified than regular workers, with more than half of the former having graduate and above degrees.

Two interesting changes are observed. First, the share of graduates and above in engineering has gone up. Second, the share of graduates and those with higher qualifications among the casual category has gone up (Table 14.7). However, as observed earlier, the share of casual workers in employment in the ICT sector is hovering around 3 per cent.

The IT–ITES industry had the highest proportion of workers having graduate and above qualifications in 2004–5, followed by trade (50.8 per cent), telecommunication (33.5 per cent), and manufacturing (27.5 per cent). In the telecommunication and IT–ITES sub-sectors, the proportion of graduate and above educated workers increased by about 5 percentage points each from 1999–2000 to 2004–5 (Table 14.8). The increase in share of graduate and above-qualified in both IT and ITES sectors was mainly due to the emerging ITES sector, where graduates with good spoken English get jobs as BPO workers.

Table 14.8: Share of Graduates and Above in Different Segments of ICT

Sector	% Share of Graduates & Above	
	1999–2000	2004–5
Manufacturing	29.6	27.5
Trade	74.8	50.8
Telecommunication	28.5	33.5
IT–ITES Services	67.3	72.0

Source: NSS, Unit Level Data, 55th Round (1999–2000) and 61st Round (2004–5).

WAGES AND EARNINGS

In this section, a comparison is made between the daily wages of regular workers in the ICT sector and other (non-ICT) workers. To make the comparison more meaningful, we have limited the database to four groups at one-digit level National Industrial Classification (NIC) 1987 classification, which have the presence of ICT sub-sector. These are manufacturing, transport, storage and communication services, trade and financial, insurance and business services.

Wage Structure and Its Trends

It is widely discussed in literature that workers in the ICT sector earn much more than non-ICT sector workers. This is clearly seen in the total ICT sector and its two sub-sectors, manufacturing and services, in 1999–2000 and 2004–5. The gap in wages between ICT and other workers was higher in services than in manufacturing during the same period. The difference of wage level was higher in the formal part of the service segment. Within the service sub-sector, the wage gap between ICT and others has widened substantially between 1999–2000 and 2004–5 in the formal segment. However, for informal sector workers, the wage gap between ICT and others in both manufacturing and services sub-sectors has not increased considerably during the same period (Table 14.9).

Table 14.9: Daily Wages/Earnings by Formal/Informal Sector, 1999–2000 and 2004–5 (at 2004–5 prices)

	Formal		Informal		Total	
	1999–2000	2004–5	1999–2000	2004–5	1999–2000	2004–5
Manufacturing						
ICT	226	244	195	96	221	178
Others	175	161	115	79	157	130
All	176	162	117	79	160	131
Services						
ICT	294	377	182	157	275	349
Others	243	229	103	83	177	152
All	244	244	104	84	180	164
All						
ICT	259	354	185	125	247	308
Others	203	193	106	81	167	142
All	206	203	108	82	168	149

Source: NSS, Unit Level Data, 55th Round (1999–2000) and 61st Round (2004–5).

Table 14.10: Growth Rate of Wages during 1999–2000 to 2004–5 in the Formal Sector (in %)

	Formal Sector
Manufacturing	
ICT	1.54
Others	−1.66
All	−1.60
Services	
ICT	5.10
Others	−1.21
All	−0.03
All	
ICT	6.43
Others	−1.03
All	−0.28

Source: NSS, Unit Level Data, 55th Round (1999–2000) and 61st Round (2004–5).

The analysis of growth of wages makes the picture clear. The growth rate of wages of ICT formal sector workers has been 6.43 per annum for the period 1999–2000 to 2004–5. Wages of workers in both formal manufacturing and services sectors have also shown positive growth rate during the same period. However, non-ICT formal workers experienced negative wage growth rate in both manufacturing and services (Table 14.10).

It is generally believed that ICT workers in the corporate segment receive higher wages than their counterparts in public and private services. This was true for 2004–5. In the manufacturing sub-sector, even in 1999–2000, public sector workers received higher salaries than workers in the corporate sector. This is no longer true. In the service segment of the ICT sector, corporate sector workers receive much higher wages than public sector workers. The gap in wages between ICT and non-ICT workers is highest in the corporate sector and much lower in the public sector (Table 14.11).

In the public sector, real wages of ICT and non-ICT workers grew at 3.85 per cent and 2.10 per cent respectively. The growth rate of wages is highest in ICT services within the public sector. In the corporate sector, highest growth has been observed in manufacturing ICT sector from 1999–2000 to 2004–5 but this growth is from a low base (Table 14.12).

Table 14.11: Daily Wages/Earnings by Enterprise Type, 1999–2000 and 2004–5, Constant Prices (2004–5 Prices) (in Rs)

	Public		Private		Corporate		All	
	1999–2000	2004–5	1999–2000	2004–5	1999–2000	2004–5	1999–2000	2004–5
Manufacturing								
ICT	278	295	167	111	193	305	221	190
Others	288	330	117	90	210	186	157	131
All	286	329	117	90	210	189	160	133
Services								
ICT	294	343	185	233	368	447	275	355
Others	289	317	105	95	254	279	177	154
All	289	319	108	98	263	318	180	166
All								
ICT	281	339	177	190	286	423	247	320
Others	288	319	109	92	220	210	167	144
All	287	321	110	95	223	228	168	151

Source: NSS, Unit Level Data, 55th Round (1999–2000) and 61st Round (2004–5).

Table 14.12: Growth Rate of Wages during 1999–2000 and 2004–5 by Enterprise Type, Constant Prices (2004–5 Prices) (in %)

	Public	Private	Corporate
Manufacturing			
ICT	1.23	–7.87	9.51
Others	2.80	–5.10	–2.35
All	2.82	–5.02	–2.10
Services			
ICT	3.13	4.72	3.96
Others	1.85	–2.11	1.92
All	1.99	–1.86	3.91
All			
ICT	3.85	1.48	8.16
Others	2.10	–3.21	–0.94
All	2.27	–2.99	0.49

Source: NSS, Unit Level Data, 55th Round (1999–2000) and 61st Round (2004–5).

Wage Rate by Status of Education

It is presumed that workers with higher qualification in the ICT sector get a much higher level of salary. To get a clear idea of the wage differential, wages at different levels of education have been calculated. It is evident

Table 14.13: Daily Wages/Earnings by Education Level, 1999–2000 and 2004–5, Constant Prices (2004–5 Prices) (in Rs)

Level of Education	Manufacturing				Services			
	ICT		Other		ICT		Other	
	1999–2000	2004–5	1999–2000	2004–5	1999–2000	2004–5	1999–2000	2004–5
Up to Primary	128	79	103	74	131	156	108	83
Middle	143	82	114	94	165	252	120	103
Secondary	218	121	154	132	194	235	165	129
Higher Secondary	223	258	231	174	196	292	190	175
Graduate & above	281	302	316	316	340	429	328	343

Source: NSS, Unit Level Data, 55th Round (1999–2000) and 61st Round (2004–5).

that workers with graduate and above degrees get considerably higher wages than other workers. In the service segment of ICT, workers are paid higher salary compared to non-ICT workers with the same qualification in 2004–5. This was not true in 1999–2000, when the wage differential was negligible (Table 14.13).

The reason for the difference lies in the rate of growth of wages. The real wages of ICT workers in the service segment have increased for all educational levels of workers, and for ICT-manufacturing workers for those with secondary and higher educational level during 1999–2000 and 2004–5 (Table 14.14). In contrast, in the non-ICT sector, a positive rate of growth of wages is observed only for workers in the service segment with education qualifications of graduate and above and that too by less than 1 per cent.

All these analyses clearly bring out that faster growth in IT–ITES and telecommunication has led to considerable enhancement in wage growth among all sections of their workforce.

Table 14.14: Growth Rate of Wages during 1999–2000 and 2004–5 by Educational Level, Constant Prices (2004–5 Prices)

Level	Manufacturing		Services	
	ICT	Other	ICT	Other
Up to Primary	–9.22	–6.26	3.65	–4.98
Middle	–10.49	–3.81	8.89	–3.05
Secondary	–11.19	–3.05	3.92	–4.81
Higher Secondary	2.94	–5.51	8.31	–1.64
Graduate & above	1.43	–0.02	4.75	0.91

Source: NSS, Unit Level Data, 55th Round (1999–2000) and 61st Round (2004–5).

Kernel Distribution of Wage

As mentioned earlier, in 1999–2000, workers with graduate and above degrees got only marginally higher wages in the service segment of ICT compared to other service sector workers. Rather, workers with lower levels of education got relatively higher wages in the ICT sector compared to other workers in the other (non-ICT) service segment. The Kernel distribution of regular workers between ICT and other workers in the service segment makes this point more clear (Figure 14.1).

The modal point of wages of ICT workers lies to the right of other workers, implying concentration at higher level of wages. However, we can also observe several peaks in ICT workers at higher level of wages, which is not seen in the case of other workers (which is quite flat), reflecting higher wages received by larger proportion of ICT workers.

The scenario has changed substantially in the span of five years. ICT workers with graduate degrees and above are getting substantially higher salaries than those in the non-ICT sector. The ICT kernel distribution has become clearly multimodal with several peaks (Figure 14.2). The first modal point, unlike in 1999–2000, does not lie to the right of the other (non-ICT) workers. In that sense, the initial part of the ICT kernel distribution seems to have shifted to the left. Clearly, there is an entry of some workers into ICT who no longer get salaries higher than non-ICT sector workers at entry level. However, there is a substantial increase in ICT workers at mid-level whose presence was not clearly seen earlier. Further, there is a

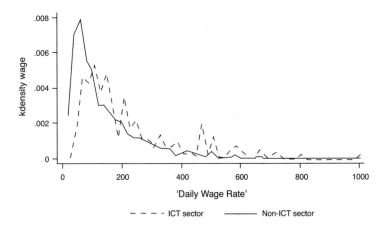

Figure 14.1: Kernel Distribution Graphs of Service Segment of Regular Workers (NSS 55th Round)

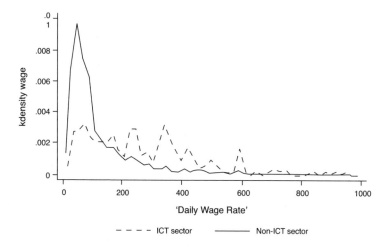

Figure 14.2: Kernel Distribution of Service Segment of Regular Workers (NSS 61st Round)

larger increase in workforce at higher level as well. All these point to the increase in inequality in the ICT sector as a whole.

INEQUALITIES IN EARNINGS

Generalized Entropy Measures

The Gini coefficient shows that inequality is comparatively higher among other (non-ICT) sectors' workers. Inequality trends according to Generalized Entropy (GE) measures depend on the measure used because of the different weights given to different parts of the wage distribution. Inequality by all three types of GE measures shows that inequality is higher among other workers.

The inequality in wages is higher in GE(2) that gives higher weightage to upper half of the distribution. It shows much higher level of inequality in the upper half for workers belonging to other (non-ICT) sectors as compared

Table 14.15: Generalized Entropy Measures

Year	Sector	GE(0)	GE(1)	GE(2)	Gini
1999–2000	ICT	0.235	0.233	0.280	0.375
	Others	0.318	0.346	0.566	0.436
2004–5	ICT	0.351	0.313	0.377	0.432
	Others	0.390	0.423	0.674	0.479

to the ICT sector (Table 14.15). This finding is quite contrary to the general perception that a small section of ICT workers gets much higher wages as compared to small sections in other sectors of the Indian economy. As a whole, wage distribution is more equitable in the ICT sector than in other sectors. But over the span of five years, the scenario has changed quickly. Inequality by all measures except for GE(2) shows that inequality in the ICT sector is increasing at a faster rate than in the non-ICT sector. Further, it is disturbing to note that between 1999–2000 and 2004–5, inequality has increased substantially in both ICT and non-ICT segments.

However, this is a very general measure. It does not control for various attributes that are likely to be quite different in different sectors. A regression analysis has been performed to see the relative return to education by controlling various attributes.

Relative Returns to Education

After controlling areas (rural and urban), location (regions of India), age, sex, and sector (formal and informal), relative returns to education is calculated for two years: 1999–2000 and 2004–05 (Figures 14.3 and 14.4).

The returns to education in ICT service was far more equitable in comparison to the non-ICT sector in 1999–2000. In ICT, return to graduates was 2.78 times that of middle school, whereas in the non-ICT sector it was 7.4 times that of middle school. The scenario was quite different in 2004–5. The ICT sector is increasingly looking more like the non-ICT sector. Only return to graduates continues to remain high. In ICT, return to graduates

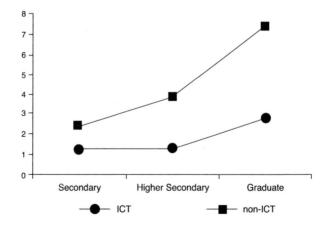

Figure 14.3: Relative Returns to Education (with respect to middle school) for 1999–2000

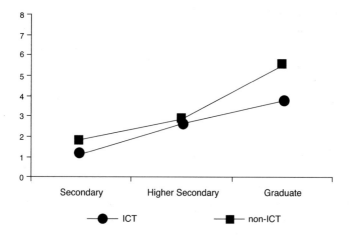

Figure 14.4: Relative Returns to Education (with respect to middle school) for 2004–5

is 3.78 times that of middle school, whereas in the non-ICT sector, it has fallen to 5.52 times that of middle school. At the higher secondary level, there is virtually no relative difference between these two sectors.

QUALITATIVE MEASURES OF DECENT WORK

The qualitative part of decent work has been argued as a better measurement of decent work in the ICT sector for developing countries like India. In this section, qualitative indicators like social security, unionization, nature of job contract and reasons for job change, working hours, and working conditions have been analysed for the regular employed in the ICT sector. The data available for these indicators are scanty; therefore, references from various websites and newspapers have also been incorporated besides the NSS data.

Social Security

The protection which society provides for its members through a series of public measures against the economic and social distress that otherwise would be caused by the stoppage or substantial reduction of earnings resulting from sickness, maternity, employment injury, invalidity and death; the provision of medical care; and the provision of subsidies for families with children. (ILO, 1984)

A social security scheme in India includes provident fund, pension, health care service, maternity benefits, and gratuity (NSS, 61st Round,

2004–05). However, in the ICT sector, many other fringe benefits are also provided. About 60 per cent of the workers have been availing some social security benefits in the ICT sector in comparison to around 31 per cent in non-ICT sectors during 2004–5. Out of total workers, about 35 per cent in the ICT sector and 15 per cent in non-ICT sector are getting all the social security benefits (PF/pension, gratuity and health care, and maternity benefits).

Further, the analysis revealed that in the formal sector, almost three-fourths (71 per cent) of the workers in ICT and more than half (52 per cent) of non-ICT workers are enjoying some social security benefits. Contrary to this, in the informal sector only 11 per cent of ICT workers and 5 per cent of non-ICT workers were in the social safety net in 2004–5. This reveals that contrary to general belief, social security benefits are more in the ICT sector than in the non-ICT sector. However, social security benefits of informal

Table 14.16: Social Security Benefits of IT and Non-IT Sectors among Regular Workers (in %)

		ICT			Other		
		Formal	Informal	Total	Formal	Informal	Total
1	Eligible for only PF/Pension	12.03	4.90	10.72	11.75	1.56	7.21
2	Only Gratuity	0.42		0.35	1.29	0.37	0.88
3	Only Health Care & Maternity	2.93	0.22	2.43	1.52	1.14	1.35
4	Only Gratuity and Health Care & Maternity Benefits	4.24	0.34	3.52	2.15	0.14	1.25
	1+2+3+4	*19.62*	*5.46*	*17.02*	*16.71*	*3.21*	*10.69*
5	Only PF/Pension and Gratuity	3.86	2.67	3.64	3.65	0.38	2.19
6	Only PF/Pension, Health Care, and Maternity	4.94		4.03	4.82	0.53	2.91
	5+6	*8.80*	*2.67*	*7.67*	*8.47*	*0.91*	*5.10*
7	PF/Pension Gratuity, Health Care & Maternity Benefits	42.58	2.62	35.21	26.72	0.96	15.23
8	Not covered under any Social Security Benefit Scheme	28.99	89.25	40.10	48.11	94.92	68.98
	Total	100.00	100.00	100.00	100.00	100.00	100.00

Source: NSS, Unit Level Data, 61st Round (2004–5).

sector workers, both ICT and non-ICT, are almost negligible, which is more severe in the case of the non-ICT sector, where the proportion of informal workers is very large (Table 14.16).

Nature of Job Contract

The availability of a long-term written contract is a possible indicator of a secured job or extent of job security. Around 43 per cent workers in ICT and 22 per cent in non-ICT sectors have job contracts of more than three years, whereas 42 per cent in ICT and 74 per cent in non-ICT sectors have no job contract. The gap of job contract between formal and informal is more pronounced in the ICT sector (45 points) than in the non-IT sector (32 points). This analysis also revealed the same as social security benefits that job security (more than three years' job contract) in ICT sector is more in comparison to non-ICT sector. However, contractual job (an indicator of low security) up to three years (about 15 per cent) tells the other side of the story in the ICT sector (Table 14.17).

Table 14.17: Nature of Job Contracts (in %)

	ICT			Other		
	Formal	Informal	Total	Formal	Informal	Total
No written job contract	34.78	73.64	41.95	58.35	93.53	74.04
Written job contract for 1 year	8.73	18.30	10.49	2.35	1.33	1.89
Written job contract for 1 to 3 years	5.32	2.76	4.85	2.73	0.85	1.89
Written job contract for more than 3 years	51.17	5.31	42.71	36.57	4.30	22.18
Total	100.00	100.00	100.00	100.00	100.00	100.00

Source: NSS, Unit Level Data, 61st Round (2004–5).

Unionization

The presence of a union and any worker association/forum represents rights of workers and enhances their bargaining power. In the ICT sector, even though the unions have not talked much, the presence of an association/workers' forum in the activity has gained momentum over the years. Around 36 per cent workers in ICT and nearly 30 per cent in the non-ICT sector reported the presence of union/association in their activities. In the formal sector, almost 90 per cent in ICT and 85 per cent in non-ICT have membership of these associations. The union/association membership in the

Table 14.18: Union Presence (in %)

	ICT			Non-ICT		
	Formal	Informal	Total	Formal	Informal	Total
Any Union/Association in your Activity	40.41	20.68	36.39	44.61	11.70	29.58
Member of any Association	89.38	6.63	79.78	85.02	65.03	81.41

Source: NSS, Unit Level Data, 61st Round (2004–5).

informal part of non-ICT (major part of non-ICT) is significantly higher than the ICT sector (Table 14.18).

Reason for Change in Jobs

Among qualitative factors, 'reasons for changing job' based on the perception of workers (see Table 14.19) revealed that better income/ remuneration is the main reason for change of job (71 per cent in ICT and 53 per cent in non-ICT sector). The other factors attributed by the employees were 'not satisfied with job' (6.80 per cent) and loss of job due to retrenchment/layoff (4.63 per cent) in the ICT sector for change of job. However, lack of work in the enterprise (7.39 per cent), loss of job due to retrenchment/layoff (6.43 per cent), closure of unit (5.31 per cent), and lack of job security (3.25 per cent) are the reasons for change of job

Table 14.19: Reasons for Change in Jobs

	ICT			Non-ICT		
	Formal	Informal	Total	Formal	Informal	Total
Loss of Job due to Retrenchment/Lay off	4.87		4.63	9.11	3.02	6.43
Closure of Unit				5.46	5.11	5.31
For Better Income/ Remuneration	70.69	78.02	71.05	49.73	57.40	53.10
No Job Satisfaction	7.15		6.80	2.39	5.89	3.93
Lack of Work in the Enterprise				9.73	4.41	7.39
Lack of Job Security				4.13	2.13	3.25
Work Place Too Far	0.43		0.41	2.12	2.48	2.28
Promotion/Transfer				1.73	3.36	2.45
Others	16.86	21.98	17.11	15.61	16.19	15.87
All	100.00	100.00	100.00	100.00	100.00	100.00

Source: NSS, Unit Level Data, 61st Round (2004–5).

in the non-ICT sector. Better income/remuneration in both formal and informal parts of the ICT and non-ICT sectors, and no job satisfaction in the formal part of ICT and both formal and informal parts of non-ICT are the main factors for job change. The lack of job security in the ICT sector for changing jobs have not been reported, which indicates that this sector has better quality/decent employment.

Working Conditions in the ICT Sector and Associations/Unions

There are various evidence available of associations/unions and working conditions in the ICT sector. Some of them have been collected from websites and newspapers and are discussed in Boxes 14.1 and 14.2.

> **Box 14.1: Association/Union and Working Conditions**
>
> The IT professionals Forum in Bangalore was launched at a public meeting in the city, held in late 2000, and since then, it has also developed an offshoot in the smaller city of Mysore, about 140 km to the southwest. According to its secretary H.S. Amar, about 300 people have enrolled as members and at least a thousand other people have been in contact with the organisation. Approximately 150 IT professionals attended its most recent public meeting, held in Bangalore in January of this year. Its sister IT professional's Forum in Hyderabad was also launched in 2000, and has a similar level of support, judging from the 250 or so people who filled a hotel conference room in the city for a public meeting of the Forum recently.
>
> The IT professional's forum have been strongly supported organizationally in their development by the international trade union federation, Union Network International (UNI), and have recently become UNI affiliates in their own right. However, the forums very clearly say that they do not wish to describe themselves as trade unions, a term which they fear could prove off putting to potential members. Any talk of seeking confrontation with employers is most definitely eschewed. The work which they are undertaking for their members would be familiar to many trade unions. The Banglore Forum has been concerned by the number of suicides in the IT sector, something it attributes to work related stress, and back pain problems, eye-strain problems, and excessively long hours of working are some of the other items on the agenda. Some workers reported they and their colleagues do work unofficially on Saturdays and Sundays as well owing to work pressure, although it is not mentioned in the contract.
>
> *Source*: ILO, *World of Work*, 2002.

> **Box 14.2: Unionization in IT/ITES Sector**
>
> Centre of Indian Trade Unions (CITU) forwarded a list of several complaints it received from the employees in this sector to the labour ministry for taking suitable action. The CITU stressed that steps must be taken to see that this sector respects labour laws of the country and creates proper working and living conditions for the employees. The employees are working around 12 hours a day without getting any overtime payment. In many call centres/BPO establishments, employees are forced to work only in night shifts, in contravention of ILO convention on frequency of night shift and compensatory allowance for doing night duty. There is no grievance redresses machinery and the employees working in the industry face summary dismissal if one even tries to raise any complaint about working conditions. Several undertakings do not give even appointment letters to the employees so that they can be dismissed from service without even giving notice.
>
> *Source*: W.R. VardaRajan (2006).

CONCLUSION

This chapter has analysed, both quantitatively and qualitatively, decent work/quality of work. Labour market patterns, trends, and wages of workers have been studied quantitatively, while the qualitative aspects studied include social security, unionization, nature of job contract, reasons for job change, working hours, and conditions of workers in the ICT sector. Also, it had a quick look at the contributions of this sector to national income and exports over the past decade, from 1997 to 2007.

The contributions of the ICT sector to GDP and employment have increased manifold, and presently its share in GDP stands at one-twentieth and its contribution to the country's export earnings is one-fifth.

More than that, the growth of the ICT sector has led to the emergence of a 'new economy' in the country and it is also a sizeable provider of better paid jobs. The contribution of this sector to total employment is small; its share in total employment is currently 0.65 per cent. But employment growth in this sector is six times that of the whole economy, and employment growth per annum has almost reached the double-digit level.

Despite this high level of growth, the sector continues to comprise a small share of national employment. Very little information is available for the indirect employment benefits of the ICT sector. However, a recent study commissioned by NASSCOM foundation and undertaken by Deloitte claimed that (on the basis of a survey of 123 NASSCOM member companies) for every job created in this sector, four are created in the economy (NASSCOM, 2008).

It is a predominantly urban-dominated sector and its share in total urban employment is more than 2 per cent. In the rural areas the telecommunication segment of ICT does provide some employment. In the ICT sector, more than 80 per cent are employed in the formal segment and it is completely dominated by regular workers. More than half of these workers are employed in the public and corporate sectors. Education plays an important role in ICT sector employment, where graduates and above constitute more than 45 per cent of the workforce. Interestingly, self-employed workers are relatively more qualified than regular workers. The new emerging sector of IT and ITES also has more than 70 per cent workforce who are graduates and above.

The earnings are the outcome that reflect the value of jobs in any sector. The wage level of ICT workers is higher than that of non-ICT workers. The gap of wages between ICT and other workers is higher in the services segment than in manufacturing. Workers with lower levels of education get relatively higher wages in the ICT sector as compared to non-ICT sector workers in the service segment. As a result, wage inequality is comparatively higher among other (non-ICT) sector workers than among ICT workers. The returns to education in the ICT sector is more equitable in comparison to the non-ICT sector. But wage inequality in the ICT sector is increasing at a faster rate than in the non-ICT sector. Also, the gap in relative returns to education between the ICT and the non-ICT sectors is fast diminishing. The ICT sector is quickly developing labour market characteristics of the old economy, but with one significant difference. It creates a substantial proportion of middle-salary level jobs, as was observed in the Kernel density graphs.

Contrary to general belief, social security benefits are more in the ICT sector than the non-ICT sector. However, social security benefits of informal sector workers, both in ICT and non-ICT, are almost negligible, which is more severe in the case of non-ICT where the proportion of informal workers is very large.

On the one hand, long-term job contract, that is, more than three years' contract, in the ICT sector is more in comparison to the non-ICT sector. However, contractual job up to three years (about 15 per cent), which is an indicator of low security, tells the other side of the story in the ICT sector. In the ICT sector, even though the unions have not talked much, the presence of associations/workers' forums in the activity has gained momentum over the year. Around 36 per cent workers in the ICT sector and nearly 30 per cent in the non-ICT sector reported the presence of unions/associations in their activity.

The reasons for changing job based on the perception of workers revealed that better income/remuneration is the overwhelming reason for change of job in the ICT sector. The lack of job security as a reason for changing jobs has not been reported in the ICT sector. But lack of job satisfaction as a reason for changing jobs is comparatively higher than the non-ICT sector.

These findings show that the ICT sector is largely urban and is a provider of regular and formal sector employment. But it has low union/association presence, and a substantial segment is not covered under social security benefits. These problems are more pronounced in the ITES sector than the IT sector, and these are aggravated by the fact that the sector has experienced high and unprecedented growth of employment in the past decade. It has been argued by some researchers that the conditions of employment for the 'low skilled' segment of the ITES sector are in fact not very good, provoking the term 'Cyber Coolies' (Babu, 2004). In this regard, there is a need for new regulations on workers' safety and social security.

However, the ICT sector has many indirect effects on economic growth, such as growth of productivity of workers and efficiency of ICT-using industries and services. Hardly any research has been done to estimate the indirect benefits of the ICT sector. But surely the ICT sector deserves to be further promoted, as its growth has many positive consequences. This sector has been a creator of new jobs for skilled and highly educated persons; a major foreign exchange earner through exports; and attractor of foreign investment. These performances are conducive for higher national and regional economic development.

NOTES

1. Software Services (IT).
   The Indian IT services and software products are categorized into core IT services, which include project-oriented services, IT outsourcing, support and training, R&D services, and software products. Software products in turn include product development, design and development of embedded systems, and sales of packaged/proprietary software (NASSCOM, 2007).

Information Technology Enabled Services (ITES). The ITES sector has the following main sub-segments: Customer care (database, marketing, customer analytics, telesales/telemarketing, inbound call centres, web sales and marketing, sales and marketing administration); Finance (billing services, accounting transactions, tax consulting and compliance, risk management, financial reporting, and financial analysis); Human resources (HR) (benefits administration, education and training, recruiting and staffing, payroll services, hiring administration, record management); Payment services (tax processing, claim processing, asset management, document management, transcription, and translation); and Content development (engineering design, animation, network consultancy, and management biotech research).

REFERENCES

Babu, P. Ramesh (2004), 'Labour in Business Process Outsourcing: A Case Study of Call Centre Agents', Working Paper Number 051/2004, National Labour Institute, Uttar Pradesh.

Basant, Rakesh and Uma Rani (2004), 'Labour Market Deepening in India's IT: An Exploratory Analysis', *Economic and Political Weekly*, Vol. 50: 5317–26.

Bescond David, Anne Châtaignier, and Farhad Mehran (2003), 'Seven Indicators to Measure Decent Work: An International Comparison', *International Labour Review*, 'Special Issue: Measuring Decent Work', 142(2): 179–211.

Biradar, R.R. (2005), 'Structure of Employment in ICT Sector in India: Emerging Issues and Prospects', *The Indian Journal of Labour Economics*, 48(4): 837–52.

Bonnet Florence, José B. Figueiredo, and Guy Standing (2003), 'A Family of Decent Work Indexes', *International Labour Review*, 'Special Issue: Measuring Decent Work', 142(2): 213–38.

Fields, S. Gary (2003), 'Decent Work and Development Policies', *International Labour Review*, 'Special Issue: Measuring Decent Work', 142(2): 239–62.

Ghai, Dharam (2003), 'Decent Work: Concept and Indicators', *International Labour Review*, 'Special Issue: Measuring Decent Work', 142(2): 113–15.

Heeks, R. (1996), *India's Software Industry: State Policy, Liberalisation and Industrial Development*. New Delhi: Sage Publications.

ILO (1984), *Into the Twenty-first Century: The Development of Social Security*. Geneva: International Labour Organization.

ILO (2002) (available at http://www.ilo.org/public/english/bureau/inf/magazine/42/itindia.htm, *World of Work*, No. 42, March 2002, accessed on July 2008).

Joseph, K.J. and K.N. Harilal (2001), 'Software and Growth of India's IT Exports: Implication of an Export-Oriented Growth Strategy', *Economic and Political Weekly*, 36(34): 3263–70.

Kumar, Nagesh (2001), 'Indian Software Development: International and National Perspectives', *Economic and Political Weekly*, 35(45): 4278–90.

Kumar, Nagesh and K.J. Joseph (2005), 'Export of Software and Business Process Outsourcing from Developing Countries: Lessons from the Indian Experience', *Asia Pacific Trade and Investment Review*, 1(1): 91–110.

Mehta, B.S. (2007), 'Employment and Quality of Employment in ICT Sector in India', M. Phil Thesis, India.

NASSCOM (2007), *National Association of Software and Service Companies*, 2007 (available at http://www.nasscom.org/Nasscom/templates/LandingPage.aspx?id=4946, accessed October 2007).

NASSCOM (2008), 'Indian IT-BPO Industry: Creating Widespread Economic and Social Impact', *NASSCOM Newsline*, 75, January (available at http://www.nasscom.org/bpo_newsline/, accessed on 21 November 2008).

OECD (1998), DSTI/ICCP/AH/M(98)1/REV1. Paris: OECD.

Parthasarathy, A. and K.J. Joseph (2002), 'Limits to Innovation Set by Strong Export Orientation: The Experience of India's Information and Communication Technology Sector', *Science, Technology and Society*, 7(1): 13–49.

Sarkar, S. and B.S. Mehta (2007), 'Employment Profile of the ICT Sector in India', in N.S. Sddharthan and H.R. Hasim (eds), *High-Tech Industries, Employment and Global Competitiveness*, pp. 195–216. New Delhi: Routledge.

Schware, R. (1992), 'Software Entry Strategies for Developing Countries', *World Development*, 20(2): 143–64.

Sen, P. (1995), 'Indian Software Exports: An Assessment', *Economic and Political Weekly*, 30(7&8): 2053–58.

VardaRajan, W.R. (2006), 'Role of IT/ITES Sector and Its Unionisation', *People's Democracy* (Weekly Organ of the Communist Party of India [Marxist]), 30(2), 8 January (available at http://pd.cpim.org/2006/0108/01082005_wrurajan.htm, accessed on 21 November 2008).

ANNEXURE 14.1

In our study, we have gone up to 5-digit industrial classification of India and included/excluded certain activities from the ICT sector. Therefore, our definition is more restrictive than the OECD definition.

The following 5-digit codes have been included/excluded in our ICT definition:

- Under 4-digit code 6420 excluded: 64201 and 64204
- Under 4-digit code 5150 included: 51506
- Under 4-digit code 5239 included: 52392

CONCLUSION

Dev Nathan and Anne Posthuma

The sectoral case studies in this volume have shown that engagement of Indian firms with global production networks (GPNs) has brought mixed outcomes. The prominent benefits shared by all sectors examined in this volume include: growth in the size and number of firms due to new market opportunities, especially in export markets; receipt of new investment (both foreign and domestic); rising output in all sectors; increases in the employment and wages of skilled workers; and new job creation, much of this involving women workers. Most first-tier suppliers in the value chain that are in direct contact with global producers have improved product quality, adopted new production practices, assumed a greater coordination role over other local suppliers in the value chain, and acquired higher rates of profit.

The case studies also reveal that benefits are mirrored with strong challenges. Rising formal employment in many upgraded firms is complemented in many cases by the use of casual, contract, and other such informal work arrangements that are poorly paid and without social protection. Evidence was found of flexible work arrangements being introduced even among the regular workforce. Firms continuing in the low value-added segments of product markets or in lower tiers of global value chains have more modest profits and pay lower wages to workers and often operate with poor working conditions. In many ways, engagement with global production shows signs of perpetuating, even intensifying, unequal outcomes on both economic and social indicators.

How to achieve both economic and social upgrading and how they are related and reinforcing (or not) are critical issues. Research findings raised in this volume indicate that there is a strong role for institutions, policies, and economic and social actors in achieving more widespread and inclusive economic upgrading and social upgrading.

VARIETIES OF UPGRADING

The manner of participation in GPNs and the possibilities of transiting from one form of engagement to another depend on a combination of five main factors: (*i*) firm-level productive capacities and forms of industrial organization that enable developing country firms to upgrade their participation in GPNs; (*ii*) industrial policies and innovation policies that set a framework, make resources available and provide incentives for upgrading that is based upon dynamic competitive advantage (not only based upon low labour costs); (*iii*) the labour market policies, institutions and regulatory mechanisms that protect workers' rights and develop labour force skills, enabling developing country workers to secure a greater share of the benefits from upgrading; (*iv*) the quality and standardization requirements of the market being served, whether export or domestic markets; and (*v*) the role of government agencies, associations of employers and workers, global buyers and organized civil society organizations (CSOs) in promoting compliance with international labour standards and national labour legislation, the provision of technical assistance and remediation services among firms, as well as representation of informal and unorganized workers.

One important factor influencing firm-level labour practices is the type of market served. More demanding clients in terms of product quality, and technical standards can encourage a process of upgrading, especially when customers/global buyers provide technical assistance and technology transfer to help developing country suppliers improve their production practices and techniques. In contrast, when buyers fail to ensure a sustained sourcing relationship, or technical expertise that supports economic upgrading, as well as fair price and delivery schedules, the pressure upon suppliers may compel them to adopt practices that lead towards 'low road' production and labour practices.

As noted in one of the case studies of the automotive components sector, 'segmented marketing strategies lead to segmented labour practices' (Awasthi et al., this volume). There is a connection between the two. Original equipment manufacturers (OEM) suppliers to the global market or the domestic market have to meet quality standards. However, there is also a large after-market, both domestic and foreign, for poor quality spares.

While OEM suppliers to both Indian and global markets may tend to adopt formal labour practices for their core workers (such as employing more skilled labour with generalized training and retaining them with efficiency wages), non-OEM firms supplying at lower tiers of value chains and to the low-end replacement market may tend to adopt low-level labour practices (for example, workers that are paid by low piece rates, and laid-off when there are no job orders).

Three of the four types of economic upgrading mentioned in the Introduction were found in the sectors studied.[1] There has been *process upgrading*—changing the production process to become more efficient and productive such as moving from craft-like to industrial, assembly-line production, seen in garments, leather products, and automotive components. Such process upgrading provides for standardization of products and economies of scale in production. *Product upgrading* (improving product design, operation, or sophistication) was found in the garments, leather products, and automotive components industries. The third form is *functional upgrading*, moving into higher stages of value added, by coordinating more parts of the value chain or moving into full package supply; from onshore to offshore work in information technology (IT) and from clinical testing and validation to earlier stages of bio-pharmaceutical research (Chaturvedi, 2007) or even from something simpler, such as to grading, marketing, and home-based processing in NTFP.[2]

There are two kinds of firm location in economic upgrading that emerge from the case studies. The first is the shift from production for the domestic market to integration into GPNs. This is most prominently the case with automotive components. There were already well-established component manufacturers prior to external market-oriented liberalization, for instance, in Tamil Nadu and Punjab. Over the 1990s and up to the present a number of these component manufacturers, which earlier supplied the domestic market, have gone on to become OEM suppliers to global networks for a variety of assemblers, including GM, Ford, Hyundai, Mercedes Benz, Chrysler, Audi, Renault, Komatsu, Piaggio, and Fiat.

The second kind of firm location in economic upgrading is that by firms and small-scale producers who were in sectors that emerged to service overseas customers; hence, they began already embedded within the GPNs. Initially IT companies in India supplied cheaper engineers for onshore work in US companies (or 'bodyshopping' as it is known in the trade). Later, however, they switched to offshore work, located in India. The contribution of offshore work to total revenue in the IT sector increased from 5 per cent in 1990–1 to 58 per cent in 2002–3 (NASSCOM, 2003), and has continued growing since then. This shift from merely supplying service personnel to supplying IT services deepened the labour market in the IT sector and enabled the business to utilize the segmentation of the labour market to reduce costs.

Within offshore work too there has been an increase in the technological competence of IT firms. They have diversified into a wider range of activities including high-end consulting and building domain expertise and packaged software, though these are still on a low scale. Some firms have also moved into providing end-to-end services, for which they have set up offices in onshore locations too. Depending upon the production segment involved, a large share of IT services can also involve the provision of low-skilled, low-cost back-office services (Upadhya, this volume).

In pharmaceuticals, there has been a shift from chemistry-driven to biology-based drug development. Indian companies initially supplied the post–drug development clinical trial services needed to test and secure approval of new drugs. More recently, some firms have taken up more sophisticated segments of drug development and small biopharmaceutical firms participate in earlier stages of basic and applied research. However, testing and validation still remain the most common activities in which Indian biopharmaceutical companies participate in global networks (Chaturvedi, 2007).

In garments, there have been all three types of economic upgrading: from manufacture of garments to full package supply, with even some original design manufacture (ODM) and original brand manufacture (OBM) of garments by large firms, such as Raymonds and Arvind (Ramaswamy, 2007; Hirway, this volume; Tewari, this volume). There was also a shift from small-scale to larger-scale production, as in Tiruppur, which was accomplished by moving from craft-like to industrial production (Tewari, this volume). Generally, there was an increase in the design content of garment production. Around Delhi this remained at a craft-level (Tewari, this volume), but with more design and decorative work.

In leather products, there has been a shift from production of shoe uppers and other components to full package supply of shoes and other leather products, mainly by firms in Chennai (Damodaran, this volume). A few firms in Kanpur have emerged as full package suppliers of saddlery and shoes (Akbar, 2007).

Finally, in the case of agricultural products there has been product upgrading to supply higher quality produce (Papola and Mamgain, 2007; Singh, this volume). Vegetables and NTFP, were also undertaking some grading and processing (Kelkar et al., this volume; Singh, this volume).

There are a number of factors, including industrial policy, contributing to this economic upgrading. For instance, in automotive components, the Indian government's import policy places higher tariffs on imported components, thus encouraging domestic production. Along with this, Indian conditions (such as poor roads and the pervasive use of professional drivers) made necessary some 'localization' of design, which enabled development of domestic design capacities in automotive components. In the case of leather products in Chennai, the European Union ban on use of certain chemicals was implemented by combining small producers with large suppliers, such as Tata Chemicals, to bring about necessary changes and upgrading in the production systems.[3]

An important question concerns whether the upgrading observed can be continued, and whether constraints to moving into higher value-added functions are transitional, a sign of path dependence, or a more structural effect of transnational corporation (TNC) chain governance that inhibits developing country suppliers from upgrading.

CAN DEVELOPING COUNTRY FIRMS AND WORKERS OBTAIN ANY SHARE OF THE RENTS IN THE CHAIN?

In looking at upgrading, there are two critical questions that need to be answered. First, do developing country firms obtain any share of the rents in the production chain? Second, if developing country firms do get a share of rents, then does labour in those firms also obtain a share of the rents?

In the Prebisch–Singer analysis of exports of primary commodities, competition among the innumerable producers and monopoly among buyers meant that the benefits of increased productivity were transferred to the buyers. Does the same situation hold for manufactures and services? This depends on the extent to which productive capacities have been spread around the developing world. If management and labour capabilities are widespread, as is the case with the assembly of garments or electronic products, one would not expect the developing country firms to receive more than normal profits over the cost of production or supply price. On the other hand, as in full package supply or end-to-end business process services, if the capabilities are available in only a few locations and firms, then one would expect the developing country firms to obtain more than just normal profits over costs; they could capture a share of rents too.

Investigating this question empirically, how do we judge whether a firm is earning any rents? One way would be to look at profit rates. Are they higher for those in GPNs as compared to similar firms producing for the domestic market? Or do they increase when firms upgrade?

Case studies in this book show that economic upgrading is likely to increase the margin that Indian firms earn. In one instance, with a shift from low quality to high quality garments (Tewari, this volume), the margin increased from 5 per cent to 35 per cent. There is no reason to think that this instance is representative, but it is likely that upgrading would increase the margin that Indian firms obtain. This, in turn, creates conditions in which social upgrading is more likely.

Another approach would look at earnings of employees in that firm. If those employees earn more than the going market rate for the types of workers required, then can one conclude that the firm is earning some rent, part of which is being passed on to workers? It seems reasonable to make such a conclusion. A firm that earned no rent (that is, no excess over normal profits in the sector) would not be able to pay its workers more than the going wage rates for the types of skill involved.

In the most globally integrated sector of all (where more than 90 per cent of total revenues come from export of services), ICT-workers were paid a higher salary than non-ICT workers with the same qualifications (Mehta and Sarkar, this volume). Hence, not only training and skills but also the sector's, or production segment's, dynamism influences wage rises and earnings.

Does this premium for education in ICT mean that the sector is able to retain a higher share of surplus in its operations and share some of that with its employees? Given that India accounts for as much as 65 per cent of the global outsourcing of IT services, this is not unlikely. Indian IT service companies offer not only cheaper services, but also may be more efficient. If they are more efficient, then they could well earn a premium for their services as compared to competitors. With the need to retain employees, some part of the rent earned by the firm could be passed on to its employees. Companies are compelled to share more when skilled labour shortages or trade union demands put pressure on them.

The case studies in this volume that analysed whether firms obtained a higher share from economic upgrading are very limited. This question needs to be investigated on a wider scale. Exploring rates of profit at different production levels then needs to be followed up with an analysis of the factors that make such higher returns possible.

DID LABOUR BENEFIT?

What is the relationship between process, product, and functional upgrading (that is, economic upgrading) and any improvement in the wage and working conditions of workers (that is, social upgrading)? As discussed in the Introduction, the term social upgrading is used to refer to improvements in the quality of employment, as well as enhancement of the capabilities and entitlements of workers as social actors. Social upgrading includes *measurable rights* such as wages, hours worked, and category of employment, and *enabling rights* such freedom of association and collective bargaining (see Barrientos, et al., 2008).

At one level, does economic upgrading improve the well-being of workers? The rock and hard place analogy of Kaplinsky (2005) would conclude that developing country firms and workers can derive little or no benefits from engagement with globalization.

Before we go on to consider the lessons from the sectors or sub-sectors studied in this volume, we can point out that each of the aforementioned kinds of upgrading requires more skilled labour. Thus, to the extent that economic upgrading is accompanied by an increase in the employment of skilled labour, there could be shortages in some segments of particular kinds of skilled labour. Further, if the volume of production increases sufficiently, there could be an increase in the employment of low-skilled labour, leading to at least regional shortages of low-skilled labour. At the same time, changes in the rural and agrarian situation that reduce seasonal migration could also result in shortages of low-skilled labour.

Recalling the earlier discussion in the 'Introduction', the outsourcing practices of TNC lead firms and Indian first-tier firms are important—when companies pass costs and risks down the value chain, as well as large fluctuations in order volume, this adds pressure upon suppliers to adopt flexible and low-cost labour practices that can work against upgrading and skills strategies. At the same time, it should be remembered that there are always two paths to reducing costs—one is to increase productivity (intensification) and the other is to reduce wages and increase working hours (sweated labour of the extensive variety).

Similarly, labour flexibility, whether numerical or functional (due to, say, seasonal orders), can also be managed in two ways. The firm can lay off workers when there is no demand. Or, the firm can pay a retainer wage (as some firms in leather exports have begun to do) or even take up a mix of orders for the various seasons (as some garment suppliers have begun to do).

Which of the two forms of labour practices are adopted—upgrading or downgrading—also depends on the national labour market structure and institutions (for example, whether there is still a Lewisian unlimited supply of low-skilled labour at low wage rates or the alternative incomes that can be earned from agriculture and other rural economic activities). All these national labour market factors combine with pressure from outsourcing practices of TNCs and Indian first-tier firms to produce the particular labour outcomes that are observed.

EMPLOYMENT, SKILLS, AND WAGES

Incorporation into GPNs has led to an increase in employment in the industrial and service sectors studied in this volume: garments, leather products, automotive components, and ICT. The increase in employment in the textiles and apparel sector enabled manufacturing in the period 1999–2000 to 2004–5 to move away from the jobless growth scenario (Ramaswamy, 2007). The growth of employment in the ICT sector, mainly attributed to growth in IT services and information technology enabled services (ITES), is well-known. In the ICT sector as a whole, 2.75 million people were working in 2004–5; the ITES part of the sector generated total direct employment of 1.7 million in 2006–7. The workforce in the IT/ITES sub-sector increased more than eight-fold over the decade 1998 to 2007 (Mehta and Sarkar, this volume).

In this increase in employment, there was overall a greater rise in skilled compared to low-skilled employment (Palit, 2007). Though in some knowledge-intensive sectors (pharmaceuticals and IT), there was a greater increase in low-skilled employment, this may be due to the domination of the not-so-skilled ITES section in IT. But what is more interesting is that even in labour intensive, low technology sectors, such as garments and leather products, there was an increase in the employment of skilled labour. The case studies by Meenu Tewari (this volume) and Indira Hirway (this volume) in garments and A.K. Akbar (2007) in leather products show such an increase in skilled employment. As expected, in automotive components, with integration into GPNs, there was an increase in the proportion of skilled workers (Palit, 2007; Awasthi et al., this volume).

The increase in demand for skilled workers led to high premiums for them. Meenu Tewari reports that in various garment manufacturing centres across the country, skilled workers received as much as 10 times the wages of low-skilled workers. '[A]verage unskilled wages are between $30 and $50 a month depending upon the region, skilled wages can range six or seven times, and be as high as $300–450 or even $600 per month depending upon the region, gender, and nature of task' (Tewari, this volume).

The demand for labour in general—and the demand for skilled workers in particular—has led to labour shortages in different sectors and regions of the country. The wages of low-skilled workers do not show increases as for skilled workers. But there seem to be regional shortages emerging. For instance, T.G. Suresh (this volume) reports that in Tamil Nadu the growth of employment in garments (the internationally famous knitted-garments node of Tiruppur is in this state) has made it difficult for unorganized units in automotive components to recruit workers. In Punjab's automotive components sector, Awasthi et al. (this volume) report, even units in the unorganized sector are increasing wages and incentives in order to retain workers. In the ICT sector, real wages have increased by 6.43 per cent per annum between 1999 and 2005, the highest for any sector in the country (Sarkar and Mehta, this volume).

In general, in units that have upgraded, there is an increase in the proportion of regular workers. In some cases, more work seems to be conducted in-house. For instance, global OEM suppliers in Punjab reportedly conducted 95 per cent own manufacturing, 3 per cent done through unorganized units, and 2 per cent of the job done through specialized job workers (Awasthi et al., this volume). Where smaller and informal firms are unable to meet strict quality requirements, there is hardly any sub-contracting between the OEM suppliers and firms in the unorganized sector. This finding shows that there is limited contact between upgraded OEM suppliers and small units with low productive capacities in the unorganized sector, which suggests in this case study that the benefits of upgrading are not being passed on to the mass of small units in the unorganized sector.

On the other hand, whether in garments, leather, or automotive components, it is in low value-added segments, even among suppliers linked to GPNs, that there is widespread sub-contracting (Barrientos et al., this volume). The quality control needed in the higher value-added segments, it would seem, cannot be achieved by sub-contracting to unorganized sector units with low-skilled workers. Firms that have upgraded require better quality work. Even in labour-intensive garment production, higher productivity is linked with better wages and working conditions.

Emerging full package suppliers also have a few highly controlled suppliers, with strict delivery schedules (just in time) and tight quality control. In automotive components, these are medium-sized firms with, for instance, computerized numerical control (CNC) and other automated tools. Or, in garment and leather products, they would be suppliers of accessories (buttons, studs, zippers, etc.), from which products may be just purchased in the market or sub-contracted. The labour systems in these supplier firms are not clear, but they definitely have a requirement of reasonably well-trained workers, with generalized knowledge and not just on-the-job training. The full package suppliers push a lot of the risk and quality control onto these capable sub-contracted parts suppliers, some of whom may even be unorganized sector suppliers.

On the other hand, there continues to exist a large mass of unorganized firms with poor working conditions. They participate in low end, low value-added export supply, or the low-end domestic market.

What is not clear from the case studies is whether the full package supplier, while adopting intensive methods of production in-house, and even main parts suppliers, may also depend on some parts from the old, sweated labour type of extensive production in India's vast informal sector. Further study of the value chain of full package suppliers is needed to work out the details of the value chain, how these inter-firm relationships change and the implications as regards social upgrading for workers when economic upgrading takes place.

The case studies bring out the clear differences between upgraded units and others in terms of conditions in the workplace. The unorganized sector units in automotive components manufacture are referred to as 'junkyards' (Awasthi et al., this volume) or 'slum-like clusters' (Suresh, this volume). OEM producers for the global chain 'mostly comply with safety requirements' (Awasthi et al., this volume).

There are differences even with regard to training of workers. The OEM units prefer technically educated freshers, since it is difficult for experienced workers to unlearn old production methods in order to learn new ones. Considerations to control wage rises and possible worker organization may also be related to this preference for inexperienced workers. On the other hand, in the unorganized units, learning is only by observing (working as a 'helper' to a craftsman) and doing. There is no formal training (Awasthi et al., this volume).

Training, however, is also used to create multiple internal labour markets within the firm (Suresh, this volume). The larger OEM producers have many sections of workers—regular employees, temporary workers, trainee workers, apprentices, and contract workers. Trainees and apprentices, for instance, do the same work as regular workers but at a much lower wage that is termed a stipend.

To sum up from the aforementioned: integration into GPNs has increased employment and the wages/salaries of skilled workers. In upgraded GPN units, working in high value-added segments, there are more regular workers than in the unorganized sector units working in low value-added segments, where there is a high level of sub-contracting. Economic upgrading has also led to an increase in the gap between wages of skilled and low-skilled persons. At the same time, there are emerging regional shortages even of low-skilled workers—for example, in Tamil Nadu—because of the overall expansion of GPN-related work. These tight labour markets may have implications for workers' scope to obtain higher wages, pressure to improve education and vocational training facilities, as well as possibly improving disposition of workers to organize themselves into representative organizations and trade unions.

There is a need for future research to explore further if these improvements in wages, skills, formal employment, and working conditions signal an absolute upgrading of employment and labour conditions as a result of engagement in GPNs, or how the dual trend of core/periphery workers observed at the level of the firm might also operate at the level of the production chain. In the latter case, poor conditions, low wages, informality, and unskilled work may tend to be pushed down the chain to more vulnerable workers and firms.

ROUTINIZATION

There is a world of difference between scientists and professionals and the run-of-the-mill bio-pharmaceuticals or IT workers. The latter are knowledge-intensive workers, in that they require advanced degrees. However, their work may become so routinized that little creativity is involved. Further, they are also subject to new forms of Taylorism—ways of checking how many lines of computer programme they write, their speed, how many key strokes they make in an hour, and so on. These new forms of Taylorism have created a routinization of skill even among knowledge workers. It is not clear if that is a 'deskilling' in the sense that Harry Braverman used the term—the removal of skill from the worker and its incorporation into a CNC or computer programme. While there is no deskilling of the work, as Carol Upadhya points out, there may be an employment of over-qualified persons who are not carrying out tasks related to their skills. A routinization of skill is occurring with a likely resulting alienation.

To an extent, such routinization is tackled by incorporating Volvo–Toyota methods into IT work. In the group responsibility started by Volvo and then extended by Toyota, the assembly line with its deadening routine (famously represented by Charlie Chaplin in *Modern Times*) is replaced by cars being assembled by groups of workers, working as a team. It also brings a sense of identification with the product. Similarly, in IT, project groups are formed, incorporating the various levels of skills required for the project, ranging from high-level domain workers to programme writers. It is likely that this type of combination of workers in project teams could involve the whole group in problem solving and thus create a greater sense of identification with the work. Routine work too then can be seen as part of the integrated whole of a project and its problem solving tasks.

GENDER ISSUES

Wage inequality, unsurprisingly, features in the labour-intensive sectors, such as garments and leather products. What is surprising is that in Chennai, where leather products are manufactured in medium to large units, the gender difference in wages had disappeared in 2006 (Damodaran, this volume). The reasons for this are unclear and need to be investigated.

It is clear that there is a difference in women's participation in the garment labour force in north India, where craft-like manufacture predominates, and south India, where industrial-type manufacture predominates (Tewari, this volume). Men as professional tailors are the traditional skilled workers, giving a gender bias to the definition of skill. This is another issue for future research to explore: whether existing gender-based divisions of labour, notions of skill, and discrimination that underlie wage differentials between men and women may be changed, or replicated in new forms, as more women enter the industrial labour force in export production, work with higher productivity equipment and production methods, and bring higher skills (as in knowledge-intensive sectors).

With industrial manufacturing, employers preferred to employ women who could be paid less than men. Employers in Chennai pressed women to move the courts against the paternalistic ban on women working in night shifts, in order to be able to pay women unequal wages for equal work. With ITES, there has been a large-scale entry of educated young women into the workforce. However, the numerous incidents of assaults on some of these young women working night shifts have only revealed the poor state of public safety. The *Delhi Human Development Report* (2007) pointed to the urgent need to make public transport and public spaces safer for women.

In acquiring skills or in pursuing careers in IT, women face the problem of combining professional work with domestic responsibilities. Meenu Tewari reports some interesting initiatives by the New Trade Union Initiative (NTUI) to introduce washing machines and crèches in the villages around Chennai where many women commute to work in the garments factories clustered in that region. Yet, among IT professionals there is clear difficulty in combining domestic responsibilities, including child-bearing and child care, with professional careers, especially where frequently long workdays, including weekends and overtime, may disadvantage women's career prospects (Upadhya, this volume).

Analytically too, it is necessary to go beyond the workplace and wages earned to how wages are spent within the household. Both in NTFP production and in garments (Kelkar et al., this volume) men often monopolize the use of women's earnings. Enabling women to gain control over the use of their earnings becomes necessary to ensure that higher incomes translate into improved welfare outcomes for women and their families. Violence against women in the household has been seen to go down where women control income and own assets (ibid.). While it is customary to analyse household and market separately as disconnected domains of existence, it is argued here that the two need to be understood and analysed as interacting domains. The essays in this volume (Kelkar et al., Hirway, Tewari, Barrientos et al.) point to the pervasive problem of household–market relations in enabling women to benefit from participation in global production.

While upgrading may create opportunities for increasing women's employment, it also highlights the inadequacy of public and private provision of facilities that would change the nature of these household–market interactions. For women workers, it is particularly relevant to have forms of worker organization that also address their double burden of workplace and domestic responsibilities.

APPROACHES TO ENCOURAGE UPGRADING OF WORK IN GPNS

There have been many initiatives to improve work conditions in developing countries within global production. Stephanie Barrientos et al. (this volume) point out that audits are good at catching violations of 'visible' work and health conditions in the workplace. Dinesh Awasthi et al. (this volume) also report that buyers are more concerned with matters like the incidence of child labour, but not so good at picking up violations of wage and contract conditions. There clearly is a role for trade unions or other forms of workers' organizations to be part of processes for arriving at implementing improvements in wage and working conditions (D'Mello, 2003).

Peter Knorringa (this volume) argues that the reach of fair trade and corporate social responsibility (CSR) is limited by the extent to which consumers are willing to pay extra for products manufactured responsibly. Such CSR would be limited but can be reasonably deep in selected areas.

Like other civil society initiatives for CSO or community-based social insurance systems (Srinivas, 2007), they would be limited in reach. There is inevitably a need for states to step in and regulate minimum conditions, whether in wages, types of wage contracts, or working and safety conditions. This issue goes beyond national borders. Standards can be set for agreements that go beyond specific corporate initiatives. However, as noted by Posthuma (this volume), a rift has often formed between private and public regulation of labour conditions in GPNs. 'If Starbucks wants to improve conditions for coffee producers, why not support an international agreement to stabilize coffee prices?' (Vogel, 2005:173).

There is clearly a need to move beyond governance as market facilitation to governance as regulation to set minimum labour standards.[4] A recent study has observed this would work at the national level, but could well require some forms of international coordination. Such international coordination would be required even for trade unions that take up the challenges of decent work in global value chain forms of production, 'focusing on the global value chain, rather than the nation state, as the locus of labour organization' (Tewari, this volume). This type of union organization is still in its infancy. In some ways, it is not even clear what this change of focus would involve, and is another area requiring further research.

INEQUALITY

Many of the sector studies (IT, leather, garments, automotive components) point to growing inequality in wages, particularly between skilled and low-skilled workers. Sandip Sarkar and Balwant Singh Mehta (this volume) point out that this is a general feature of industry in India. Inequality in wages between skilled and low-skilled workers has gone up with the increased demand for skilled workers in globalized production, linked to skill-biased technological change arising from imports of more sophisticated capital goods. This has occurred both in developed and in developing countries (Nathan, this volume).

At the same time, there is also a growing inequality between profits and wage shares, or, more broadly, property and labour incomes. This rising share of profits after the mid-1970s reversed the post-Second World War trend that saw a rise in the share of wages. This increasing share of profits, it is argued, makes the expansion of capitalism unstable, as investment needs to be correspondingly high. There is always the threat of a downturn in consumption, in turn leading to a fall in the high investment rates. Rising inequality is manifest in the housing mortgage-based financial crisis in the US. Various forms of international coordination will be needed to deal with the resulting downturn.

RECESSION AND THE VULNERABILITY OF OUTSOURCING?

It is not uncommon to think that jobs linked to globalized outsourcing are more vulnerable than those tied to production for the domestic market. Fluctuations in the global economy surely have their impact, but it is necessary to be more nuanced in seeing this impact. In the case of consumer products, such as garments and shoes, a drop in consumption demand in developed countries will surely lead to a fall in export demand. What about back office services, such as IT services? In such cases there will be two opposite effects. A contraction of the principal company's business, say mortgage banks in 2008, will lead to a fall in demand for outsourced services. However, an opposite tendency is also at work. In a recession, when demand falls and competition rises, there is greater pressure to economize on costs which tends to increase the extent of outsourcing. It should not be forgotten that the great push toward globalization of production took place in the aftermath of the mid-1970s' recession and led to the shifting of whole segments and even whole lines of production to Asia.

Thus, recession in the US and other developed countries may not reduce the extent of outsourcing of business processes per unit of output. It might, in fact, strengthen that tendency as firms try to cut costs to stay competitive in a shrinking market. This, however, has to be balanced against the reduction in the volume of production until the US and global economy recover.[5] There will certainly be reductions in margins, at least in the immediate recessionary period. The rates of growth of Indian IT firms have slowed down. Call-centre jobs are not growing at the same rates as earlier, and reports show that this has reduced attrition rates—those leaving jobs would not be so sure that they would immediately secure another job.

While it is acceptable that firms (rather, their owners) may have to face the ups and downs of competition in markets, both in India and around the world, there is a question with regard to how workers in these firms will cope. How can workers in these firms be protected against the welfare losses? Putting in place a system of social insurance would help buffer workers against the fluctuations in earnings and benefits associated with the ups and downs of business. It is interesting to note that the slowing down of growth and the pressure on workers to increase production have brought signs of increasing unionization among IT and aviation workers, who formerly thought they did not need unions.

IMPLICATIONS FOR THE INDIAN LABOUR MARKET

Product, functional, and process upgrading increase the demand for skilled labour, leading to a tightening of the labour market. Even in the condition of overall unemployment, or underemployment, there can be tightening of the labour market in specific segments, particularly those for different kinds of skilled labour, which occurs with upgrading. An insufficient increase in the supply of skilled labour leads to increasing wage payments to skilled workers in a number of ways, including the payment of retention wages during slack periods in order to retain skilled labour.

For the vast number of low-skilled workers in the informal sector, an increase in income can come about through a number of interventions such as shortening the chain of intermediaries, or through moving up in value-added processing. The existence of alternative buyers in the market is useful in assuring higher prices.

For low-skilled workers, the minimum earned in agriculture is an important benchmark. The employment provided under the National Rural Employment Guarantee Act (NREGA) has increased wages at the lowest level in rural areas and probably even reduced seasonal migration. In terms of policy, given that considerable unemployment and underemployment still exists, there is an important role for a public works employment programme to raise the floor of wage and related incomes.

At the same time, the bottom level is where international competition is most intense. Asia as a whole is undergoing an industrial transformation leading to a large Lewisian supply of labour from agriculture. There is intense competition among countries to secure employment for these urban migrants. With low-skilled workers, competition basically concerns the price of labour.

This international competition at the lowest level has led some countries to abandon minimum wage legislation in an attempt to attract more international capital to utilize low-skilled labour. Such international competition is often referred to as the 'low road' of industrializing in labour-intensive industries.

One important policy measure to reduce reliance on 'low road' competition is to eliminate preferences for small-scale units, which have existed historically in India. These reservation and preferential policies are now being eliminated and have resulted in scale increases in labour-intensive manufacture and the shift from craft-like to industrial manufacture. Nevertheless, there is still a considerable path dependency resulting in a very slow transformation of these small units, with poor labour conditions.

We have already mentioned the importance of public works employment in raising wages at the lowest level. However, its likely international effects must be considered. Could this reduce competitiveness with a negative effect on employment of low-skilled labour? In order to avoid lowering the wages of low-skilled labour, new initiatives would be necessary to achieve some coordination between countries in establishing minimum wages. This could be at the level of governments and even among trade unions. The NTUI in India is collaborating with unions in countries like Vietnam to establish an 'Asia floor wage'.

Such international coordination is welcome but faces an inherent limitation when countries entering the international market seek to set a lower wage or income level than those already established in the market. This has been observed not only in manufactures but also in the markets for agricultural commodities, such as coffee, bananas, and tea. While an Asian minimum wage would help to reduce competition within Asia, and is desirable, it will not circumvent the likely attempt by other countries and regions to enter labour-intensive manufactures. Such coordination efforts will need to extend beyond Asia as new countries enter the international labour market. Ultimately, such initiatives would need to raise the floor internationally to address 'low road' competition.

Indian discussions on labour market reforms have emphasized, from the side of employers, the importance of flexibility in employment; that is, the right to lay-off workers, due to seasonality of orders in garments, leather products, and other items of fashion. Studies of both garments and leather sectors show there are ways of dealing with seasonality without this type of flexibility. Larger units or combinations of units can obtain flexibility by taking orders for various seasons and reallocating labour as needed. As pointed out (Tewari, this volume), garment units have been quite keen to utilize the facilities of cheap land and good infrastructure in private apparel parks, where there are no special exemptions from existing labour legislation.

The question of flexible employment provisions is also brought up with regard to IT employees. In most states of India, IT and ITES units are exempt from labour laws, including the right of representation. There is an attempted individualization of grievance procedures as a substitute for the right to organize and have a collective voice. From the side of the employees too, as emphasized in Upadhya (this volume), there is a reluctance to organize.

It is important for union representatives to adopt ways of organizing such employees. The survey by the National Sample Survey (NSS) of IT and ITES employees finds a surprisingly high level of forms of organizing, though there is an expressed denial of the need for unions (Sarkar and Mehta, this volume). This could mean that flexibility of unions in forms of organizing, utilizing community forums, and other issue-based movements, could yield benefits in organizing these employees. An analysis of high-tech workers in Bangalore and the Silicon Valley points out, 'It is, therefore, critical to develop and strengthen local collaboration between unions and these diverse social movements if workers' rights are to be protected' (Ferus-Comelo, 2007: 5). The example of a call centre in Morocco shows that such employees are not completely opposed to organizing (Maghreb Civil Society Portal, 2008). The Scandinavian countries, in particular, have a long history of unions among officials, and technical professionals. As pointed out earlier, the pressures on jobs, overtime, etc., brought about by the current recession has increased the scope for unionization among IT and aviation professtionals, those who formerly thought themselves outside the pale of unionism.

The need for some new approaches to organization is discussed with regard to the self-employed and other workers in India's vast informal economy (Papola and Mamgain, 2007; Srinivas, 2007; Barrientos et al., this volume; Kelkar et al., this volume). The non-governmental organizations (NGOs), women's groups, cooperatives, and community forms of organization play roles in securing benefits for workers. This is particularly important where the number of workers, under one employer or in one place, is not very large.

An extension of forms organizing also brings a broadening of the issues taken up for consideration. Given the interaction between household and market (whether in the case of own-account, self-employed, or formal employees), gender concerns figure among issues of concern of workers' organizations. These range from women's control over their earnings (Kelkar et al., this volume) to combining interventions on domestic tasks, such as washing clothes or child care, in order to enable women to increase their benefits from market-based economic activity. Safety of women employed in night shifts and the issue of sexual harassment at the workplace, both figure prominently for women workers, including for employees of call centres.

GOVERNANCE OF LABOUR STANDARDS

There has been a proliferation of labour and technical standards and also of agencies that audit the observance of these standards. As pointed out (by Anne Posthuma in this volume), internationally we are likely at an inflexion point in the matter of public and private regulation—from a long period of pre-eminence of private standards, we are moving towards a renewed recognition of the important role of state-determined and enforced minimum Core Labour Standards.

Along with standards, there has also been a proliferation of agencies involved in auditing compliance. Most of them, however, carry out snapshot checks (Barrientos et al., this volume) that assess implementation of 'visible' standards, such as safety factors and employment of child labour, but are not very good at capturing violations of wages, overtime, or freedom of association. While accepting that roles have developed for various types of agencies in monitoring standards, there has to be a key involvement of workers' organizations.

Workers and their unions face various challenges in the context of global production. The major problem is with regard to low-skilled workers, who have left poor alternative incomes in agriculture or other traditional rural livelihoods. As the various case studies by the contributors to this volume show, there are, in fact, fast emerging shortages of skilled labour and corresponding increases in wages. Competition between developing country firms does not seem to eliminate higher returns from economic upgrading, which makes it possible for workers' unions to press for increases in wages and improvement in working conditions. Of course, government and employers too must recognize a role for unions in improving labour conditions in upgrading (Pegler and Knorringa, 2007).

A greater sharing of returns from economic upgrading is required. A study of India and Brazil points out, 'Mutual gains to workers and their firm based on concepts such as trust and cooperation may require a unique combination of unions being both recognized and representative and workers showing allegiance to both company and union' (Pegler and Knorringa, 2007: 43). Unions in Scandinavia have related their demands to increases in productivity, thus enabling firms to retain competitiveness and reducing the threat of global production shifting to cheaper locations.

The threat of relocation is often greater for the low-skilled, labour intensive parts of manufacture. For the upgraded portions of manufacture, the threat of relocation tends to be a medium-term rather than a short-term affair. For instance, if the TVS group in India supplies all radiator caps to

GM cars, can this company face the threat of relocation in the short term? Further, to the extent that IT knowledge enters into the production of components, the duplication of such manufacture would not be so likely in the short term—within the period in which wage negotiations are usually carried out. What does change is that in GPNs, unions and workers too have to be concerned with maintaining or increasing competitiveness of the firms in which they work. One may find forms of corporatism, with trade unions closely linked to firms, emerging in the context of global production.

What the case studies in the book show is that even within the globalized sector of production there is only a section that upgrades production systems and improves labour conditions. There is a kind of 'enclave' development of a few firms that upgrade and improve labour conditions, while a vast base of small firms continues with poor labour conditions. Is it possible to strengthen the effect, whereby improved conditions in the upgrading enclaves lead to benefits down the value chain? Trickle-down benefits seem to exist primarily for upgraded firms. For instance, in automotive components, small firms that become part of the OEM chain shift from manual to CNC machine tools. However, this involves only a part of the small firms that continue to produce non-OEM parts for the local replacement market.

Similarly, in leather and garments, one would expect that accessory suppliers to upgraded firms would also have to improve their production facilities in order to standardize and raise the quality of their products. Yet, there still remain large numbers of small firms that supply to the low-quality market, both external and domestic, that do not upgrade production facilities or improve labour conditions.

HOW TO SPREAD THE BENEFITS? RESEARCH QUESTIONS AND POLICY ISSUES

The chapters in this volume do not cover all globalized segments of production in India, but they do identify important trends in relation to the impacts of participation in GPNs on firms and workers. In extending the research agenda, some critical questions emerge from this volume.

First, how does upgrading affect Indian (or developing country) firm margins? Some results in this volume show that with upgrading, firms' margins do rise. Greater expertise and higher value-added in a particular segment of production, reduces the likelihood that the Prebisch–Singer thesis of developed country firms capturing all the benefits (see Prebisch, 1950), through a fall in supply price, would apply. This, however, needs to be investigated for different sectors and segments of production.

The globalization of production networks shifts emphasis from an analysis at the level of products to that of segments of production and global value chains. High-tech products, such as IT or business services, do contain low-tech segments, such as packaging. Similarly, low-tech products, such as garments and leather products, do contain some high-tech segments, such as product design. We need to investigate not just sectors or products but also particular segments of production for the overall knowledge requirement and whether or not this knowledge is widespread or not easily available. This could be a critical factor in determining how much of the gains developing country firms are able to capture and how much is lost to developed country buyers through a fall in price.

A second issue for research relates to the nature of knowledge generation and distribution in globalized production. With the spread of manufacturing, service, and even research capabilities, there is also a spread of related knowledge. Does this change the dynamics of knowledge creation, namely, innovation; and if so, how does this happen? Does this affect bargaining within the networks that create the new products and processes? Does greater knowledge creation and market share overseas among large Indian firms create the necessary conditions for these firms to become transnational producers that create their own GPNs?

These two issues relate to the nature of the globalization of production, that is, the creation of new nodes and firm-level bargaining within these networks. For labour to obtain a share of the resulting gains that developing country firms are able to capture, what institutions are needed? What needs to be investigated are the roles of different labour market-related institutions, such as public labour administration and inspection services; private codes of conduct and corporate governance; trade unions; women's and community-based organizations; and other CSOs. The studies in this volume point to the need to investigate the changing roles of all these public, private, and civil society organizations. How is the increased demand for skilled workers observed across all sectors in this volume affecting wages, the terms and conditions of employment, and the relative bargaining power of workers?

New forms of rule-making are coming into play through the globalization of production, sometimes in ways that by-pass the state and traditional labour market institutions. These new forms of rule-making, the global content, and global context of these forms of rule-making, and the development of new forms of countervailing power—all these factors are beginning to be seen. There is scope to investigate the globalization of forms of rule-making, their contexts, and dynamics.

Finally, a major research question relates to the level of workers' incomes. Can individual countries raise the wage floor, without risking a loss of competitiveness? Is coordination required to raise the floor? Or can large economies, such as China, India, and Brazil, take initiatives on their own that could then impact on other economies in their regions? As the floor of a country's base income rises, is there pressure on firms in that country to move up and upgrade in the production networks? With China, India, and Brazil all taking measures to raise their national floors, it will be important to examine their impacts on wage and income inequality both within the countries and in their respective regions.

We now turn to the major policy issues arising from the studies in this book. The first issue concerns how to spread the positive effects of upgrading in GPNs. Some of these benefits are attained through changes in the structure of production and of the labour market, emphasizing the important role for unions to generalize and extend these benefits. The private governance of standards in global production and oversight by new types of private and civil society actors are relatively recent labour market interventions in addition to public labour regulation. What the analysis in this volume shows is that while there is scope for labour market interventions that improve the condition of labour in a developing country, labour market interventions must involve national action, as well as international action, as this addresses a section of the workers within global production.

A much bigger task involves efforts to spread the benefits of global production beyond the enclaves of upgraded production to the vast majority of firms and workers that are often embedded in less visible layers within global production, for which action to raise the social minimum may be critical. Benefits for labour are neither inevitable nor automatic; they require intervention and regulation. With the current global downturn, there will be setbacks in social upgrading but short-term issues should not cloud these long-term trends and goals.

NOTES

1. The classification of forms of economic upgrading is based on Gerefii (2005) and Schmitz and Knorringa (2000).

2. Examples were not found of the fourth form of economic upgrading—chain upgrading—and, therefore, this aspect is not considered in the discussion here.
3. For more details see Nathan and Kalpana (2007), and Tewari and Pillai (2003).
4. See Gereffi (2006) for a distinction between market facilitating, regulatory, and redistributive functions of governance and the inadequacy of global governance in addressing the second regulatory, leave alone the third (redistributive) function.
5. Thanks to Will Milberg for bringing this double movement to our attention—the increase in the rate of outsourcing per unit of output, as against the volume of output; these two tendencies together would determine the volume of outsourced work.

REFERENCES

Akbar, M. (2007), 'Human Resource Asset Specificity, Transaction Costs and Decent Work in Global Production Netwoks (GPNs): A Case Study from Kanpur–Unnao Leather Cluster', Paper presented at ICSSR–IILS–IHD Seminar on Global Production Networks and Labour in India. Bangalore: Institute for Social and Economic Studies.

Barrientos, Stephanie, Gary Gerrefi, and Arianna Rossi (2008), 'What are the Challenges and Opportunities for Economic and Social Upgrading?', Concept Note presented at the 'Capturing the Gains Workshop', Manchester, December.

Braverman, Harry (1974), *Labour and Monopoly Capital: The Degradation of Work in the Twentieth Century*. New York: Monthly Review Press.

Chaturvedi, Sachin (2007), 'Global Production Networks and Indian Biopharmaceutical Industry: Emerging Linkages and Prospects', Paper presented at ICSSR–IILS–IHD Seminar on Global Production Networks and Labour in India, Bangalore, ISEC.

D'Mello, Bernard (2003), 'Reebok and the Global Footwear Sweatshop', *Monthly Review*, 54(9): 26–41.

Ferus-Comelo, A. (2007), 'Paving the Way to Unionization of High-tech Sweatshops', in V. Schmidt (ed.), *Trade Union Responses to Globalization: Informing Strategic Development*. Geneva: ILO.

Gereffi, Gary (2005), 'The Global Economy: Organization, Governance and Development', pp. 160–182, in Neil J. Smelser and Richard Swedberg (eds.), *The Handbook of Economic Sociology*, 2nd edition. Princeton, New Jersey: Princeton University Press and Russell Sage Foundation.

—— (2006), *Global Production and Social Protection*. IILS, Lecture Series. Geneva: International Institute for Labour Studies.

Government of Delhi (2007), *Delhi Development Report*. New Delhi.

Kaplinsky, Raphael (2005), *Globalization, Poverty and Inequality: Between a Rock and a Hard Place*. Cambridge: Polity Press.

Maghreb Civil Society Portal (2008), 'Morocco's First Unionised Call Centre' (available at http://www.e-jousor.net/en/node/1396, accessed on 19 August 2008).

NASSCOM (2003), *Indian ITES-BPO Industry*, NASSCOM Newsline, New Delhi.

Nathan, Dev and V. Kalpana (2007), 'Issues in the Analysis of Global Value Chains and Their Impact on Employment and Incomes in India', IILS Discussion Paper. Geneva: International Institute for Labour Studies.

Pegler, Lee and Peter Knorringa (2007), 'Integrating Labour Issues in Global Value Chain Analysis', in Verena Schmidt (ed.), *Trade Union Responses to Globalization*. Geneva: ILO.

Papola, T. S. and R.P. Mamgain (2007), 'A Study of Vegetable Supply Chain', Paper presented at ICSSR-IILS-IHD Seminar on Global Production Networks and Labour in India, Bangalore, ISEC.

Palit, Amitendu (2007), 'Evolution of Global Production Systems and Their Impact on Employment in India', ILO Working paper. New Delhi: ILO.

Prebisch, Raul (1950), *The Economic Development of Latin America*. Santiago: ECLA.

Ramaswamy, V.K. (2007), 'Global Market Opportunities and Local Labour Markets: A Study of Indian Textile and Apparel Industry', Paper presented at ICSSR-IILS-IHD Seminar on Global Production Networks and Labour in India, Bangalore, ISEC.

Schmitz H. and P. Knorringa (2000), 'Learning from Global Buyers', *Journal of Development Studies*, 37(2): 177-205.

Srinivas, Smita (2007), 'Cost, Risk, and Dual Labour Models: The State and Sticky Institutions in Global Production Networks', Paper presented at ICSSR-IILS-IHD Seminar on Global Production Networks and Labour in India, Bangalore, ISEC.

Tewari, Meenu and Poonam Pillai (2003), *Negotiated Collective Action and Adjustment in Tamil Nadu's Leather Industry*, Report, India Program, Center for International Studies, University of North Carolina at Chapel Hill.

Vogel, David (2005), *The Market for Virtue: The Potential and Limits of Corporate Social Responsibility*. Washington DC: The Brookings Institution Press.

CONTRIBUTORS

MEENAKSHI AHLUWALIA, Independent Researcher, UNDP, Geneva, Switzerland.

DINESH AWASTHI, Professor and Director, Entrepreneurship Development Institute of India, Gandhinagar, Gujarat.

STEPHANIE BARRIENTOS, Associate Professor, School of Environment and Development, University of Manchester, UK.

SUMANGALA DAMODARAN, Senior Lecturer, Department of Economics, Lady Shri Ram College for Women, University of Delhi, New Delhi.

GARY GEREFFI, Professor, Department of Sociology and Director, Center on Globalization, Governance & Competitiveness, Duke University, USA.

ESRA GÜLER, Research Associate, Terry Sanford Institute of Public Policy, Duke University, USA.

INDIRA HIRWAY, Director, Centre for Development Studies, Ahmedabad, Gujarat.

GOVIND KELKAR, Regional Programme Coordinator, Economic Security & Rights, UNIFEM, South Asia Office, New Delhi.

MEENAKSHI KUMAR, Independent Researcher, New Delhi.

PETER KNORRINGA, Associate Professor, Institute for Social Studies, Erasmus University, The Hague, The Netherlands.

KANCHAN MATHUR, Professor, Institute of Development Studies, Jaipur and Coordinator of the Women's/Gender Studies Unit.

BALWANT SINGH MEHTA, Associate Fellow-cum-Systems Manager, Institute for Human Development, New Delhi.

DEV NATHAN, Visiting Professor, Institute for Human Development, New Delhi.

SANJAY PAL, Associate Senior Faculty, Entrepreneurship Development Institute of India, Gandhinagar, Gujarat.

ANNE POSTHUMA, Senior Researcher, International Institute for Labour Studies, Geneva, Switzerland.

SANDIP SARKAR, Senior Fellow, Institute of Human Development, New Delhi.

SUKHPAL SINGH, Associate Professor, Centre for Management in Agriculture, Indian Institute of Management, Ahmedabad, Gujarat.

ATUL SOOD, Associate Professor, Centre for the Study of Regional Development, Jawaharlal Nehru University, New Delhi.

T.G. SURESH, Assistant Professor, Centre for Political Studies at the School of Social Sciences, Jawaharlal Nehru University, New Delhi.

MEENU TEWARI, Associate Professor, University of North Carolina, Chapel Hill, USA.

CAROL UPADHYA, Associate Professor, National Institute of Advanced Studies, Bangalore.

JIGNASU YAGNIK, Faculty, Entrepreneurship Development Institute of India, Gandhinagar, Gujarat.